National Courts and the Application of EU Law

This book presents the case-law of Polish courts, namely the Supreme Court, administrative courts, and the Constitutional Tribunal, in which the principles of EU law have been successfully applied. It discusses how Polish courts apply principles of consistent interpretation, primacy, and direct effect of EU law in their daily adjudicating practice in order to ensure *effet utile* of EU law, resulting in effective protection of individuals' rights derived from the EU legal order. The book explores the legal nature of these principles and, in particular, the requirement that national rules that are found to be incompatible with legally binding and enforceable EU law should be disapplied by the domestic courts. It explains Polish courts' reasoning concerning the inseparable relationship between the principle of primacy of EU law and the remedy of disapplication of national law. As the guidelines provided for the national courts by the Court of Justice of the European Union are often quite vague, the work will be important and useful for academics and practitioners from different European jurisdictions to observe the manner in which these principles of EU law are applied in jurisdictions other than their own.

Monika Domańska is Adjunct Professor in the Department of European Law at the Institute of Law Studies, Polish Academy of Sciences, Warsaw, Poland; judicial assistant at the Labour and Social Security Chamber of the Supreme Court of Poland since 2001; and member of the Polish Association of European Law.

Dawid Miąsik is Adjunct Professor in the Department of European Law at the Institute of Law Studies, Polish Academy of Sciences, Warsaw, Poland. Since 2014, he has been justice at the Labour and Social Security (until April 2018 the Labour, Social Security and Public Affairs) Chamber of the Supreme Court of Poland. As a judge rapporteur, he has adjudicated various issues of EU labour, social security, state aid, competition, telecommunications, energy, commercial and consumer protection law, and the rule of law. Dawid was a member of judicial panels that made most of the preliminary references originating from the Polish Supreme Court, including C-585/18 A.K.

Monika Szwarc is Professor in the Department of European Law at the Institute of Law Studies, Polish Academy of Sciences, Warsaw, Poland, and the Head of the Centre for Research on Judicial Application of EU Law (CEREJA-EU).

National Courts and the Application of EU Law

Lessons from Poland

Monika Domańska, Dawid Miąsik,
Monika Szwarc

Routledge
Taylor & Francis Group
LONDON AND NEW YORK

First published 2024
by Routledge
4 Park Square, Milton Park, Abingdon, Oxon OX14 4RN

and by Routledge
605 Third Avenue, New York, NY 10158

Routledge is an imprint of the Taylor & Francis Group, an informa business

British Library Cataloguing-in-Publication Data
A catalogue record for this book is available from the British Library

ISBN: 978-1-032-44625-7 (hbk)
ISBN: 978-1-032-45224-1 (pbk)
ISBN: 978-1-003-37601-9 (ebk)

DOI: 10.4324/9781003376019

Typeset in Galliard
by Apex CoVantage, LLC

Publication financed under the program of the Minister of Science and Higher Education under the name "DIALOG" in the years 2019–2023 as part of the project "Excellence in Legal Research. Promoting Polish Achievements in the Area of Legal Sciences Abroad" implemented under the leadership of Celina Nowak by the Institute of Law Studies of the Polish Academy of Sciences.

DIALOG

Contents

Tables

Boxes

1 Introduction

Monika Domańska, Dawid Miąsik, Monika Szwarc

Preliminary remarks

The decentralised system for the application and enforcement of European Union law depends on the national courts of Member States. As a result, 'every national court in the European Community is now a Community law court',[1] exercising European mandate.[2] When fulfilling this function of 'EU law court', national courts aim for the effective application of EU law and the judicial protection of rights of individuals, which they derive from EU law. The role, such as this, of the national courts became obvious and was commonly accepted by EU law researchers and legal practitioners throughout the 60 years of European integration. Even if such a statement is not explicitly inserted in the Treaties, it is rooted in the principle of loyal cooperation enshrined in Article 4 (3) TEU and the case-law of the CJEU. The involvement of national courts in the decentralised application of EU law rests on the principles of primacy and direct effect (which are always relevant, 60 years after the *Van Gend en Loos* and *Costa v. ENEL* cases), completed by the principle of consistent interpretation (as formulated in *von Colson and Kamman*). Still,

1 J Temple Lang, The Duties of National Courts under Community Constitutional Law, *European Law Review*, 1997, no. 3, p. 3; this term – in the context of Polish courts – is commonly used in the Polish literature since: A. Wróbel, Pytania prawne sądów państw członkowskich do Europejskiego Trybunału Sprawiedliwości (Sądu Pierwszej Instancji) [Preliminary References of National Courts to European Court of Justice], in: A. Wróbel (ed.), *Stosowanie prawa Unii Europejskiej przez sądy* [Application of EU law by courts], Zakamycze, 2005, p. 778; D. Kornobis-Romanowska, Kompetencje wspólnotowe sądów krajowych – przegląd zagadnień [Community Competence of National Courts – Preliminary Issues], in: D. Kornobis-Romanowska (ed.), *Stosowanie prawa wspólnotowego w prawie wewnętrznym z uwzględnieniem prawa polskiego* [Application of Community Law in Domestic Order with Account of Polish Law], Dom Wydawniczy ABC, 2004, p. 14; A. Wróbel, Sądy administracyjne jako sądy Unii Europejskiej [Administrative Courts as EU Courts], *Zeszyty Naukowe Sądownictwa Administracyjnego*, 2005, no. 5, pp. 474–496.

2 M. Claes, *The National Courts' Mandate in the European Constitution*, Hart Publishing, 2006, pp. 58–68.

DOI: 10.4324/9781003376019-1

the dialogue between the CJEU and national courts, on the EU duties of national courts, is constantly developing, as the evolution of social, economic, and legal circumstances provokes new challenges to the jurisdictions across the European Union.

The case-law of the CJEU on the principles of primacy, direct effect, and consistent interpretation, and its consequences for EU law development, has been analysed and discussed by EU researchers and practitioners. The results of these analyses are published in numerous monographs, collected volumes, and national reports. This is not the case for the practices of the national courts. The analyses of the application of EU principles by national courts in their daily adjudication (in the framework of domestic law) have been very few.[3] Yet, in this context, we share the view expressed by M. Claes, 'In order to gain a better understanding of the functioning of Union law it must be looked at from a double perspective top-down from the Community perspective and bottom-up from the national angle'.[4] As she rightly indicates, 'If the national courts had not taken up their mission as Community law courts and if they had not assisted in enforcing compliance with Community law and protecting Community rights of individuals, Community law would probably have remained a sub-set of international law, where compliance depends on the co-operation of the legislative, executive and administrative organs of the Member States'.[5] The same assumption was formulated in other words: 'what

3 Still, it is worth noting recent FIDE publication by M. Botman, J. Langer (eds.), *National Courts and the Enforcement of EU Law: The Pivotal Role of National Courts in the EU Legal Order*. The XXIX FIDE Congress in the Hague 2020 Congress publications vol. 1, Eleven International Publishing, 2020; there are also several specific publications: 1) focusing on the judicial application in specific EU law field, including M.A. Jarvis, *The Application of EC Law by National Courts: The Free Movement of Goods*, Oxford University Press, 1998; S. Sciarra (ed.), *Labour Law in the Courts: National Judges and the European Court of Justice*, Hart Publishing, 2001; J. Jans, R. Macrory, A.M. Moreno Molina, *National Courts and EU Environmental Law*, Europa Law Publishing, 2013; 2) focusing on comparative studies to a limited extent including A.-M. Slaughter, A. Stone Sweet, J.H.H. Weiler, *The European Court and National Courts: Doctrine and Jurisprudence: Legal Change in It's Social Context*, Hart Publishing, 1998; J.M. Beneyto, I. Pernice (eds.), *Europe's Constitutional Challenges in the Light of the Recent Case-Law of National Constitutional Courts: Lisbon and Beyond*, Nomos, 2011; M. Florczak-Wątor (ed.), *Judicial Law-Making in European Constitutional Courts*, Routledge, 2021; and 3) focusing on application of international law and fundamental rights by national courts, including P. Popelier, C. Van de Heyning, P. Van Nuffel, *Human Rights Protection in the European Legal Order: The Interaction Between the European and the National Courts*, Intersentia, 2011; P.J. Castillo Ortiz, *EU Treaties and the Judicial Politics of National Courts: A Law and Politics Approach*, Routledge, 2017; A. Wyrozumska (ed.), *Transnational Judicial Dialog on International Law in Central and Eastern Europe*, Wydawnictwo Uniwersytetu Łodzkiego, 2017.

4 M. Claes, *The National Courts' Mandate in the European Constitution*, Hart Publishing, 2006, p. 14.

5 Ibidem.

national courts do not apply in reality, does not exist in practice'.[6] Thus, recognising that EU law only functions via the prism of national legal cultures, the authors decided to examine the judicial application of EU principles of consistent interpretation, primacy, and direct effect by Polish courts with the view to filling, to some extent, the existing research gap. In order to create a broad research perspective on the application of EU law, it is a must to have a closer look at the practices of national courts in this context.

The need to undertake research on the judicial practice, in the application of EU law, seems crucial in times when national courts found themselves amid the turbulent discussions connected to their role and functions, in addition to their independence and impartiality. Currently, the European mandate of national courts is questioned and, sometimes, even denied. This is not, however, a book about the rule of law crisis in Poland and reaction of Polish courts to it in their daily adjudication. This subject calls for a separate in-depth analysis.

Courts in Poland

The duties and challenges under review in this monograph became a reality for Polish courts on 1 May 2004 with the accession of Poland to the European Union. This volume is about how Polish courts since that date have fulfilled their functions as EU courts, thus ensuring *effet utile* of EU law and protecting individuals' rights. Before explaining the aims and scope of our research, let us briefly present the Polish judicial system. Currently,[7] it consists of three judicial regimes with different jurisdictions: 1) the Constitutional Tribunal, a constitutional court dealing with issues relating to the constitutionality control; 2) administrative courts, including voivodship administrative courts and the Supreme Administrative Court overlooking the activities of public administration and 3) courts of general (common) jurisdiction, with the Supreme Court at the top, hearing all other cases that are not reserved, by law, to the competence of other courts.

The Supreme Court supervises the adjudication of courts of general jurisdiction (common courts) that adjudicate in civil, criminal, family, and labour law matters, as well as military courts. It is the court of the last resort of appeal against judgments of the lower courts. It mostly hears cassations (appeals of the point of law) and complaints against procedural (formal) rulings of the lower courts. It also passes resolutions on preliminary references, made by the courts of second instance, in complex cases on issues relating to the interpretation of law. The Supreme Court consists of chambers. The 'old' chambers include the Civil Chamber, the Criminal Chamber, and the Labour

6 J. Jans, R. Macrory, A.M. Moreno Molina, *National Courts and EU Environmental Law*, Europa Law Publishing, 2013, p. 3.

7 Since the entry into force of the Constitution of the Republic of Poland of 1997.

and Social Security Chamber. The 'newly' established chambers were created in 2018: The Chamber of Extraordinary Control and Public Matters and the Disciplinary Chamber. This monograph is devoted to the jurisprudence of the 'old' Chambers of the Supreme Court, with some exceptions, in which we demonstrate how these new Chambers apply principles of EU law following C-585/18 *A.K. and others* and what their jurisprudence may mean for the future of national application of EU law.

The administrative courts in Poland were created as a separate branch of the judicial system following the entry into force of the Polish Constitution of 1997[8] and are grounded in its 175 and 184. Since 1 January 2004, Poland has introduced a two-tier system of administrative judiciary: the voivodship administrative courts (VAC) and the Supreme Administrative Court (SAC).[9] The voivodship administrative courts hear, as to the principle, all administrative matters, except for matters reserved for the jurisdiction of the Supreme Administrative Court. There are now 16 voivodship administrative courts, whose jurisdictions coincide with the divisions of Poland into voivodships. The administrative courts exercise, to the extent specified by statute, control over the performance of the public administration. Such control shall also extend to judgments on the conformity to statute of resolutions issued by the organs of local government and normative acts of territorial authorities of government administration. The controlling function of the administrative courts means that, should they find a decision of a national administrative authority to be in violation of national or European law, they may only set such a decision aside and remand the case back to the authority for further deliberation. The detailed competences and jurisdiction of the administrative courts are regulated in laws adopted by the Parliament, namely the Act of 25 July 2002, the Law on the system of administrative courts, and the Act of 30 August 2002, the Law on proceedings before administrative courts. The jurisdiction of the administrative courts includes a) individual complaints brought against the administrative decisions, or orders subject to complaint, termination of proceedings, or in determining the substance of the case; b) orders issued in executive proceedings and proceedings to secure claims; c) written interpretations of tax issued in individual cases; d) disputes regarding local enactments issued by territorial governments or other territorial authorities or by regional authorities of the state administration; and e) complaints concerning the failure of the administration to act.

The Constitutional Tribunal is responsible for four areas of the jurisdiction of the Constitutional Tribunal: a) reviewing norms (both abstract and

8 This part has been elaborated on the basis of the information from the Supreme Administrative Court itself https://nsa.gov.pl/en.php.

9 In detail, see J. Chlebny, W. Piątek, The Systemic and Competence Evolution of the Administrative Courts System, *Zeszyty Naukowe Sądownictwa Administracyjnego*, 2021, no. 1–2, pp. 37–62.

specific, a posteriori and a priori); b) settling disputes over authority between the central constitutional organs of State (Article 189 of the Constitution); c) deciding on the conformity to the Constitution of the purposes or activities of political parties (Article 188 subpara. 4 of the Constitution); and d) determining whether or not there exists an impediment to the exercise of the office by the President of the Republic (Article 131 para. 1 of the Constitution). The list of the competences of the Tribunal is exhaustive, and its extension by the legislator in the form of a statute must be considered impermissible.

The Supreme Court, common courts, and administrative courts may review the legality of regulations issued by the executive and may refuse to apply such a regulation in a particular case. However, they cannot decide on the validity of a regulation since this lies solely within the competence of the Constitutional Tribunal. As opposed to other constitutional courts, the Polish Constitutional Tribunal does not review rulings or decisions issued in individual cases but rather controls normative acts serving as legal grounds for a given ruling or decision.

The Polish Constitutional Tribunal does not take an active approach in the review of the constitutionality of normative acts. In adjudicating a case, the Tribunal is bound by the limits of the submitted application, question of law, or complaint. The obligation to identify the grounds for the alleged unconstitutionality of a challenged provision is imposed on the participants in the proceedings. This concept of constitutional judiciary is based on the presumption of the constitutionality of the law. The Polish Constitutional Tribunal reviews domestic statutes implementing EU legislation in the same manner as other national, legal acts. Statutes implementing EU law are subject to preventive and subsequent control by the Constitutional Tribunal. The preventive control may start at the stage of implementation of EU law (i.e., before the statute enters into force). This can only be initiated by the President who may, before signing a statute, refer it to the Constitutional Tribunal for adjudication of its conformity to the Constitution (Article 122 (3) of the Constitution).

Aim and scope of the work

The aim of this work is to analyse how Polish courts, namely the Supreme Court, administrative courts, and the Constitutional Tribunal, apply EU principles of consistent interpretation, primacy, and direct effect in their daily adjudication. The main assumption underlying such research is that EU law researchers and legal practitioners in the Member States of the EU struggle with similar legal problems as Polish researchers and practitioners in terms of the judicial application of EU law and that the selected case-law of Polish courts may be a valuable source of good practices in this context. Thus, this volume is addressed principally to all researchers and practitioners, in particular judges and legal representatives, who look for inspiration and good ideas on how to effectively apply EU law in their domestic legal orders, including the consistent interpretation of national law, primacy, and direct effect of EU law.

As a result of the earlier considerations, this book focuses on the practices of domestic courts and not the case-law of the Court of Justice of the EU as such. The latter, concerning, EU principles of primacy, direct effect, and consistent interpretation, has been widely and thoroughly discussed in the literature. The authors assume that a reader already has knowledge of this case-law of the CJEU and, therefore, there is no need to discuss it in a separate chapter or subchapters. Still, the leading cases of the CJEU are concisely presented at the beginning of each chapter in order to confront the state of EU case-law with national case-law. In detailed considerations, the case-law of the CJEU is only referred to and explained in connection with specific cases adjudicated by Polish courts, if a specific judgment of the CJEU played a role in the grounds of judicial decision adopted at the national level.

The structure of the book highlights the interplay of various motives and factors that affect judicial decision-making. It reflects the objectives of the research and corresponds with the general methodology of judicial application of EU law. It begins by identifying whether a given case before a national court is an 'EU case'. The concept of an 'EU case' or 'a case with an EU element' provides national courts with an analytical tool helping them to establish whether facts of the case or even an incidental, yet contentious, issue falls within the scope of EU law and hence requires the application of its principles. Once the EU nature of the dispute has been established and applicable provisions of EU have been identified, national courts have to respect the principle of consistent interpretation. They must do so not only when they establish, initially, the incompatibility of national law and EU law and try to circumvent the limitations of direct effect on certain sources of EU law and hence secure the effectiveness of EU law without recourse to the principle of primacy. In order to secure the effectiveness of EU law and respect the principles of its uniform interpretation and application, national courts should always follow the guidelines stemming from consistent interpretation when they interpret the national provisions falling within the scope of EU law.

According to the methodology discussed earlier, the volume is divided into three chapters devoted accordingly to definition of 'EU case' and hence determination of the scope of application of EU law (Part I), principle of consistent interpretation (Part II), and principles of primacy and direct effect (Part III). The subject of consideration in Part I is the issue of how Polish courts understand and identify EU elements in particular cases pending before them. In Part II, the analysis focuses on how Polish courts understand their duties, resulting from the principle of consistent interpretation; what challenges they have encountered; and how they filled, with actual practice, the vague guidelines of the CJEU that 'the principle of interpreting national law in conformity with European Union law has certain limitations' by means of general principles of law prohibition of an interpretation of national law *contra legem*.[10] Part III presents the case-law of Polish courts exemplifying inter alia: how the

10 For example, case C-282/10, *Maribel Dominguez*, EU:C:2012:33, para. 24–25.

remedy of disapplication works in practice at the level of national courts; how Polish courts establish incompatibility between Polish law and EU law; which kind of provisions form the grounds of judicial decision, once the *Simmenthal* rule has been applied; how Polish courts perceive the relationship between the principles of primacy and direct effect and between the primacy of EU law and the primacy of national constitution. The latter issue is of utmost importance for the coherence and the effectiveness of EU law in the times of turmoil connected to the rule of law breakdown in some Member States, a breakdown supported in Poland by a politically dependent constitutional court.

Parts I, II and III are then divided into chapters concerning accordingly the Supreme Court, administrative courts, and the Constitutional Tribunal. The research scheme reflects more specific questions and was developed in such a way as to allow judges and other practitioners to quickly search for a potential legal solution to the problem concerning the application of EU law by national courts. Each chapter was divided into smaller detailed sections, corresponding to a specific issue. To each of these smaller units, the authors attributed the most interesting cases, in which that particular issue of judicial application of EU law played a significant role. These chapters end with preliminary conclusions, which are then recapitulated in the final Conclusions.

Method

As already stated, the book aims at presenting the involvement of Polish courts in the application of EU law in terms of the principles of consistent interpretation, primacy and direct effect. As a result, it focuses on the case-law of Polish courts, with only minimal reference to the case-law of the CJEU.

As indicated by the plan outlined earlier, the analyses were not conducted according to the fields of law, such as social, environmental, and tax law. It was assumed instead that the axe of research is the application of the particular EU law principle (namely consistent interpretation, primacy, and direct effect) to decide an individual case pending before a given Polish court. Put another way, it was not that important which field of law a given case was grounded in but rather which of the aforementioned EU principles was a tool for a given Polish court to decide a case and to ensure *effet utile* of EU law. Thus, this book discusses the manner 'EU cases', pending before Polish courts, have been resolved so far and the consequences of the judicial decisions pertaining to the rights of individuals in these national proceedings. Such an approach enabled the authors to formulate conclusions for the domestic courts and to build a valuable record of good practices exercised by national courts. Additionally, despite the high degree of fragmentation and great differences in national procedures, the case-law of Polish courts, belonging to different types of jurisdictions, show a certain homogeneity with regard to the effects of EU law principles.

The perspective, adopted by the authors, remains strictly a lawyer's one. The sources of information were the legal texts (laws, regulations, courts' rulings) and literature including commentaries. No empirical studies, including, for example, interviews or statistical studies, were conducted. Thus, this is case-law-based research. The research comprised a lot of rulings. The authors assumed that readers not established in Poland are not necessarily familiar with its legal system. Accordingly, the cases sometimes had to be explained in a rather lengthy manner. This was necessary to give readers the descriptive elements necessary to understand the factual and legal context of a particular case and its importance for the scope of EU law and its principles.

The choice of cases reviewed in this monograph was made according to the best knowledge of the authors. Firstly, cases dealing expressly with the scope of application of EU law, consistent interpretation, direct effect, and primacy were identified in each jurisdiction. The initial selection of judgments was made with the use of keywords used to describe legal institutions under consideration and the preliminary rulings of the CJEU. Secondly, cases which form good examples of judicial application of EU law, at a national level that can be followed in the future, or that explained issues unresolved by the CJEU were taken into consideration. Thirdly, cases from different Polish jurisdictions were grouped with the use of a common research matrix. Fourthly, it was decided to elaborate in more detail on such cases that either followed preliminary reference to the CJEU (as it will be easier for foreign readers to become familiar with more details of the case and consider its impact on the application of EU law by national courts by comparing our assertions with preliminary ruling of the CJEU) or had peculiar facts. Again, the focus is, therefore, not on what the national courts ought to decide to give the effect to EU law principles and interpretation of the CJEU but how, or to what extent, their judgments can be reconciled with the idea of ensuring the effectiveness of EU law.

The authors used differentiated tools in searching for the material for the conducted research. Many important judgments, concerning the application of EU law by national courts, has regularly been reported in the *Europejski Przegląd Sądowy* (European Judicial Review), a leading Polish legal law journal devoted to issues of EU law.[11] Rulings delivered by the Supreme Court are also publicly available in Polish at www.sn.pl/orzecznictwo/SitePages/Najnowsze_orzeczenia.aspx and in two commercial legal databases. All judgments reported in the manner discussed earlier have been thoroughly examined from the perspective of their impact on the application of EU law by the Supreme Court and courts of common jurisdiction. Different keywords were used, relating to the issues or the case-law of the CJEU, which are important for each of the chapters of our monograph.

As to the rulings of administrative courts, there is a publicly available database at https://orzeczenia.nsa.gov.pl/cbo/query which contained, at the end of

11 The heading devoted to the EU caselaw of the Supreme Court was initially developed and run by Dawid Miąsik, then by Monika Domańska and, for a couple of years, has been run by Dr Michalina Szpyrka, Dawid's legal assistant at the Supreme Court.

2021, nearly 194,000 records (as well as in two commercial databases). The identification and choice of relevant jurisprudence was thus a challenge and inevitably the most time-consuming part of the research. The starting point for the research was the experience of the voivodship administrative courts and the Supreme Administrative Court in the framework of preliminary rulings procedure: the references to the Court of Justice of the European Union and the rulings delivered by these courts, taking into account the rulings of the CJEU.[12] The list of references, with relevant documents, is kept up to date at https://nsa.gov.pl/pytania-prejudycjalne-wsa-i-nsa.php. Similarly, to the method applied for the jurisprudence of the Supreme Court, judgments were selected in the first step using different keywords relating to the issues or the CJEU's case-law, important for each of the chapters of our monograph. The rulings found, according to such methods, were thoroughly analysed in order to verify whether they could match each chapter of this book.

Rulings delivered by the Constitutional Tribunal are publicly available in English: http://trybunal.gov.pl/en/ and also in other Polish commercial legal databases. The case-law, concerning EU law, was also gathered by the Constitutional Tribunal Publication Office in *Selected rulings of the Polish Constitutional Tribunal concerning the law of the European Union (2003–2014)*, vol. LI, Warsaw 2014. http://trybunal.gov.pl/publikacje/wydawnictwa/art/7070-tom-li-selected-rulings-of-the-polish-constitutional-tribunal-concerning-the-law-of-the-european-un/. All judgments of the Constitutional Tribunal, concerning EU law, were analysed in detail. The most important, and most influential judgments, are reported in this book. Some of them (the most recent) still do not have justification published but are crucial for some of the EU law aspects that are contained in the text.

The analysis of the jurisprudence of the Constitutional Tribunal is carried out in view of the fact that, since 2016, there have been significant, systemic changes in Poland leading to the so-called constitutional crisis. At the end of 2015, the first statutes limiting the systemic role of the CT were adopted, and three judges were elected to the Constitutional Tribunal in violation of the Constitution. The currently binding statutes, concerning the Constitutional Tribunal, in the opinion of the vast majority of experts, raise grave, constitutional concerns regarding the politicisation of the CT composition and judicial independence.[13]

It must be noted, however, that discussion of and search for national case-law has limitations. It was possible to take account only of these rulings which had been reported. Additionally, the case-law of Polish courts is publicly accessible mainly in Polish with few exceptions from the Constitutional Tribunal. Thus, all the cases were translated by the authors and references made in the

12 On the practice of administrative courts from the perspective of the preliminary ruling procedure in detail, see P. Wróbel, Dialogue of Administrative Courts with the Court of Justice of the European Union, *Zeszyty Naukowe Sądownictwa Administracyjnego*, 2021, 1–2, no. 94–95, pp. 175–195 and the literature referred therein.

13 See Judgment of the ECHR of 7 May 2021, Xero Flor w Polsce sp. z o.o. v. Poland, 4907/18.

volume are directed to the Polish versions of rulings. Finally, it was not possible to take account of all the rulings of Polish courts due to the volume of that case-law. To keep the material manageable, the analysis does not cover all the case-law concerning EU law. The work thus aims to demonstrate those judgments which focus on pragmatic solutions to complex problems in order to ensure the effectiveness of the EU principles. Therefore, the book presents the case-law selected by the authors according to the criteria of suitability for the research objective and the understandability for readers coming from legal systems other than Polish.

The book is based on the results of the research financed under the program 'DIALOG' of the Minister of Science and Higher Education in the years 2019–2022. This study strives to state the case law as of 1 November 2022.

Literature

Beneyto J.M., Pernice I. (eds.), *Europe's Constitutional Challenges in the Light of the Recent Case-Law of National Constitutional Courts: Lisbon and Beyond*, Nomos, 2011.

Botman M., Langer J. (eds.), *National Courts and the Enforcement of EU Law: The Pivotal Role of National Courts in the EU Legal Order*, The XXIX FIDE Congress in the Hague 2020 Congress Publications vol. 1, Eleven International Publishing, 2020.

Castillo Ortiz P.J., *EU Treaties and the Judicial Politics of National Courts: A Law and Politics Approach*, Routledge, 2017.

Chlebny J., Piątek W., The Systemic and Competence Evolution of the Administrative Courts System, *Zeszyty Naukowe Sądownictwa Administracyjnego*, 2021, no. 1–2, pp. 37–62.

Claes M., *The National Courts' Mandate in the European Constitution*, Hart Publishing, 2006.

Florczak-Wątor M. (ed.), *Judicial Law-Making in European Constitutional Courts*, Routledge, 2021.

Jans J., Macrory R., Moreno Molina A.M., *National Courts and EU Environmental Law*, Europa Law Publishing, 2013.

Jarvis M.A., *The Application of EC Law by National Courts: The Free Movement of Goods*, Oxford University Press, 1998.

Kornobis-Romanowska D., Kompetencje wspólnotowe sądów krajowych – przegląd zagadnień [Community Competence of National Courts – Preliminary Issues], in D. Kornobis-Romanowska (ed.), *Stosowanie prawa wspólnotowego w prawie wewnętrznym z uwzględnieniem prawa polskiego* [Application of Community Law in Domestic Order with Account of Polish Law], Dom Wydawniczy ABC, 2004.

Popelier P., Van de Heyning C., Van Nuffel P., *Human Rights Protection in the European Legal Order: The Interaction Between the European and the National Courts*, Intersentia, 2011.

Sciarra S. (eds.), *Labour Law in the Courts: National Judges and the European Court of Justice*, Hart Publishing, 2001.

Slaughter A.-M., Stone Sweet A., Weiler J.H.H., *The European Court and National Courts: Doctrine and Jurisprudence: Legal Change in It's Social Context*, Hart Publishing, 1998.

Temple Lang J., The Duties of National Courts under Community Constitutional Law, *European Law Review*, 1997, no. 3, p. 3.

Wróbel A., Pytania prawne sądów państw członkowskich do Europejskiego Trybunału Sprawiedliwości (Sądu Pierwszej Instancji) [Preliminary References of National Courts to European Court of Justice], in A. Wróbel (ed.), *Stosowanie prawa Unii Europejskiej przez sądy* [Application of EU Law by Courts], Zakamycze, 2005, p. 778.

Wróbel A., Sądy administracyjne jako sądy Unii Europejskiej [Administrative Courts as EU Courts], *Zeszyty Naukowe Sądownictwa Administracyjnego*, 2005, no. 5, pp. 474–496.

Wyrozumska A. (ed.), *Transnational Judicial Dialog on International Law in Central and Eastern Europe*, Wydawnictwo Uniwersytetu Łodzkiego, 2017.

Part I

The concept of the EU case – scope of application of EU law before Polish courts

The national courts are obligated to ensure the effectiveness of EU law, as explained in the Introduction. However, this obligation arises exclusively in such cases, pending before national courts, which fall within the scope of EU law. Thus, each national court must verify – in each case – whether the dispute falls within the EU law or not. Exclusively in the first situation, a national court will act as an 'EU court'. A case in the second situation will be treated as a 'purely internal' one, where a national court will act as a 'purely national' court. The idea of an 'EU case' – a case that falls into the scope of EU law – is easy to grasp at a theoretical level. It is much more difficult to be applied in the daily practice of national courts, and yet – crucial for ensuring the effectiveness of EU law in the Member States.

Therefore, the opening chapter of this book is devoted to the question of how Polish courts identify these cases in which they should apply EU law and its principles. The authors attempted to select, analyse, and then present systematically the case-law of the Supreme Court, administrative courts, and the Constitutional Tribunal, where this issue was considered in detail to identify and reconstruct the legal basis for adjudicating a particular case.

Let us briefly remind that the Court of Justice applied different words to embrace this issue, such as 'a situation with/without a link to Community/Union law', 'case not covered by Article 39 EC';[1] 'situations including those involving the exercise of the fundamental freedoms guaranteed by the Treaty and those involving the exercise of the right to move and reside within the territory of the Member States, as conferred by Article 18 EC;[2] application of EU law remaining in 'relation to the actual facts of the main action or its purpose';[3] 'a situation such as that in the main proceedings falls within the scope of Community law, and in particular of Article 18(1) EC'.[4] In these cases, the Court of

1 Case C-520/04, *Turpeinen*, EU:C:2006:703, para. 17.
2 Case C-209/03, *Bidar*, EU:C:2005:169, para. 33 and case-law referred to therein.
3 Case C-36/02, *Omega*, EU:C:2004:614, para. 21.
4 Case C-499/06, *Nerkowska*, EU:C:2008:300, para. 20.

DOI: 10.4324/9781003376019-2

Justice had to decide whether directly effective provisions of the Treaty were to be applied by referring national courts in domestic proceedings. Cases with various forms of a cross-border (interstate) element are the classic academic example of national judicial proceedings belonging to the category of cases that are governed by EU law. Still, the existence of the cross-border element often is difficult to establish.[5]

When the Charter of Fundamental Rights entered into force, the Court of Justice started to answer preliminary questions from national courts on the applicability of the Charter in domestic proceedings. This is a consequence of the wording of Article 51 (1) of the Charter, according to which it is addressed 'to the Member States only when they are implementing Union law', which again requires a national court in a particular case to decide whether it is a situation of implementing Union law or not. Following the entry into force of the Charter, two main situations have been identified in respect of EU fundamental rights, when national courts act within the scope of EU law: 1) when national measures to be applied by the court implement EU or apply EU law (the so-called *Wachauf* line of cases) and 2) when national measures derogate from EU law (the so-called *ERT* line of cases).[6] So, the Charter alone is not applicable, if other sources of EU law do not apply to the facts of the case, but it is applicable – just as applicable are the general principles of EU law – when other acts of EU law apply and prohibit the Member States from doing something, or when EU law applies and permits the Member States to do something.[7]

Apart from the discussion on the scope of 'implementation of EU law' for the purpose of application of the Charter, it shall be reminded that national courts act as EU courts when they apply directly applicable provisions of EU

5 Compare, for example, case C-286/81, *Oosthoek's Uitgeversmaatschappij BV*, EU:C:1982:438; case C-112/00, *Schmidberger*, EU:C:2003:333; case C-60/00, *Carpenter*, EU:C:2002:434 and C-318/00, *Bacardi-Martini*, EU:C:2003:41.

6 Explanatory Notes to the Charter; see also: X. Groussot, I. Pech, G.T. Petursson, *The Scope of Application of Fundamental Rights on Member States Action: In Search of Certainty in EU Adjudication*, Eric Stein Working Paper no 1/2011, pp. 1–2; K. Lenaerts, Exploring the Limits of the EU Charter of Fundamental Rights, *European Constitutional Law Review*, 2012, 8, no. 3, pp. 375–403, p. 382; F. Fontanell, Implementation of EU Law Through Domestic Measures after Fransson: The Court of Justice Buys Time and 'Non-Preclusion' Troubles Loom Large, *European Law Review*, 2014, 39(5), pp. 682–700, pp. 683–684; A. Ward, Article 51, in: S. Peers, T. Harvey, J. Kenner, A. Ward (eds.), *The EU Charter of Fundamental Rights. A Commentary*. Second Edition, Hart Publishing, 2021, pp. 1553–1610; A. Wróbel, Artykuł 51 [Article 51], in: A. Wróbel (ed.), *Karta Praw Podstawowych Unii Europejskiej. Komentarz. Drugie wydanie* [The Charter of Fundamental Rights of the European Union. Commentary. Second edition], C.H. Beck, 2020, pp. 1249–1288; for the domestic abundant literature on the scope of application of the Charter, see further: M. Szwarc, Zakres związania państw członkowskich Kartą praw podstawowych Unii Europejskiej w kontekście stosowania prawa karnego (uwagi na tle orzecznictwa TSUE) [The Scope of Application of the Charter of Fundamental Rights of the European Union by the Member States in the Criminal Law Context (Remarks on the Recent CJEU Case-Law)], *Studia Prawnicze*, 2017, no. 3, pp. 47–79.

7 F. Fontanell, Implementation of EU Law . . ., p. 687.

secondary acts (mostly regulations), national provisions implementing EU secondary legislation (mostly directives), and national provisions derogating from provisions of the TFEU. The analysis of preliminary rulings of the CJEU allows us to conclude that, in addition to the aforementioned, a case falls within the scope of EU law, when national law prohibits reverse discrimination stemming from a privileged situation enjoyed by those, whose legal position is covered directly by EU law[8] and when national law refers to EU law.[9] This means that there is a variety of factors that must be taken into the account by any national court adjudicating any type of proceedings before it can ascertain that it is supposed to act as an EU court. The use of the concept of 'purely internal' situations or cases[10] may be helpful, but it also requires the same analysis, of whether a given dispute is governed by EU law. Apart from that, it often happens that the actual scope of application of EU law is determined by the CJEU only after a preliminary reference has been made by a national court seeking to establish whether it is required to apply EU law.[11]

8 A. Somek: *Reverse Discrimination Revisited. Coping with an Incongruity Between Community Law and Member States Legislation*, Vienna Working Papers in Legal Theory, Political Philosophy and Applied Ethics No 9, Vienna, 1998, p. 6; J. Krommendijk, Wide Open and Unguarded Stand Our Gates: The CJEU and References for a Preliminary Ruling in Purely Internal Situations, *German Law Journal*, 2017, 18, no. 1359, p. 1360; see also R. White, A Fresh Look at Reverse Discrimination? *European Law Review*, 1993, 18, no. 6, pp. 527–532; C. Ritter, Purely Internal Situations, Reverse Discrimination, Guimont, Dzodzi and Article 234, *European Law Review*, 2006, 31, no. 5, pp. 690–710; P. Van Elsuwege, St. Adam, Belgium: The Limits of Constitutional Dialogue for the Prevention of Reverse Discrimination, *European Constitutional Law Review*, 2009, 5, no. 2, pp. 327–339; C. Dautricourt, S. Thomas, Reverse Discrimination and Free Movement of Persons under Community Law: All for Ulysses, Nothing for Penelope?, *European Law Review*, 2009, 34, no. 3, pp. 433–454; D. Kochenov, Reverse Discrimination in EC Law, *European Law Review*, 2010, 35, no. 1, pp. 116–118; P. Van Elsuwege, European Union Citizenship and the Purely Internal Rule Revisited: Decision of 5 May 2011, Case C-434/09 Shirley McCarthy v. Secretary of State for the Home Department, *European Constitutional Law Review*, 2011, 7, no. 2, pp. 308–324; St. Adam, P. Van Elsuwege, Citizenship Rights and the Federal Balance Between the European Union and its Member States: Comment on Dereci, *European Law Review*, 2012, 37, no. 2, pp. 176–190; K. Eisele, A.P. van der Mei, Portability of Social Benefits and Reverse Discrimination of EU Citizens Vis-a-vis Turkish Nationals: Comment on Akdas, *European Law Review*, 2012, 37, no. 2, pp. 204–212; C. Ginter, Free Public Transport of Tallinn, Estonia: A Case to Justify (Reverse) Discrimination on the Basis of Residence, *European Law Review*, 2017, 42, no. 6, pp. 894–908.

9 Compare judgments C-297/88 and C-197/89, *Dzodzi*, EU:C:1990:360; C-298/15, *Borta*, EU:C:2017:266, and C-195/21, *Smetna palata na Republika Bulgaria*, EU:C:2022:239 with C-346/93 *Kleinwort Benson*, EU:C:1995:85; C-217/05, *Confederación Española de Empresarios de Estaciones de Servicio*, EU:C:2006:784; see also S. Lefevre, The Interpretation of Community Law by the Court of Justice in Areas of National Competence, *European Law Review*, 2004, 29, no. 4, pp. 501–516.

10 For example, S. Iglesias Sanchez, Purely Internal Situations and the Limits of EU Law: A Consolidated Case-Law or a Notion to be Abandoned? *European Constitutional Law Review*, 2018, 14, no. 1, pp. 7–36.

11 For example, whether certain rights stem from an EU directive, see C-569/16 and C-570/16, *Stadt Wuppertal v. Maria Elisabeth Bauer and Volker Willmeroth v. Martina Broßonn*, EU:C:2018:871.

The term 'Community case' started to be applied in the Polish literature quite early,[12] as a tool to identify those cases which required including a Community/EU law element into the legal grounds for deciding/adjudicating. Soon after, the doctrinal concept of the 'EU case' have been developed in Polish literature[13] with the view to provide the national courts with guidelines enabling them to determine whether a case to be adjudicated by them falls within the scope of the EU law. Pursuant to this concept, an 'EU case' is a case in which the dispute between the parties – even partially – falls within the temporal, personal, and material scope of application of EU law. In other words, there must be a link between the facts of the whole case or the contentious issue and EU law. This link is also called the 'EU element' of a case. It may take the form of 1) an interstate (cross-border) element, 2) a legal basis of the claim being derived from directly effective provisions of EU law, 3) application of national provisions implementing EU secondary legislation, 4) reverse discrimination, and 5) referral to EU law in national legislation.

The following chapters of this part present examples of different types of EU cases, in the meaning given earlier, which were selected from the case-law of the Supreme Court, administrative courts, and the Constitutional Tribunal.

12 D. Kornobis-Romanowska, *Sąd w prawie wspólnotowym* [Court in Community Law], Wolters Kluwer, 2007; A. Wilk, P. Wróbel, Orzecznictwo sądów administracyjnych w sprawach wspólnotowych [Case-Law of Administrative Courts in Community Cases], *Europejski Przegląd Sądowy*, 2005, no. 2, s. 49.

13 See D. Miąsik, Sprawa wspólnotowa przed sądem krajowym [A Community Case Before a National Court], *Europejski Przegląd Sądowy*, 2008, no. 9, pp. 16–22; D. Miąsik, Pojęcie sprawy wspólnotowej z perspektywy właściwości Izby Pracy, Ubezpieczeń Społecznych i Spraw Publicznych Sądu Najwyższego (zarys problematyki), [The notion of a community case from the perspective of the jurisdiction of Labour, Social Security and Public Affairs Chamber of the Supreme Court (outline of issues)], in: K. Ślebzak, W. Wróbel (ed.), *Studia i Analizy Sądu Najwyższego*, Vol. II, Warszawa, 2008, pp. 227–269.

2 The concept of the EU case in the case-law of the Supreme Court

Dawid Miąsik

Introduction

The Supreme Court's case-law analysis shows that the 'EU' case concept is rarely mentioned. One of the few examples in which that concept was used is the order of the Supreme Court of 18 July 2018, case III UZ 10/18.[1] The Supreme Court ruled that under the concept of the 'EU case', one should understand judicial proceedings in the course of which 'the court is under the duty to take into account European Union law and its principles when formulating the legal basis for the decision to be taken' and that such an 'obligation results from the temporal, personal and material scope of the EU law'. Case III UZ 10/18 concerned an appeal of the Polish Pension Office against a judgment revoking one of its decisions. The case was sent back to the office by the court of the second instance because the court considered the decision to have been issued prematurely. The Court of Appeals thought that the challenged decision concerning the application of Article 13 of Regulation 883/2004[2] could not be issued by the Polish Pension Office before a decision of a competent pension office of another Member State, excluding a Polish entrepreneur from the social security scheme of that other State, becoming final. The office appealed to the Supreme Court. The proceedings before the Supreme Court were limited to a strictly procedural issue as pursuant to the national procedure, the Supreme Court was not allowed to rule on the merits of the case. It could only determine whether the court of the second instance was entitled to revoke the decision of the Polish Pension Office. This issue may seem to be

1 By this order, the panel of three judges of the SC made a reference to the panel of seven judges of the SC, which in turn, made a preliminary reference to the European Court of Justice (CJEU) in C-522/18 DŚ vs. Zakład Ubezpieczeń Społecznych Oddział w Jaśle (EU:C:2020:42) on issues concerning Directive 2000/78, as this panel consisted of two judges covered by new legislation lowering the retirement age of judges from 70 to 65 years.

2 Regulation (EC) No 883/2004 of the European Parliament and of the Council of 29 April 2004 on the coordination of social security systems, OJ L 166, 30.04.2004, p. 1 with later amendments.

DOI: 10.4324/9781003376019-3

covered by national law alone pursuant to the principle of national procedural autonomy, as the EU law does not regulate when and whether a national court may revoke the decision of the pension office issued under Regulation 883/2004. Yet even in such proceedings, the assessment of the legality of the judgment of a court revoking an administrative decision depends upon the results of interpretation of EU law (Regulation 883/2004 and Regulation 987/2009),[3] since that EU law regulates the rights and duties of competent pension authorities of different Member States. Hence, a purely procedural issue concerning the legality of a national court's ruling (revocation of a decision instead of judgment on the case's merits) was held to fall within the scope of EU substantive law.

The fact that the concept of the EU case has been referred to not infrequently does not mean that the Supreme Court had not followed the guidelines resulting from that concept. In those cases where the EU element is evident in the proceedings, there is no need to explain that the proceedings concerned fall within the scope of EU law. Such is the case when the Supreme Court applies national provisions implementing sources of EU secondary law. It then emphasises that principles of EU law such as direct effect and primacy 'apply in cases which are of European proceedings by their nature due to the courts' application of national law provisions implementing the European Union directives'.[4] On the other hand, the Supreme Court refers directly to the concept of the EU case when the courts of lower instances have not noticed the EU aspect of a case or when – in the light of the parties' positions taken before the Supreme Court[5] or controversies articulated in the public opinion or legal doctrine[6] – the admissibility of applying EU law is called into question.

An insignificant number of direct references to the concept of the EU case in the case-law of the Supreme Court results from a relatively good understanding, by that court, of when Polish courts should apply the EU law. Only a few instances of deciding the outcome of EU cases without applying EU law and its principles may be indicated. Such an example is provided by the issue

3 Regulation (EC) No 987/2009 of the European Parliament and of the Council of 16 September 2009 laying down the procedure for implementing Regulation (EC) No 883/2004 on the coordination of social security systems, OJ L 284, 30.10.2009, pp. 1–42 with later amendments.

4 See, for example, judgments of the Supreme Court (SC) of 14 April 2010, case III SK 1/10; of 21 September 2010, case III SK 8/10.

5 See, for example, the order of the panel of seven judges of the SC of 29 August 2019, case III UZP 3/17 following C-545/17, *Pawlak*, EU:C:2019:260, where the applicability of EU law (directive 97/67) was questioned by the panel of three judges of the Supreme Court making preliminary reference to the panel of seven judges of the Supreme Court.

6 See also the judgment of SC of 5 December 2019, case III PO 7/18 implementing C-585/18, *A.K.*, EU:C:2019:982, where the applicability of EU law (both Directive 2000/78 and Article 47 CFR) was challenged before the CJEU by the representatives of Poland and by the public officials in the media.

of the impact of Directive 97/67[7] (the Postal Market Directive) on the application of a national procedural provision regarding the meeting of the procedural time limit in the event of posting a procedural document at a post office of the postal operator instead of lodging it directly before the court (Article 165 § 2 Code of Civil Procedure – from now on referred to as CCP). Previously, before the reference for a preliminary ruling in Case C-545/17 *Pawlak*[8] was made, the Supreme Court had repeatedly adjudicated under Article 165 § 2 CCP alone without considering Directive 97/67. Some judgments even denied the directive's impact on such national regulations.[9]

The concept of the 'EU case' and application of EU law *ex officio*

The insignificant number of cases in which the Supreme Court would clarify courts of lower instances as well as the general public, whether a particular case should be considered as a case with an 'EU element', can be explained by the attention of the Supreme Court given to the duty of Polish courts to apply EU law in its early judgments delivered in the EU proceedings. In those cases, the Supreme Court focused on the admissibility of the so-called *ex officio* application of EU law. This issue is of great practical importance for the case-law of the Supreme Court. The court is bound with the grounds for appeal in cassation raised by the pleading party. While the courts of the lower instances apply the principle of '*iura novit curia*' and hence are free to apply any provision of Polish or European law that is suitable for the resolution of the dispute between the parties (within limits set by the statement of claims or the appeal), the Supreme Court examines the appeal in cassation only within the set of provisions listed in the grounds of this appeal by the professional lawyer representing the party. That binding of the Supreme Court with the grounds of appeal could mean that in the event of a lack of reference to the provisions of EU law in the grounds for the appeal, the Supreme Court would not apply EU law at all, even where the need to apply it would be obvious. Such a failure to raise issues of EU law in cassation proceedings could result from the initial failure to apply EU law by the courts of lower instances or from the attorney's incompetence. Therefore, quite early in the case-law of the Supreme Court, the admissibility of applying EU law *ex officio* was adopted. This occurs both on the grounds for the appeal without referral to the provisions of EU law and when such a reference had been made, albeit to inappropriate EU law

7 Directive 97/67/EC of the European Parliament and of the Council of 15 December 1997 on common rules for the development of the internal market of Community postal services and the improvement of quality of service, OJ L 15, 21.01.1998, pp. 14–25.

8 EU:C:2019:260.

9 See judgments of the SC listed in the preliminary reference made in order of the panel of seven judges of the SC of 19 July 2017, case III UZP 3/17, and order of the panel of seven judges of the SC of 29 August 2019, case III UZP 3/17, adopted following the judgment of CJEU in C-545/17, *Pawlak*, EU:C:2019:260.

provisions.[10] It was sufficient that the plea covered provisions of Polish law that implemented EU law or that fell within the scope of EU law.

For the first time, the Supreme Court has encountered that problem in cases relating to the protection of employees in the event of an employer's insolvency. Those cases had been clearly of the EU nature (as falling within the scope of Directive 80/987).[11] Back in 2006, this aspect, however, was not noticed at all by the courts of both instances, as well as by the representatives of the employees filing cassation. Applying the provisions of the national law alone led to the issuance of a decision depriving employees of the protection they were entitled to under Directive 80/987. However, the fact that the national rules were contrary to Directive 80/987 was found only at the stage of the cassation proceedings, where the EU aspect appeared for the first time as a result of the *ex officio* activity of the Supreme Court. While under the principle of the national procedural autonomy following *van Schijdel*,[12] the Supreme Court could completely ignore the issue of incompatibility of statutory provisions with Directive 80/987 for the sake of EU law effectiveness, the Supreme Court held that although 'in principle that Court is not required to consider any potential infringement of EU law provisions, if the party bringing the appeal in cassation has not raised the infringement of those provisions in the grounds for the appeal', nevertheless, it is 'competent to apply the EU law provisions when assessing the correctness of applying the provisions of Polish law by the court of the second instance, when the provisions of Polish law referred to in the appeal in cassation fall within the scope of EU law regulatory framework'. Thus, it turned out that the Supreme Court determined the admissibility of applying EU law *ex officio* by referencing the concept of the EU case.

10 Judgment of the SC of 5 December 2006, case II PK 18/06.

11 Council Directive 80/987/EEC of 20 October 1980 on the approximation of the laws of the Member States relating to the protection of employees in the event of the insolvency of their employer, OJ L 283, 28.10.1980, pp. 23–27 with amendments.

12 Joint cases C-430/93 i C-431/93, *van Schijndel et al.*, EU:C:1995:441, para. 22; see more S. Prechal, Community law in national courts: the lessons from van Schijndel, *CMLRev.* 1998, pp. 681–706. For further discussions, see: A. Wallerman, Towards an EU Law Doctrine on the Exercise of Discretion in National Courts? The Member States' Self-Imposed Limits on National Procedural Autonomy, *CMLRev.*, 2016, 53, no. 2, pp. 339–360; T. Heukels, Joined Cases C-430/93 and C-431/93, Van Schijndel and Van Veen v. Stichting Pensioenfonds voor Fysiotherapeuten; and Case C- 312/93, Peterbroeck, Van Campenhout, *CMLRev.*, 1996, 33, no. 2, pp. 337–353, N. Shelkoplyas, National Procedures, Public Policy and EC Law. From Van Schijndel to Eco Swiss and Beyond, *European Review of Private Law*, 2004, 12, no. 5, pp. 589–611, H. Schebesta, Does the National Court Know European Law? A Note on 'Ex Officio' Application after Asturcom, *European Review of Private Law*, 2010, 18, no. 4, pp. 847–880, A.M. Mancaleoni, The Obligation on Dutch and Italian Courts to Apply EU Law of Their Own Motion, *European Review of Private Law*, 2016, 24, no. 3, pp. 553–578, C.M. Kakouris, Do the Member States Possess Judicial Procedural 'autonomy', *CMLRev.*, 1997, 34, no. 6, pp. 1389–1412, see also M. Baran, *Stosowanie z urzędu prawa UE przez sądy krajowe* [Application of EU law by national courts ex officio], Wolters Kluwer Polska, 2014, especially pp. 127–257.

The Supreme Court presented a similar approach regarding the application *ex officio* of Article 21 TFEU and Regulation No. 1408/71.[13] In the case I UK 59/11,[14] the problem was whether the provisions mentioned earlier of EU law applied to the right to further payment of the benefit to the Polish national entitled to a social pension (the social security benefit for people who had become unable to work before starting their professional activity, and for that reason could not acquire the right to pension for incapacity for work) who decided to study in another Member State. Polish legislation made the right to the payment of that benefit conditional upon the fact that the recipient remained in the territory of Poland.[15] Before the assessment of whether EU law (and the right to retain the payment of the benefit in the event of moving to another Member State) covered a social pension, the Supreme Court needed to decide whether it could *ex officio* examine the compliance of Polish legislation with the provisions of Regulation No. 1408/71. These provisions had not been referred to in the appeal in cassation that had been limited to alleged the infringement of Article 21 TFEU only.

It is also worth noting that the Supreme Court allowed for the '*ex officio*' application of EU law not only to decide the case in which infringement of provisions of Polish law implementing EU directives had been raised but also, more importantly, from the perspective of the effectiveness of EU law, at an earlier stage when the Supreme Court considers before the adjudication, whether it is necessary to refer for a preliminary ruling to the Court of Justice.[16] This means that it is admissible for the Supreme Court to apply EU law *ex officio* to verify, with the help of CJEU, whether the case is an EU case at all. Once again, Case C-545/17 *Pawlak*[17] provides an excellent example of the *ex officio* application of EU law, this time at the stage of making preliminary reference to the CJEU. No issues of EU law were raised in the appeal to the Supreme Court nor in the referral from the panel of three judges of the Supreme Court to an extended panel of seven judges that took over the case and made the reference.

Other examples of *ex officio* application of EU law by the Supreme Court, which are discussed in more detail in other parts of this monograph, include cases II 504/17 and III PK 53/19.

To sum up this part, it follows from the case-law of the Supreme Court that if the appeal in cassation includes the ground of misinterpretation or improper

13 Regulation (EEC) No. 1408/71 of the Council of 14 June 1971 on the application of social security schemes to employed persons and their families moving within the Community, OJ L 149, 5.07.1971, pp. 2–50 with amendments.

14 Judgment of the SC of 20 September 2011, case I UK 59/11.

15 Similarly as in the case regarding another benefit from the social security scheme C-499/06, *Nerkowska*, EU:C:2008:132.

16 Judgments of the SC: of 5 December 2006, case II PK 18/06; of 18 December 2006, case II PK 17/06; of 4 January 2008, case I UK 182/07.

17 EU:C:2019:260.

application of a provision of Polish law, such a plea in law will implicitly cover the plea of interpretation incompatible with EU law or the application of a Polish law provision incompatible with EU law. On the other hand, if a plea regarding failure to apply a provision of Polish law is raised, it will also include the plea of faulty determination of inconsistencies between Polish law and EU law.[18] This means that – except cases in which national courts apply directly effective provisions of European regulations – any plea raising wrongful interpretation or application of a provision of Polish law that falls within the scope of application of EU law also encompasses a plea of a wrongful interpretation or application of a provision of EU law.

The concept of the 'EU case' and substantive or procedural law

EU law affects mainly the area of substantive law in the Member States and its application. Therefore, the majority of EU cases are judicial proceedings, in which national courts apply directly effective provisions of EU substantive law or national provisions of substantive that fall within the scope of EU law. In the latter group of cases, EU law is applied indirectly. It serves either as a source of an interpretative standard for the principle of consistent interpretation (e.g., what does the notion of 'transfer of undertaking' mean? Does it encompass the transfer of cleaning tasks from the employer to an external servicing company?)[19] or as a source of a legal norm that must be applied according to the principles of direct effect and primacy (e.g., is a provision of national law that makes practical effectiveness of an exclusive right to an active substance of a patented drug dependent upon commencing production in Poland compatible with Article 34 TFEU?).[20]

However, as Case C-545/17 *Pawlak*[21] (III UZP 3/17 before the SC) shows, substantive provisions of EU law may affect the application of national procedural rules. Thus, the *Pawlak* case is an exciting example of the practical difficulties experienced when determining the actual scope of the application of EU law.[22] It also shows that the duty of national courts to apply EU law is not only activated when the whole dispute or the essence of the case falls within the scope of EU law. It is sufficient that an incidental issue to the main proceedings is even indirectly governed by EU law. Of course, in such

18 Judgment of the SC of 20 September 2011, case I UK 59/11, discussed in more detail in the section on 'seemingly EU cases'.

19 Judgment of the SC of 3 March 2015, case I PK 187/14.

20 See judgment of the SC of 10 February 2006, case III CSK 112/05 discussed in more details further subsequently.

21 EU:C:2019:260.

22 For more detailed discussion, see D. Miąsik, M. Szwarc, Effectiveness of EU Directives in National Courts – Judicial Dialogue Continues: The Court of Justice's Judgment in C-545/17 Pawlak, *Polish Yearbook of International Law*, 2020, pp. 267–286.

circumstances, a national court will be obliged to apply EU law only in resolving that incidental issue.

In the *Pawlak* case, the main dispute arose between a Polish farmer living in Poland and *Kasa Rolniczego Ubezpieczenia Społecznego* (a unit governed by public law dealing with paying benefits for farmers – from now on KRUS). It concerned the refusal of the KRUS to pay compensation to the farmer for an accident at work, which had taken place in Poland. Such compensation payments fall totally outside the scope of EU law. Yet, an issue calling for the application of EU law arose in incidental proceedings. Their subject matter was limited to the question of whether the KRUS had failed to meet the deadline for filing an appeal against the judgment of the court of the first instance by delivering its appeal by a postal operator who was not a designated operator as required by the Polish code of civil procedure. The problem to be solved was whether such an issue was covered by Directive 97/67,[23] which does not directly deal with national civil procedures. Because of that – before the reference for a preliminary ruling was made to CJUE in C-545/17 *Pawlak* – the impact of the EU postal law on the national procedural law had not been realised at all in the prevailing case-law of the Supreme Court.[24] As a result, it had been ruled by the Supreme Court that posting a procedural document at the Polish postal office of an operator that had not been the designated operator meant that the party had missed the time limit when the document was received by the competent court after the expiry of the statutory time limit to perform a procedural act. This resulted in a given procedural act (e.g., submitting an appeal) being ineffective and subject to dismissal without looking at the case's merits. Since Directive 97/67 was focused on the creation of the internal market for postal services, it remained to be solved by the CJEU, whether its scope also encompassed national procedural provisions. The positive reply to that question in C-545/17 *Pawlak* meant that the case before the Supreme Court – concerning a minor procedural problem – turned out to be an EU case calling for the use of the principle of consistent interpretation. The lesson to be learned from C-545/17 *Pawlak* is that even when the subject matter of the main proceedings falls outside of EU law, one cannot exclude a situation in which an EU law element calls for the application of EU law and its principles when resolving an incidental issue, which must be adjudicated before examining the merits of the case.

Another interesting example of the interweaving of the EU substantive law – this time one of the freedoms of the internal market – with national procedure

23 Directive 97/67 on common rules for the development of the internal market of Community postal services, OJ L 15, 21.01.1998, p. 14.

24 Orders of the Supreme Court: of 3 June 2015, case V CZ 33/15; of 8 June 2015, case III SW 41/15; of 14 July 2015, case II UZ 10/15; of 25 August 2015., case II UZ 16/15; of 14 April 2016, case IV CZ 15/16; of 20 April 2016, case II UZ 75/15 and of 17 May 2016, case II PZ 2/16.

concerns the issue of the nullity of proceedings based on the claim of the failure to secure the party with rights of defence. In the case decided by the judgment of the Supreme Court of 10 April 2019, case II UK 504/17, an objection was raised by the Prosecutor General that the proceedings before the court of the second instance were invalid on the ground that a party had been deprived of the right to defence as a result of being represented by a professional legal representative who had no right to stand before Polish courts. The party, on whose behalf the public prosecutor brought the appeal, had been represented by a Polish lawyer, running a law firm in Germany under the freedom of establishment. The prosecutor argued that such a lawyer could not be the party's representative in the proceedings before Polish courts, since he had not been entered into the list of foreign lawyers providing legal services in the territory of Poland. However, the Supreme Court held that the proceedings were not invalid, since a Polish lawyer running a law firm in Germany was providing legal services in Poland under Article 56 TFEU and hence was covered by the free movement of services and Council Directive 77/249/EEC of 22 March 1977 to facilitate the effective exercise by lawyers of freedom to provide services.[25] The presence of the cross-border element and the EU directive sufficed to determine the case's character – although limited to the issue of nullity of the proceedings. The reference to C-99/16, Jean – Philippe Lahorgue,[26] helped the Supreme Court to assess the claim in the light of the existing caselaw of the CJEU without making preliminary reference.

Another example of the impact of EU substantive rules on the national procedure is found in the already discussed order of the Supreme Court of 18 July 2018, case III UZ 10/18. The problem was whether the decision of the Polish pension authority declaring that the Polish entrepreneur was subject to the Polish social security scheme instead of being subjected to the system of another Member State (with lower social security contributions) was premature when that entrepreneur had challenged before Slovak's courts the decision of the Slovak pension authority on the exemption from Slovak legislation and that decision was quashed in the course judicial proceedings. The case was referred back to the Slovak pension authority for reconsideration.[27] The case, which before the Supreme Court was limited to a purely procedural issue, was held to fall within the scope of EU law; since the coordination of social security systems was based on the principle of a single jurisdiction, EU law regulated the cooperation procedure between pension authorities of different Member States, including the results of provisional determination of

25 OJ L 78, 26.03.1977, pp. 17–18 with amendments.

26 EU:C:2017:391.

27 The extended panel of the Supreme Court established to examine that legal problem, referred to the Court of Justice a question for preliminary ruling on the compatibility with EU law of the provisions on the retirement of Supreme Court judges at a new reduced age, order of the panel of seven judges of the SC of 2 August 2018, case III UZP 4/18 (C-522/18).

applicable legislation. Although the grounds for annulling or changing a decision were subject to the legislation of a respective Member State, the application of these grounds had to respect those principles of EU social security law.

The category of EU cases in which EU law affects the way procedural rules are applied should also include the judgment of the Supreme Court of 5 December 2016, case III SK 18/14, issued following the preliminary reference to CJEU in C-231/15 *Petrotel*.[28] In this judgment, the problem of compatibility – with Article 47 of the Charter of Fundamental Rights and the right to an effective legal remedy – of the practice developed in national case-law was decided. The courts developed a practice of revoking such decisions of *Prezes Urząd Komunikacji Elektronicznej* (the President of the Office of Electronic Communications, national regulatory authority – NRA) that executed its original (regulatory) decisions. The latter decisions imposed specific regulatory obligations upon dominant operators. They also specified the asymmetric rates for call termination to be applied between operators and a schedule to introduce them in practice. The executing decisions enforced this schedule when operators could not reach an agreement compatible with the regulatory decisions of the NRA. The executing decisions depended on the content and existence of the regulatory decision. Since that decision was quashed in other judicial proceedings only after the national regulatory authority had issued the executing decisions, lower courts took the opinion that the executing decision, enforcing the rates to be applied between telecom operators stipulated in the original decision together with the schedule, lost its factual and legal basis for introducing rates stipulated in the regulatory decision into agreements between operators. While the substance of decisions issued by the President of UKE was governed by Polish Telecommunications Law implementing various EU telecommunications directives, those directives were silent regarding the effects of revocation of national regulatory offices' decisions. However, in parallel to Article 47 CFR, these directives obliged the Member States to provide telecom operators with the right to effective judicial remedy against the decision of the national regulatory authority. The Supreme Court thought, both in the preliminary reference in C-231/15 *Petrotel* and the judgment delivered following the preliminary ruling, in this case that Article 47 CFR mandated such revocation of executing decisions of the national regulatory authority with a retroactive effect, instead of a *pro futuro* effect advocated by the administration and mandated by the Polish code of administrative procedure. Here the link with EU law took the form of an effective remedy that had to be provided to telecom operators under directives and Article 47 CFR.

The EU case and the temporal scope of EU law

While substantive (material) and personal scope of application of EU law play a dominant role in establishing whether a national court is hearing the

28 EU:C:2016:769.

'EU case', the temporal aspects of EU law also need to be taken into account. Above all, problems of that kind arise in relation to the accession of new Member States. They decided to take into account, first of all, the provisions of the Accession Treaty and, secondly, the principles of EU intertemporal law.[29] According to the latter, EU law applies to new facts of the case, to new results of old facts of the case (e.g., the length of service), and the new results of legal relations continuing at the accession date. Therefore, a case concerning the facts that 'have been completed' before the accession date is not an EU case.[30]

Another group of cases, when courts are required to consider the temporal scope of application of EU law, are cases concerning retirement pensions and similar benefits, where various insurance periods had been completed before the accession to the EU. Here, a fine example is provided by the issue of the application of Directive 76/207[31] in proceedings relating to a pension due at a reduced age.[32] The employment and insurance periods were developed years before Poland accessed the European Union. However, since the earlier retirement age had been reached by an employee (the orchestra conductor) after the accession of Poland to the European Union, it was admissible to apply the provisions of Directive 76/207 prohibiting discrimination on the grounds of gender in the area of acquisition the right to a pension at a reduced age. The use of directive 76/207 allowed the Supreme Court to verify whether the provisions of national law originating in 1983 were compatible with EU law (more extensively on this case, see the chapter on the principles of direct effect and primacy). The CJEU had already established that the Directive concerned also covered the conditions for acquiring pension rights at a reduced age. This resulted in a judgment granting the pension, contrary to the court's rulings of lower instances and previous practice of the Supreme Court.

In an 'old' Member State, the temporal aspect of the scope of EU law takes a different form: it relates to the date of entry into force of the acts of Union law from the position of legal assessment of the facts of the case. For example, in the resolution of the Supreme Court of 19 November 2008, I PZP 4/08, it was noticed, when selecting the EU legal basis for the reconstruction of

29 See more broadly S. Kaleda, *Przejęcie prawa wspólnotowego przez nowe państwa członkowskie* [Takeover of Community law by new Member States], Wydawnictwo Prawo i Praktyka Gospodarcza, 2003; N. Półtorak, Ratione Temporis Application of the Preliminary Rulings Procedure, *CMLRev.*, 2008, 45, no. 1357, pp. 1357–1381.

30 Judgment of the SC of 9 August 2006, case III SK 6/06 concerning a cartel fined prior to the accession.

31 Council Directive 76/207/EEC of 9 February 1976 on the implementation of the principle of equal treatment for men and women as regards access to employment, vocational training and promotion, and working conditions, OJ L 39, 14.02.1976, pp. 40–42.

32 Judgment of the SC of 4 January 2008, case I UK 182/07.

the appropriate interpretation standard, that Directive 2006/54,[33] which repealed, among others Directive 76/207, did not apply to the facts of that case, since Directive 2006/54 'entered into force after termination of the employment contract with the claimant and after she had acquired pension rights'. Consequently, the legal situation of the claimant should have been assessed in the light of Directive 76/207 alone.

An example of the impact on the temporal scope of application of EU law of the entry into force of amendments to EU legislation is found in the judgment of the Supreme Court of 20 September 2011, case I UK 59/11. Here the date of entry into force of the amendment of the Annex to Regulation No. 1408/71 was crucial. At the time, when the pension office suspended payment of a social pension (social security benefit for people who had become not capable of working before starting a professional activity and, thus, could not acquire the right to a pension for incapacity to work) to a disabled Polish student who moved to the UK to pursue academic education, the social pension was listed in Annex IIa to Regulation No. 1408/71 among other benefits, for which a Member State could rightfully exclude the transfer of benefits paid in the event of a change of residence to another Member State. The listing in Annex IIa was not taken into account by the lower courts, who based their judgment on C-499/06 *Nerkowska,* which also concerned the issue of transfer of residence to another Member State, but there the benefit at issue was not covered by the EU rules on coordination of social security systems

The EU case and the personal scope of EU law

Where the temporal scope confirms the application of EU law to the facts of a case, a court must verify whether these provisions fall within the personal scope of the application of EU law. The question to be answered is whether a party to the proceedings (most often the one who pursues a claim but also a party defending itself against liability for infringement of national law) is an addressee of an EU rule, from which an outcome of the case favourable to them could result. Here one can distinguish two situations.

The first occurs when parties to the proceedings are aware that there is a norm in EU law that they consider to be favourable to their legal situation. Then in the appeal in cessation, they wrongfully raise an objection alleging an infringement of law by the court of the second instance consisting of the failure to apply EU law when deciding a case. It is then for the court to verify whether the personal scope of the invoked provision of EU law

33 Directive 2006/54/EC of the European Parliament and of the Council of 5 July 2006 on the implementation of the principle of equal opportunities and equal treatment of men and women in matters of employment and occupation (recast), OJ L 204, 26.07.2006, pp. 23–36.

covers the claimant. An example of an EU case, in which that aspect of the personal scope was of crucial importance, is the order of the Supreme Court of 3 October 2013, case III SK 11/13, in which the appeal in cessation has been refused to be heard. The application for a granting ***writ of certiorari*** to the Supreme Court was based on the need to solve a legal issue, whether cooperative savings and credit union, registered and operating in Poland, was an undertaking within the meaning of Article 54 and Article 101 TFEU. The Supreme Court rejected hearing the case on the following grounds. Firstly, there was no issue of EU law requiring the application of EU law since Article 54 TFEU defined the company's concept only for the internal market. The applicant had not made use of such freedom. Secondly, that case did not concern the application of EU competition rules, including Article 101 TFEU, but only Polish provisions implementing directive 98/27.[34] Hence, the facts of the case were outside the personal scope of Articles 101 and 54 TFEU. It was then evident that the Court of Appeals could not have breached these provisions as they were inapplicable to the claimant.

The second situation demands a detailed examination of the personal scope of EU law. It arises much more frequently in cases where the Supreme Court is about to apply provisions of Polish law implementing various acts of EU law. In such cases, it is necessary to decide whether EU law demands that national provisions cover a party to the proceedings within their scope. An example of analysing EU law's personal scope is the Supreme Court resolution of 9 September 2015, case III SZP 2/15. In this case, the Supreme Court had searched in various consumer directives for an EU standard that would justify the modification of a legal definition of the consumer under Article 22 of the Civil Code,[35] to cover within that term an injured party pursuing claims from the insurance company under the policy against civil liability insurance in respect of the use of motor vehicle issued by such a company for the perpetrator. Since there was no general definition of consumer in the European legislation, each consumer directive had a different personal scope of application and Directive 209/103[36] was silent in that respect; the Supreme Court ruled that it was

34 Directive 98/27/EC of the European Parliament and of the Council of 19 May 1998 on injunctions for the protection of consumers' interests, OJ L 166, 11.07.1998, pp. 51–55.

35 Pursuant to that provision, 'The consumer is a natural person who has entered with an entrepreneur into a legal act which is not directly related to his or her business or profession'. The contentious issue was whether the requirement to 'enter into legal act' with an entrepreneur (insurance undertaking) is fulfilled, when injured party demands damages from the insurance company of the perpetrator.

36 Directive 2009/103/EC of the European Parliament and of the Council of 16 September 2009 relating to insurance against civil liability in respect of the use of motor vehicles, and the enforcement of the obligation to insure against such liability, OJ L 263, 7.10.2009, pp. 11–31.

not under the duty to interpret Article 22 of the Civil Code extensively to align it with EU law.

Another example is a situation in which the personal scope of an act of EU law requiring implementation is broader than the scope of application of the implementing provisions. That was the issue decided in the judgment of the Supreme Court of 4 December 2018, I PK 181/17. It concerned a provision of Polish law that excluded employees of 'the association entered into the register of entrepreneurs' from the scope of application of the national law implementing Directive 2008/94.[37] Such exclusion of this group of workers from the personal scope of protection mandated by Directive 2008/94 was considered contrary to EU law.

The EU case and the material scope of EU law

EU cases including a cross-border element

Cases which include a cross-border element are typical for EU law. Such cases result from applying national provisions that fall within the scope of the internal market freedoms or EU competition rules. However, such cases rarely appear before the Supreme Court and lower courts.

One of the very few examples of such a type of EU case is case III CSK 112/05[38] (discussed in greater detail in the section devoted to primacy and direct effect). In that case, a foreign pharmaceutical entrepreneur was the claimant, and a Polish pharmaceutical manufacturer was the defendant. The dispute concerned an infringement of the exclusive rights to a pharmaceutical product granted to the claimant. The exclusive rights, equivalent to a patent, were granted based on an episodic law adopted at the beginning of an economic transformation of Poland in the 1990s when patent protection was reintroduced for chemical and pharmaceutical inventions. To secure foreign investment, *quasi-patent* protection was provided to such inventions which could not benefit from the patent protection in the territory of Poland before 1990. However, the primary condition for the effectiveness of that protection was to manufacture the subject matter of the invention in the territory of the Republic of Poland. Thus, when the claimant brought the action for infringement of his exclusive right, the defendant (preparing to market a generic drug based on the exclusive right) alleged that the *quasi-patent* right was ineffective against him since the claimant was not manufacturing a drug patented in the territory of the Republic of Poland. The drug containing the 'patented' substance was imported to Poland from the other Member States. The EU nature of the case had been unseen by the lower courts which adjudicated the

37 Directive 2008/94/EC of the European Parliament and of the Council of 22 October 2008 on the protection of employees in the event of the insolvency of their employer, OJ L 283, 28.10.2008, pp. 36–42.

38 Judgment of the SC of 10 February 2006, case III CSK 112/05.

case without verifying the compatibility of the requirement to produce the 'patented' substance in Poland with Articles 34 and 36 TFEU. Yet, the EU character of the case was evident to the Supreme Court (albeit had gone unnoticed by the lower courts), since the CJEU had already adjudicated twice upon the Commission's complaint against the Member States that Article 34 TFEU applied to such national provisions.[39]

A more significant group of EU cases that include the cross-border element – albeit not covered by the TFEU – and have been adjudicated by the Supreme Court covers two categories. The first of them includes various types of cases in the area of coordinating social security systems. The latter category includes cases of judicial cooperation in civil and criminal matters. Legal problems specific to Poland are the attempts to avoid being subject to Polish legislation by individuals conducting economic activity in Poland who undertake, as it usually turns out, a marginal or even a fictitious operation in the other Member States under an employment contract, to be exempt from an obligation to pay social security contributions in Poland.[40] The second problem in that area, which very often occurs in the judicial practice, is the issue of workers posted by Polish entrepreneurs or temporary work agencies in the other Member States still subject to Polish social security legislation.[41] The third category of EU cases of that group is the cases relating to suspending the right to a social security benefit when residing abroad (such a requirement is generally considered contrary to EU law).[42]

The EU cases with a cross-border element are also the state aid cases[43] and the cases relating to the parallel application of EU and national competition law,[44] which appear much less frequently in the judicial practice of the Supreme Court. A particular example of an EU case relating to state aid was a social security case concerning the recovery of unlawful state aid which initially took the form of cancellation of the social security contributions.[45]

EU cases without a cross-border element

The cases of that category are predominant in the judicial practice of the Supreme Court. This should not be a surprise, given EU law's extensive

39 Case C-235/89, *Commission v. Italy*, EU:C:1992:73 and C-30/90, *Commission v. UK*, EU:C:1992:74.

40 For example, judgments of the SC of 25 November 2016, case I UK 370/15; of 10 May 2017, case I UK 456/16; of 14 June 2018, case II UK 179/17.

41 See judgments of the SC of 11 January 2018, case II UK 650/16; of 31 October 2018, case II UK 331/17; order of the SC of 19 September, case II UK 241/18.

42 Judgment of the SC of 8 December 2009, case I BU 6/09.

43 Judgments of the SC of 14 March 2017, case III SK 92/13; of 28 November 2017, III SK 30/14; of 3 March 2017, case I CSK 86/16.

44 Judgment of the SC of 25 October 2018, case III SK 38/16.

45 Judgment of the SC of 7 October 2014, case I UK 395/13.

harmonisation of national laws. To better illustrate the most compelling examples of EU law application, they should be divided into smaller groups depending on the source of EU law that is applied. Verifying the EU nature of a case sometimes requires an analysis of interactions between provisions contained in various acts of EU law. In such a case, a situation might arise when the provisions of secondary law exclude the application of the provisions of primary law. Therefore, deciding a case based on the latter could be erroneous.[46]

As regards primary law, the cases in which the Charter of Fundamental Rights is applied prevail in those cases in which Polish courts apply the provisions of national law implementing EU directives. That application is carried out in two ways. Firstly, the Charter of Fundamental Rights (the Charter) is used as a standard influencing the interpretation of the provisions of directives and then, indirectly, national law. Examples of such an application are the cases concerning the imposition of a financial penalty by *Prezes Urzędu Komunikacji Elektronicznej* (the President of the Office for Electronic Communications, UKE). In a series of rulings, it has been found that it is not possible to impose a financial penalty after carrying out an autonomous procedure for the imposition of the penalty if the President of the UKE becomes aware of infringements of telecommunications law only after having initiated an inspection procedure which has not been exhausted according to the original wording of Directive 2002/20.[47] Under Article 10 Directive 2002/20 and Polish implementing legislation, discovery of irregularities by the national regulatory authority was to be followed by the order addressed to the undertaking concerned, mandating specific measures to be taken. Fine could be imposed only after failing to perform that order within the time limit specified by the NRA.[48] However, the President of the UKE developed a practice under which he would initially open an inspection procedure to search for potential violations of telecommunications laws and then – without awaiting correction on behalf of the telecom operator concerned – immediately initiate separate fining proceedings. Another example of that category is the judgment of the Supreme Court of 5 December 2016, case III SK 18/14. Reference to Article 47 of the

46 See Judgment of the SC of 20 September 2011, case I UK 59/11, discussed in more details under heading False EU case.

47 Directive 2002/20/EC of the European Parliament and of the Council of 7 March 2002 on the authorisation of electronic communications networks and services (Authorisation Directive), OJ L 108, 24.04.2002, pp. 21–32.

48 Judgment of the SC of 21 September 2010, case III SK 8/10 – if Prezes Urzędu Komunikacji Elektronicznej (the President of the Office of Electronic Communications, the UKE) has obtained information on a breach, by a telecom entrepreneur, of an obligation under the Telecommunications Law in the course of an inspection procedure initiated under Article 199 and the subsequent ones of that Law, he may not impose a financial penalty on the entrepreneur for infringements, which were the subject of the inspection procedure in question, after carrying out a separate procedure for the imposition of a financial penalty under Article 210 (1) read in conjunction with Article 209 (1) of the Telecommunications Law.

Charter was made in that case to justify the choice of the operative form of the judgment and to explain the effects of the judgment annulling the decision of the national regulatory authority to ensure the effective judicial remedy. The Supreme Court ruled that the annulment of the decision setting rates to be applied between incumbent telecoms and newcomers had the *ex tunc* effect (*ab initio*), instead of *ex nunc* effect (for the future only) as mandated in the Polish administrative procedure, case-law, and legal doctrine. That category of EU cases also includes several preliminary references relating to the protection of the rule of law, when the Supreme Court attempted to derive, from Article 47 of the Charter, the right to declare that a given decision issued by the judges who had been appointed based on national provisions challenged in C-585/18 *A.K. and others*, does not produce any legal effects.[49]

Secondly, those provisions of the Charter for which the Court of Justice ruled on their direct effect are used as delivering legal standards for reviewing the compatibility of Polish law with EU law to apply the *Simmenthal* rule. Here, the best examples are the cases decided after the judgment of the Court of Justice C-585/18 *A.K. and others*, in which the panel of judges from the Labour and Social Security Chamber of the Supreme Court refused to apply provisions of the Supreme Court Law providing for the jurisdiction of the Disciplinary Chamber, which could not be regarded as a court in the meaning of EU law.[50]

In any case, the application of the Charter is dependent upon the fact of the cases falling within the scope of application of EU secondary law, as clearly mandated by Article 51 (1) of CFR and C-617/10 *Fransson*.[51] This group of EU cases – cases with facts and contentious issues governed by EU secondary legislation – is most often adjudicated by the Supreme Court. In the event of the EU cases falling within the material scope of the application of Regulations without a cross-border element, the EU nature of the proceedings is evident from the outset, where the Regulation is a source of claims (as it is the case with the Regulations relating to EU intellectual property protection rights as community trademarks and designs)[52] or where the Regulation concerns EU funds.[53] However, the category of EU cases without cross-border elements

49 See a preliminary reference made by order of the panel of seven judges of the SC of 21 May 2019, case III CZP 25/19, judgment of CJEU in C-487/19, *proceedings brought by W.Ż.*, EU:C:2021:798.

50 Judgment of the SC of 5 December 2019, case III PO 7/18 and orders of the SC of 15 January 2020, cases III PO 8/18 and III PO 9/18.

51 EU:C:2013:105.

52 For example, judgments of SC of 2 February 2017, case I CSK 778/15, and of 27 July 2017, case I CSK 413/16.

53 For example, judgments of the Civil Chamber of SC of 30 March 2017, V CSK 256/16, and of 6 September 2017, I CSK 563/16, and order of the Criminal Chamber of SC of 27 September 2010, case V KK 179/10 – preliminary reference of the SC in case C-489/10, *Łukasz Marcin Bonda*, EU:C:2012:319.

that dominate in the judicial practice of the Supreme Court is the one encompassing these cases, in which the provisions of national law implementing EU Directives are applied.[54] Just by limiting the overview to cases heard by the Labour and Social Security Chamber of the Supreme Court, we can point out cases concerning equal treatment as regards remuneration,[55] claims against direct discrimination[56] or unequal treatment,[57] occupational health and safety in the field of noise protection,[58] working time,[59] transfer of the workplace to another employer,[60] collective redundancies,[61] the rights of temporary and part-time workers,[62] protection of women during pregnancy, protection of motherhood and parenthood,[63] and protection of employees in the event of employer's insolvency.[64] Here the practical difficulty often was that this EU element of a case (directive) had been overlooked by the lower courts and

54 Judgment of SC of 21 September 2010, case III SK 8/10.

55 Judgment of SC of 14 March 2019, case II PK 310/17, as regards the admissibility of differentiated remuneration for employees with different length of service employed at the same work positions only if longer work experience of the better paid employees translates into the larger productivity and better quality of work performed by them.

56 As regards discrimination on the grounds of age, in the event of dismissal of an employee due to reaching a reduced retirement age – the resolution of the panel of seven judges of SC of 21 January 2009, case II PZP 13/08. As regards the concept of discrimination and unequal treatment as well as the rules for calculating compensation awarded for the breach of the principle of equal treatment – the judgment of 9 May 2019, case III PK 50/18.

57 Judgment of the SC of 26 September 2019, case III PK 126/18 – as regards the right of an employee whose employment contract has expired under Article 51 (7) (3) of the Act of 10 February 2017 – provisions introducing the National Centre for Agricultural Support Law (Dz.U. [Journal of Laws] of 2017 item 624 as amended) to compensation, when failure to make him/her an offer of employment is classified as a manifestation of inequal treatment or discrimination.

58 Order of SC of 4 June 2020, case III UK 444/19.

59 Resolution of SC of 3 June 2008, case I PZP 10/07; resolution of a panel of seven judges of SC of 13 March 2008, case I PZP 11/07.

60 Judgment of SC of 7 February 2007, case I PK 269/06.

61 Judgment of SC of 10 October 2019, case I PK 196/18 – as regards the concept of collective redundancy and when the termination of the employment contract, as a result of not accepting new employment conditions, falls within the concept of collective redundancy in the meaning of Article 1 (1) first paragraph (a) of the Council Directive 98/59/EC of 20 July 1998 on the approximation of the laws of the Member States relating to collective redundancies, OJ L 225, 12.08.1998, pp. 16–21 with later amendments.

62 Judgment of SC of 6 June 2006, case I PK 263/05.

63 As regards the rules for determining compensation for discriminatory practices on grounds of maternity, see the judgment of 9 May 2019, case III PK 50/18; as to the requirement for treating, by the court, a claim for reinstatement as including also the claim for admission to work, when an employee acting in a mistaken belief caused by her employer that her employment relationship had ended, claimed the reinstatement only, see the judgment of SC of 7 February 2019, case I PK 242/17.

64 As regards *ratione personae* of protection and an admissible exemption therefrom – see judgment of SC of 4 December 2018, case I PK 181/17, and Article 1 sec. 2 and Article 12 of Directive 2008/94.

even professional representatives, as evidenced *inter alia* by the judgment of 18 November 2020, case III PK 53/19 discussed in full in Part II, Chapter 5. In that case, concerning the right of a father to parental leave, both courts of the lower instances properly acknowledged the EU character of the case. They upheld the claim by reference to the principle of consistent interpretation of the Polish Labour Code and Articles 4 and 9 of Directive 2006/54. Yet in the appeal for cessation, the professional representative of the defending employer omitted EU aspects of the case and limited the grounds of appeal and arguments to national provisions only.

An example of an EU case falling into this category that calls for a broader presentation is the judgment of the Supreme Court of 6 April 2017, case III SK 15/16. It concerned the succession of administrative-criminal liability (fine for infringement of the collective interests of consumers under legislation implementing Directive 2009/22)[65] in the event of acquisition or merger of undertakings during administrative proceedings concerning the imposition of a penalty. The courts of lower instances correctly identified the issue of succession of such legal responsibility as falling within the scope of the application of Directive 2011/35.[66] This in turn structured the interpretation of the Polish Code of Commercial Companies and allowed the courts to uphold the decision of the Competition and Consumer Protection Office imposing a fine on an undertaking that was taken over after the date of issuing the fining decision but before the date of delivery of this decision to the acquiring company (since the acquired company ceased to exist in the meantime).

The EU cases adjudicated by the Supreme Court also include cases that fall within European decisions' scope. An example of such a case is the judgment of the Supreme Court of 14 March 2017, case III SK 92/13, regarding the 'stranded costs' support scheme for electricity producers. The interpretation of Article 4 (2) of the Commission Decision 2009/287/EC of 25 September 2007 on 'State Aid awarded by Poland as part of Power Purchase Agreements and the State Aid which Poland is planning to award concerning compensation for the voluntary termination of Power Purchase Agreements', as adopted by the Court of Justice in its judgment of 15 September 2016, C-574/14 *PGE*,[67] played a vital role in the interpretation and application of national rules governing the support scheme.

A very peculiar EU case falling into this category concerned the use of Directive 2000/78 together with Article 19 TEU in a preliminary reference

65 Directive 2009/22/EC of the European Parliament and of the Council of 23 April 2009 on injunctions for the protection of consumers' interests (Codified version), OJ L 110, 1.05.2009, pp. 30–36.

66 Directive 2011/35/EU of the European Parliament and of the Council of 5 April 2011 concerning mergers of public limited liability companies, OJ L 110, 29.04.2011, pp. 1–11.

67 EU:C:2016:686.

made amid the rule-of-law crisis in Poland by the panel of seven judges of the Supreme Court of 2 August 2018, III UZP 4/18. Prohibition of discrimination based on age, stemming from Articles 2, 9, and 11 of Directive 2000/78, allowed the Supreme Court to adjudicate in the preliminary reference made under the Polish civil procedure in the already discussed case III UZ 10/18 (concerning procedural aspects of the coordination of social security systems), to make the reference to the CJEU on the issue of a prematurely forced retirement of Supreme Courts judges (including two members of the adjudicating panel). Sadly the reference was dropped by the CJEU following the legislative changes introduced by the Polish government to avoid CJEU's judgment.[68]

The concept of the 'EU case' also covers the cases in which the facts fall within the scope of the application of non-binding EU legal instruments. In III SK 92/13, referred to earlier, such an instrument was the methodology for calculating stranded costs.[69] On the other hand, in case III SK 16/09 Commission guidelines on the relevant market analysis were applied,[70] which the national regulatory authority had been required to apply under Directive 2002/21.[71]

Reverse discrimination and referral to EU law

While reviewing the case-law of the Supreme Court, we have yet to come across judgments that would perfectly fit into the categories of cases encompassing reverse discrimination and referral to EU law. However, we have found one novel example of a referral to EU law to protect Polish citizens against reverse discrimination in purely national proceedings, resulting from raising divergencies between the standards of protection of fundamental rights. The source of these divergences is the activity of legislative and executive powers backed by the case-law of the Constitutional Court since 2017, under which any legal solution or interpretation that limits the power of the political will of the ruling party is unconstitutional. Hence, if the parliament or the executive is of the opinion that the European standard of a right to fair trial may be used to limit how the political will want to shape the judiciary system and judicial procedure in Poland, then such a standard is declared unconstitutional by the Constitutional Court or newly appointed judges (since April 2018). So far,

68 Order of CJEU of 29 January 2020, C-522/18, *DŚ przeciwko Zakładowi Ubezpieczeń Społecznych Oddział w Jaśle*, EU:C:2020:42.

69 Commission Communication relating to the methodology for analysing State Aid linked to stranded costs, see more extensively the judgment of the Court of Justice C-574/14 PGE referred to earlier.

70 Guidelines on market analysis and the assessment of significant market power (OJ C 165, 11.07.2002, pp. 6-31).

71 Directive 2002/21/EC of the European Parliament and of the Council of 7 March 2002 on a common regulatory framework for electronic communications networks and services (Framework Directive), OJ L 108, 24.04.2002, pp. 33–50.

the Supreme Court has tried to prevent these divergences, and we think that these judgments should be attributed to the EU cases concerning both reverse discrimination (worse treatment of parties to judicial proceedings in purely internal matters than in proceedings falling within the scope of EU law) and referral to EU law (EU standard of protection of fundamental rights forms the lowest standard of protection applicable in Poland in any proceedings). This thesis is rooted in the Constitutional Court case-law before 2017 where provisions (or the interpretation thereof) introduced unfavourable treatment to legal entities in purely internal situations compared to legal entities, who could invoke EU law, were held unconstitutional.[72]

Following C-585/18 *A.K. and others* and the judgments of the Supreme Court in proceedings in which preliminary references, in this case, were made (judgment of 5 December 2019, III PO 7/18, and orders of 15 January 2020, III PO 8 and 9/18), the Supreme Court adopted the resolution of the formation of the combined Civil Chamber, Criminal Chamber, and Labour Law and Social Security Chamber of 23 January 2020, BSA I-4110-1/20 under which

> A court formation is unduly appointed within the meaning of Article 439(1)(2) of the Code of Criminal Procedure or a court formation is unlawful within the meaning of Article 379(4) of the Code of Civil Procedure also where the court formation includes a person appointed to the office of a judge of the Supreme Court on the application of the National Council for the Judiciary formed by the Act of 8 December 2017 amending the Act on the National Council for the Judiciary and certain other Acts (Journal of Laws of 2018, item 3).

This resolution allows any party to the proceedings before the Supreme Court in which the judicial decision was adopted by judges nominated in the procedure evaluated by the CJEU in C-585/18 *A.K. and others* and C-487/19 *W.Ż.*,[73] as well as C-824/18 *A.B. and others*,[74] to raise the plea of nullity of proceedings. At the same time, the sentence of the resolution does not mention any provisions of EU law and deals with the procedural issue (nullity of proceedings) that in general falls outside of the scope of EU law; the reasoning behind that resolution was based, among others, on the application of the standard of protection of fundamental rights stemming from Article 47 CFR. The resolution of 23 January 2020, BSA I-4110-1/20, followed the approach adopted by the Supreme Court in III PO 7/18. In that case, which beyond any doubt fell within the scope of EU law due to the infringement of the prohibition of discrimination on grounds of age resulting from

72 Judgment of CT of 21 April 2004, case K 33/03 (bio-components in gasoline and diesel).
73 EU:C:2021:798.
74 EU:C:2021:153.

Directive 2000/78, the Supreme Court thought that the constitutional standard of protection of the fundamental right to a fair trial before an independent and impartial court established by law in purely national situations cannot be lower than the standard resulting from Article 47 CFR and Article 6 ECHR. So it ruled that failure to meet the threshold established in the case-law of the CJEU and the ECHR resulted not only in the breach of the respective provisions of EU law or European Convention but also in violation of the right to a fair trial protected by Article 45 of the Polish Constitution. In the resolution of 23 January 2020, BSA I-4110-1/20, it was explained more fully that an obligation of the Supreme Court to consider, in its interpretations and reviews of the law, the case-law of the ECtHR and the Court of Justice of the European Union follows directly from the constitutional position of the Supreme Court as a body responsible for the administration of justice within the meaning of Article 175 (1) of the Constitution of the Republic of Poland and the role of the Supreme Court in the judicial system of the European Union as a guardian, together with other judicial bodies, of the rights and freedoms safeguarded under the Charter or ECHR.

That reasoning was not based directly on the notions of reverse discrimination or referral to EU law in national legislation. However, it means that when it comes to the EU's fundamental rights and values of the Union of law, these rights and values, as defined by the CJEU or ECHR, form the lowest standard of protection of fundamental rights under the Polish Constitution. While the constitutional standard may by higher, it cannot drop below the threshold resulting from CFR and ECHR. So it can be implied that, on one hand, failure to meet this 'lowest' standard in cases falling outside of the scope of EU law would result in discriminatory treatment of the parties to judicial proceedings, who cannot invoke the EU standard directly. On the other hand, while there is no direct referral to EU fundamental rights in the Polish constitution, it follows from the membership in the Union that the national standard of protection of fundamental rights must not be lowered following the accession.[75]

False EU cases

While previous examples regularly considered cases in which the EU element had been raised for the first time either by the Supreme Court itself or in the cassation, the following examples consider cases, where the existence of an EU element was wrongly raised either by a lower court or by the claiming party.

In the judgment of the Supreme Court of 2 September 2009, case II UK 30/09, the appellant alleged infringement of Regulation No. 1408/71 demanding that at the stage of calculating initial pension capital (which then is

75 This corresponds to the interpretation of Article 2 TEU adopted by the CJEU in Joined Cases C-83/19, C-127/19, C-195/19, C-291/19, C-355/19 and C-397/19, *Asociația 'Forumul Judecătorilor din România',* EU:C:2021:393, para. 162.

used for the calculation of a monthly pension), periods of his employment in the Czech Republic should be taken into the account. The Supreme Court dismissed that claim arguing that the determination of an initial pension capital did not fall within the scope of Regulation No. 1408/71. Periods of insurance completed in the other Member States were to be taken into consideration only at the stage of granting retirement pension (Article 45) or calculating its amount (Article 48), while the calculation of initial pension capital was not forming part of the procedures covered by any of the aforementioned articles of Regulation No. 1408/71.

One of the best examples of the defective application of EU law to the facts of the case by lower courts is the judgment of the Supreme Court of 20 September 2011, case I UK 59/11. The case related to the compliance with EU law of the national provision conditioning the payment of a social pension upon 'residing in the territory of the Republic of Poland', resulting from Article 2 (1) of the Social Pension Law.[76] The court of a lower instance found that condition contrary to Article 21 (1) TFEU in the case where the social pension payment was suspended to a Polish national who had studied in another Member State. The view of the court of the lower instance was based on the judgment of the Court of Justice in C-499/06 *Nerkowska*. The CJEU held that

> Article 18 (1) EC precludes legislation of a Member State under which it refuses, generally and in all circumstances, to pay to its nationals a benefit granted to civilian victims of war or repression solely, because they are not resident in the territory of that State throughout the period of payment of the benefit, but in the territory of another Member State.

The Supreme Court pointed out that although Article 21 TFEU had been interpreted broadly by the Court of Justice and also encompassed the provisions of national social law, which made the exercise of acquired rights conditional upon continuing to reside in the territory of that Member State,[77] it followed from Article 21 (1) TFEU itself that the scope of its application might be affected by the provisions of secondary law. The Supreme Court concluded that 'a national rule restricting the exercise of rights covered by Article 21 (1) TFEU cannot be regarded as contrary to that provision if it introduces derogations from that provision, allowed by specific provisions of the EU law'. The social pension at issue in that case turned out to be a benefit covered by the social security coordination system in contrast to the benefits due to combatants (covered by the *Nerkowska* case). However, as resulted from the Annexes to Regulation No. 1408/71, that regulation was not applicable in that case,

76 The Act of 27 June 2003 – the Social Pension Law, Dz.U. [Journal of Laws] No 153, item 1227 as amended.

77 With references to C-192/05, *Tas Hagen and Tas*, EU:C:2006:676.

since Poland listed the social pension in Annex IIa among other benefits, for which – under EU law – a Member State could rightfully exclude the transfer of benefits paid in the event of a change in the residence to another Member State. The interpretation of the Regulation provisions, made by the Supreme Court (Article 10a (1) of Regulation No. 1408/71) as to such effects, had been confirmed by the judgment of the Court of Justice concerning a benefit under the Dutch Law on the provision of incapacity benefit to disabled young people,[78] essentially of the same nature as the social pension in the case concerned, which was also listed in Annex IIa to Regulation No. 1408/71. The Court of Justice explicitly considered the requirement of residence in the Netherlands throughout the period of receiving the benefit and withholding its payment, when the entitled person who had obtained the right left the territory of that state, to be compatible with EU law.

Additionally, the Supreme Court did not agree to apply EU law to waive the fine imposed on the electricity undertaking that had not discharged its obligation to purchase energy produced from more environmentally friendly sources located in the territory of the State.[79] *Prima facie*, it seemed that the requirement to purchase energy from domestic sources was incompatible with Article 34 TFEU. However, Article 34 TFEU was held inapplicable to the facts of the case. The fined undertaking had not fulfilled its duty at all. It had not attempted to discharge this obligation by purchasing 'green' energy abroad in the other Member States. Article 34 TFEU would be applicable should this undertaking have purchased 'green' energy in another Member State instead of buying it from energy sources located in Poland and be fined for the failure to comply with the duty to purchase from the national energy source.

Conclusions

The overview of judgments of the Supreme Court on issues relating to the scope of EU law has evidenced a proper understanding of the spectrum of the various types of civil and criminal proceedings that fall within the scope of EU law and hence demand the application of its principles by national courts. Cases falling within the concept of 'EU cases' dominate in the European case-law of the Supreme Court, including those with a cross-border element (few), covered by EU Regulations (much more), and those decided based on national provisions implementing EU Directives accounting for most EU cases. However, we were surprised to note that in a significant number of European proceedings before the Supreme Court, the EU link has been either omitted by the lower instance courts or ignored by the professional representative filling the appeal for cassation on behalf of the party. These omissions often

78 With references to C-154/05, *J.J. Kersbergen-Lap, D. Dams- Schipper*, EU:C:2006:449.

79 Judgment of SC of 28 November 2017, case III SK 30/14, the facts of the case discussed in the judgment of the CJEU C-329/15, *ENEA*, EU:C:2017:671.

happen in cases falling within the scope of European directives, when EU law is applied indirectly, primarily by consistent interpretation.

The primary function of the EU case concept in the case-law of the Supreme Court is to provide guidelines to national courts of lower instances when they should adjudicate as EU courts and have to respect various principles of EU law.

Another function of the EU case concept is to provide either the Supreme Court or the lower courts with additional arguments to change the established case-law to assure compatibility between Polish and EU legal standards. Two examples may be provided. The first relates to the judicial review of the activities of administrative authorities imposing financial penalties, such as the competition authority or national regulatory authorities in the field of communications and energy. Decisions of these authorities may be appealed to a special court of common jurisdiction (instead of an administrative court), and such appeals are adjudicated under the rules of civil procedure. In settled case-law established in the 1990s, it was accepted that any defects in the administrative proceedings were not taken into account by the courts hearing appeals. The Supreme Court ruled that the focus of the judicial proceedings was on assessing the substantive – but not procedural – correctness of the decision that the authority had issued (e.g., whether the authority proved that there was a cartel, but not whether proof was legitimately obtained). The reference to EU law served to break that line of case-law and to gradually develop the standard for protection of an entrepreneur's rights in the proceedings resulting in the imposition of a financial penalty through verification of whether the procedure before administrative authority leading to the fine being imposed for the failure to comply with national legislation implementing EU directives had met the requirements stemming from Polish law and general principles of EU law applicable to fining proceedings.[80] The Supreme Court concluded, both from EU law and the European Convention on Human Rights, on the criminal nature of regulatory authorities' fines. Such a qualification resulted in stricter judicial review of fining decisions. The starting point for the development of that line of case-law, which was subsequently transferred into pure national affairs, had been an assumption that the national court had to apply the standard for protection of fundamental rights developed in fining proceedings by EU courts when ruling on a fine imposed on the undertaking which failed to discharge its obligations stemming from Polish laws implementing EU directives.

The other example of such an application of the concept of the EU case is the resolution of a panel of seven judges of the Supreme Court of 28 September 2016, case III PZP 3/16. In that decision, it was held that an employee did not have to bring an action against his former employer for wrongful termination of the employment contract (Article 45 § 1 of Polish Labour Code)

80 Judgments of SC of 14 April 2010, case III SK 1/10; of 21 September 2010, case III SK 8/10; of 7 July 2011, case III SK 52/10.

if that employee wanted to claim from the employer only the damages for a discriminatory reason for the termination or a discriminatory reason for the selection of an employee to be dismissed from work (Article 18 (3d) of the Labour Code). In the previous case-law, established before the accession to the EU, it had been held that awarding such compensation was dependent upon an appeal against the employer's decision to dismiss an employee. In case III PZP 3/16, the approach adopted in the previous case-law was considered as undermining the effectiveness of EU law.

The Supreme Court has also demonstrated the ability to perceive non-obvious EU cases. These are the cases where the dispute between the parties falls outside the scope of EU law, but an incidental issue that the court must adjudicate happens to be within reach of EU rules. The best examples are provided by III UZP 3/17, where the issue concerned the impact of EU substantive law (e.g., postal law) on the interpretation and application of national procedural rules concerning delivery of pleadings, and II UK 504/17, which demanded the application of EU rules concerning the different modes of providing services, by members of the legal professions, to evaluate a claim of nullity of proceedings for the failure to provide a party to the proceedings with rights of defence.

It remains to be seen how the Supreme Court itself and lower courts will try to apply the judgment of the CJEU, C-585/18 A.K., and other judgments concerning the newly established Disciplinary (Star) Chamber and the Chamber of Extraordinary Control, in cases that do not strictly fall within the scope of the application of EU law.

While the judgment in case III UZP 3/17 provides a perfect example of an indirect impact of EU law upon the national procedure and hence application of procedural provisions, this case also delivers one of the very few examples in the case-law of the Supreme Court which shows an initial failure in the correct understanding of the scope of the application of EU law. In several cases before III UZP 3/17, the Supreme Court had applied Polish procedural rules without any reference to directive 67/7. However, it must be emphasised that the failure, such as this, to see the EU element in a case adjudicated by the Supreme Court has been sporadic.

From the point of view of the principle of effectiveness of EU law *sensu largo*, it is worth pointing out that the Supreme Court has adopted a very favourable view on the so-called application of EU law *ex officio*. This allowed the Supreme Court, as the court of law, to circumvent the national legislation limiting its capacity to rule on legal issues that the appealing party has not raised. It must be emphasised that the Supreme Court had not hidden behind the shield of the principle of national procedural autonomy. The Supreme Court had also not applied the principle of effectiveness *sensu stricto* to depart from this autonomy. It adopted the position that a claim alleging that a specific provision of Polish law had been wrongfully applied (or interpreted) by a lower court also covers a claim that this provision had been applied (or interpreted) in a manner inconsistent with EU law. Such an approach has significantly increased the effectiveness of the judicial application of EU law, at least at the level of the Supreme Court.

Literature

Baran M., *Stosowanie z urzędu prawa UE przez sądy krajowe* [Application of EU law by national courts ex officio], Wolters Kluwer Polska, 2014.

Heukels T., Joined Cases C-430/93 and C-431/93, Van Schijndel and Van Veen v. Stichting Pensioenfonds voor Fysiotherapeuten; and Case C- 312/93, Peterbroeck, Van Campenhout, *CMLRev.*, 1996, 33, no. 2, pp. 337–353.

Kakouris C.M., Do the Member States Possess Judicial Procedural 'Autonomy', *CMLRev.*, 1997, 34, no. 6, pp. 1389–1412.

Kaleda S., *Przejęcie prawa wspólnotowego przez nowe państwa członkowskie* [Takeover of Communit law by new Member States], Wydawnictwo Prawo i Praktyka Gospodarcza, 2003.

Mancaleoni A.M., The Obligation on Dutch and Italian Courts to Apply EU Law of Their Own Motion, *European Review of Private Law*, 2016, 24, no. 3, pp. 553–578.

Miąsik D., Szwarc M., Effectiveness of EU Directives in National Courts – Judicial Dialogue Continues: The Court of Justice's Judgment in C-545/17 Pawlak, *Polish Yearbook of International Law*, 2020, pp. 267–286.

Półtorak N., Ratione Temporis Application of the Preliminary Rulings Procedure, *CMLRev.*, 2008, 45, no. 1357, pp. 1357–1381.

Prechal S., Community Law in National Courts: The Lessons form van Schijndel, *CMLRev.*, 1998, 35, pp. 681–706.

Schebesta H., Does the National Court Know European Law? A Note on 'Ex Officio' Application after Asturcom, *European Review of Private Law*, 2010, 18, no. 4, pp. 847–880.

Shelkoplyas N., National Procedures, Public Policy and EC Law. From Van Schijndel to Eco Swiss and Beyond, *European Review of Private Law*, 2004, 12, no. 5, pp. 589–611.

Wallerman A., Towards an EU Law Doctrine on the Exercise of Discretion in National Courts? The Member States' Self-Imposed Limits on National Procedural Autonomy, *CMLRev.*, 2016, 53, no. 2, pp. 339–360.

3 The concept of the EU case in the case-law of the administrative courts

Monika Szwarc

Introduction

The first part of the analysis of the administrative courts' case-law addresses an issue when these courts decide to take into account the EU element in adjudicating a particular case. As previously explained in the general remarks opening this chapter, these cases are referred to as 'EU cases' or 'EU proceedings' or cases with an 'EU element'.[1] Still, the 'EU case' as a concept or term is rarely explicitly mentioned or discussed by administrative courts in their decisions. It may be explained by the fact that in the cases where the EU element is evident, there is no need to explain that the particular case concerned falls within the scope of EU law. In general, administrative courts do not have difficulty in establishing the EU element in the factual and legal situations of a given case, where the ground of adjudication includes national provisions implementing EU directives or directly applicable provisions of EU regulations.

The existence of the 'EU element' is however discussed in such cases in which the existence of the EU element had not been obvious but required from the court in question the preliminary consideration as to whether the rules derived from EU law should be included in the normative basis for adjudicating. In order to identify and select cases of administrative courts where this issue was discussed, the available database of judgments has been searched according to the following keywords: 'the Community case', 'the EU case', [a case] 'including the Community element', and [a case] 'including the EU element'. All the cases that had been identified in that way were analysed in order to determine, whether, in a given case, the court considered the 'EU nature' of a particular case or whether the keyword appeared only in the procedural documents of the parties to the proceedings. In addition, examples of the comprehension of the 'EU case' concept are provided by the questions

1 D. Miąsik, Sprawa wspólnotowa przed sądem krajowym [A Community Case Before a National Court], *Europejski Przegląd Sądowy*, 2008, no. 8, pp. 16–22.

DOI: 10.4324/9781003376019-4

referred for a preliminary ruling by administrative courts available on the website of the Supreme Administrative Court.

On the basis of that analysis, it can be concluded that the courts inconsistently use each of these terms: 'the EU case', 'the Community case',[2] 'a case including the Community element',[3] and 'a case including the EU element'.[4]

Administrative courts find that 'a Community/EU case' is the one where a given issue is governed by Community (EU) law'[5] or 'whose subject matter is related to EU law', and in that respect refer directly to the view of the Supreme Court.[6] In their judicial practice, voivodeship administrative courts and SAC hardly ever separately discuss in their reasoning why EU law is applicable in a case concerned. Thus, they rarely use the term 'the EU case', although in general they have no difficulty in identifying the EU rules applicable in the case in question. Therefore, that concept is under consideration only in those cases in which acts of EU secondary legislation, or national law provisions implementing directives, are not applicable and, thus, where additional analysis is needed as to whether other provisions of EU law, that is, the Charter of Fundamental Rights or the Treaties, could be applicable.

The judgment of the Supreme Administrative Court of 23 October 2013 serves as an example of the argumentation adopted by this court, in which it held that the Code of Administrative Procedure was applicable, not only in purely internal situations but also to the EU cases, that is, which are administrative cases with the so-called cross-border element where a party to the proceedings has a claim of public law nature based on the directly effective EU provisions, in particular, the party has exercised one of the internal market freedoms (stemming from the Treaty on the Functioning of the European Union).[7]

In recent case-law of administrative courts, the concept of an 'EU case' appears in the context of verifying whether the provisions of the Charter of Fundamental Rights are applicable in a case. In the context of the case relating to the right to deduct the value-added tax, the VAC held that this right was in principle protected by Article 17 (1) of the Charter of Fundamental Rights, and also, referring to the judgment in Case *Fransson*,[8] that VAT cases were the

2 For example, judgment of the VAC in Gliwice of 6 May 2008, case III SA/Gl 1654/07.

3 For example, judgments of the SAC: of 17 March 2008, case II GSK 464/07; of 30 March 2016, case I FSK 1948/14.

4 For example, judgments of the SAC: of 5 May 2015, case I FSK 479/14; of 27 May 2015, case I FSK 117/14.

5 Judgment of the VAC in Gliwice of 6 May 2008, case III SA/Gl 1654/07; judgments of the SAC: of 2 April 2009, case I FSK 4/08; of 4 November 2011, case I FSK 873/10.

6 Order of the Supreme Court of 20 February 2008, case III SK 23/07.

7 Judgment of the SAC of 23 October 2013, case I OSK 1164/13; citing A. Wróbel, Komentarz do artykułu 1, in: A. Wróbel et al. (eds.), *Kodeks postępowania administracyjnego. Komentarz*, Wolters Kluwer, 2020, do art. 1, Stosowanie kodeksu do spraw unijnych, uw. 1).

8 Case C-617/10, *Fransson*, EU:C:2013:105.

EU cases in which the provisions of the Charter of Fundamental Rights were applicable (in accordance with its Article 51 (1)).[9]

It is also important to draw attention to the specificity of the activities of administrative courts. As was indicated in the introduction, these courts ensure the legality of individual administrative decisions delivered by national administrative authorities. Therefore, as is underlined in the legal writing, the purpose of the proceedings before an administrative court is an assessment not only of whether a complaint (concerning the activities of administrative authority) is well-founded (justified) or not but also of whether this administrative authority acted according to the legal provisions.[10] In other words, an administrative court must first reconstruct the legal standard for review of the challenged administrative decision and only then it shall proceed to decide about the complaint itself (well-founded or not). Therefore, in rulings of administrative courts, in particular VACs, in cases where the court found the complaint justified and declared the administrative decision invalid – the same court provides the administrative authority (obligated to initiate the administrative proceedings again) with the legal standard it has to apply in order to end with legal result (legal administrative decision). It means that when an administrative court relies in its reasoning on the consistent interpretation (of national law with EU law) or primacy and/or direct effect of EU provision, it is not only to annul the administrative decision which is subject to judicial review but equally to provide the administrative authority with the legal standard to handle the given administrative case, the standard that is conform to EU law.[11]

It seems also useful to explain here that in general, administrative courts are competent to review administrative decisions, which regulate the individual situation of an individual in specific circumstances of a given case. In addition, however, in tax cases administrative authorities are competent to issue so-called tax interpretations: general tax interpretations are issued by the Minister of Finances and individual tax interpretations issued by competent regional tax authorities. These interpretations may also be challenged before administrative courts, and then their legality, including conformity with EU law, is reviewed. In general, this aspect of procedural effects was not indicated in the following considerations, as the main focus was on the activities of administrative courts. Still, it must be remembered that in both instances, namely

9 Judgment of the VAC in Warsaw of 30 April 2020, case III SA/Wa 2525/19; judgments of the VAC in Gliwice: of 1 February 2022, case I SA/Gl 1436/21 and I SA/Gl 1437/21; of 19 January 2022, case I SA/Gl 1232/21.

10 M. Kamiński, Konstruowanie wzorca legalności decyzji administracyjnej na podstawie prawa UE przez polskie sądy administracyjne, cz. I [Reconstructing by Polish administrative courts of the standard of legality for administrative decision pursuant to EU law, part I], *Europejski Przegląd Sądowy*, 2011, No. 4, pp. 22–27, at 22.

11 See also M. Kamiński, Bezpośrednie i pośrednie stosowanie dyrektyw unijnych przez polskie sądy administracyjne [Direct and indirect application of EU directives by Polish administrative courts], *Przegląd Sądowy*, 2011, no. 1, pp. 24–37.

administrative decisions and interpretations, a given administrative court establishes the standard for legality, including conformity with EU law, of the activities undertaken by administrative bodies.

The notion of EU case and application of EU law *ex officio*

It raises no doubts that the courts of the first instance (voivodeship administrative courts) are obliged, when hearing cases, to take account of the elements of EU law. The bases for such a statement is the procedural provision, according to which a voivodship administrative court 'is not bound by the pleas in law and submissions of the complainant'.[12] The SAC interprets this provision in such a way that the court 'is obliged to hear the case that has been decided by the contested decision from the point of view of legality'.[13] Therefore, a voivodship administrative court is bound by a duty to examine *ex officio* whether a contested act (action) issued by an administration authority infringes EU law directly or indirectly, which will affect the assessment of its legality.[14] That position was confirmed by the SAC when adjudicating that

> acceptance of the provision that an administrative court of first instance is not bound by the pleas in law and submission of the complainant results in acceptance of a duty resting on such a court to raise *ex officio* arguments based on EU law.[15]

Another situation takes place in the event of an appeal in cassation (an appeal on the point of law) to the Supreme Administrative Court, which serves to review the rulings of voivodeship administrative courts.[16] Unlike, as in the case of voivodship administrative courts not bound by pleas in law, the Supreme Administrative Court 'hears an appeal in cassation (an appeal on the point of law) within the limits of [its] pleas, taking into account *ex officio* only invalidity of the proceedings'.[17]

However, the analysis of settled case-law of the SAC enables to draw the following conclusions. On the one hand, there are no rulings which would expressly break the aforementioned 'limitation' resulting from the procedural

12 Article 134 para 1 – of the Law on the Proceedings before Administrative Courts.
13 Judgment of the SAC of 2 February 2005, case II FSK 44/05; judgment of the SAC of 11 April 2007, case II OSK 610/06.
14 Further on this issue in the Polish literature M. Baran, *Stosowanie z urzędu prawa Unii Europejskiej przez sądy krajowe* [Application of EU law by national c ex officio], Wolters Kluwer Polska, 2014, pp. 399–434.
15 Judgment of the SAC of 7 October 2014, case II OSK 637/13.
16 Article 173 and subsequent of the Law on the Proceedings before Administrative Courts.
17 Article 183 (1) of the Law on the Proceedings before Administrative Courts.

provisions. It is worth noting that this limitation has been overcome as far as the rulings of the Constitutional Tribunal are concerned. The SAC held:

> In a situation, where the Constitutional Tribunal found that a normative act, under which a ruling under appeal had been made, was not in conformity with the Constitution and such an unconstitutional provision (as declared by the CT) has not been indicated in the grounds for cassation, the Supreme Administrative Court should apply directly the provisions of Article 190 (1) and (4) of the Constitution of the Republic of Poland and take into account the judgment of the Tribunal without being bound by the wording of Article 183 § 1 of the Act of 30 August 2002 the Law on the Proceedings before Administrative Courts.[18]

However, there is no analogous statement in the SAC case-law in relation to a situation in which the incompatibility of the domestic provision results from the ruling of the CJEU and such a provision has not been referred to in the pleas in law for cassation.[19] What is more, the SAC consistently repeats that being bound by the grounds for an appeal in cassation results in the requirement for a complainant to determine pleas in law in the appeal itself, which means *inter alia* to invoke specific legal provisions which – according to the applicant – had been infringed by the court and to determine in what form the infringement at issue was, to justify the alleged infringement. Additionally, when the appeal contains an allegation of infringement of procedural law – to demonstrate that the alleged infringement could have a significant impact on the outcome of the case. When a pleading in cassation does not meet those constitutive requirements, it prevents the court from assessing its merits. Due to the requirements for an appeal in cassation, it is obligatory to be prepared by a professional legal adviser.[20] As it has been emphasised by the SAC, that obligation is based on the assumption that a qualified lawyer will draw up a pleading in cassation of the appropriate substantive and formal quality, enabling the court of the second instance to review the judgment under appeal.[21]

However, on the other hand, in no way does Article 183 (1) of the Law on the Proceedings before Administrative Courts prevent the SAC from taking into account, in the course of the cassation proceedings, the provisions of EU

18 Resolution of seven judges of the SAC of 7 December 2009, case I OPS 9/09; this ruling has been vastly discussed in the literature: J. Sułkowski, *Zeszyty Naukowe Sądownictwa Administracyjnego*, 2010, no. 3, pp. 160–165; W. Kręcisz, *Zeszyty Naukowe Sądownictwa Administracyjnego*, 2010, no. 3, pp. 147–159; M. Szubiakowski, Wyrok Trybunału Konstytucyjnego o niezgodności z Konstytucją aktu normatywnego wydanego po wniesieniu skargi kasacyjnej – granice rozpoznania skargi kasacyjnej. Glosa do uchwały NSA z dnia 7 grudnia 2009 r., I OPS 9/09, *Orzecznictwo Sądów Polskich*, 2010, no. 6, pp. 409–418.

19 Discussion on that topic in the Polish literature cf. M. Baran, *Stosowanie z urzędu . . .*

20 Article 175 § 1–3 the Law on the Proceedings before Administrative Courts.

21 Judgment of the SAC of 28 December 2018, case I OSK 1723/18.

law which are functionally linked to the provisions of national law referred to in the appeal in cassation. The analyses of the SAC case-law lead to the conclusion that in a situation where a judgment of the VAC is under review which, in turn, relate to administrative decisions issued on the basis of directly applicable provisions of EU Regulations or national legislation transposing EU directives into Polish law, the SAC takes into account those 'EU elements' when constructing a basis for adjudication of a case (irrespective of the fact of whether a relevant provision of EU law has been referred to in the pleading). In addition, an important role in identifying the provisions of EU law applicable in a given case is undoubtedly played by the parties' representatives submitting the appeals in cassation.

The EU case and the material scope of EU law

EU cases including the cross-border element

More doubts arise in those cases in which adjudicating is based neither on national provisions which implement the provisions of EU directives nor on directly applicable provisions of EU regulations. However, it seems that administrative courts immediately after the accession began to correctly identify those cases in which the directly effective provisions of the Treaty on the functioning of the European Union (TFEU) guaranteeing the freedoms of the internal market should be incorporated into the legal basis for adjudication. This is particularly evident in the area of non-harmonised taxes.

Administrative courts encountered one of the first problems related to the application of EU law in Poland as early as 2007, when they began to receive complaints concerning the decisions of tax authorities assessing the amount of the excise duty on second-hand motor vehicles imported from other Member States after 1 May 2004. The payment of the assessed tax was necessary to register such a vehicle, but at the same time, the persons concerned questioned the amount of those duties (requested the tax authorities to reimburse of the excise duty), based on the unfavourable way in which the amount of that tax in the case of vehicles purchased in the context of intra-Community acquisition was calculated. The VAC in Warsaw, when referring questions for a preliminary ruling to the Court of Justice in case *Brzeziński,* drew attention to the fact that the Polish legislation did not differentiate – directly – domestic products from imported products, however, only certain types of goods – in this case, second-hand motor vehicles not registered in the territory of the State – were subject to excise duty. Therefore, according to the VAC, it was possible to admit that the responsibility for the tax liability depended on the occurrence of a specific characteristic feature of goods (failure to register a vehicle in the territory of Poland). However, a single-payment excise duty was required in Poland – at a certain trading stage – from an entity selling a passenger car before its first registration in the territory of the State, which, in practice, meant that the tax concerned was also paid on cars that were not imported but bought in Poland and purchased once again, since each time the amount of excise duty (paid before the first registration) was included in the transaction price.

In order to verify whether such national legislation conformed with the EU law, it was crucial, firstly, to determine which provisions of the latter should serve as the standard for a review of the administrative decision and – as a consequence – of the national legislation being the legal basis thereof. The VAC in Warsaw examined both former Article 25 EC (now Article 30 TFEU), prohibiting customs duties and charges having equivalent effect, and former Article 90 EC (now Article 110 TFEU), prohibiting discriminatory and protectionist taxation. Then the VAC considered the possibility of applying for this purpose former Article 28 EC (now Article 34 TFEU), prohibiting measures having equivalent effect to quantitative restrictions, and Article 3 of Directive 92/12 on the general arrangements for products subject to excise duty and on the holding, movement, and monitoring of such products,[22] taking into account additional requirements such as a need to submit a simplified tax return and pay excise duty.[23] The Court of Justice had confirmed the need to analyse the provisions of the Polish Act on Excise Duty (which were the legal basis for the refusal to reimburse excise duty) from the perspective of prohibition of discriminatory and protectionist taxation,[24] which was later accepted by administrative courts.[25]

In 2007, cases concerning the possibility of applying deductions for the purposes of annual tax returns of natural persons were heard before administrative courts on a number of occasions. On the basis of then applicable provisions of the Personal Income Tax Law, the taxable amount could be reduced only by the amount of contributions for social security in Poland, and the amount of tax could be reduced only by the amount of health insurance contributions paid in Poland. Those provisions were contested by applicants in Poland from the perspective of various provisions of the TFEU, both in the context of operating for profit and in the context of people living in Poland and enjoying the status of an EU citizen.

22 OJ L 76, 23.03.1992, p. 1, no longer in force.

23 Order of the VAC in Warsaw of 22 May 2005, case III SA/Wa 679/05.

24 Case C-313/05, *Brzeziński*, EU:C:2007:33, para. 24; see also commentaries: D.A. Mangialardi, Tributi interni – Tasse sugli autoveicoli usati importati, *Giurisprudenza italiana*, 2007, pp. 290–291; E. Bernard, Droit d'accises sur les véhicules d'importation en Pologne, *Europe*, 2007 Mars Comm. no. 85 pp. 13–14; B. Makowicz, Polnische 'Akzise' auf eingeführte Gebrauchtfahrzeuge, *Zeitschrift für Zölle und Verbrauchsteuern*, 2007, pp. 129–131; K. Lasiński-Sulecki, Sprzeczność polskich przepisów dotyczących opodatkowania używanych samochodów osobowych z europejskim prawem wspólnotowym [Incompatibility with the Community Law of Polish Regulation on Taxation of Second-Hand Cars], *Przegląd Podatkowy*, 2007, no. 4, pp. 41–43; A. Rigaux, Taxe d'effet équivalent, *Europe*, 2017 Décembre no. 12 pp. 23–24.

25 Judgment of the VAC in Warsaw of 6 March 2007, case III SA/Wa 254/07; on the judicial application of the *Brzeziński* ruling, see chapter 9 on primacy and direct effect.

Firstly, those provisions had been challenged by nationals of other Member States residing in Poland who were not pursuing any activity for profit. One of such cases was heard by the VAC in Wrocław, examining the legality of the decision of the tax authority under which an applicant was denied the possibility of reducing the income tax which he was liable to pay in Poland in respect of the occupational pension which he received in another Member State by the amount of health insurance contributions paid in that Member State.[26] In that case, the applicant claimed that Polish legislation was incompatible with Regulation (EEC) No 1408/71 of the Council of 14 June 1971 on the application of social security schemes to employed persons and their families moving within the Community[27] and the former Article 39 EC (now Article 45 TFEU), that is, free movement of workers. The VAC, as a standard for review of the administrative decision (refusal to reduce income tax) – and as a consequence – of the national provisions being the legal basis thereof, took into account the principle of equal treatment (Article 12 EC, now Article 18 TFEU), the free movement of workers (Article 39 EC, now Article 45 TFEU), as well as the provisions of Regulation No. 1408/71 and Regulation No. 574/72.[28] The Court of Justice held that '[p]ersons who have carried out all their occupational activity in the Member State of which they are nationals and who have exercised the right to reside in another Member State only after their retirement, without any intention of working in that other State, cannot rely on freedom of movement as a worker' and that '[a] situation such as that of Mr Rüffler is covered by the right of free movement and residence in the Member States of citizens of the European Union. Persons who, after retirement, leave the Member State of which they are nationals and in which they have carried out all their occupational activity in order to set up residence in another Member State exercise the right which Article 18 (1) EC confers on every citizen of the European Union to move and reside freely within the territory of the Member States'.[29] Thus, the situation before the national court had to be analysed pursuant to the principle of non-discrimination, as enshrined in former Article 12 TEC (now Article 18 TFEU) in connection with freedom to move and reside freely, as enshrined in former Article 18 TEC (now Article 21 TFEU).[30]

26 Judgment of the VAC in Wrocław of 25 August 2009, case I SA/Wr 946/09.

27 OJ L 149, 5.07.1971, p. 2.

28 Order of the VAC in Wrocław of 3 October 2007, case I SA/Wr 971/07.

29 Case C-544/07, *Rüffler*, EU:C:2009:258, for commentaries, see A.-L. Mosbrucker, F. Kauff-Gazin, Fiscalité directe, *Europe*, 2009 Juin Comm. no. 214, pp. 9–11; P. Kubicki, Einkommensteuer ermäßigbar durch Abzug der in anderem Mitgliedstaat gezahlten Krankenversicherungsbeiträge, *Europäische Zeitschrift für Wirtschaftsrecht*, 2009, pp. 543–545; H.-D. Steinmeyer, Freizügigkeit – Besteuerung von Krankenversicherungsbeiträgen, *Zeitschrift für europäisches Sozial- und Arbeitsrecht*, 2010, pp. 78–80.

30 On the judicial application of the *Rüffler* ruling, see Chapter 9 on primacy and direct effect.

Secondly, those provisions were challenged by applicants (usually Polish nationals), pursuing an economic activity on self-employment basis in the territory of other Member States (e.g., the Netherlands) and who were at the same time subject to unlimited tax liability in Poland but in their annual statements could include neither social security contributions nor health insurance contributions that had been incurred in Member States other than Poland. Administrative courts heard disputes between the complainants, in these cases taxpayers, and the tax administration authorities refusing the possibility of applying the deductions of contributions that had been paid outside Poland. In those contexts, to begin with, it was necessary to determine which provisions of EU law were applicable, since applicants most often had referred to the infringement of ex-Article 39 EC (now Article 45 TFEU). Whereas, administrative courts found that in such cases, due to the fact that the complainants were self-employed, the provisions of ex-Article 43 EC (now Article 49 TFEU) should have been applied.[31] The correctness of such legal classification was confirmed by the Court of Justice in its judgment in the Case *Filipiak*,[32] where it had been held that 'the situation of a taxpayer such as Mr Filipiak, who is a member of a partnership under Netherlands law, the organisational structure of which corresponds to that of a general partnership under Polish law, suggests that that taxpayer was able personally to perform tasks associated with the economic activity of that partnership and that he had a degree of control over that activity', but at the same time stipulating that 'while such a situation may come under Article 43 EC, it may also come under the provisions of the Treaty on freedom to provide services because it cannot be ruled out that Mr Filipiak, while a taxpayer resident in Poland, not only has a degree of control over the economic activity of the Netherlands partnership of which he is a member, but also provides services in the Netherlands' and for that reason '[t]he situation of a taxpayer such as Mr Filipiak may therefore be examined in light of the principle of freedom of establishment laid down in Article 43 EC and of the principle of freedom to provide services provided for in Article 49 EC'.[33]

Thirdly, those provisions were challenged by applicants subject to unlimited tax liability in Poland but receiving income in another Member State in which the employer had also made health insurance and social security contributions. Due to the fact that in accordance with Polish legislation they were only the contributions referred to in the 'Law on the Social Security System' (Article 26 (1)) and in 'the Law on Publicly Funded Health-Care Benefits'

31 Order of 30 May 2008, case I SA/Po 1006/09 (preliminary questions in Case C-314/08 *Filipiak*; case I SA/Po 1756/07; case I SA/Po 1757/07; case I SA/Po 371/10).

32 Case C-314/08, *Filipiak*, EU:C:2009:719, for commentaries, see further K. Tetlak, *Highlights & Insights on European Taxation*, 2010, no. 2, pp. 65–66.

33 *Filipiak*, para. 53, 56–57; on judicial application of this judgment, see Chapter 9 on primacy and direct effect.

(Article 27b (1)(2)) that were taken into account in the annual statement, the applicants could not take into account contributions that had been paid in accordance with the laws of another Member State in which the work had been provided. The VAC in Gliwice, in a series of judgments, held that those facts of the case fell within the scope of EU law application, since the free movement of workers was applicable (former Article 39 EC, now Article 45 TFEU).[34] In this case, the VAC held that it was not necessary to make a reference for a preliminary ruling, since that matter had been sufficiently clarified by the Court of Justice in cases *Rüffler* and *Filipiak*.

In addition, administrative courts heard the cases in which there were doubts as regards the compliance of provisions of the Corporate Income Tax Law with EU law in so far as treating investing in investment funds operating outside Poland was concerned. In accordance with Polish legislation, only the investment funds operating in accordance with the Polish Law on Investment Funds could benefit from the exemptions from dividends and interest specified in the Corporate Income Tax Law. Such wording of the legal provisions resulted in tax authorities refusing to benefit from that exemption (administrative decisions refusing to recognise and refund an overpayment of flat-rate corporation tax), when it was claimed by the funds established outside the territory of Poland (both those established in other EU Member States and those established in third countries). The need to apply the TFEU provision on the free movement of capital in those cases was confirmed by the SAC,[35] which made it possible to shape the EU standard for review of tax authorities' administrative decisions and – as a result – of provisions regarding income received by investment funds.[36]

The doubts as to the compatibility of that solution with EU law have also appeared in relations between tax authorities and the funds established outside the EU, that is, in a third country. In a case that later became the basis for a preliminary ruling in Case *Emerging Markets*, an investment fund with the registered office in the United States of America, and having Polish companies forming one part of its business, requested from the Polish tax authority the refund of an overpayment of flat-rate corporation tax which had been applied, at a rate of 15%, to dividends which had been paid to it by those companies which were established in Poland. The applicant claimed that it was entitled to obtain that refund on the basis of national legislation read in conjunction with the double taxation convention between the United States and Poland. The tax authorities rejected this claim on the ground that as an

34 Judgments of the VAC in Gliwice of 10 January 2012, in cases: I SA/Gl 446/11; I SA/Gl 447/11; I SA/Gl 448/11; I SA/Gl 452/11; I SA/Gl 453/11.

35 Judgment of the SAC of 28 June 2012, case II FSK 1308/11.

36 The VAC in Warsaw previously took into account either the principle of non-discrimination on grounds of nationality (now Article 18 TFEU) – judgment of the VAC in Warsaw of 14 March 2008, case III SA/Wa 1577/07, or the principle of non-discrimination and freedom of establishment (now Article 49 TFEU), which does not seem to be fully correct.

investment fund established in the United States of America, the applicant in the main proceedings did not satisfy the exemption conditions set out in Article 6 (1) (10) of the law on corporation tax, namely, that it was not an investment fund operating in accordance with the Polish law on investment funds.

The applicant in the dispute with the tax authority referred to the free movement of capital (now Article 63 TFEU), whereas tax administration claimed that in the case of the acquisition of shares in companies by the fund, the freedom of establishment should be applied (now Article 49 TFEU). Due to the fact that in the dispute concerned the fund had been established outside the EU, it could not exercise the freedom of establishment. Consequently, the VAC in Bydgoszcz, hearing an appeal against an administrative decision (refusing to award a tax exemption), had to establish, in the first place, which of the freedoms should be applied as a basis for the assessment of national provisions.[37] On the one hand, it took into account the fact that the nature of the investments made by the applicant did not allow them to exert a real impact on the decisions taken by the Polish company, in which they had invested capital (since it was a share below 10%).[38] However, it was considered by the VAC that an extensive personal exemption, including, among others, investment funds, was subject to fulfilling additional conditions, among others, the conditions of operation under Polish legal provisions on investment funds. For that reason, the VAC in Bydgoszcz, firstly, asked:

> Does [Article 63 TFEU] apply to an assessment by a court, in respect of a personal tax exemption of general scope, of the permissibility of the application by a Member State of provisions of national law which draw a distinction between the legal situation of taxable persons in such a way that they grant an exemption from flat-rate corporation tax on dividends received by investment funds established in a Member State of the European Union but do not provide for such an exemption for an investment fund which is resident for tax purposes in the United States?

The Court of Justice held in Case *Emerging Markets*:

> [t]hat Article 63 TFEU on the free movement of capital applies in a situation, such as that at issue in the main proceedings, where, under national tax legislation, the dividends paid by companies established in a Member State to an investment fund established in a non-Member State

37 Order of the VAC in Bydgoszcz of 28 March 2012, case I SA/Bd 1035/11 – order with preliminary questions addressed to the ECJ.

38 The VAC took into account, in this regard, judgment of the Court of Justice C-157/05 *Holböck*, EU:C:2007:297, para. 35, from which it follows that the freedom of establishment may be applicable if the shares held by the shareholder enable him to participate effectively in the management of that company or in its control.

are not the subject of a tax exemption, while investment funds established in that Member State receive such an exemption.[39]

An interesting example is also a dispute under Polish pharmaceutical law relating to the marketing authorisation under parallel imports. In proceedings before the VAC in Warsaw, the applicant (who appealed against the decision refusing to issue a parallel import licence) claimed incompatibility of a provision of Polish law with prohibition of quantitative restrictions and measures having equivalent effect, as enshrined in Article 34 and Article 36 TFEU. The VAC shared doubts of the claimant and referred preliminary question to the CJEU.[40] Such an approach was confirmed by the CJEU in its ruling in *Delfarma*.[41]

EU cases without a cross-border element

Administrative courts, entrusted with the power to review the legality of administrative decisions issued by public authorities hear, above all, the cases where administrative decisions have been issued on the basis of directly applicable regulations or national provisions transposing the EU directives. The EU nature of those cases does not raise any doubts of administrative courts, since they are considered as cases with the EU element.[42]

The rulings of voivodship administrative courts and the SAC presented in Chapter 3 (concerning the principle of consistent interpretation) and Chapter 4 (devoted to the principles of primacy and direct effect of EU law) represent

39 Case C-190/12, *Emerging Markets*, EU:C:2014:249, para. 35; for commentaries see further K. Dickson, T. O'Shea, Non-EU Funds Can Be Charged Withholding Tawes, ECJ Advocate General Says in Emerging Markets, *Tax Notes International*, 2014, pp. 541–550; K. Von Brocke, Emerging Markets Series: Equal Tax Treatment for U.S. Regulated Investment Companies in Europe, *Tax Notes International*, 2014, pp. 327–333; P. Baker, The CJEU Judgment in the Emerging Markets Series Case, *Tax Journal*, 2014, no. 1215, pp. 14–15; E. Pinetz, Der Rechtfertigungsgrund der wirksamen steuerlichen Kontrolle und Drittstaaten, *Ecolex*, 2014, p. 568; A. Patzner, EuGH: Auf Ausschüttungen an Drittstaaten-Fonds erhobene Kapitalertragsteuer verstößt gegen Kapitalverkehrsfreiheit, *Recht der Finanzinstrumente*, 2014, pp. 253–254; A. Maitrot de la Motte, Cour de justice, 1re ch., 10 avril 2014, Emerging Markets Series of DFA Investment Trust Company c/ Dyrektor Izby Skarbowej w Bydgoszczy, aff. C-190/12, ECLI:EU:C:2014:249, *Jurisprudence de la CJUE 2014 (Ed. Bruylant – Bruxelles)*, 2014, pp. 418–421; V. Michel, Traitement fiscal des dividendes sortants, *Europe*, 2014 Juin no. 6 pp. 29–30; W. Nykiel, M. Wilk, Swoboda przepływu kapitału w stosunkach z państwami trzecimi – glosa do wyroku Trybunału Sprawiedliwości z 10 April 2014 r. w sprawie C-190/12 Emerging Markets Series of DFA Investment Trust Company przeciwko Dyrektorowi Izby Skarbowej w Bydgoszczy [Free Movement of Capital with Third States – Commentary on C-190/12 Emerging Markets], *Europejski Przegląd Sądowy*, 2015, 6, pp. 37–43.

40 Order of the VAC in Warsaw of 18 April 2018, case VI SA/Wa 2256/17.

41 Case C-387/18, *Delfarma*, EU:C:2019:556.

42 Judgment of the VAC in Kielce of 17 October 2006, case I SA/Kc 219/06.

a wide range of instances, where applicable national provisions were implementation of EU directives in such areas as value-added tax, excise duty, telecommunications law, environmental protection law, EU funds and direct payments, migration law, and notification of technical regulations. In principle, they will be discussed in the following chapters.

An EU case? Or not? When doubts arise

In the practice of the administrative courts, there are still many instances when it is necessary to decide whether it is an EU case at all. It seems that the main challenge of administrative courts is exactly this field of exploration.

The issue, as to whether a particular case contains 'the EU element', is of particular importance in the context of the possibility of declaring the unlawfulness of the final ruling of the administrative court. The purpose of such proceedings is to declare that a given administrative court breached the law and, as a result, to open way for interested individuals to claim compensation from the state (financial liability of the public authority for breaches of law). In principle, pursuant to Article 285a of the Law on Proceedings before Administrative Courts, that option is available when appealing against the final rulings of voivodeship administrative courts but not against the rulings of the SAC. Only exceptionally, a final ruling of the SAC may be declared unlawful, when non-compliance results from the serious violation of the European Union law. Therefore, the claim under Article 285a of the Law on Proceedings before Administrative Courts against a ruling of the SAC is admissible only when this court applied EU law. For the purposes of applying this provision, the SAC interprets EU law as legal rules resulting from sources of European Union law, in particular, provisions of law issued on the basis of the applicable Treaties, that is, TEU, TFEU, and EAEC. The SAC also states that the violation of EU law may result from failure to apply a directly effective provision of EU law, which should have been applied in the case, or the application of a provision of national law which is contrary to EU law or the application of national law in a way that is incompatible with the requirements of EU law.[43] Since the provisions governing the administrative court proceedings do not constitute the EU law rules, therefore, the mere application of such provisions cannot constitute a violation of EU law rules. That means that an action for a declaration of the unlawfulness of a final judgment cannot be used to verify each ruling of the Supreme Administrative Court and that this legal remedy is thus not applicable to cases without an EU law element.[44]

43 Judgment of the SAC of 27 April 2017, case II FNP 1/17.

44 Judgment of the SAC of 19 December 2013, case I GNP 2/13; consequently referred to in judgments of the SAC: of 1 June 2015, case II FNP 1/14; of 27 April 2017, case II FNP

An interesting example is a case in which administrative courts settled the dispute with the Minister of State Treasury, who had issued a decision refusing to confirm the right to compensation for the so-called property beyond the Bug River (real estate that was left outside the current territory of Poland due to the considerable modification of borders in the East) and the heir of the person entitled to such compensation. It should be clarified that the dispute took place under the Law on the Exercise of the Right to Compensation for leaving real estate outside the current borders of the Republic of Poland, in which it was provided that only the heir of the person entitled to compensation who also had Polish citizenship could be entitled to compensation. The Minister's decision refusing to confirm the right to compensation was challenged by the heirs of the entitled person who although were EU citizens did not have Polish citizenship or – which turned out to be decisive in that case – had never lived in Poland. Since the VAC in the first instance held that regulating the right to compensation for the so-called property beyond the Bug River was not subject to the Treaty regulation (therefore, this matter was a purely internal matter), it was the SAC that was hearing that case in the cassation proceedings. The applicants in both instances raised, among others, the infringement of Article 18 and Article 20 TFEU. It should be welcomed that the SAC correctly noticed the possibility of the dispute, such as that at issue, to fall within the scope of EU law on the ground that the European Union citizen concerned had exercised his freedom of movement and residing within the territory of the Member States and also considered the possibility of applying, in the case in question, case-law of the Court of Justice on compensation for civilian war victims.[45] In the question referred for a preliminary ruling, it asked for an interpretation of Article 18 TFEU only, without reference to Article 21 TFEU and only to Article 20 TFEU (the one referred to by the applicants).

The Court of Justice, however, refused to provide an answer on the ground that there was no relevance to EU law, since in the light of the facts set out in the files referred to the Court, a situation such as that at issue in the main proceedings bore no relation to any of the situations covered by the Treaty provisions on the free movement of persons, and in particular Article 21 TFEU. What is more, the purely hypothetical prospect of exercising that right of movement does not make a sufficient link to EU law, which would justify the application of those provisions of the Treaty.[46] Consequently, the pleas included in the appeal on a point of law, based on the infringement of EU law, have been dismissed by the SAC.

The parties to the proceedings before administrative courts also raise, as one of the pleas against administrative decisions, the infringement of the provisions

1/17, case II FNP 2/17, case II FNP 3/17; of 22 August 2019, case II FNP 2/19; order of SAC of 25 October 2019, case II ONP 3/19.

45 Order of the SAC of 30 April 2013, case I OSK 2024/11.

46 Case C-370/13, *Teisseyre*, EU:C:2014:2033, para. 34–35.

of the Charter of Fundamental Rights. The SAC held that although the Charter of Fundamental Rights, as primary law, is part of the European Union's legal order, an allegation of infringement of its provisions can be effectively raised only if the provisions of EU law, other than the Charter, are applicable or should be applied to the case. Thus, the concept of law application in the meaning of Article 51 (1) of the Charter requires that there is a link to EU law, which means that the application of the Charter by the court may take place in the 'EU case', that is, the one in which the facts of the case are subject to EU law, whereas the Charter is not applicable in a case of a purely domestic nature.[47] This was a case for example in disputes concerning Polish construction law dispositions (right to good administration),[48] execution of duties (right to good administration, but at the same time underlying that this right stems from the domestic legal order).[49]

Conclusions

In general, the administrative courts adequately identify proceedings which fall within the scope of EU law and hence require the application of EU principles by national courts, as is reflected by their case-law discussed earlier. It represents a wide range of instances in which the national law implementing EU directives was applied in such areas as value-added tax, excise duty, telecommunications law, environmental protection law, EU funds and direct payments, migration law, and the notification of technical regulations. Thus, similarly to what has been concluded in terms of the case-law of the Supreme Court, in administrative courts dominate cases which clearly fall within the notion of 'EU cases'. In the Polish literature on administrative law and administrative procedure, it is widely accepted that since Poland's accession to the European Union one has witnessed the so-called 'Europeanisation of administrative law and administrative procedure'.[50]

The administrative courts in Poland hardly ever distinguish, on the grounds for their judgments, a separate element justifying why EU law is applicable in the case concerned. Thus, they rarely use the term 'the EU case'. That concept is under consideration only in those cases where additional analysis is needed, thus when adjudicating a case is based neither on national provisions,

47 Judgment of the SAC of 26 November 2019, case II OSK 30/18, p. 11.

48 Ibidem.

49 Judgments of the VAC in Wrocław of 4 November 2021, cases: I SA/Wr 173/21, I SA/Wr 156/21, I SA/157/21 and I SA/Wr 158/21.

50 In particular see: D. Miąsik, A. Wróbel, Europeizacja prawa administracyjnego – pojęcie i konteksty, w: R. Hauser, Z. Niewiadomski, A. Wróbel (eds.), *System Prawa Administracyjnego*, t. 3, *Europeizacja prawa administracyjnego*, C.H. Beck, 2014; N. Półtorak, Efektywność prawa Unii Europejskiej a polska procedura administracyjna i sądowoadministracyjna' [Effectiveness of the EU Law and Polish Administrative and Judicial-Administrative Procedure], *Zeszyty Naukowe Sądownictwa Administracyjnego*, 2014, no. 3, pp. 37–53.

which implement the provisions of EU directives, nor on the directly applicable provisions of EU regulations. However, it seems that the administrative courts, immediately after the accession, began to correctly identify those cases in which the directly effective provisions of the TFEU, guaranteeing the freedoms of the internal market, should be incorporated as grounds for the ruling. This is particularly evident in the area of non-harmonised taxes.

The main challenge for the future seems the correct application of the Charter and, as a result, correct identification of whether a given case is 'implementation of EU law' in the meaning of Article 51 (1) of the Charter. As applicants and their legal representatives acquire knowledge of the Charter, they invoke its provisions in their claims more frequently. Consequently, administrative courts are faced with this new dimension of EU law more frequently.

Literature

Baker P., The CJEU Judgment in the Emerging Markets Series Case, *Tax Journal*, 2014, no. 1215, pp. 14–15.

Baran M., *Stosowanie z urzędu prawa UE przez sądy krajowe* [Application of EU law by national courts ex officio], Wolters Kluwer Polska, 2014.

Bernard E., Droit d'accises sur les véhicules d'importation en Pologne, *Europe*, 2007 Mars Comm, 2007, no. 85, pp. 13–14.

Dickson K., O'Shea T., Non-EU Funds Can Be Charged Withholding Tawes, ECJ Advocate General Says in Emerging Markets, *Tax Notes International*, 2014, pp. 541–550.

Kamiński M., Bezpośrednie i pośrednie stosowanie dyrektyw unijnych przez polskie sądy administracyjne [Direct and Indirect Application of EU Directives by Polish Administrative Courts], *Przegląd Sądowy*, 2011, no. 1, pp. 24–37.

Kamiński M., Konstruowanie wzorca legalności decyzji administracyjnej na podstawie prawa UE przez polskie sądy administracyjne, cz. I [Reconstructing by Polish Administrative Courts of the Standard of Legality for Administrative Decision Pursuant to EU Law, Part I], *Europejski Przegląd Sądowy*, 2011, no. 4, pp. 22–27, at 22.

Kręcisz W., Commentary to the Resolution of 7 Judges of the SAC of 7 December 2009, Case I OPS 9/09, *Zeszyty Naukowe Sądownictwa Administracyjnego*, 2010, no. 3, pp. 147–159.

Kubicki P., Einkommensteuer ermäßigbar durch Abzug der in anderem Mitgliedstaat gezahlten Krankenversicherungsbeiträge, *Europäische Zeitschrift für Wirtschaftsrecht*, 2009, pp. 543–545.

Lasiński-Sulecki K., Sprzeczność polskich przepisów dotyczących opodatkowania używanych samochodów osobowych z europejskim prawem wspólnotowym [Incompatibility with the Community Law of Polish Regulation on Taxation of Second-Hand Cars], *Przegląd Podatkowy*, 2007, no. 4, pp. 41–43.

Maitrot de la Motte A., Cour de justice, 1re ch., 10 avril 2014, Emerging Markets Series of DFA Investment Trust Company c/ Dyrektor Izby Skarbowej w Bydgoszczy, aff. C-190/12, ECLI:EU:C:2014:249, *Jurisprudence de la CJUE 2014* (Ed. Bruylant – Bruxelles), 2014 p. 418–421.

Makowicz B., Polnische 'Akzise' auf eingeführte Gebrauchtfahrzeuge, *Zeitschrift für Zölle und Verbrauchsteuern*, 2007, pp. 129–131.

Mangialardi D.A., Tributi interni – Tasse sugli autoveicoli usati importati, *Giurisprudenza italiana*, 2007, pp. 290–291.

Miąsik D., Sprawa wspólnotowa przed sądem krajowym [A Community Case Before a National Court], *Europejski Przegląd Sądowy*, 2008, no. 9, pp. 16–22.

Miąsik D., Wróbel A., Europeizacja prawa administracyjnego – pojęcie i konteksty, w R. Hauser, Z. Niewiadomski, A. Wróbel (red.), *System Prawa Administracyjnego, t. 3, Europeizacja prawa administracyjnego*, C.H. Beck, 2014.

Michel V., Traitement fiscal des dividendes sortants, *Europe*, 2014 Juin, no. 6, pp. 29–30.

Mosbrucker A.-L., Kauff-Gazin F., Fiscalité directe, *Europe*, 2009 Juin Comm., no. 214, pp. 9–11.

Nykiel W., Wilk M., Swoboda przepływu kapitału w stosunkach z państwami trzecimi – glosa do wyroku Trybunału Sprawiedliwości z 10.04.2014 r. w sprawie C-190/12 Emerging Markets Series of DFA Investment Trust Company przeciwko Dyrektorowi Izby Skarbowej w Bydgoszczy [Free Movement of Capital with Third States – Commentary on C-190/12 Emerging Markets], *Europejski Przegląd Sądowy*, 2015, no. 6, pp. 37–43.

Patzner A., EuGH: Auf Ausschüttungen an Drittstaaten-Fonds erhobene Kapitalertragsteuer verstößt gegen Kapitalverkehrsfreiheit, *Recht der Finanzinstrumente*, 2014, pp. 253–254.

Pinetz E., Der Rechtfertigungsgrund der wirksamen steuerlichen Kontrolle und Drittstaaten, *Ecolex*, 2014, p. 568.

Półtorak N., Efektywność prawa Unii Europejskiej a polska procedura administracyjna i sądowoadministracyjna' [Effectiveness of the EU law and Polish Administrative and Judicial-Administrative Procedure], *Zeszyty Naukowe Sądownictwa Administracyjnego*, 2014, no. 3, pp. 37–53.

Rigaux A., Taxe d'effet equivalent, Europe 2017 décembre no. 12, pp. 23–24.

Steinmeyer H.-D., Freizügigkeit – Besteuerung von Krankenversicherungsbeiträgen, *Zeitschrift für europäisches Sozial- und Arbeitsrecht*, 2010, pp. 78–80.

Sułkowski J., Commentary to the Resolution of 7 Judges of the SAC of 7 December 2009, Case I OPS 9/09, *Zeszyty Naukowe Sądownictwa Administracyjnego*, 2010, no. 3, pp. 160–165.

Szubiakowski M., Wyrok Trybunału Konstytucyjnego o niezgodności z Konstytucją aktu normatywnego wydanego po wniesieniu skargi kasacyjnej – granice rozpoznania skargi kasacyjnej. Glosa do uchwały NSA z dnia 7 grudnia 2009 r., I OPS 9/09, *Orzecznictwo Sądów Polskich*, 2010, no. 6, pp. 409–418.

Tetlak K., Commentary to Case C-314/08, Filipiak, EU:C:2009:719, *Highlights & Insights on European Taxation*, 2010, no. 2, pp. 65–66.

Von Brocke K., Emerging Markets Series: Equal Tax Treatment for U.S. Regulated Investment Companies in Europe, *Tax Notes International*, 2014, pp. 327–333.

Wróbel A., Komentarz do artykułu 1, in A. Wróbel et al. (eds.), *Kodeks postępowania administracyjnego*, Komentarz, Wolters Kluwer, 2020, do art. 1, Stosowanie kodeksu do spraw unijnych, uw. 1).

4 The concept of the EU Case in the case-law of the Constitutional Tribunal

Monika Domańska

Introduction

The number of rulings of *Trybunał Konstytucyjny* (hereafter referred to as the Constitutional Tribunal and the CT) in which legal problems related (directly or indirectly) to EU law have been resolved amounts to over a thousand cases. At the beginning of the interaction of the CT with EU law, there was a clear upward trend in the number of EU cases, and it lasted until 2009. Subsequently, that amount remained at a level of 50–60 (fifty-sixty) cases a year (except for the year 2015, in which more than 80 (eighty) cases were recorded). However, following this, a decreasing trend could be observed. Currently, the CT issues less than 20 judgments per year (in all matters falling within its competence). There were 19 judgments in 2021 and only 14 in 2022.

The analysis of case-law of the CT covering the cases related to European Union law must, in the first place, cover the determination of what characterises a case that is classified, by the CT, as so-called EU cases. It should be emphasised that the CT determines easily whether a particular case falls within the category of EU cases. In general, it can be found that the CT includes in that category those cases in which it issues the rulings that resolve legal problems relating to the membership of Poland in the European Union and the position of EU law in the Polish legal order.[1] When making a more detailed analysis, it is noted that the CT includes in the category of EU cases also those rulings which consider whether a given case (in the area of legal regulation or the facts of the case) requires the reference to EU law, that is, whether it is covered by the regulatory framework of EU law. The latter aspect relates to the need to refer to the EU law system as a source of a

1 The challenges that national, subnational, and European territorial entities within a multi-level framework face are defined as 'asserting jurisdictional integrity over the selected territory' and 'securing relational integrity in terms of legitimacy, consensus and accountability', see S. Piattoni, *The Theory of Multi-level Governance. Conceptual, Empirical and Normative Challenges*, Oxford University Press, 2010, p. 27.

DOI: 10.4324/9781003376019-5

reviewed or reviewing rule, in addition to determining the content of an EU law rule as a method to support the line of argument adopted by the CT in a particular case.

It should be emphasised that determining the scope of application of EU law is essential for defining the *ratione materiae* of an obligation to ensure the consistency of National Law with EU law by the CT. On the other hand, the obligation in question has a limited scope, in the sense, that it extends to matters covered by EU law legislation but not beyond.

Another very important issue, from the perspective of the analysis under consideration, is that the Polish Constitutional Tribunal is not the law-applying body,[2] the meaning, in which the application of the law is based on the procedure applicable to administrative courts, the courts of general jurisdiction, in addition to the proceedings before the Supreme Court.[3] It should be recalled that the Polish Constitutional Tribunal is an independent constitutional body of the State and, under Article 10 (2) of the Constitution, its essential task is to review the hierarchical compliance of legal rules. The Polish Constitutional Tribunal does not take an overly active approach to the reviewing of the constitutionality of normative acts. A characteristic feature of the proceedings before the CT is, among others, that the documents initiating the procedure before the Court (the applications, the constitutional complaints) contain as a detailed presentation of the conflict of the rules as possible (according to a person submitting a document concerned) together with extensive grounds for such a view. In that respect, the arguments relating to EU law are presented. Thus, the CT does not search for the EU provisions (rules) applicable in a case, relevant to the ruling being issued, on its own. Such a concept of the constitutional judiciary is a derivative of the presumption of constitutionality of the law and the principle of stability of the legal order.[4]

2 About the Polish legal system in nowdays, see D. Szumiło-Kulczycka, The Organisation and Management of Courts in Poland, in: D. Szumiło-Kulczycka, K. Gajda-Roszczynialska (eds.), *Judicial Management Versus Independence of Judiciary*, Wolters Kluwer Polska, 2018, pp. 61–82. For more, with respect to judicial idependence, see instead of multiple K. Gajda-Roszczynialska, Judicial Idependence as Part of the 'Court of Law' Concept Versus the Law on the Organisation of Common Courts Amended in 2015–2018, D. Szumiło-Kulczycka, K. Gajda-Roszczynialska (eds.), *Judicial Management Versus Independence of Judiciary*, Wolters Kluwer Polska, 2018, pp. 83–115.

3 Judgment of the CT of 19 December 2006, case P 37/05. The Tribunal discontinued the proceedings as the ruling was inadmissible.

4 The comparative overview reveals that Constitutional courts do not by definition take a more activist approach within a legitimation strategy. They are embedded in the constitutional systems and as a rule will take a position in line with the strategy from the constitutional system as a whole, see P. Popelier, 'Europe Clauses' and Constitutional Strategies in the Face of Multi-Level Governance, *Maastricht Journal of European and Comparative Law*, 2014, 21, no. 2, pp. 300–319; see also comparative studies in: *Transnational Judicial Dialogue on International Law in Central and Eastern Europe*, A. Wyrozumska (ed.), Wydawnictwo Uniwersytetu Łódzkiego, 2017, p. 500.

Definition of the EU case

As the CT points out

> it is only the Constitutional Tribunal that is legally empowered to rule, in an operative part of a judgment and with *erga omnes* effect, on how to understand a legal rule in compliance with the Constitution. . . . The doctrine aptly defines the function of the constitutional judiciary as the control of norms, that is, the control of the rules of conduct established by state authorities, <<encoded>> in legal provisions (P 57/07).[5]

Since the imposition on Poland of the obligation to adapt its National Law to the standards resulting from the EU (Community) legal order, the CT should also consider the EU (Communities) *acquis* in its case-law. The CT in its case-law places emphasis on examining whether a particular EU legal act offers an adequate level of protection of rights and freedoms, rather than taking the EU legal system in general into consideration. It was within that practice that the definition of 'the EU/Community case' began to be developed in the CT case-law.

Based on the analysis of the case-law of the CT, it could be concluded that the CT takes EU law into account, both directly and indirectly, thus, creating a line of judgments in 'EU cases' and the line of judgments 'in cases with an EU element'. The former should include all the cases in which the CT examines the consistency of EU legislation with the provisions of the Constitution in addition to the provisions 'implementing' EU legislation to a national [legal] order or refers to a question for a preliminary ruling to the Court of Justice to determine the meaning (validity) of EU laws. In other words, these are the cases that cannot be heard in isolation from relevant EU legislation.

The second category of cases, that is, the cases with an EU element covers all other rulings of the CT in which the Tribunal has referred *acquis communatuire* to support the arguments justifying the view of the CT in a case concerned.

Pre-accession case-law

Before Poland began to participate in EU structures, that is, still in the pre-accession period, the CT had taken the position that all national authorities were obliged to interpret the law (in the scope to be adapted) considering the EU standards.[6] In this regard, a clear example here is the judgment issued in

5 Judgment of the CT of 15 December 2008, case P 57/07.

6 The concept of 'direct applicable' or 'self-executing' treaty provisions had been well established by Polish courts long before the Constitution was adopted (1997). When Poland became a member of the EU, Polish courts started to follow the formula devised by the CJEU for conditions of direct applicability of EU law established in 26/62, *Van Gend en Loos* and other cases without references to this sources (silent dialog), see A. Wyrozumska, The Central and Eastern European judiciary and Transnational Judicial Dialog on international Law, in: A. Wyrozumska (ed.), *Transnational Judicial Dialog on International Law in Central and Eastern Europe*, Wydawnictwo Uniwersytetu Łódzkiego, 2017, p. 22.

Case K 33/03[7] relating to the constitutionality of the provisions contained in the contested Law of 2 October 2003 on bio-components used in liquid fuels and liquid biofuels[8] and their relation in connection with constitutional rights and freedoms.[9] The grounds for this judgment had been very specific to an EU case before the CT, and the direction of this reasoning was followed in the case-law of the CT, also in the EU cases heard after the joining of the EU structures by Poland. In the judgment under analysis, the Tribunal has aptly observed that

> the case cannot be heard in isolation from European Union legislation on biofuels *sensu largo*. Directive 2003/30/EC of the European Parliament and the Council of 8 May 2003 on the promotion of the use of biofuels and other renewable fuels for transport is of fundamental importance in this place. . . . Since the accession to the European Union Poland has been obliged to comply with the principles of interpretation resulting from *acquis communautaire*. This also applies to the methods of interpretation applied in the case-law of the Constitutional Tribunal, including the present case, in which there is a need to interpret the limits of the concept of economic freedom (Article 22 of the Constitution). This is even more necessary, that this judgment will be published in the official journal only after 1 May 2004, that is, after the formal accession.

In the pre-accession period, the suggestion that EU law be used as an interpretative inspiration for the Constitutional Tribunal means, first, that the use of that law to reconstruct the constitutional standard in reviewing the constitutionality. This is neither the same as 'applying' EU law by the Constitutional Tribunal nor as the treating, thereof, as a direct and exclusive reference point for the constitutionality review. It must be underlined that in those days there was no obligation to comply with the consistent interpretation of National Law with EU law but the CT assessed that the contested acts, from the point of view of their compatibility (or incompatibility) with the Constitution, but also, as that text refers to the terminology, concepts, and principles of EU law, with the concepts and principles known in *acquis* of the EU. The Constitutional Tribunal noticed in its judgments[10] that although EU law is not binding in Poland, nevertheless, the provisions of Article 68 and Article 69 of the Europe Agreement establishing an association between the European Communities and their Member States, of one part, and the Republic of Poland, of the other part, have already, now, obliged Poland to make every effort to ensure the compliance of its future legislation with the Community legislation.

7 Judgment of the CT of 21 April 2004, case K 33/03.
8 Dz.U. [Journal of Laws] No. 199, item 1934.
9 B. Rakoczy, Glosa do wyroku TK z dnia 21 kwietnia 2004 r., K 33/03 [Commentary on the CT judgment of 21 April 2004, K 33/03], *Przegląd Sejmowy* 2005, no. 3, pp. 153–158.
10 Judgments of the CT: of 28 January 2001, case K 2/02; of 21 April 2004, case K 33/03; of 27 May 2003, case K 11/03.

One of the first judgments, qualified as a case including the EU law (or rather Community law) element, is the judgment in Case K 11/03.[11] Although the CT refers, on the grounds for the judgment, not so much to EU (Community) law itself but the practice of the EU Member States. Nevertheless, it is a very important case in the context of assessing the legality of the procedure for the expression of the consent of Polish nationals to the accession of Poland to the EU. The Tribunal examined the compatibility of the provisions of the National Referendum Law of 14 March 2003[12] with the Polish Constitution. The CT referred to the constitutional principle of favouring the process of European integration and cooperation between Member States. According to the CT, 'the interpretation of the binding legislation should take into account the constitutional principle of favouring the process of European integration and cooperation between states (cf. Preamble and Article 9 of the Constitution)'. The constitutionally preferred interpretation of the law is, that it serves the implementation of the indicated constitutional principle.[13]

Case-law after 1 April 2004

As early as 31 May 2004, that is, less than a month after the accession of Poland to EU, the Tribunal in Case K 15/04 ruled on the constitutionality of Article 8 of the Act, Electoral Law for the European Parliament[14] insofar as [it granted] the right to elect Members of the European Parliament in the Republic of Poland to citizens of the Union who were not Polish nationals and Article 9 of said Law, in the scope of which [it provided] the right to be elected to the European Parliament in the Republic of Poland to EU citizens who were not Polish nationals.[15] In that case, the legal status was based on a National Law [statute], which had implemented the EU directive and had

11 Judgment of the CT of 27 May 2003, case K 11/03.

12 Dz.U. [Journal of Laws] No. 57, item 507.

13 P. Radziewicz, Glosa do wyroku TK z dnia 27 maja 2003 r., K 11/03 [Commentary on the CT judgment of 27 May 2003, K 11/03], *Przegląd Sejmowy* 2004, no. 2, p. 191; P. Sarnecki, Glosa do wyroku TK z dnia 27 maja 2003 r., K 11/03 [Commentary on the CT judgment of 27 May 2003, K 11/03], *Przegląd Sejmowy* 2003, no. 5, pp. 92–96.

14 The Act of 23 January 2004 – Electoral Law for the European Parliament (*Dz.U.* [Journal of Laws No 25, item 219).

15 Another ruling of the CT delivered in the EU case with a similar subject is the judgment of the CT of 20 February 2006, case K 9/05. *Rzecznik praw obywatelskich* (the Polish Ombudsman) applied for examination of constitutionality of Article 6 (1) read in conjunction with Article 5 (1) and Article 7 (1) as well as Article 6a (1) read in conjunction with Article 5 (1) and Article 7 (1) of the Act of 16 July 1998 – Electoral law for municipalities councils, *poviats* councils, and voivodships assemblies (*Dz. U.* [Journal of Laws] of 2003 No. 159, item 1547 as amended); hereinafter: electoral law, the Act of 16 July 1998) in so far as those regulations deprive the right to elect (an active election right), as well as to be elected (the passive election right) to the municipal council and to the position of *voit* (town mayor, president of a city) the Polish nationals and the citizens of the European Union who are not Polish nationals entered into the permanent register of voters, kept in the municipality, less than 12 months before the election day.

entered into force even before the accession of Poland to the European Union, but those provisions were to be applied from the perspective of elections to the European Parliament, which were to take place after the accession of Poland to the EU structures.

In this case, the CT stated that there is no uniform election procedure for the European Parliament for all Member States and each State regulates this procedure by internal law. In this case, the constitutional regulation was unjustified. Firstly, because the regulation of elections to EU institutions is a matter of EU law. Secondly, taking into account the Polish perspective, it is enough to adopt regulation at the statutory level.[16]

It is worth mentioning that Statutes implementing EU law are subject to preventive and subsequent control by the CT. At the stage of implementation of EU law (before the statute enters into force), a Statute may be subject to preventive control. This control can be initiated only by the President of Poland who – before signing a statute – has the competence to refer such a project to the CT for adjudication of its conformity to the Constitution. Such control was initiated by the President in case Kp 1/09[17] concerning the Act of 5 December 2008 concerning the organisation of the fish market implementing Council Regulation 1224/2009 establishing a Community control system for ensuring compliance with the rules of the common fisheries policy.[18] The main subject of the analysed ruling, however, was the issue of constitutional requirements that must be met in a situation of limiting the exercise of the freedom of economic activity. The CT recalled that the freedom of economic activity may be subject to limitations due to the international obligations of Poland, which may be considered an 'important public interest'. That is why the scope of the regulatory freedom of the Polish legislator, regarding limitation of the freedom of economic activity, requires, in each case, the fact of integration with the EU to be taken into account.[19]

The CT reviews domestic statutes implementing EU legislation in the same manner as the other parliamentary statutes or legal acts issued by central organs of the state.[20] An individual submitting a constitutional complaint

16 A. Chmielarz-Grochal, J. Sułkowski, (Nie)obecność Unii Europejskiej w Konstytucji Rzeczypospolitej Polskiej z 2 kwietnia 1997 r. w kontekście zjawiska globalizacji – wyzwania dla państwa suwerennego [The (non)presence of the European Union in the Constitution of the Republic of Poland of April 2, 1997 in the context of the phenomenon of globalization - challenges for a sovereign state], in: A. Domańska, K. Skotnicki (eds.), *Zagadnienia prawa konstytucyjnego. Zasada suwerenności. Problemy wybrane* [Constitutional law issues. Principle of sovereignty. Selected problems], Wydawnictwo Uniwersytetu Łódzkiego, 2017, p. 25; M. Płachta Michał, R. Wieruszewski, Glosa do wyroku TK z dnia 27 kwietnia 2005 r., P 1/05 [Commentary on the CT judgment of 27 April 2005, P 1/05], *Państwo i Prawo*, 2005, no. 9, pp. 117–125.

17 Judgment of the CT of 13 October 2010, case Kp 1/09.

18 OJ L 343, 22.12.2009, pp. 1–50.

19 A. Krzywoń, Glosa do wyroku TK z dnia 13 października 2010 r., Kp 1/09 [Commentary on the CT judgment of 13 October 2010, Kp 1/09], *Przegląd Sejmowy*, 2011, no. 5, pp. 133–143.

20 Judgment, of the CT: of 27 April 2005, case P 1/05; of 5 October 2010, case SK 26/08.

that challenges the conformity of an act undermines the level of protection of rights and freedoms, in comparison with the level of protection guaranteed by the Constitution. The Brussels I judgment of the Polish CT was the first case in which the CT of an EU Member State directly reviewed the constitutionality of secondary EU law and issued a ruling on the merits.[21] In case SK 45/09[22] the CT adjudicated that Article 41, the second sentence of the Brussels I Regulation,[23] was consistent with the right to a fair hearing and equal rights of parties to court proceedings – Article 45 (1) in conjunction with Article 32 (2) of the Constitution. The CT has the competence to control EU secondary legislation (normative acts) only where the Constitution explicitly refers to the review of normative acts. According to Article 79 (1) of the Polish Constitution, an individual may in a constitutional complaint challenge the conformity of a statute or other normative act – being the basis for the court's judgment in an individual case – with the Constitution. The CT stated that the 'normative act' is also a legal act issued by an organ of an international organisation (Article 79 (1) of the Constitution). In the justification of the judgment, the CT assumed also that the examination of constitutional complaints constitutes a different type of procedure from the review of hierarchical compliance of norms. This thesis allowed the CT to include Brussel I Regulation within the scope of its jurisdiction.[24] Doubts as to this thesis are primarily related to the narrow subject scope of a constitutional complaint, characteristic of the Polish legal system, which may only concern the constitutionality of normative acts and not acts of applying the law.[25]

21 S. Biernat, M. Kawczyńska, The Role of the Polish Constitution (Pre-2016): Development of a Liberal Democracy in the European and International Context, in: A. Albi, S. Bardutzky (eds.), *National Constitutions in European and Global Governance: Democracy, Rights, the Rule of Law*, Springer, 2019, pp. 755–756.

22 Judgment of the CT of 16 November 2011, case SK 45/09.

23 Council Regulation 44/2001 of 22 December 2000 on jurisdiction and the recognition and enforcement of judgments in civil and commercial matters, OJ L 12, 16.1.2001, pp. 1–23.

24 This judgment is called also the most controversial case in the pre-2016 jurisprudence of the CT on EU metters. A crucial argument of the CT was that such control should be treated as independent, but also subsidiary, to the jurisdictional competence of the ECJ. The CT underlined that clearly stated a ruling of the non-compliance of EU law with the Polish Constitution should be the ultima ratio and should occur only when no other ways to resolve a conflict in issue with the norms of the EU's legal order are possible. As to the detailed analysis, see A. Sołtys, The Court of Justice of the European Union in the Case Law of the Polish Constitutional Court: The Current Breakdown in View of Polish Constitutional Jurisprudence Pre-2016, *Hague Journal of the Rule Law*, 2022, 15, pp. 23–24. https://link.springer.com/article/10.1007/s40803-022-00186-6, https://doi.org/10.1007/s40803-022-00186-6

25 Instead of many, see P. Bogdanowicz, P. Marcisz, Szukając granic kontroli. Glosa do wyroku TK z dnia 16 listopada 2011 r., SK 45/09 [Seeking the limits of control. Commentary on the CT judgment of 16 November 2011, SK 45/09], *Europejski Przegląd Sądowy* 2012, no. 9, pp. 47–52; T. Jaroszyński, Dopuszczalność kontroli zgodności unijnego prawa pochodnego z Konstytucją. Glosa do wyroku TK z dnia 16 listopada 2011 r., SK 45/09 [The Admissibility

An important guideline relating to the classification of a [given] case as the EU case, as the category of cases falling within the scope of judicial competence of the CT, is the view contained in the ruling P 37/05.[26] Whilst ruling on the basis of a question of law submitted by the VAC, the CT discontinued the proceedings on the grounds that the delivery of the ruling was inadmissible. On those grounds, it emphasised, among others, that 'the essential problem in the case concerned lies in the application, and not the binding force of law'. Judges, in the process of applying the law, are dependent and subject to the Constitution and Laws (Article 178 (1) of the Constitution). 'The conflict-of-laws rule, expressed in Article 91 (2) imposing a duty to refuse to apply a Law [statute] in the event of a conflict with an international agreement ratified by the Law [statute] is related to that principle. The principle of precedence applies also to Community law (Article 91 (3) of the Constitution). Therefore, if the court has no doubts as to the content of a rule of Community law – it should refuse to apply such a provision of a Law [statute], which is contrary to Community law, and apply directly a provision of Community law; alternatively, if it is not possible to apply the rule of Community law directly, look for the possibility of interpreting national law in conformity with Community law. In the event of interpretation doubts in the context of Community law, the National Court should refer a question to the Court of Justice for a preliminary ruling on that issue. Expecting the CT to eliminate such provisions of the Law would mean expecting the Tribunal to ensure the effectiveness of the implementation of the Community law, and this is the issue of the application of law. The Tribunal is not competent to rule on individual issues relating to the application of the law, including Community law'.[27]

The CT has no jurisdiction to declare that the acts of EU institutions are invalid. However, like other National Courts, the CT may consider the validity of an EU act. In July 2015, the CT decided to submit its first reference

---

of checking compliance of EU secondary law with Constitution. Commentary on the CT judgment of 16 November 2011, SK 45/09], *Państwo i Prawo*, 2012, no. 9, pp. 130–135; A. Kustra, Model skargi konstytucyjnej jako czynnik kształtujący orzecznictwo sądów konstytucyjnych w sprawach związanych z członkostwem państwa w Unii Europejskiej [Model of constitutional complaint as a factor shaping the jurisprudence of constitutional courts in matters related to the EU membership], *Państwo i Prawo*, 2015, no. 3, pp. 34–56.

26 Judgment of the CT of 19 December 2006, case P 37/05.

27 A. Wyrozumska, Stosowanie prawa wspólnotowego a art. 91, 188 ust. 2 i 193 Konstytucji RP. Glosa do postanowienia TK z dnia 19 grudnia 2006 r., P 37/05 [Application of Community law and Art. 91, 188 sec. 2 and 193 of the Constitution of the Republic of Poland. Commentary on the decision of the Constitutional Tribunal of 19 December 2006, P 37/05], *Europejski Przegląd Sądowy*, 2007, no. 3, pp. 39–43; T. Kozieł, Rozstrzyganie sprzeczności ustawy ze wspólnotowym prawem pierwotnym. Glosa do postanowienia TK z dnia 19 grudnia 2006 r., P 37/05 [Settling the contradictions of an act with the Community's primary law. Commentary on the decision of the Constitutional Tribunal of 19 December 2006, P 37/05], *Europejski Przegląd Sądowy*, 2009, no. 5, pp. 42–48.

for a preliminary ruling concerning the validity of the provisions of Directive 2006/112 on the common system of value-added tax.[28] The CT referred to the CJEU with questions concerning the rate of VAT on books published in digital form and other electronic publications (K 61/13).[29] The CJEU stated in its judgment that despite different VAT rates on electronic and printed publications, the contested provisions were valid.[30]

The CT listened to the voice of the CJEU expressed in the *Melki and Abdeli* judgment,[31] accepting

> the principle according to which constitutional courts of the Member States should refer a question for a preliminary ruling on the validity of a directive when they adjudicate on the constitutionality of a national law implementing binding provisions of the directive, and the charges against this act are based on fundamental rights, protected both in national law and in EU law.[32]

28 Council Directive 2006/112/EC of 28 November 2006 on the common system of value added tax, OJ L 347, 11.12.2006, pp. 1–18.

29 Resolution of the CT of 7 July 2015, case K 61/13.

30 Case C-390/15 *RPO*, EU:C:2017:174. Notes on Academic Writings: F. Grube, Derzeit geltender Ausschluss des ermäßigten Steuersatzes auf Zurverfügungstellung sog. E-Books unionsrechtskonform – Rzecznik Praw Obywatelskich (RPO), *Mehrwertsteuerrecht*, 2017, p. 317; P. Dodos, R. Heilmeier, Steuerrecht: Mehrwertsteuersatz bei digitalen Büchern, *Europäische Zeitschrift für Wirtschaftsrecht*, 2017, pp. 439–440; L. Dobratz, Die Beschränkung des ermäßigten Steuersatzes für Bücher auf Lieferungen auf physischem Träger ist mit dem Grundsatz der Gleichbehandlung des Unionsrechts vereinbar – Keine Notwendigkeit einer erneuten Parlamentsanhörung wenn die finale Richtlinienfassung in ihrem Wesen nicht vom Wortlaut des Richtlinienvorschlags abweicht, *Umsatzsteuer-Rundschau*, 2017, pp. 399–401; R. Szudoczky, RPO. VAT Rate. Difference in Treatment Between Printed Publications and Digital Publications is Valid. Court of Justice, *Highlights & Insights on European Taxation*, 2017, no. 8, pp. 34–36; M. Bainczyk, Die praktische Anwendung des Unionsrechts in Polen – Anmerkung zum Urteil des EuGH v. 7.3.2017, Rs. C-390/15 (RPO), und zum Beschluss des polnischen Verfassungsgerichtshofes v. 17.5.2017, Akz. K 61/13, *Europarecht*, 2017, pp. 725–743; E. Prejs, Zakres zastosowania obniżonej stawki podatku od wartości dodanej dla dostaw książek, gazet i czasopism. Glosa do wyroku TS z dnia 7 marca 2017 r., C-390/15 [The scope of application of reduced VAT rate for books, newspapers and periodicals – commentary to judgment of the European Court of Justice of 7 March 2017, C-390/15], *Europejski Przegląd Sądowy*, 2017, no. 8, pp. 34–38; A. Denys, Zasada równego traktowania w świetle przepisów o obniżonej stawce podatku od wartości dodanej dla dostaw książek, gazet i czasopism [The principle of equal treatment in the light of the provisions on the reduced rate of value added tax for supplies of books, newspapers and magazines], *Prawo Europejskie w praktyce*, 2018, no. 9/10, pp. 45–51.

31 Joint cases C-188/10 *Aziz Melki* and C-189/10 *Selim Abdeli*, EU:C:2010:363.

32 L. Garlicki, Przegląd orzecznictwa Trybunału Konstytucyjnego za 2015 rok, *Przegląd Sądowy*, 2016, no. 7–8, pp. 188–211; M. Wróblewski, Karta Praw Podstawowych UE w orzecznictwie Trybunału Konstytucyjnego – stan obecny i perspektywy [The European Union Charter of Fundamental Rights in the (Polish) Constitutional Court jurisprudence. The current state and prospects], *Europejski Przegląd Sądowy*, 2015, no. 10, pp. 19–24; R. Grzeszczak, 'Mapa' Judykatury Trybunału Konstytucyjnego Dotyczących

This case is important also for another reason. This example showed that the CT was open to a dialogue with the CJEU, that Poland was a good legal environment for the application of EU law, and that CT judges were familiar with the case-law of the CJEU and its procedures. In many cases, the judges apply foreign law without any reference to international courts' decisions. From a functional perspective, dialogue between judiciaries in the European legal space is interdependent. According to K. Lenaerts, 'with regard to judicial transparency . . . there is a somewhat interdependent relationship between communication and trust since without communication there is no trust and without trust, there is no communication'.[33]

The judgment that was issued in Case P 1/05,[34] which led to the amendment of the Constitution, should also be considered an important EU case. The Tribunal noted that

> the provision challenged in the question of law had been introduced to the Code of the Criminal Procedure by (the above mentioned) Act of 18 March 2004 amending the law, the Law Criminal Code, the Law, the Code of Criminal Procedure and the Law, the Code of Petty Offences. The amendment to the Code of the Criminal Procedure was made to implement, to the national order, the Council Framework Decision

Członkostwa Polski w Unii Europejskiej "Mapa" judykatury Trybunału Konstytucyjnego dotyczącej członkostwa Polski w Unii Europejskiej ['The Map' of the Judicature of the Constitutional Tribunal Concerning Poland's membership in the European Union], in: A. Bodnar, A. Płoszka (eds.), *Wokół kryzysu praworządności, demokracji i praw człowieka. Księga jubileuszowa Profesora Mirosława Wyrzykowskiego* [Around the crisis of the rule of law, democracy and human rights. Jubilee book of Professor Miroslaw Wyrzykowski], Wolters Kluwer Polska, 2020, p. 795.

33 K. Lenaerts, The Court of Justice and national Courts: A transparent Dialogue, in: P. Šámal, G. Raimondi, K. Lenaerts et al. (eds.), *Binding Effect of Judicial Decisions – National and International Perspectives*, Kluwer Law International, 2018, p. 204.

34 Judgment of the CT of 27 April 2005, case P 1/05. This judgment created lots of controversies in Polish doctrine. Instead of many, see D. Leczykiewicz Trybunal Konstytucyjny (Polish Constitutional Tribunal), Judgment of 27 April 2005, No. P 1/05, Glosa do wyroku TK z dnia 27 kwietnia 2005 r., P 1/05, *CMLRev.*, 2006, pp. 1181–1191; K. Grajewski, Europejski nakaz aresztowania – konstytucyjność regulacji kodeksowej. Glosa do wyroku TK z dnia 27 kwietnia 2005 r., P 1/05 [European arrest warrant - constitutionality of the code regulation. Commentary on the judgment of the Constitutional Tribunal of 27 April 2005, P 1/05], *Gdańskie Studia Prawnicze - Przegląd Orzecznictwa*, 2006, no. 1, pp. 161–166; P. Kruszyński, Glosa do wyroku TK z dnia 27 kwietnia 2005 r., P 1/05 [Commentary on the CT judgment of 27 April 2005, P 1/05], *Palestra*, 2005, no. 7–8, p. 289; M. Płachta, R. Wieruszewski, Glosa do wyroku TK z dnia 27 kwietnia 2005 r., P 1/05 [Commentary on the CT judgment of 27 April 2005, P 1/05], *Państwo i Prawo*, 2005, no. 9, pp. 117–125; P. Hofmański, Glosa do wyroku TK z dnia 27 kwietnia 2005 r., P 1/05 [Commentary on the CT judgment of 27 April 2005, P 1/05], *Państwo i Prawo*, 2005, no. 9, pp. 113–117; W. Czapliński, Glosa do wyroku TK z dnia 27 kwietnia 2005 r., P 1/05 [Commentary on the CT judgment of of 27 April 2005, P 1/05], *Państwo i Prawo*, 2005, no. 9, pp. 107–111.

2002/584/JHA of 13 June 2002, on the European arrest warrant and the surrender procedures between the Member States.[35]

That circumstance was discussed more broadly by the Constitutional Tribunal, since it was considered to be important for the understanding of the intentions of the Polish legislature, for the restrictions to which it was subject under EU law, in addition to the subsequent assessment of the effects of finding unconstitutionality of an implementing Law.[36]

The judgment of the CT issued in case K 18/04[37] resolved the doubts in the EU case which should have been qualified so, given the content of the conclusions submitted to the Tribunal. Those conclusions, as a main review subject, pointed to the Treaty of Accession of the Republic of Poland to the European Union (signed in Athens on 16 April 2003), together with the Act concerning the conditions of the accession of the Republic of Poland and the adjustments to the Treaties on which the European Union is founded in addition to the Final Act of the Athens conference, which are the integral parts of the Accession Treaty. The grounds [for applications] were directed against the Treaty and the Acts referred to, either in their entirety or against their individual provisions, as set out in the applications, and any reference to EU primary law, as a subject of review, was made indirectly only, that is, through the Accession Treaty and its respective provisions. It is an important issue due to the fact that the CT is not authorised to assess the constitutionality of EU primary law. However, it has such a competence towards a ratified international agreement, for example, the Accession Treaty (Article 188 item 1 of the Constitution). The applicants' objections corresponded to the two basic claims: a) that the Constitution does not allow accession to the legal system of the European Union, which assumes the primacy of Community law over Polish law; since this leads, as the applicants claimed, to a violation of a constitutional principle, expressed in Article 8 (1); b) that a number of the provisions of the Constitution, including those relating to the ownership, the family, the family farm, were incompatible with the rules resulting, according to the applicants, from primary or secondary Community law. In this situation, two sets of problems required an answer: whether a legal system of the European Union is embedded in the Constitution of the Republic of Poland; whether the objections concerning respective Community provisions justify their contradiction with the Polish Constitution, and what is more, whether the grounds for applications had been based on appropriate premises and duly supported with arguments.

35 OJ L 190, 18.07.2002, pp. 1–20.

36 A broader discussion of the judgment see the chapter: The effect of consistent interpretation of national law in the case-law of the Constitutional Tribunal of this volume. In terms of application of the provisions or the implementation of the European Arrest Warrant the CT ruled also in the judgment of 5 October 2010, case SK 26/08.

37 Judgment of the CT of 11 May 2005, case K 18/04.

In the operative part, the CT had not declared the unconstitutionality of an act of EU law referred to in the applications, or a specific EU provision referred to, and the CT discontinued the proceedings in the scope of the assessment of the constitutionality of EU primary law. The justification of the judgment is the most extensive and the most serious, at that time, statement of the CT on the EC/EU and their legal system. It contains an analysis of many issues falling within the scope of both Polish constitutional law and international and community law. Above all, the arguments of the CT concerning the main systemic problems of the EU and the position of the state constitution in European constitutionalism are essential for the CT's legal reasoning in other cases.[38]

In the context of the aforementioned ruling of the CT and, at the same time in terms of the definition of an 'EU case', it should be noted that the current panel of the Tribunal had changed the interpretation direction set in that case, as regards the scope of its own competencies, as well as the competences entrusted to the European Union by Poland, which caused some judicial instability. The Tribunal found that it had sufficient competencies to review the constitutionality of EU primary law. It is enough to make a reference, at this juncture, to the rulings issued in the EU cases including P 7/20[39] (in which the CT held – that Article 4 (3) the second subparagraph TEU, read in conjunction with Article 279 TFEU, in the scope, in which the Court of Justice imposed *ultra vires* obligations on Poland, in its capacity as a Member State of the European Union, [by] issuing interim measures relating to the organisation and jurisdiction of the Polish courts, in addition to the procedure to be followed before those courts, was incompatible with the Constitution of the Republic of Poland, and in that respect, was not covered by the principles of primacy and of direct applicability set out in Article 91 (1) to (3) of the Constitution), or Case K 3/21,[40] in which the CT also ruled on unconstitutionality of the provisions of TEU under review, that is, the first and the second subparagraphs of Article 1, in conjunction with Article 4 (3) TEU; the second subparagraph of Article 19(1) TEU; and the second subparagraph of Article 19 (1) and Article 2 TEU.

By openly questioning the basic foundations of European integration, such as the primacy of EU law and the EU understanding of judicial independence,

38 A broader discussion of the judgment see the chapter: The effect of consistent interpretation of national law in the case-law of the Constitutional Tribunal of this volume.

39 Judgment of the CT of 14 July 2021, case P 7/20. The judgment of the CT is closely connected with the Decision of the CJEU of 8 April 2020, C-791/19 R *European Commission v. Republic of Poland*, EU:C:2020:277. A broader discussion of the judgment of the CT see the chapter: The effect of consistent interpretation of national law in the case-law of the Constitutional Tribunal this volume.

40 Judgment of the CT of 7 October 2021 r., case K 3/21. A broader discussion of the judgment see the chapter: The effect of consistent interpretation of national law in the case-law of the Constitutional Tribunal of this volume.

the CT marked the end of cooperation with the CJEU and escalated the tensions between those two Tribunals in the area of their competences. On one hand, it resulted in a new model on constitutional adjudication but on the other hand, the CT changed the approach to the use of EU law (considering EU cases) by other national courts. The CT limits the scope of application of EU law in issues sensitive to the Polish government (constitutional complaints were brought by entities representing government bodies) by declaring various sources of EU law to be unconstitutional as falling outside the scope of competences granted to the EU in the founding treaties.

This new line of the case-law of the CT is an element of the years-long 'rule of law crisis' in Poland.

Case-law with an EU law element

When focusing on the category of cases with an EU element, it is sufficient to show the main differences arising in the scope of reasoning of the CT, to refer to those examples of the rulings, where both in the application (complaint) addressed to the CT and in the operative part of the ruling, there are no provisions (acts) of EU law. Nevertheless, the CT makes a clear reference to the EU law system in these cases. This way the Tribunal confirms and enhances the relevance of the view taken in the case.

Thus, Case P 1/11,[41] which related to the principles of carrying out the development policy (the rights and obligations of applicants applying for funds from regional operational programs), could be an example. The Tribunal noticed:

> [f]inally, it is needed to refer to thesis, arising during the proceedings, that a need, to regulate in the implementation systems the rights of participants of the project competitions, is determined not only by the provisions challenged but also by the acts of European Union law, and in particular, Regulation No. 1083/2006. That argument is important, as the EU Regulations are of 'the general application', are binding in whole, and are directly applicable in all Member States. . . . The EU law does not provide in what type of legal acts the rights and obligations of entities applying for funds from regional operational programs should be regulated. . . . However, the freedom of Member States in the above-mentioned area is relative, because it is limited by the obligation to respect the general structural principles of the European Union. . . . Therefore, the change in the way in which the rights and obligations of the participants in competitions are regulated, resulting from that judgment, will at the same time, cause restoring the situation of constitutionality and more effective implementation of the obligations arising from the membership of Poland in the European Union.

41 Judgment of the CT of 12 December 2011, case P 1/11.

On the other hand, for example, in judgment P 25/06[42] on the method of submitting monthly information as a condition for obtaining co-financing of salaries for disabled employees, the Tribunal merely mentions, in the grounds of the case, what the connection between the case concerned and EU law is. It finds:

> [t]he provisions of Article 26c (1) (1) and (2) and (1a) and (6) of the Rehabilitation Law, referred in the question of law, have been introduced into that Act by the Act of 20 April 2004 on the amendment and repeal of certain acts in connection with the accession of the Republic of Poland to the European Union (*Dz. U.* [Journal of Laws] No. 96, item 959); and that Act in Article 28 has amended the Rehabilitation Law in such a way that Directive 2000/78/EC of 27 November 2000 establishing a general framework for equal treatment in employment and occupation (Journal of Laws EC L 303 of 2 December 2000) has been implemented within the scope of its regulation. . . . The effect of implementing Directive No 2000/78/EC has been the adoption by Poland, [in its capacity] as a Member State, an obligation to implement its recommendations by establishing generally applicable provisions of national law, the application of which would make it possible in practice to achieve the objective of the Directive i.e. the equal opportunities also for people with disabilities on the labor market, in particular, in terms of the high level of employment and social protection, equal treatment in employment and occupation.

In case K 41/05[43] The Tribunal stated

> [a]lthough – which should be clearly emphasized – the Constitutional Tribunal does not control the compliance of the anti-money laundering act with the law of the European Communities, however – given the implementation nature of the reviewed act – the content of the Directive 2005/60/EC is not without significance for the outcome of this proceeding.

These rulings are a clear example that the CT draws a significant line between the need to assess the compliance of national law with EU law and the obligation to review of the constitutionality of normative acts. In this respect, it is an easy way to strike the right balance between different but interconnected legal systems, and consequently to find harmony in diversity.

Conclusions

The EU cases and the cases with an EU law element in the case-law of the Constitutional Tribunal provide for a certain standard, which is applicable in

42 Judgment of the CT of 6 February 2007, case P 25/06.
43 Judgment of the CT of 2 July 2007, case K 41/05.

the proceedings before the CT. It seems to be a rule that EU (Community) legislation is considered whenever it should be applied to the interpretation of the national legal provisions, and it is reconstructed not only on the basis of the Treaty provisions, which are the foundation of the EU, but also on the basis of all provisions of secondary law.

A characteristic feature of the case-law of the CT in the EU cases *sensu largo* is limiting of the deliberations contained on the grounds of the issue currently being decided in a case concerned. It is strictly related to the limits of claim, and such action of the Constitutional Tribunal is completely justified. Such a practice does not differ from the decision-making process of the Constitutional Tribunal carried out in cases applying solely domestic law or classical international law.

Bearing in mind the previous examples of CT rulings in EU law cases, it should be stated that EU (related) issues are present in the case-law of the CT in a significant number of judgments; however, few of them can be considered characteristic. They illustrate the issues that were faced by the Polish CT under EU law – in connection with either the development of national law or changes in EU law. As the proceedings before the CT are not initiated *ex officio*, the subject of the review and its scope are set by the entities initiating the proceedings. Therefore, some constitutional issues in the matter under examination have been considered in the case-law of the Tribunal more intensively than others, and some have not yet received judicature positions.

Literature

Bainczyk M., Die praktische Anwendung des Unionsrechts in Polen – Anmerkung zum Urteil des EuGH v. 7.3.2017, Rs. C-390/15 (RPO), und zum Beschluss des polnischen Verfassungsgerichtshofes v. 17.5.2017, Akz. K 61/13, *Europarecht*, 2017, pp. 725–743.

Biernat S., Kawczyńska M., The Role of the Polish Constitution (Pre-2016): Development of a Liberal Democracy in the European and International Context, in A. Albi, S. Bardutzky (eds.), *National Constitutions in European and Global Governance: Democracy, Rights, the Rule of Law*, Springer, 2019, pp. 755–756.

Bogdanowicz P., Marcisz P., Szukając granic kontroli. Glosa do wyroku TK z dnia 16 listopada 2011 r., SK 45/09 [Seeking the limits of control. Commentary on the CT judgment of 16 November 2011, SK 45/09], *Europejski Przegląd Sądowy*, 2012, no. 9, pp. 47–52.

Chmielarz-Grochal A., Sułkowski J., (Nie)obecność Unii Europejskiej w Konstytucji Rzeczypospolitej Polskiej z 2 kwietnia 1997 r. w kontekście zjawiska globalizacji – wyzwania dla państwa suwerennego [The (non)presence of the European Union in the Constitution of the Republic of Poland of April 2, 1997 in the context of the phenomenon of globalization - challenges for a sovereign state], in; A. Domańska, K. Skotnicki (eds.) *Zagadnienia prawa konstytucyjnego. Zasada suwerenności. Problemy wybrane* [Constitutional law issues. Principle of sovereignty. Selected problems], ed. A. Domańska, K. Skotnicki, Wydawnictwo Uniwersytetu Łódzkiego, 2017, p. 25.

Czapliński W., Glosa do wyroku TK z dnia 27 kwietnia 2005 r., P 1/05 [Commentary on the CT judgment of of 27 April 2005, P 1/05], *Państwo i Prawo*, 2005, no. 9, pp. 107–111.

Denys A., Zasada równego traktowania w świetle przepisów o obniżonej stawce podatku od wartości dodanej dla dostaw książek, gazet i czasopism [The principle of equal treatment in the light of the provisions on the reduced rate of value added tax for supplies of books, newspapers and magazines], *Prawo Europejskie w praktyce*, 2018, no. 9/10, pp. 45–51.

Dobratz L., Die Beschränkung des ermäßigten Steuersatzes für Bücher auf Lieferungen auf physischem Träger ist mit dem Grundsatz der Gleichbehandlung des Unionsrechts vereinbar – Keine Notwendigkeit einer erneuten Parlamentsanhörung wenn die finale Richtlinienfassung in ihrem Wesen nicht vom Wortlaut des Richtlinienvorschlags abweicht, *Umsatzsteuer-Rundschau*, 2017, pp. 399–401.

Dodos P., Heilmeier R., Steuerrecht: Mehrwertsteuersatz bei digitalen Büchern, *Europäische Zeitschrift für Wirtschaftsrecht*, 2017, pp. 439–440.

Gajda-Roszczynialska K., Judicial Independence as Part of the 'Court of Law' Concept Versus the Law on the Organisation of Common Courts Amended in 2015–2018, in: D. Szumiło-Kulczycka, K. Gajda-Roszczynialska (eds.), Wolters Kluwer Polska, 2018, pp. 83–115.

Grajewski K., Europejski nakaz aresztowania – konstytucyjność regulacji kodeksowej. Glosa do wyroku TK z dnia 27 kwietnia 2005 r., P 1/05 [European arrest warrant - constitutionality of the code regulation. Commentary on the judgment of the Constitutional Tribunal of 27 April 2005, P 1/05], *Gdańskie Studia Prawnicze - Przegląd Orzecznictwa*, 2006, 1, pp. 161–166.

Grube F., Derzeit geltender Ausschluss des ermäßigten Steuersatzes auf Zurverfügungstellung sog, E-Books unionsrechtskonform – Rzecznik Praw Obywatelskich (RPO), *Mehrwertsteuerrecht*, 2017, p. 317.

Grzeszczak R., "Mapa" judykatury Trybunału Konstytucyjnego dotyczącej członkostwa Polski w Unii Europejskiej ['The Map' of the Judicature of the Constitutional Tribunal Concerning Poland's membership in the European Union], in A. Bodnar, A. Płoszka (eds.), *Wokół kryzysu praworządności, demokracji i praw człowieka. Księga jubileuszowa Profesora Mirosława Wyrzykowskiego* [Around the crisis of the rule of law, democracy and human rights. Jubilee book of Professor Miroslaw Wyrzykowski], Wolters Kluwer Polska, 2020, p. 795.

Hofmański P., Glosa do wyroku TK z dnia 27 kwietnia 2005 r., P 1/05 [Commentary on the CT judgment of 27 April 2005, P 1/05], *Państwo i Prawo*, 2005, no. 9, pp. 113–117.

Jaroszyński T., Dopuszczalność kontroli zgodności unijnego prawa pochodnego z Konstytucją. Glosa do wyroku TK z dnia 16 listopada 2011 r., SK 45/09 [The Admissibility of checking compliance of EU secondary law with Constitution. Commentary on the CT judgment of 16 November 2011, SK 45/09], *Państwo i Prawo*, 2012, no. 9, pp. 130–135.

Kozieł T., Rozstrzyganie sprzeczności ustawy ze wspólnotowym prawem pierwotnym. Glosa do postanowienia TK z dnia 19 grudnia 2006 r., P 37/05 [Settling the contradictions of an act with the Community's primary law. Commentary on the decision of the Constitutional Tribunal of 19 December 2006, P 37/05], *Europejski Przegląd Sądowy*, 2009, no. 5, pp. 42–48.

Kruszyński P., Glosa do wyroku TK z dnia 27 kwietnia 2005 r., P 1/05 [Commentary on the CT judgment of 27 April 2005, P 1/05], *Palestra*, 2005, 7–8, p. 289.

Krzywoń A., Glosa do wyroku TK z dnia 13 października 2010 r., Kp 1/09 [Commentary on the CT judgment of 13 October 2010, Kp 1/09], *Przegląd Sejmowy*, 2011, no. 5, pp. 133–143.

Kustra A., Model skargi konstytucyjnej jako czynnik kształtujący orzecznictwo sądów konstytucyjnych w sprawach związanych z członkostwem państwa w Unii Europejskiej [Model of constitutional complaint as a factor shaping the jurisprudence of constitutional courts in matters related to the EU membership], *Państwo i Prawo*, 2015, no. 3, pp. 34–56.

Leczykiewicz D., Glosa do wyroku TK z dnia 27 kwietnia 2005 r., P 1/05 Trybunal Konstytucyjny (Polish Constitutional Tribunal), Judgment of 27 April 2005, No. P 1/05, *CMLRev.*, 2006, 4, pp. 1181–1191.

Lenaerts K., The Court of Justice and National Courts: A Transparent Dialogue, in P. Šámal, G. Raimondi, K. Lenaerts et al. (eds.), *Binding Effect of Judicial Decisions – National and International Perspectives*, Kluwer Law International, 2018, p. 204.

Piattoni S., *The Theory of Multi-level Governance. Conceptual, Empirical and Normative Challenges*, Oxford University Press, 2010, p. 27.

Płachta M., Wieruszewski R., Glosa do wyroku TK z dnia 27 kwietnia 2005 r., P 1/05 [Commentary on the CT judgment of 27 April 2005, P 1/05], *Państwo i Prawo*, 2005, no. 9, pp. 117–125.

Prejs E., Zakres zastosowania obniżonej stawki podatku od wartości dodanej dla dostaw książek, gazet i czasopism. Glosa do wyroku TS z dnia 7 marca 2017 r., C-390/15 [The scope of application of reduced VAT rate for books, newspapers and periodicals – commentary to judgment of the European Court of Justice of 7 March 2017, C-390/15], *Europejski Przegląd Sądowy*, 2017, no. 8, pp. 34–38.

Radziewicz P., Glosa do wyroku TK z dnia 27 maja 2003 r., K 11/03 [Commentary on the CT judgment of 27 May 2003, K 11/03], *Przegląd Sejmowy*, 2004, no. 2, p. 191.

Sarnecki P., Glosa do wyroku TK z dnia 27 maja 2003 r., K 11/03 [Commentary on the CT judgment of 27 May 2003, K 11/03], *Przegląd Sejmowy*, 2003, no. 5, pp. 92–96.

Szudoczky R., RPO. VAT Rate. Difference in Treatment Between Printed Publications and Digital Publications is Valid. Court of Justice, *Highlights & Insights on European Taxation*, 2017, no. 8, pp. 34–36.

Szumiło-Kulczycka D., The Organisation and Management of Courts in Poland, in D. Szumiło-Kulczycka, K. Gajda-Roszczynialska (eds.), *Judicial Management Versus Independence of Judiciary*, Wolters Kluwer Polska, 2018, pp. 61–82.

Wróblewski M., Karta Praw Podstawowych UE w orzecznictwie Trybunału Konstytucyjnego – stan obecny i perspektywy [The European Union Charter of Fundamental Rights in the (Polish) Constitutional Court jurisprudence. The current state and prospects], *Europejski Przegląd Sądowy*, 2015, 10, pp. 19–24.

Wyrozumska A., Stosowanie prawa wspólnotowego a art. 91, 188 ust. 2 i 193 Konstytucji RP. Glosa do postanowienia TK z dnia 19 grudnia 2006 r., P 37/05 [Application of Community law and Art. 91, 188 sec. 2 and 193 of the Constitution of the Republic of Poland. Commentary on the decision of the Constitutional Tribunal of 19 December 2006, P 37/05], *Europejski Przegląd Sądowy*, 2007, no. 3, pp. 39–43.

Wyrozumska A. (ed.), *Transnational Judicial Dialogue on International Law in Central and Eastern Europe*, Wydawnictwo Uniwersytetu Łódzkiego, 2017.

Part II

The principle of consistent interpretation of Polish law with EU law

The previous part focused on the question with regard to how Polish courts define and identify cases falling within the scope of EU law, so-called EU cases. Once a national court has established that – either alone (*acte clair*),[1] or with the indirect (*acte éclairé*),[2] or direct (in reply to preliminary reference) help of the CJEU, then it is clear that certain provisions of EU law must be taken into account when adjudicating the case or the contentious issue. Except for cases falling within the scope of the directly applicable provisions of EU regulations (which constitute the self-standing legal basis of the judicial decision), national courts usually adjudicate EU cases on the basis of national provisions, including these implementing provisions of EU directives. In such cases, the effectiveness of EU law demands, from national courts, the interpretation of national provisions in a manner that is harmonious with the respective provisions of EU law. This duty is called the consistent or conforming interpretation of national law.

Let us recall briefly that the principle of consistent interpretation has been formulated by the Court of Justice of the EU. Accordingly, national judges are obligated to interpret national law (in particular in cases of conflict between Union and national law), as far as possible and subject to fundamental principles (such as legality and non-retroactivity), in conformity with any relevant provision of EU law.[3] The principle of consistent interpretation is most often involved and invoked in cases in which the subject matter is governed by

1 Case 283/81, *Cilfit and others*, EU:C:1982:335.

2 Pursuant to Article 99 of the Rules of Procedure of the Court of Justice, CJEU rules in the form of order, see, for example, case C-275/14, *Jednostka Innowacyjno-Wrożeniowa*, EU:C:2015:75; case C-491/18 *Mennica Wrocławska*, EU:C:2018:1042; case C-2/21, *Rzecznik Praw Obywatelskich*, EU:C:2022:502.

3 Starting with case 14/83, *von Colson and Kamann*, EU:C:1984:153; followed by, in particular: C-106/89, *Marleasing*, EU:C:1990:395; joint cases C-397/01 to C-403/01, *Pfeiffer*, EU:C:2004:584.

DOI: 10.4324/9781003376019-6

directives,[4] but it is equally binding and important in all other EU cases, including also cases where the facts of the case or the contentious issues are governed by sources of EU law not requiring implementation, such as founding treaties. In any type of EU case, national courts are under the duty to interpret national law in compliance with the requirements of EU law before invoking direct effect and primacy.[5] It is only where such an interpretation is impossible that the national court must directly apply the principles of direct effect and primacy of EU law if the source of EU law in question is capable of producing a direct effect.[6] Since not all provisions of EU law meet the requirements of the direct effect test, and not all sources of EU law can produce a direct effect, the scope of the application of conforming interpretation is much wider than the actual scope of the application of two other principles of EU law under consideration in this monograph.

Therefore, the interpretation of national law that is consistent with EU law is, beyond any doubt, the most important tool from the point of view of the effectiveness of EU law.[7] Should a national court make use of consistent

4 Case 14/83, *von Colson and Kamann*, EU:C:1984:153, para. 28; case C-550/19, *Obras y Servicios Públicos*, EU:C:2021:514, para. 76; case C-282/19, *YT and others*, EU:C:2022:3, para. 121.

5 Case C-282/20, *ZX and Spetsializirana prokuratura*, EU:C:2021:874, para. 40; case C-573/17, *Popławski I*, EU:C:2019:530, para. 57.

6 D. Miąsik, M. Szwarc, Primacy and direct effect – still together: Popławski II, *CMLRev.*, 2021, pp. 571–590.

7 From abundant legal writing, see in particular: P. Craig, Directives, Direct Effect and te Construction of National Legislation, *European Law Review*, 1997, 22, no. 6, pp. 519–538; Skouris, Effet Utile Versus Legal Certainty: The Case-law of the Court of Justice on the Direct Effect of Directives, *European Business Law Review*, 2006, 17, no. 2, pp. 241–255, p. 246; S. Drake, Twenty Years after Von Colson: The Impact of 'Indirect Effect' on the Protection of the Individual's Community Rights, *European Law Review*, 2005, 30, no. 3, pp. 329–348, pp. 330–334; M. Klamert, Judicial Implementation of Directives and Anticipatory Indirect Effect: Connecting the Dots, *CMLRev.*, 2006, pp. 1251–1275; in the Polish literature in particular: S. Biernat, Wykładnia prawa krajowego w zgodzie z prawem Wspólnoty Europejskiej [Interpretation of National Law in Conformity with Law of the European Community], in: C. Mik (ed.), *Implementacja prawa integracji europejskiej w krajowych porządkach prawnych* [Implementation of Law of European Integration into National Legal Orders], TNOIK, 1998; K. Kowalik-Bańczyk, Prowspólnotowa wykładnia prawa krajowego [Interpretation of national law consistent with Community law], *Europejski Przegląd Sądowy*, 2005, no. 3, pp. 9–18; A. Wróbel, Pośredni skutek dyrektyw, czyli wykładnia prawa państwa członkowskiego zgodnie z prawem wspólnotowym [Indirect Effect of Directives – Interpretation of Member State's Law in Conformity with Community Law], in: A. Wróbel (ed.), *Stosowanie prawa Unii Europejskiej przez sądy. Tom I* [Application of EU Law by Courts], Zakamycze, 2005; M. Domańska, *Implementacja dyrektyw unijnych przez sądy krajowe* [Implementation of EU Directives by National Courts], Wolters Kluwer Polska, 2014, pp. 176–246; A. Sołtys, *Obowiązek wykładni prawa krajowego zgodnie z prawem unijnym jako instrument zapewniania efektywności prawa Unii Europejskiej* [The Obligation to Interpret National Law in Conformity with EU Law as an Instrument to Ensure Effectiveness of EU Law], Wolters Kluwer Polska, 2015; R. Wiatrowski, *Wykładnia prounijna Naczelnego Sądu Administracyjnego w zakresie przepisów dotyczących podatku od towarów I usług* [Consistent interpretation of the Supreme Administrative Court concerning VAT], Wolters Kluwer Polska, 2021 and the literature referred therein.

interpretation, then there is no need to resort to the principle of primacy and the remedy of the disapplication of national law. A given case before the national court will be decided on the basis of national provisions applied directly alone, with the provisions of EU law serving exclusively as a source of the normative standard to be achieved by the interpretation of national law. Remedies such as the reopening of judicial[8] or administrative[9] proceedings or for claims for damages[10] are also unnecessary since the effectiveness of EU law has been secured by the initial decision of a national court or administrative authority to apply provisions of national law in such a manner as to achieve the result required by the provisions of EU law.[11]

As has been already mentioned previously, the duty of consistent interpretation is binding, irrespective of the source of provisions of EU law and their direct effect.[12]

Such an interpretation can also, in cases where there is a conflict of national and European legal norms, allow the national court to deliver a judicial decision that will be compatible with EU law when, without such an interpretation, a national court would have been unable to use the principles of direct effect and primacy. This is the case of judicial proceedings falling within the scope of application of directives and framework decisions, which have not been implemented at all or have been wrongly transposed into national law. Without recourse to consistent interpretation, a national court would have to deliver a judgment on the basis of national provisions incompatible with EU law, since such national provisions may not be disapplied in any proceedings that either concern individuals and the facts of the case fall within the scope of a directive (direct effect of EU directive provision in disputes between individuals is excluded)[13] or are governed by framework decisions (direct effect of framework decisions has been excluded in the Treaties).[14] Hence, the CJEU consistently holds that

> the principle that national law must be interpreted in conformity with EU law, by virtue of which the national court is required, to the greatest

8 Case C-234/04, *Kapferer*, EU:C:2006:178.
9 Case C-453/00 *Kühne & Heitz*, EU:C:2004:17.
10 Case C-224/01, *Köbler*, EU:C:2003:513; C-173/03, *Traghetti del Mediterraneo*, EU:C:2006:391.
11 On the effectiveness of EU law and instruments to ensure it in national courts, see in particular N. Półtorak, *European Union rights in national courts*, Kluwer Law International 2015.
12 Case C-106/89, *Marleasing*, EU:C:1990:395, paras 6 and 8.
13 Case C-152–154/07, *Arcor and others*, EU:C:2008:426, para. 35–44; case C-351/12, *OSA*, EU:C:2014:110, para. 46, 47; case C-122/17, *Smith*, EU:C:2018:631, para. 49; case C-193/17 *Cresco Investigation*, EU:C:2019:43, para. 73.
14 Case C-573/17, *Popławski II*, EU:C:2019:530, para. 72; case C-554/14, *Ognyanov*, EU:C:2016:835, paras. 58 and 61; S. Drake, 'Twenty Years after Von Colson: The Impact of 'Indirect Effect' on the Protection of the Individual's Community Rights', *European Law Review*, 2005, 30, no. 3, pp. 329–348; R. Loof, Temporal Aspects of the Duty of Consistent Interpretation in the First and Third Pillars, *European Law Review*, 2007, 32, no. 6, pp. 888–895.

> extent possible, to interpret national law in conformity with the requirements of EU law, is inherent in the system of the treaties, since it permits the national court, within the limits of its jurisdiction, to ensure the full effectiveness of EU law when it determines the dispute before it.[15]

To secure the effectiveness of EU law, the legal concepts used in EU directives (framework decisions) should be understood in the same manner across the whole EU and (save for the exceptions provided for in directives based on the minimum harmonisation) national provisions implementing such concepts (or containing such concepts in legislation predating directives) should be interpreted in a manner reflecting the wording and purpose of provisions of EU law and their binding interpretation delivered by the CJEU.[16]

The duty of consistent interpretation was initially placed upon national courts. However, as it was also rooted in the principle of sincere cooperation enshrined now in Article 4 para 3 TEU, there should be no doubt that this duty has also bound administrative authorities, who are, just as the court are, bodies of the state bound by that principle.[17] This was only confirmed in *Popławski II*, where the CJEU ruled that the obligation to interpret national law in conformity with the EU binds all Member State authorities, including members of the executive, like the Minister of Justice.[18]

The duty of consistent interpretation means that national law should be interpreted in conformity with EU law 'to the greatest extent possible'[19] in the light of the wording and purpose in order to achieve the results sought by EU law.[20] The exercising of this duty by a court or authority means that a particular case or an issue will be decided differently than initially expected. Whilst the wording of a national provision interpreted in conformity with the EU will remain the same, consistent interpretation will allow for the altering of the content of a legal norm derived from such a provision. Thus, such

15 Case C-84/12, *Koushkaki*, EU:C:2013:862, paras. 75 and 76; case C-554/14, *Ognyanov*, EU:C:2016:835, para. 59; case C-579/15, *Popławski I*, EU:C:2017:503, para. 31; case C-573/17, *Popławski II*, EU:C:2019:530, para. 55; see also joined cases C-397/01 to C-403/01 *Pfeiffer and Others*, EU:C:2004:584, para. 114; joined cases C-378/07 to C-380/07 *Angelidaki and Others*, EU:C:2009:250, paras. 197 and 198; and case C-555/07 *Kücükdeveci*, EU:C:2010:21, para. 48.

16 Especially when national provisions reproduce those of EU law, Ch. N.K. Franklin, Limits to the Limits of the Principle of Consistent Interpretation? Commentary on the Court's Decision in Spedition Welter, *European Law Review*, 2015, 40, no. 6, pp. 910–924, p. 917.

17 Case C-103/88, *Costanzo*, EU:C:1989:256, para. 31.

18 Case C-573/17, *Popławski II*, EU:C:2019:530, para. 94.

19 Case C-573/17, *Popławski II*, EU:C:2019:530, para. 57.

20 For example, case C-282/19, YT and others, EU:C:2022:3, para. 118; case C-760/18, *M.V. and Others*, EU:C:2021:113, para. 69; in respect of framework decisions, see case C-105/03, *Pupino*, EU:C:2005:386, para. 43; case C-42/11, *Lopes Da Silva Jorge*, EU:C:2012:517, para. 54; case C-554/14, *Ognyanov*, EU:C:2016:835, para. 59; case C-579/15, *Popławski*, EU:C:2017:503, para. 31.

interpretation influences the application of national law since it should be applied in a manner enabling the achievement of results expected by the EU lawmaker. This may result in either the imposition of certain obligations on an individual or a limitation of his or her rights. The types of proceedings, as well as the body of law, are irrelevant. The consistent interpretation may lead to the modification of the interpretation of national public or private law[21] to the detriment, or to the advantage, of an individual or the state (its agency).

When executing the duty of consistent interpretation, national courts must: 1) 'do whatever lies within their jurisdiction',[22] 2) take 'the whole body of domestic law into consideration'[23], and 3) apply 'the interpretative methods recognized by domestic law'.[24] The CJEU explicitly demands that national courts follow this duty when national law permits the court to give a broad interpretation to the provision of national law.[25] National court must not avoid consistent interpretation by claiming that 'it can't interpret a provision of national law in a manner that is consistent with EU law merely because that provision has consistently been interpreted [or applied] in a manner that is incompatible with EU law'.[26] However, the CJEU does not expect the national court, when exercising the duty of consistent interpretation, to do the impossible. Instead, national courts are expected to verify, on a case-by-case basis, whether such a consistent interpretation of the national provisions is possible with due consideration given to the various interpretative methods of legal texts accepted and used in domestic legal practice, on one hand, and safeguards against the maverick interpretation, that individuals derive from the general principles of EU law, on the other.

The principle of consistent interpretation has certain limits. The obligation of a national court to interpret and apply national law in conformity with EU

21 Case C-282/19, *YT and others*, EU:C:2022:3, para. 118; case C-760/18, *M.V. and Others*, EU:C:2021:113, para. 69.

22 Case C-282/19, *YT and others*, EU:C:2022:3, para. 124; case C-550/19, *Obras y Servicios Públicos and Acciona Agua*, EU:C:2021:514, para. 78.

23 Case C-212/04, *Adeneler and Others* EU:C:2006:443, para. 111; case C-282/10, *Dominguez*, EU:C:2012:33, para. 27; case C-282/19, *YT and others*, EU:C:2022:3, para. 124; case C-550/19, *Obras y Servicios Publicos and Acciona Agua*, EU:C:2021:514, para. 78; case C-42/11, *Lopes Da Silva Jorge*, EU:C:2012:517, para. 56; case C-579/15, *Popławski I*, EU:C:2017:503, para. 34; case C-492/18 PPU, *TC*, EU:C:2019:108, para. 68, however, sometimes the CJEU departs from this obligation by demanding national courts to interpret and apply only those national provisions that were designed to implement EU law, see Ch. N.K. Franklin, Limits to the Limits of the Principle of Consistent Interpretation? Commentary on the Court's Decision in Spedition Welter, *European Law Review*, 2015, 40, no. 6, pp. 910–924, p. 918.

24 Case C-282/19, *YT and others*, EU:C:2022:3, para. 124; case C-550/19, *Obras y Servicios Públicos and Acciona Agua*, EU:C:2021:514, para. 78.

25 Case C-282/20, *ZX and Spetsializirana prokuratura*, EU:C:2021:874, para. 42.

26 Case C-573/17, *Popławski II*, EU:C:2019:530, paras 79 and 95; case C-554/14, *Ognyanov*, EU:C:2016:835, para. 69; case C-684/16, *Max-Planck-Gesellschaft zur Förderung der Wissenschaften*, EU:C:2018:874, para. 60; case C-282/20, *ZX and Spetsializirana prokuratura*, EU:C:2021:874, para. 42.

law is limited by the general principles of law, and it cannot serve as the basis for the interpretation of national law *contra legem*.[27]

The CJEU has, most often, mentioned the principle of legal certainty and the resulting, therefrom, the principle of non-retroactivity,[28] as the general principles of EU law setting limitations on the duty to secure the effectiveness of EU law. These principles preclude the duty of consistent interpretation from leading to the criminal liability of individuals being determined or aggravated.[29] Recently, the CJEU added respect for the rights of the defence of the accused person[30] and the right of the accused person to effective judicial protection[31] as guiding principles when determining whether a certain conforming interpretation of national law is possible.

Most of the time, the CJEU limits itself to the repetition of the general duty of consistent interpretation and the stating of the effects of such interpretation in the case at hand, whilst leaving the national court to focus on the actual interpretative element. However, it has happened recently that the CJEU has abandoned this comfortable habit of dictating to the national court what they should do, without explaining how they should arrive at the desired interpretation. For example, in *Popławski II* the CJEU, faced with a returning preliminary reference after *Popławski I*, engaged in providing the national court with guidance on whether a certain interpretation of national law in conformity with a framework decision was actually possible.[32]

The following considerations aim to present how Polish courts have accepted, and applied, the principle of consistent interpretation. Again, three jurisdictions will be presented, namely: the Supreme Court, administrative courts, and the Constitutional Tribunal. The synthesis is presented in the most coherent manner possible and includes examples of case-law that concern the reception of the principle of consistent interpretation, its structural elements and sources, in addition to the consequences of the consistent interpretation for courts and the rights of individuals.

27 Joint cases C-397/01 to C-403/01, *Pfeiffer*, EU:C:2004:584, para. 114; case C-105/03, *Pupino*, EU:C:2005:386, paras. 44 and 47; case C-282/19, *YT and others*, EU:C:2022:3, para. 123; case C-550/19, *Obras y Servicios Públicos and Acciona Agua*, EU:C:2021:514, para. 77.

28 Case C-282/19, *YT and others*, EU:C:2022:3, para. 123; case C-550/19, *Obras y Servicios Públicos and Acciona Agua*, EU:C:2021:514, para. 77.

29 Case 80/86, *Kolpinghuis Nijmegen*, EU:C:1987:431, para. 14; case C-168/95, *Luciano Arcaro*, EU:C:1996:363, para. 42; case C-321/05, *Kofoed*, EU:C:2007:408, para. 45; joined cases C-74/95 and C-129/95 *X*, EU:C:1996:491, para. 24, and joined cases C-387/02, C-391/02, and C-403/02, *Berlusconi and Others*, EU:C:2005:270, para. 74; case C-554/14, *Ognyanov*, EU:C:2016:835, paras. 63 to 64; case C-579/15 *Popławski*, EU:C:2017:503, para. 32; case C-573/17, *Popławski II*, EU:C:2019:530, para. 75.

30 Case C-282/20, *ZX and Spetsializirana prokuratura*, EU:C:2021:874, para. 42.

31 Case C-282/20, *ZX and Spetsializirana prokuratura*, EU:C:2021:874, para. 43.

32 Case C-573/17, *Popławski II*, EU:C:2019:530, para. 87; case C-167/17, *Klohn*, EU:C:2018:833, para. 68; case C-665/20 PPU, *X*, para. 66.

5 The principle of consistent interpretation in the case-law of the Supreme Court

Dawid Miąsik

Introduction

This sub-chapter presents how the Supreme Court of the Republic of Poland discharges its obligation to interpret national provisions in conformity with EU law (the principle or the duty of consistent interpretation). To illustrate this, the most interesting and important Supreme Court rulings were selected, in which the court had explicitly referred to that obligation or explained its scope and application *in concreto*.[1] Initially, the perception of the Supreme Court of the sources of the obligation of consistent interpretation will be discussed, with the elements of the legal structure of these obligations, its *ratione personae* and *ratione materiae*, in addition to the functions to be subsequently presented. Subsequently, the method used by the Supreme Court of reconstructing the EU standard for interpretation and the limits of that interpretation shall be presented using selected examples. Next, the generalised effects of the interpretation, in conformity with EU law, on the content of a national legal rule and the consequences of its application when resolving various categories of cases will be discussed.

Reception of the principle of consistent interpretation

The case-law developed so far clearly shows an extensive acceptance of the obligation of interpretation in conformity with EU law in a form and to the extent that results from the existing case-law of the Court of Justice.[2] The duty of

1 When selecting the rulings of the Supreme Court, it was impossible to refer only to those cases, which included references to CJEU case-law on the consistent interpretation, since in numerous judgments in which such an interpretation had been applied there were no references to the CJEU judgments in that respect. The *von Colson* judgment has been – altogether – cited 22 times, *Marleasing* 16 times, *Adeneler* 16 times, *Pfeifer* 12 times, and *Dominguez* 11 times, whereas quite often in the Dominguez Supreme Court referred in its ruling to all of the aforementioned cases of the CJEU.

2 It cannot be excluded that changes in that respect could arise in relation to the appointment to the Supreme Court of persons appointed under the conditions leading to establishing a body which in not a court in the meaning of Article 19 TEU, Article 267 TFEU, and Article 47 of

DOI: 10.4324/9781003376019-7

consistent interpretation is understood in the case-law of the Supreme Court as an obligation, resulting from the case-law of the Court of Justice, to interpret national law 'to the fullest extent possible in the light of the wording and purpose' of the EU law, by 'referring to the methods of interpretation recognised by the national order in such a way as to ensure the full effectiveness' to EU law rules and, as a result of such an interpretation, to issue a ruling consistent with the aims of the European Union law.[3] This obligation is regarded as

> an instrument intended to ensure the effectiveness of EU law in the national legal order using appropriate interpretative measures by an entity applying the law (as far as possible) to achieve the aim that had been pursued by the EU legislature and was incorrectly fulfilled by the national legislature.

One of the best examples of the consistent interpretation of a provision of national law, incorrectly implementing an EU directive, is the judgment of the SC of 4 March 2014, case III SK 34/13. It points out that, in accordance with the interpretation made by the CJEU in Case C-435/11 *CHS Tour Services GmbH*,[4] to qualify a commercial practice as misleading, there is no need to refer to the criterion of professional diligence under Article 5 (2) (a) of Directive 2005/29[5] (the equivalent of which was the clause of principles of morality under Article 4 (1) of the Law on Preventing Unfair Commercial Practices).[6] To qualify the behaviour of an entrepreneur as a misleading commercial practice, it is sufficient to find that the conditions referred to in Article 6 (1) of Directive 2005/29 (Article 5 (1) of the Law respectively) have been met. Therefore, there was no need to demonstrate separately that the entrepreneur's conduct infringed the principles of morality (professional diligence in the meaning of Directive 2005/29). However, such a demonstration was

---

the Charter of Fundamental Rights, since in the rulings, issued by adjudicating panels with their participation, this recognition is limited only to those EU cases, in which the standard for the interpretation in conformity with EU law does not lead to issuing a ruling with a content not corresponding to the expectations, expressed in the media, of the political authorities or the status of those persons as national judges.

3 Orders of the panel of seven judges of the SC of 19 July 2019, case III UZP 3/17 (preliminary reference in case C-545/17, *Pawlak*, EU:C:2019:260) and of 29 August 2019 (delivered following the ECJ's judgment).

4 EU:C:2013:574.

5 Directive 2005/29/EC of the European Parliament and of the Council of 11 May 2005 concerning unfair business-to-consumer commercial practices in the internal market and amending Council Directive 84/450/EEC, Directives 97/7/EC, 98/27/EC and 2002/65/EC of the European Parliament, and of the Council and Regulation (EC) No 2006/2004 of the European Parliament and of the Council ('Unfair Commercial Practices Directive'), OJ L 149, 11.06.2005, pp. 22–39.

6 The Law of 23 August 2007 on Preventing Unfair Commercial Practices, consolidated text: *Dz. U.* [Journal of Laws] of 2017 item 2070 as amended.

explicitly required by Article 4 (1) of the Law, including the definition of unfair commercial practice[7] implementing that Directive. The Supreme Court ruled that it was enough to apply the provision recognising the conduct of the entrepreneur misleading a consumer as unfair commercial practice (Article 5 (1) of the Law).

The Supreme Court has respected the primary role of the duty of consistent interpretation by treating the principle of primacy and the resulting remedy of disapplication of national provisions as a tool to be used as a last resort. The Simmenthal rule should be used 'where it is impossible to interpret provisions of national law in conformity with EU law and where a provision of EU law, with which national law provisions are incompatible, is directly effective'. The Supreme Court refers to the principle of direct effect and primacy of EU law only when the interpretation, in conformity with EU law, is impossible or highly doubtful and, at the same time, an 'adventurous' interpretation of Polish law that would achieve the aims of EU law; it is not necessary to ensure the effectiveness of EU law in a case concerned since it is possible to apply primacy and direct effect due to the participation of a Member State or its emanation as a party to the proceedings. For these reasons, the Supreme Court has already corrected the position of national courts, which claimed wrongfully that the lack of direct effect of the provisions of Directives prevented the outcomes of consistent interpretation, whose results would be detrimental to individuals. The Supreme Court takes a utilitarian assumption, according to which the interpretation in conformity with EU law serves mainly to ensure the effectiveness of EU law. It is not about the protection of the rights of individuals.[8] That protection is provided to individuals by the limits of the consistent interpretation imposed by the Court of Justice and resulting from the general principles of EU law, particularly the principle of legal certainty and the prohibition of interpretation *contra legem*.[9]

From the point of view of the reconstruction of the foundations of that obligation, the preference to referring to traditional judgments in the Cases of *von Colson*[10] and *Marleasing*[11] can be noticed. The Supreme Court, less often, refers to the more recent judgments of the Court of Justice, detailing the

7 'A commercial practice used by entrepreneurs towards consumers is unfair, if it is *contrary to the principles of morality* (a disputed element – annotation DM) and significantly distorts or is likely to distort the market behaviour of an average consumer before, during or after the conclusion of a product contract'.

8 Resolution of the SC of 13 May 2010, case III SZP 2/10.

9 Judgments: of the SC of 7 July 2011, case III SK 52/10; of 8 May 2019, case I PK 41/18; of 18 November 2020, case III PK 53/19.

10 Judgment of the SC of 14 February 2012, case II PK 137/11; resolution of the SC of 3 June 2008, case I PZP 10/07; judgment of the SC of 7 February 2019, case I PK 242/17.

11 Resolution of the SC of 9 September 2015, case III SZP 2/15; judgment of the SC of 4 December 2018, case I PK 181/17.

content of the obligation to interpret national law in conformity with EU law and its limits. Three rulings deserve attention in this respect.

In the first one (case III SK 52/10), the *Adeneler* formula has been accepted, according to which, since the date on which a Directive has entered into force, the national courts should refrain from interpreting domestic law provisions in a manner that might 'seriously compromise the attainment of the result prescribed by [that directive]'.[12] The *Adeneler* formula should have served the Supreme Court to accept an argument by the national regulatory authority (Chairman of the Office for Electronic Communication) that the Court should depart from its steady case-law. Under that case-law developed under the original version of Directive 2002/20,[13] the authority could not impose fines for breaches of Telecommunications Law discovered during the control procedure envisaged to provide the authority with information about any irregularities in the activities of telecoms. This procedure set severe limits on the authority's power to fine telecommunications undertakings by requiring it to demand corrections within a specific time limit before the initialising fining procedure for failure to abide. Through the referral to the Adeneler formula, the authority intended to bypass those limits imposed by national legislation. The Supreme Court had not followed this argument due to the limitations of the duty of consistent interpretation discussed subsequently (as the change of its case-law could lead to criminal liability being imposed on the undertakings concerned).

In the second one (case I PK 41/18), discussed in more detail, on the occasion of the limits to the interpretation in conformity with EU law, the Supreme Court used the *Dominguez* formula to justify a situation in which the national court should reconstruct the legal rule to be applied in resolving the case from the provisions of national law other than those which it would usually apply.[14] In that case, although the Supreme Court had generally allowed for such a possibility, it finally held that it could not behave following that formula since 'there is no equivalent legal solution in the Polish legal order within the meaning of Clause No. 4 (1) of the framework agreement either, which could be used *in lieu* of Article 30 (4) of the Labour Code'. The third judgment in that category, which may be regarded as an example of an approach taken by a national court in compliance with the *Dominguez* formula, is the judgment of the SC of 7 June 2016, case II PK 139/15. It was delivered in the case relating to the termination of a cooperative employment contract with the member of a cooperative solely on the ground that this member had been awarded the right to a retirement pension. The attention should be drawn to the fact that Article 187 sub-item 2 of the Cooperatives Law directly entitled the employer to

12 Judgment of the SC of 7 July 2011, case III SK 52/10.

13 Directive 2002/20/EC of the European Parliament and of the Council of 7 March 2002 on the authorisation of electronic communications networks and services (Authorisation Directive), OJ L 108, 24.04.2002, pp. 21–32.

14 Judgment of the SC of 8 May 2019, case I PK 41/18.

terminate the cooperative employment contract in such a situation. However, the Supreme Court found such a solution to violate the prohibition of discrimination on the grounds of age (although formally, it had neither applied Article 21 of the Charter of Fundamental Rights nor made a reference to the general principle of EU law prohibiting discrimination on the grounds of age nor used Directive 2000/78) and held that, from the general principle of the Polish Labour Law, as enshrined in Article 18^{3a} of the Labour Code (including the prohibition of discriminating employees, among others, on the grounds of age), a rule resulted that prohibited the termination of the employment relationship solely on the basis that an employed member of a cooperative had been granted the entitlement to a retirement pension. Thus, a consistent interpretation of a *lex generalis* provision of the Labour Code has led to the non-applying of the *lex specialis* provision, which is a consequence of the *Dominguez* formula.

Structural elements of the principle of consistent interpretation

Initially, in the case-law of the Supreme Court, a clear distinction had been made between the consistent interpretation of national law with EU law and 'the EU law-oriented interpretation'. The former term was used when the Supreme Court had found a conflict between EU law and national law and attempted, before using the principle of primacy, to remedy that conflict using an appropriate interpretation of the provisions of Polish law.[15] On the other hand, the latter term was used when there was no such conflict. Still, the Supreme Court was only concerned with determining the proper meaning to be provided to the provisions of Polish law implementing a provision of EU law into Polish law. The 'EU law-oriented interpretation' consisted of giving, when interpreting the provisions of Polish law, such meaning to national provisions as resulted from the interpretation of EU law that the CJEU had already made. That distinction has been criticised in the literature.[16] The use of this thereof seems to have been discontinued, assuming that the obligation to interpret national law in a manner consistent with EU law is a duty of national courts, regardless of whether there is a conflict between national law and EU law.[17] Nevertheless, indirectly, the Supreme Court still seems to maintain that distinction since it refers to the concept of the interpretation in conformity with EU law itself when it first finds that there is an incompatibility between a rule resulting from a provision of national law and the EU law rule.[18]

15 Judgment of the SC of 9 July 2008, case I PK 315/07; resolution of a panel of seven judges of the SC of 19 November 2008, case I PZP 4/08.

16 A. Sołtys, *Obowiązek wykładni prawa krajowego zgodnie z prawem unijnym jako instrument zapewniania efektywności prawa Unii Europejskiej*, [The Obligation to Interpret National Law in Conformity with EU Law as an Instrument to Ensure Effectiveness of EU Law], Wolters Kluwer Polska, 2015, p. 630.

17 See, for example, judgment of the SC of 8 March 2012, case V CSK 102/11.

18 See, for example, judgment of the SC of 10 October 2019, case I PK 196/18.

Before presenting numerous examples in this chapter relating to the results of interpretation in conformity with EU law, it should be noted that, in the case-law of the Supreme Court, those cases prevail without any verbal reference to the obligation of interpretation in conformity with EU law. It is assumed that, in the case of acts of national law implementing EU law to the national legal order, it is necessary to interpret the provisions contained therein in a manner that takes into account the wording and purposes of the EU legal acts, which those national provisions implement and their interpretation made by the Court of Justice.

A perfect example of such an approach is the resolution of the panel of seven judges of the SC of 21 January 2009, case II PZP 13/08, in which it was found, by referring to Directives 2000/78 and 2006/54 and at the same time without a reference to the obligation of interpretation in conformity with EU law that 'reaching the retirement age and acquiring the right to a pension cannot be the sole reason for the termination of the employment contract by an employer', and hence new meaning was given to Article 30 (4) of Labour Code (regulating the just cause of the termination of an employment contract).

Another example of such an approach is the judgment of the SC of 28 February 2019, case I PK 50/18 in the case regarding the one-off severance pay and the length of service award, [where] the Supreme Court explained Article 18^{3a} (1) of the Labour Code,[19] assuming that indirect discrimination in employment on the grounds of disability occurs when the agreement between an employer and the trade unions excludes, without any objective justification, from the right to benefits to which employees are entitled due to the transfer to a new employer, all the persons employed by the employer being acquired, who have been declared at least partially incapable of working. Moreover, the differentiating criterion in the form of having other sources of income in relation to the rules on granting the length of service award in connection with the restructuring of the employer consisting in the transfer of employees to a new employer under Article 23^1 of the Labour Code, implementing Directive 2001/23, has been considered as being deprived of an objective justification. When justifying that ruling, the Supreme Court pointed out that the Court of Justice 'considers that the concept of disability is an autonomous concept of Community law and that its interpretation should be given taking into account Council Directive 2000/78' and that 'the concept of disability in the meaning of the Directive, following the position of the Court of Justice, is not limited to the situation of a total deprivation of the possibility to participate in professional life, but also includes partial restrictions in the work performance'. That justified giving a sufficiently broad meaning to the prohibition of discrimination included in Article 18^{3a} (1) of the Labour Code as also covering the disability criterion.

The Supreme Court decided, in the same way, in the judgment of 12 September 2006, case I PK 87/06. First, the court determined how the principle

19 Consolidated text: *Dz. U.* [Journal of Laws] of 2020, item 1320, as amended.

of equal treatment in employment had been interpreted in the case-law of the Constitutional Tribunal, the European Court of Human Rights, and the Court of Justice. Subsequently, the Supreme Court assumed, in the light of those standards, that 'a provision of a company's collective agreement granting, during the period of guaranteed employment, a higher severance pay to an employee dismissed later than to an employee dismissed earlier, infringes the principle of equal treatment in employment' (Article 11^2 and Article 18^{3a} of the Labour Code).

The Supreme Court held similarly, in the judgment of 7 December 2017, case I PK 334/16, where it found that 'a reasonable accommodation', referred to in Article 23 (1) of the Law of 27 August 1997 on vocational and social rehabilitation and employment of disabled persons,[20] implementing Directive 200/78, consists of taking actions to enable a disabled employee to continue to occupy their current position and not be removed from the scope of [their] responsibilities, those duties that should be considered fundamental for the position held by the disabled employee. Therefore, such an employee should work in a properly prepared work environment (position). Still, they should not be forced to perform a different (narrower) scope of duties than provided for, in the same position, for a non-disabled person.

From the point of view of *ratione materiae* of the consistent interpretation, all provisions of Polish law, regardless of the date of their entry into force, are subject to interpretation in conformity with EU law.[21] In practice, the Supreme Court complies with the obligation to interpret Polish law in conformity with EU law in cases where EU law provisions are indirectly applicable, nevertheless shaping the content of the Polish law provisions and introducing thereof to the national legal order. This is the case in those EU proceedings in which the provisions of Polish law implementing EU Directives are applied.[22]

The Supreme Court case-law also explained that the obligation of interpretation in conformity with EU law binds national courts and national administrative authorities, such as national regulatory authorities.[23]

The obligation of interpretation in conformity with EU law is incumbent on all courts, regardless of the procedural activity and arguments of the parties to the proceedings.[24] In practice, the Supreme Court verifies whether the legal issue to be resolved in the appeal in cassation examination falls within the scope of EU law application. The issues examined by the Supreme Court extend to whether the legal issue, regarding the interpretation of provisions

20 Consolidated text: *Dz. U.* [Journal of Laws] of 2018, item 511 as amended.

21 Judgment of the SC of 5 December 2006, case II PK 18/06.

22 Judgment of the SC of 15 February 2008, case I CSK 358/07.

23 For example, Chairman of the Office for Energy Regulation (President of URE) – resolution of the SC of 15 January 2013, case III SZP 1/12.

24 See orders of the panel of seven judges of the SC of 19 July 2019, case III UZP 3/17 (preliminary reference in case C-545/17, *Pawlak*, EU:C:2019:260) and of 29 August 2019 (delivered following the ECJ's judgment) and the latest judgment of the SC of 18 November 2020, case III PK 53/19, in which this case-law was upheld.

of national law, is governed by provisions of EU law, whether Polish courts differently interpret or apply the provisions of Polish law which fall within the scope of EU law regulation, whether there has been an apparent infringement of the provisions of Polish law falling within the subject, object, or temporal scope of EU law since those provisions should be understood or applied in a way that has already been determined in the case-law of the CJEU. In principle, indicating the EU context of the case in which the Supreme Court hears an appeal is on a party. However, it should be emphasised that the Supreme Court has adopted an extraordinary adjudicating practice, which substantially mitigates the formal rigours applicable to that appeal, that is, an appeal in cassation, the primary legal remedy heard by that court (90% of rulings relate to appeals in cassation). It follows from this practice that it is sufficient to indicate only the provisions of Polish law on the grounds for the appeal in cassation. It is then for the Supreme Court to verify, on its motion, whether they fall within the scope of EU law application, whether they are compatible with it and whether they have been interpreted and applied by the court of the second instance in a way that ensures the effectiveness to EU law.[25] Therefore, from the point of view of EU law doctrine, we can talk about an obligation to apply an interpretation in conformity with EU law by the Polish courts *ex officio*.[26]

The Supreme Court recognises that it is obliged to interpret national law in conformity with EU law when EU law contains rules relating to the facts of the case and, due to the limitation of the scope of the Supreme Court's jurisdiction, falling within the grounds for the appeal in cassation (legal provisions which, according to the applicant have been allegedly infringed by the court of the second instance). Therefore, when EU law contains the rule that, due to the subject, object, or temporal scope of the act of EU law containing it, does not apply to the provisions of Polish law referred to in the appeal in cassation, the Supreme Court is not bound by the obligation to interpret national provisions in conformity with EU law.

An example illustrating that particular issue is the judgment of the SC of 26 June 2013, case V CSK 366/12. The EU copyright law did not define the concept of 'importer' for the obligation to pay so-called reprography fees. The acts of EU law, referred to by the court of the second instance, did not contain a generally applicable definition of that concept. Therefore, the reference to the

25 See especially judgments of the SC: of 18 December 2006, case II PK 17/06, OSNP 2008, no. 1–2, item 8; of 21 November 2011, case IV CSK 133/11, see also judgment of the SC of 18 November 2020, case III PK 53/19, in which this case-law was upheld.

26 See K. Kowalik-Bańczyk, *Badanie z urzędu naruszenia prawa wspólnotowego przy rozpoznawaniu skargi kasacyjnej przez Sąd Najwyższy – glosa do wyroku SN z dnia 18 December 2006*, II PK 17/06 [Examination Ex Offi cio of Infringement of EU Law When Examining the Appeal on the Point of Law by the Supreme Court – Case Note to the Judgement of the Supreme Court of 18th December 2006, II PK 17/06], *Europejski Przegląd Sądowy* 2009, no. 4, pp. 43–48; M. Baran, *Stosowanie z urzędu prawa UE przez sądy krajowe*, [Application of EU law by national courts ex officio], Wolters Kluwer Polska, 2014.

obligation of interpretation in conformity with EU law leading to the narrowing of the scope of the term 'importer' only to entrepreneurs importing to Poland reprographic devices from countries outside the European Economic Area has been considered unauthorised. Such a 'narrowing' interpretation of the 'importer' concept, corresponding to the realities and regulations of the internal market, would exclude, from the obligation to pay reprography fees, the operators importing copying devices and printers from the other Member States.

Another example of that type is the refusal to interpret the concept of the consumer in conformity with EU law. The resolution of the SC of 9 September 2015, case III SZP 2/15, concerned the issue of whether an injured party, who is a natural person not carrying out an economic activity and who claims from the insurer, within the guarantee liability under a contract of compulsory civil liability insurance of motor vehicles, should be considered a consumer within the meaning of Polish law.[27] In that case, the national provisions that implemented Directive 2009/22 were applied.[28] However, that Directive does not contain its definition of a consumer either but refers, in that regard, to other consumer directives listed in Annex I. Each of the consumer directives, to which Directive 2009/22 refers, defines the concept of consumer for its use. Hence, EU law did not define the notion of consumer for the purpose of bringing claims under compulsory motor vehicle keeper's liability insurance.

At the same time, the Supreme Court opted for the admissibility of interpreting Article 22 (1) of the Civil Code in conformity with EU law in cases where a national Law, implementing Directive 2005/29, would apply. That Directive implied the need to protect consumers not only at the stage of performing an act in law in the meaning of national law but even 'before the consumer is committed to the transaction' (Article 5 of Directive 2005/29), that is, before an 'act in law' in the meaning of Polish private law is performed. Consequently, the term 'performs an act in law' under Article 22 (1) of the Civil Code should be understood but only in matters covered by Directive 2005/29 in such a way that the concept of the consumer includes persons who are about to perform an act in law with an entrepreneur and not only those who have concluded a contract with an entrepreneur.

In cases not of an EU nature, the Supreme Court treats EU law as a source of 'intellectual inspiration' when interpreting national legislation.[29] The previous reasoning does not conflict with the position adopted in the resolution of

27 In accordance with Article 22 (1) of the Civil Code 'a natural person who performs an act in law not directly related to his/her economic or professional activity shall be deemed a consumer'. Thus, essential for recognising a natural person as a consumer was to perform 'an act in law' and in the light of domestic law 'bringing claims' is not such an act.

28 Directive 2009/22/EC of the European Parliament and of the Council of 23 April 2009 on injunctions for the protection of consumers' interests (Codified version) Text with EEA relevance, OJ L 110, 1.05.2009, pp. 30–36 with later changes.

29 So, for example, with reference to competition law and the concept of concerted practices in the pre-accession to EU cartel, judgment of the SC of 9 August 2006, case III SK 6/06.

the SC of 23 January 2019, case III PZP 5/18, in which a reference was made to the interpretation in conformity with EU law when interpreting national provisions concerning the members of the civil service corps. It was assumed there that an employee with the status of a member of the civil service corps, whose employment relationship had expired under Article 170 (1) of the Law of 16 November 2016, provisions introducing the Law on the National Tax Administration,[30] was entitled to severance pay under Article 8 of the Law of 13 March 2003, on special rules for terminating employment relationships with employees for reasons not related to employees.[31] Thus, civil servants belonging to the Civil Service Corps were covered with the protection resulting from the Law on collective redundancies, which provides additional benefits for employees made redundant as part of collective redundancies compared to employees with whom employment relationships were terminated outside this procedure. The Supreme Court pointed out that the Law on collective redundancies implements Directive 98/59,[32] aimed at increasing the level of protection of workers in the event of collective redundancies,[33] which, in turn, means that the terms used in this context, including the term 'redundancy' as defined in Article 1 (1) the first para. (a) should not be interpreted narrowly. Consequently, 'redundancy' in the meaning of the provisions of Directive 98/59 should be interpreted as all cases of termination of the employment relationship that occurred against the employee's will and, therefore, as unilateral legal acts of the employer, agreements of the parties to the employment relationship, as well as events, with which the provisions of Labour Law associate such an effect.[34] Particularly noteworthy is the fact that the Supreme Court pointed out that, in principle, Directive 98/59 did not apply to employees of public administration or public law institutions. However, it introduces a minimum standard of protection, which the Member States may extend if this serves the purposes of the Directive. According to the Supreme Court, in the case of such an extension, we are dealing with the EU case and, consequently, with an obligation of interpretation in conformity with EU law. However, it might initially seem that the scope of application of Directive 98/59 did not cover the facts of the case, in which the dismissal and any possible claims of a public administration employee were involved. However, since the Polish Legislator, in Article 11 of the Law of 13 March 2003, excluded from the scope of its application only certain employees of public administration (employed based on an appointment

30 *Dz.U.* [Journal of Laws] of 2016, item 1948.

31 Consolidated text: *Dz.U.* [Journal of Laws] of 2018, item 1969 as amended.

32 Council Directive 98/59/EC of 20 July 1998 on the approximation of the laws of the Member States relating to collective redundancies, OJ L 225, 12.08.1998, pp. 16–21 with later amendments.

33 With reference to case C-422/14, *Christian Pujante Rivera v. Gestora Clubs Dir SL* and *Fondo de Garantía Salarial*, EU:C:2015:743.

34 With reference to case C-55/02, *Commission of the European Communities v. Portuguese Republic* EU:C:2004:605.

contract), that Law and, thus, also Directive 98/59, covers the employees of public administration employed based on the employment contract.

At this juncture, it should also be noted that, in the case-law of the Supreme Court, one can find references to the obligation to interpret, in conformity with EU law, even in cases outside the scope of EU law regulation. An example of this kind is the case of the right to a trial of the prosecutor of the military prosecutor's office who is also a military officer, about the rights of the service or the cases relating to the claims of employees of the tax administration, whose employment relationships expired in 2017 in breach of Labour Law provisions not covered by EU harmonisation.[35] It should be assumed that such references to the duty of consistent interpretation do not manifest the application of this duty but only strengthen the argumentative model of the interpretation of national provisions. The references to the legal standard contained in the provisions of EU law support, in such cases, the arguments based on the interpretation of provisions containing the rules having the position of fundamental principles of a given branch of law, constitutional provisions, or the provisions of the European Convention on Fundamental Rights and Freedoms.[36] Alternatively, such references to EU law, outside the scope of its regulation, are intended to ensure the constitutional principle of equal treatment, where the EU standard present in the implementing act is higher than the standard of protection of rights of a given type provided for in a national Law [statute] regulating the same issue in purely domestic cases.[37]

A practically important issue should be raised regarding the *ratione personae* scope of the duty of consistent interpretation. Namely, in the light of the case-law of the SC, the interpretation in conformity with EU law is applicable not only in disputes between an individual and a Member State (its emanation) but also in disputes between individuals (in the meaning of EU law). The interpretation in conformity with EU law can also be applied both to the advantage and to the disadvantage of individuals, leading, for example, to imposing on them an obligation, which, when interpreted without taking into account the EU normative standard, does not result from national law.[38]

Sources of the interpretative standard for consistent interpretation

There should be no doubt that the ready-to-apply standard for interpreting Polish Law, in conformity with EU law, is included in the preliminary rulings issued in response to the court's questions, which is to hear a case concerned.

35 Judgment of the SC of 26 September 2019, case III PK 126/18.
36 Order of the SC of 29 October 2020, case III UZP 4/20.
37 Judgment of the SC of 26 September 2019, case III PK 126/18.
38 For example, by declaring an appeal brought by a pension authority admissible following the interpretation of the provisions on judicial time limits in conformity with EU law, order of the panel of seven judges of the SC of 19 July 2019, case III UZP 3/17.

In such cases, when the Supreme Court rules when implementing the preliminary ruling issued by the Court of Justice in response to its preliminary reference, it only refers to such a CJ judgment as to the ruling, including the standard for interpretation that binds the Supreme Court.[39] Much more often, when the Supreme Court uses consistent interpretation without making preliminary reference itself, it attempts to reconstruct the existing EU interpretation standard, to which it will be able to compare Polish law.[40] When there is already a case-law of the CJEU relating to the interpretation of a particular EU provision, the Supreme Court, without hesitation, reconstructs the EU normative standard based on the Court of Justice's interpretation. To determine the required European pattern of interpretation, the Supreme Court refers both to the interpretation adopted by the CJ in preliminary rulings[41] in addition to other proceedings, in particular, upon the complaint of the Commission.[42] It is also irrelevant whether the CJ has made that interpretation in response to the preliminary question arising from a Polish court[43] or the court of another Member State.[44] It is also irrelevant whether such an interpretation was given in proceedings arising from the Commission's complaint against Poland[45] or another Member State.[46] In any case, the Supreme Court assumes that the interpretation of EU law made by the CJ is binding upon it irrespective of the type of proceedings in which the CJ adopted it. That approach should be treated as the expression of acceptance for the principle of the binding force of the interpretation of EU law made by the CJ for all national courts, which the CJ itself rarely articulates.[47] This principle is a manifestation of the principle of autonomy of EU law and its uniform interpretation and application.

An example of such an approach is the resolution of the SC of 12 December 2019, case III CZP 45/19. According to Article 49 (1) of the Law of 12

39 See, for example, judgments of the SC: of 24 June 2015, case III SK 59/12; of 9 June 2016, case III SK 28/13; of 5 December 2016, case III SK 18/14; of 26 January 2017, case III SK 52/14; of 10 November 2010, case III SK 27/08; of 7 July 2011, case III SK 16/09; of 16 June 2011, case I UK 163/11; of 10 November 2016, case III SK 53/13.

40 Orders of the SC of 22 February 2007, case IV CSK 200/06; judgments of the SC: of 17 May 2012, case I PK 179/11; of 18 April 2012, case II PK 197/11.

41 Resolution of the SC of 19 November 2010, case III CZP 79/10.

42 Judgment of the SC of 10 February 2006, case III CSK 112/05.

43 For example, judgments of the SC: of 9 January 2020, case I PK 197/18; of 10 October 2019, case I PK 196/18; of 12 February 2019, case II PK 283/17 with references to case C-149/16, *Halina Socha and others*, EU:C:2017:708 and case C-429/16, *Małgorzata Ciupa and others*, EU:C:2017:711.

44 For example, judgment of the SC of 4 January 2008, case I UK 182/07; judgment of the panel of seven judges of the SC of 18 November 2015, case II UK 100/14.

45 For example, resolution of the SC of 15 January 2013, case III SZP 1/12 with references to case C-475/07 *Commission v. Republic of Poland*, EU:C:2009:86.

46 Judgment of the SC of 10 February 2006, case III CSK 112/05 with references to C-235/89, *Commision v. Italy*, EU:C:1992:73 and C-30/90, *Commision v. UK*, EU:C:1992:74.

47 Case C-8/08, *T-Mobile and others* EU:C:2009:343.

May 2011 on consumer credit,[48] in the case of the full repayment of the credit before the date indicated in the agreement, the total cost of the credit is to be reduced by the costs relating to the remaining duration of the contract, even if the consumer had borne those costs before the repayment. In that case, it was required to resolve whether, in the case of the early repayment of the credit, it is also the amount of the commission for granting the consumer credit that is subject to the proportional settlement and reduction. A response was needed in answer to the question as to whether the commission for granting a consumer credit is a cost relating to the whole duration of the contract, which in the case of repayment of the credit before the date indicated in the agreement, is reduced under Article 49 (1) of the Law of 12 May 2011 by the remaining duration of the contract, or the cost which is not dependent on the duration of the contract. The Supreme Court held that the consumer's entitlement to reduce the total cost of the credit in the case of its full repayment before the date indicated in the agreement provided for in Article 49 (1) of the Law of 12 May 2011 also covered the commission for granting credit. Such an interpretation of Article 49 (1) of the Law of 12 May 2011 was based on the assumption that this provision transposed Directive 2008/48.[49] In addition, Article 5 (6) of the Law of 12 May 2011, implementing Article 3 (g) of Directive 2008/48/EC, defines the total cost of the credit, which includes commissions. It followed from the interpretation of Article 16 of Directive 2008/48 in the judgment in Case C-383/18 *Lexitor*[50] that 'the right of the consumer to a reduction in the total cost of the credit in the event of early repayment of the credit includes all the costs imposed on the consumer'. Thus, following C-383/18 *Lexitor*, the Supreme Court ruled that this consumer right also included the commission's costs.

While the practice of the Supreme Court is to rely heavily on the doctrine of *acte eclaire*, there are also some cases of using the *acte clair* doctrine. The examples of an independent interpretation of a provision of EU law by the Supreme Court are provided by the cases resolved based on the provisions implementing Article 10 of Directive 2002/20 in its original version. The judgment in the case III SK 52/10[51] is of particular importance. The Supreme Court assumed, therein, that it was inadmissible for the National Regulatory Authority in the field of electronic communication to impose a financial penalty without first requesting a way to remedy the breaches found. In this way, the practice of the Polish national regulatory authority was questioned. The authority first initiated the control procedure to check whether the telecommunication

48 Consolidated text: *Dz. U.* [Journal of Laws] of 2019 item 1083 as amended.

49 Directive 2008/48/EC of the European Parliament and of the Council of 23 April 2008 on credit agreements for consumers and repealing Council Directive 87/102/EEC, OJ L 133, 22.05.2008, pp. 66–92 with later amendments.

50 EU:C:2019:702.

51 Judgment of the SC of 7 July 2011, case III SK 52/10. See also judgment of the SC referred to in the reasoning of this judgment.

undertaking was in breach of law. Then, instead of proceeding in the manner specified in the Polish provisions regulating the control procedure and implementing Article 10 of Directive 2002/20 by requiring the authority to demand from the undertaking concerned to remedy this breach under the threat of a fine, the authority used to immediately initiate separate and independent proceedings for the imposition of the fine for the breaches found.

The practice of the Supreme Court shows that quite often, when reconstructing the EU normative standard, it is necessary to make a complex analysis of the case-law of the Court of Justice. Occasionally, for a particular EU case heard by the Supreme Court, it is, therefore, necessary to determine how the interpretation of the case-law of the CJ has evolved and how to adjust it to the specificity of the facts of the case. An example is a judgment of the SC of 11 April 2012, case I PK 155/11, relating to the 'transfer of an undertaking or its parts' under Article 23^1 (1) of the Labour Code, which implements Directive 2001/23.[52] The Supreme Court emphasised when reconstructing that concept that

> currently there is a line of case-law under development, according to which there are different conditions for considering that there is a transfer of undertaking within the meaning of the Directive and the importance of those conditions for the resolution of each case depends on the nature of the employer's activity, i.e., the methods of production or exploitation used in the undertaking or an establishment concerned.

From that case-law line it followed, for the Supreme Court 'that taking over the tasks alone is not sufficient for the application of the Directive in a situation, where the operation of the undertaking is based, to a large extent, on the tangible substrate, which has not been taken over', clearly drawing attention to the evolution of case-law of CJEU and the adequacy of a specific line of case-law to the fact of a particular case.[53] Only after decoding an EU standard was it possible to reconstruct an appropriate domestic legal standard as to the conditions that must be met to make it possible to talk about the transfer of the undertaking and taking over the employees. Thus, the conclusion, in that case, was that 'in the case of quite simple services, the performance of which is related to the property facilities such as, e.g., catering, cleaning, for the transfer in the meaning of Article 23^1 of the Labour Code, taking over of the facilities by a new employer is required'.

52 Council Directive 2001/23/EC of 12 March 2001 on the approximation of the laws of the Member States relating to the safeguarding of employees' rights in the event of transfers of undertakings, businesses, or parts of undertakings or businesses, OJ L 82, 22.03.2001, pp. 16–20.

53 With references to case C-340/01, *Carlito Abler*, EU:C:2003:629 and joint cases C-232/04, and C-233/04 *Nurten Güney – Görres and Gul Demir*, EU:C:2005:778, from which if followed that when the hospital awards [the contract] for catering [services] to a new contractor, there is no transfer of undertaking, if that contractor uses substantial parts of [tangible] assets used by its predecessor.

Limits of consistent interpretation

The interpretation, in conformity with EU law, has its limits. Under the case-law of the Supreme Court, which specifies the views of the CJEU, those are as follows. Firstly, an ordinary court may not go beyond the express wording of the provision.[54] Secondly, the interpretation consistent with a Directive must not lead to the disapplication of a national provision.[55] Thirdly, the consistent interpretation must not lead to 'the imposition on an individual, the criminal sanctions not provided for by national law'.

Prohibition of interpretation contra legem

Regarding the first circumstance exempting a Polish court from the duty of consistent interpretation, the Supreme Court generally opted for treating the textual, literal wording of a provision of national law as a limit beyond which the interpretation in conformity with EU law would lead to the *contra legem* result. Therefore, where a national provision does not contain vague concepts or does not leave room for interpretation as it refers directly to other legal acts or legal definitions that are precisely formulated from the linguistic point of view, the Supreme Court considers that it cannot secure the effectiveness of EU law using consistent interpretation. In such cases, the Supreme Court will either attempt to refer to the principle of primacy and direct effect, or it will refer to the principle of liability for damages as means of compensating a party for the failure of a Member State to fulfil its obligations. An example of such an approach is in the judgment of 4 December 2018, case I PK 181/17. In this ruling, it was emphasised that

> given the strict exclusionary message (i.e., the direct exclusion of a certain category of workers from the scope of application of the Law implementing Directive 2008/94) included in Article (2) (2) of the Law, it is impossible to consider, using the interpretation in conformity with EU law, that the guarantee in the event of insolvency has also been extended to the employees of an association entered into the register of entrepreneurs.

Consequently, the application of primacy and direct effect should be considered to protect the rights of the employees of a bankrupt association carrying out an economic activity.

54 Judgments of the SC: of 29 January 2008, case II PK 143/07; of 21 November 2011, case IV CSK 133/11; of 4 August 2009, case I PK 64/09; of 13 August 2013, case III SK 57/12; resolution of the SC of 13 May 2010, case III SZP 2/10.

55 Judgments of the SC: of 21 November 2011, case IV CSK 133/11; of 19 October 2012, case III SK 3/12.

The interpretation in conformity with EU law was decided not to be possible to apply in Case III PK 53/19 either (see Table 5.1. Consistent interpretation of national law with Directive 96/34). A father (claimant), an employee of a court of ordinary jurisdiction (emanation of the Member State), applied for parental leave when his second child was born. His application was rejected because his wife was not entitled to maternity leave and maternity allowance since, under Polish law, she was not employed (though as permanent care provided for the first child with disabilities, she had been covered by the Polish social security system albeit with the exclusion of protection covering maternity leave and allowance). Regarding parental leave for fathers, Polish law makes their right to such leave dependent upon the mother's resignation from her right to receive maternity allowance, which, in turn, is dependent on the right

Table 5.1 Consistent interpretation of national law with Directive 96/34

Provision of EU law	This agreement, subject to Clause 2.2, grants to male and female workers an individual right to parental leave on the grounds of the birth or adoption of a child, in order to enable them to care for a child, for at least three months, until the child reaches a certain age, a maximum of eight years, as determined by the Member States and/or social partners.[56]
Provision of Polish law (Article 180 (5) Labour Code)	An employee-father bringing up a child is entitled, if the insured mother of a child resigns from receiving maternity allowance after she has used that allowance for a period of at least 14 weeks after the birth the right to a portion of the maternity leave falling after the date of resignation by the insured mother of the child, from receiving maternity allowance.
Prior interpretation	An employee-father bringing up a child is entitled to the portion of maternity leave falling after 14 weeks after the birth, also if the child's mother *no longer* receives maternity allowance.
Interpretation in conformity with EU law	An employee-father bringing up a child is entitled to the portion of maternity leave falling after the period of 14 weeks after the birth, also, if the child's mother has not been insured and has *never* received maternity allowance.
Has the interpretation in conformity with EU law been declared admissible?	No, in view of the employer's status as an emanation of a Member State, the reference has been made to the principle of direct effect and the *Jonkman* formula, granting the right to leave under Article 180 (5) of the Labour Code applied in conjunction with Article 4 and Article 9 of Directive 2006/54.

56 Clause No. 2 implemented by the Council Directive 96/34/EC of 3 June 1996 on the Framework agreement on parental leave concluded by UNICE, CEEP, and ETUC (OJ L 145, p. 4 – spec. ed. in Polish, chapter 5, vol.2, p. 285), amended by Council Directive 97/75/EC of 15 December 1997 (OJ 145, 19.6.1996, pp. 4–9).

to maternity leave. That condition (dependency of parental leave for the father on the mother's right to maternity leave and allowance) is contrary to EU law. The wording of the provision of Polish law, which was to be interpreted in conformity with EU law, together with the respective provisions of EU law and the required interpretation to be given to the former, is presented later. The Supreme Court found consistent interpretation, in this case, to be impossible and decided to apply the principles of direct effect and primacy as the employer of the father, claiming his right to parental leave, was to be considered a Member State against which an individual may invoke the provisions of a directive. It is also interesting to note that in case III PK 53/19, the courts, adjudicating in the first and second instances, granted the claimant the right to parental leave by referring to the principle of consistent interpretation, albeit without providing any hint as to how such an interpretation had been possible.

It is relatively rare that the Supreme Court, guided by the exceptions allowed in the national practice for the interpretation of legal acts and departure from the outcomes of the linguistic interpretation, departs from the results of the textual interpretation of a clearly worded provision of national law. An example of radical derogation, from the principle of treating the results of the

Table 5.2 Consistent interpretation of national law with Directive 97/67

Provision of EU law	Member States do not grant or maintain in force exclusive or special rights for the establishment and provision of postal services.[57]
Provision of Polish law (Article 165 (2) of the Code of Civil Procedure)[58]	Posting a procedural document at a Polish post office of a designated operator within the meaning of the Act of 23 November 2012 – Postal Law or at the post office of an operator providing universal service in another Member State of the European Union shall be equivalent to lodgement of that document at the court.
Prior interpretation	Only posting a procedural document at a Polish post office of a designated operator within the meaning of the Act of 23 November 2012 – Postal Law shall be equivalent to the lodgement of that document at the court.
Interpretation in conformity with EU law	Posting a procedural document at a Polish post office of any postal operator providing a universal service shall be equivalent to the lodgement of that document at the court.
Has the interpretation in conformity with EU law been declared admissible?	Yes, *rationae personae* of Article 165 (2) of the Code of Civil Procedure has been changed. The concept of the designed operator has been interpreted as covering each operator providing universal postal services.

57 Article 7 (1) of Directive 97/67.

58 The act of 17 November 1964 – the Code of Civil Procedure consolidated text: Dz.U. [Journal of Laws] of 2016, item 1822 as amended.

textual interpretation as setting a limit for the interpretation in conformity with EU law and including good argumentation, which could be used in other cases, is the order of the panel of seven judges of the SC of 29 August 2019, case III UZP 3/17 (preceded by the C-545/17 Pawlak judgment). In that case, the national provision provided clearly that only “posting a procedural document at a Polish post office of a designated operator within the meaning of the Act of 23 November 2012 – Postal Law or at the post office of an operator providing a universal service in another Member State of the European Union shall be equivalent to lodgement of that document at the court.” (see Table 5.2, Consistent interpretation of national law with Directive 97/67). Finally – after the judgment of the Court of Justice had been delivered under the procedure of Article 267 TFEU – it was interpreted, by the Supreme Court, as including a rule, according to which ‘posting a procedural document at a postal operator, which is not a designated operator shall be equivalent to lodgement of the procedural document at the court’ (Article 165 (2) of the Code of Civil Procedure read in conjunction with Article 7 (1) subpara. 1 of Directive 97/67)’.[59]

It follows from that judgment that, in order to derogate from the textual interpretation and to interpret national law in conformity with EU law, notice must be taken of the following: 1) the inconsistency of national rules with EU law confirmed directly by the judgment of the CJEU, which justifies, on systemic (constitutional) grounds, the derogation from the results of the textual interpretation; 2) the introduction of a provision containing the rule inconsistent with EU law in order to implement a directive when reading defectively an EU normative standard; 3) the amendments to the provision resulting in the applicability, in the legal system, of the provisions governing related issues and containing – depending on a legal act – the solutions consistent with or contrary to EU law; 4) the absence of any (reasonable) justification for introducing a legal solution resulting from the literal interpretation of a provision concerned; 5) issuing an unfair ruling in the case of applying a literal wording of the provision, infringing the basic principles of the legal system or a particular branch of law; 6) the existence of essential reasons for derogating from the results of the textual interpretation; and 7) the absence of disproportionately adverse effects on the other party to the proceedings, from the point of view of the principle of legal certainty.

Another option for breaking the prohibition of the *contra legem* interpretation is to modify the national normative basis of judgment by co-opting it into other provisions, whose interpretation will allow the court to make a consistent interpretation without the need to depart from the textual interpretation. An example is the judgment of the SC of 9 June 2016, case III SK

59 Directive 97/67/EC of the European Parliament and of the Council of 15 December 1997 on common rules for the development of the internal market of Community postal services and the improvement of quality of service, OJ L 15, 21.1.1998, pp. 14–25.

28/13, issued after the judgment in Case C-397/14 *Polkomtel sp. z o.o.*[60] It has been held, therein, that although Article 79 (1) of the Telecommunication Law[61] does not expressly provide for the competence of *Prezes Urzędu Komunikacji Elektronicznej* (the President of the Office for Electronic Communications, 'the President of the UKE' or NRA), to regulate the level of the wholesale rates for the connections referred to in that provision, the interpretation of Article 79 (1) read in conjunction with Article 28 of the Telecommunication Law (TL) must take account of the interpretation of Article 5 (1) and Article 8 (3) of the Access Directive read in conjunction with Article 28 of the Universal Service Directive made by CJEU in the preliminary ruling issued in that Case. In the opinion of CJEU, those provisions must be interpreted as allowing national regulatory authorities, in resolving disputes concerning pricing procedures between the operators for the access to services using non-geographic numbers, to set such wholesale rates. To make such a set of rates by the President of the UKE legal, the Supreme Court decided to decode a legal norm applicable in this case from Article 79 TL, read in conjunction with Article 28 TL. The Supreme Court noted the obligation to provide users with access to services provided through non-geographical numbers as expressly provided in national law implementing Article 28 of Directive 2002/22[62] (Article 79 TL). However, the exact content of this obligation, and how the national regulatory office could enforce this obligation was to be determined by reference to another provision of Polish legislation (Article 28 TL). Moreover, satisfying that obligation required a teleological interpretation of Article 28 TL. The Supreme Court explained that by issuing a decision under Article 28 TL, the President of the UKE resolved a dispute between the undertakings. Without any doubt, the NRA was competent in that respect. The ruling of the regulatory authority related to those issues covered by Article 79 TL and also falling within the scope of Article 28 TL, as to which the parties have not reached an agreement. At the same time, when applying Article 79 TL in the light of Article 28 TL, the President of the UKE took into consideration not only the obligations under the TL incumbent on the telecom operators in dispute under Article 79 TL but also the proposals of both parties to the dispute filed in the course of negotiations as to how they see the appropriate level of contentious wholesale rates. Therefore, the intervention of the regulatory authority was undertaken within the limits of its powers (Article 28 TL, as a general source of competence to act, was applied additionally to Article 79, which was the source of specific competence of the NRA).

60 EU:C:2016:256.

61 Consolidated text: *Dz. U* [Journal of Laws] of 2021 item 576.

62 Directive 2002/22/EC of the European Parliament and of the Council of 7 March 2002 on universal service and users' rights relating to electronic communications networks and services (Universal Service Directive), OJ L 108, 24.4.2002, pp. 51–77.

Inability to derogate from the application of a national provision

The second limitation imposed upon the duty of consistent interpretation recurring in the case-law of the Supreme Court is the inadmissibility of the disapplication of a provision of national law as a result of its interpretation in conformity with EU law. That limitation conflicts with the *Dominguez* formula. The Supreme Court referred to this formula in the judgment of 8 May 2019, case I PK 41/18. However, due to the absence of a provision in Polish law concerning the duty to give reasons for a dismissal of an employee employed for a fixed term that would be compatible with EU law, the Supreme Court decided to interpret a provision (Article 30 (4) of the Labour Code), which was usually applicable in other dismissal cases. The Supreme Court pointed out, under the general concept of the importance of the results of the textual interpretation, that Article 30 (4) of the Labour Code was clear; an obligation to provide a reason for termination applies only to a contract for an indefinite period. The Supreme Court couldn't interpret Article 30 (4) of the Labour Code in conformity with EU law. Such an interpretation would have to lead to the extension of the application of that provision to fixed-term employment contracts. Such an extension would directly contravene the wording of this provision. Consequently, the Supreme Court examined whether it was possible to disapply Article 30 (4) of the Labour Code so far that it does not provide for the obligation to provide, in the employer's statement, the reason for terminating the fixed-term employment contract. However, such a remedy of disapplication was considered inadmissible in the light of the CJ case-law as to the limited direct effect of the directives. Since, in that case, the defendant employer was not an emanation of the Member State, it could not be held liable for the unlawfulness of the incorrect implementation of Directive 99/70[63] in respect of fixed-term employees by the Polish legislator. As a result, the Supreme Court was not entitled to disapply Article 30 (4) of the Labour Code and had to rule that that provision of Polish law, while incompatible with the EU, must be applied to the facts of the case and could not have been interpreted in conformity with EU law.

Inability to fine an individual with a 'penal' sanction

The third limitation on the duty of consistent interpretation of national law arises in the case-law of the Supreme Court in the cases relating to the administrative fines imposed on individuals for breaches of national provisions implementing EU law. Such fines are regarded as criminal (penal) sanctions within Article 49 of the Charter of Fundamental Rights. Such a qualification constitutes a limit for the duty of consistent interpretation of different

63 Council Directive 1999/70/EC of 28 June 1999 concerning the framework agreement on fixed-term work concluded by ETUC, UNICE, and CEEP, OJ L 175, 10.07.1999, pp. 43–48.

provisions of Polish law governing the substantive and procedural principles of individuals' liability. The Supreme Court consistently and repeatedly relied on the limitation of the obligation to interpret in conformity with EU law resulting from the 80/86 *Kolpinghuis Nijmegen*[64] line, assuming that it also applied to administrative liability of the repressive nature and not only to strictly criminal liability.[65] For example, in the judgment of 7 July 2011, case III SK 52/10, the Supreme Court did not agree to the use the consistent interpretation in such a way that, contrary to the previous case-law developed under the original wording of Article of Directive 2002/20, would allow the national regulatory authority in the field of electronic communication, based on consistent interpretation of national provisions reflecting the new wording of Article 10 of Directive 2002/20, to impose financial penalties without exhausting the procedure provided for in the control proceedings regulated based on the provisions implementing Article 10 of Directive 2002/20 in the original version.

At this point, it is also necessary to record a controversial opinion, which requires further analyses from the point of view of compliance with the EU standard, according to which the interpretation in conformity with EU law of vague or unclear national provisions, leading to the extension of the obligations incumbent on an individual (a sanctioned rule) at the same time may result in the imposition of an administrative penalty on the individual for failure to discharge of an obligation understood in this way (based on the sanctioning rule applicable in national law). The Supreme Court has accepted so far that since national law provides for a provision containing a sanction for the breach of an obligation formulated in other legal provisions, the extensive interpretation of those other legal provisions in conformity with EU law is allowed to determine whether an individual has breached that is sanctioned by a fine.[66]

Consequences of consistent interpretation

Consequences from the perspective of the role of the Supreme Court

The consistent interpretation of national law always leads to the interpretation of national provisions with the result of a legal norm that would differ from this, which has been made so far (in the previous case-law, which now is considered to produce results incompatible with EU law and its effectiveness) or which has been adopted after the use different methods of interpretation admissible in national law, albeit not taking into account the EU normative standard. In practice, this translates into resolving a dispute differently than

64 EU:C:1987:431.
65 Judgment of the SC of 7 July 2011, case III SK 52/10.
66 Judgment of the SC of 14 April 2010, case III SK 1/10.

initially expected. The same applies not only to judgments ending the case before a court but also to a judgment delivered on some side issues in the course of proceedings (i.e., concerning the admissibility of an appeal – see case III UZP 3/17). From the perspective of the judicial application of the law by the Supreme Court as the court of the last instance whose duty is to care about unified interpretation and application of the law, the effects of the interpretation in conformity with EU law can be divided into the categories in which that leads to 1) change in the case-law line that has been developed so far (adoption of a unified legal standard for the future), 2) introduction of the derogations from the existing case-law in EU cases applied so far (adoption of a divergent standard in cases with an EU element/link and without such element/link), and 3) resolving divergences in the case-law of the Supreme Court or the lower courts.[67]

Change in the case-law line developed so far by imposing a new interpretation of the existing provisions

A classic example of using an interpretation consistent with EU law to change the previous line of case-law is to give a new meaning to vague terms or general clauses contained in existing acts of national law falling within the scope of EU law legislation. The examples of such an effect of the interpretation in conformity with EU law are the cases relating to the term an 'average consumer' in cases relating to misleading[68] or an 'informed user' in industrial property (design) law.[69] The reference to the interpretation of EU law, made by the CJEU in pre-accession cases, was intended to bring those vague notions into line with the requirements of EU law, which in both cases required derogation from the previous case-law line assuming a low level of attention of an average consumer or an informed user.

Derogations from the previous case-law

An example of that category is case III SK 24/14.[70] The Supreme Court has assumed in that judgment that the term 'principles of morality' used in national law in Article 4 (1) of the Law of 23 August 2007, implementing Directive 2005/29, must be understood by taking into account the criterion of 'professional diligence', referred to in Article 2 (h) of Directive 2005/29. Thus, the use of the conventional interpretation of the existing notion of principles of morality developed in other areas of private law that had been used

67 Resolution of the SC of 21 November 2012, case III PZP 6/12; orders of the panel of seven judges of the SC of 19 July 2019, case III UZP 3/17 (preliminary reference in Case C-545/17, *Pawlak*, EU:C:2019:260) and of 29 August 2019 (delivered following the ECJ's judgment).

68 Judgment of the SC of 4 March 2014, case III SK 34/13.

69 Judgment of the SC of 23 October 2007, case II CSK 302/07.

70 Judgment of the SC of 16 April 2015, case III SK 24/14.

for many years, for example, in the Polish law on combatting unfair competition, was excluded. The concept of the 'principles of morality', as previously understood by the Supreme Court, would define unfair commercial practice as another, broader scope of application than that provided for in Directive 2005/29. However, since that Directive is based on the maximum harmonisation of national legislation, such an extension of the scope of application of the national implementing legislation was held inadmissible. Thus, using the principle of consistent interpretation resulted in a stricter interpretation of Polish law.

Resolving divergences in the case-law of the Supreme Court

An example of using the interpretation in conformity with EU law to resolve the divergences in the case-law of Polish courts is case III UZP 3/17, referred to before. In this case, the extension of the *ratione materiae* of Article 165 para. 2 of the Code of Civil Procedure to other postal operators than a designated operator was finally opted for, while previously, such an extension was excluded in most cases decided by the Supreme Court. Another example is the resolution of the SC of 21 November 2012, case III PZP 6/12, in which the discrepancies in the case-law of the Supreme Court were resolved as regards the impact of the personal data protection law, harmonised at that time by Directive 95/46,[71] on the employer's obligation to cooperate with the trade union organisation operating in its business in matters concerning the employment relationships of individual employees protected by a respective union. The contentious issue was whether the employer was entitled to demand (and hence the trade union obliged to hand it over) from the trade unions to provide him, in advance, with the list of employees protected by trade unions operating in his undertaking. The provision of Polish law under consideration was found in the Act on trade unions[72] and only indirectly fell within the scope of the application of EU law on personal data. Since providing the employer with the names of individual workers enjoying trade unions' protection was deemed to constitute the use of personal data, the Supreme Court ruled that such a general request of an employer (made before the commencement of any actions against an individual employee) was inadmissible. Hence, the failure of the trade unions to reply to such a request did not deprive them of their powers against the employer nor lifted their protection over individual employees.

71 Directive 95/46/EC of the European Parliament and of the Council of 24 October 1995 on the protection of individuals with regard to the processing of personal data and on the free movement of such data, OJ L 281, 23.11.1995, pp. 31–50.

72 Article 30 sec. 2(1) sentence 1 of the Act of 23 May 1991, consolidated version Polish OJ 2019, position 263.

Consequences from the perspective of individuals

From the point of view of individuals and their interests, the consistent interpretation of Polish law with EU law may lead to the extension or narrowing of the national legislation's *ratione personae* or *ratione materiae*.[73] As a result of such a change, an individual may be deprived of their right (protection) or may be given such a right or receive a broader/more accessible protection thereof.[74] Alternatively, the scope of national legislation may be broader (e.g., higher compensation).[75] The consequence of acquiring an individual's right will be the imposition of the civil law obligation on another individual.[76] In addition, an administrative obligation may be imposed on an individual.[77]

Change in the personal scope of application of Polish law

An example of change in the subject-related scope of national provisions, resulting from the consistent interpretation, as a result of which a broader circle of individuals will acquire certain rights. At the same time, the individual will be obliged to discharge his or her obligation in a broader scope if the resolution of the SC of 13 May 2010, case III SZP 2/10. Article 67 (1) of TL had been interpreted in conformity with EU Law, which resulted in the obligation to provide specific data allowing telephone inquiry services under the conditions laid down in that provision. The consistent interpretation was required only for specifying the circle of entities to which data is to be made available. The interpretation of Article 67 (1) TL in conformity with EU law consisted in the recognition that 'another telecommunications undertaking providing telephone inquiry services' should be understood as also

73 Judgment of the SC of 14 February 2012, case II PK 137/11.

74 See, for example, resolution of the panel of seven judges of the SC of 28 September 2016, case III PZP 3/16 declaring that it is no longer required for an employee to challenge before a labour court the termination notice if an employee wants to claim compensation for discriminatory reason for termination or the discriminatory reason for selecting an employee to be dismissed; judgment of the SC of 8 September 2017, case II CSK 845/16 – 'After the time limit provided for the implementation of Directive 2004/39/EC of the European Parliament and the Council of 21 April 2004 on markets in financial instruments (OJ EU L 145, p. 1 – "MiFID" directive), the standard for the information obligation of the bank as regards forward financial transactions (Article 5 (2) (4) of the Act of 29 August 1997 – Banking Law, consolidated text *Dz. U.* [Journal of Laws] of 2016, item. 1988), including forward currency option contracts, had to be determined taking into account the interpretation requirement consistent with the Directive – according to the guidelines resulting from Directive 2004/39/EC', which meant that failure to comply with the standard resulting from the Directive opened the possibility of granting protection to a contractor that had not received information required by Directive 2004/39.

75 Judgment of 9 May 2019, case III PK 50/18, demanding lower courts to award higher damages from an employer for discriminatory treatment of a young mother.

76 For example, resolution of the SC of 19 November 2010, case III CZP 79/10 has such consequences.

77 Resolution of the SC of 13 May 2010, case III SZP 2/10.

covering a telecommunications undertaking which is preparing to provide such services. At the same time, the Supreme Court found that Article 67 (1) TL could not be interpreted in conformity with EU law in such a way that the right to request making available data necessary for providing telephone inquiry services would be granted to all entrepreneurs who were not telecommunications undertakings. It was assumed that it would be the *contra legem* interpretation.

The examples of the interpretation in conformity with EU law, resulting in the modification of the subject-related scope of applying national provisions, include the order in case III UZP 3/17, which has been extensively discussed. It has been adopted therein that a party to the proceedings meets the procedural time limit when a procedural document is posted at any postal operator providing universal services and not only a designated operator. Thus, the category of postal operators who could accept consignments, including procedural documents with the effect of meeting the procedural time limit, has been extended.

Acquisition of the right by an individual and the imposition of the obligation on another individual

This category includes rulings clarifying how to understand the term 'collective redundancy', contained in the Collective Redundancies Law (implementing Directive 98/59) and providing for various types of benefits for employees in situations where there have been notices amending the terms of the employment relationship of a larger number of employees. It should be recalled that, so far, an amending notice of a labour contract has not been treated in Polish law as an event falling within the concept of collective redundancy. Therefore, in a series of judgments delivered after the CJEU *Nierodzik* ruling, the line of case-law was modified.[78] It was assumed that amending notices (Article 42 of the Labour Code) made to a more significant number of employees were subject to the application of the provisions on collective redundancies when, as a result of those termination notices, at least five redundancies within the meaning of Article 1 (1) first para. (a) of Directive 98/59 had occurred.

Another example of a case falling within that category of the effects of the consistent interpretation is a case that extended the notion of collective redundancies to the termination of fixed-term employment contracts (judgment of the SC of 14 February 2012, case II PK 137/11). Thus, fixed-term workers have obtained additional protection, and the obligation to pay additional severance pay has been imposed on employers.

78 Judgments of the SC: of 9 January 2020, case I PK 197/18; of 10 October 2019, case I PK 196/18; of 12 February 2019, case II PK 283/17.

Narrowing the rights of an individual

Applying the principle of consistent interpretation may also lead to the narrowing of the party's rights to the proceedings, including an individual who is not an emanation of a Member State. An example of such a result of the interpretation in conformity with EU law is the resolution of the SC of 12 December 2019, case III CZP 48/19. Under this resolution, only costs of the 'purposeful' recovery exceeding the equivalent of an amount of EUR 40 are covered by the notion of recovery costs, referred to in Article 10 (2) of the Law of 8 March 2013 on Payment Time Limits in Commercial Transactions.[79] That resolution was adopted under the legal circumstances, where Article 10 (2) of the Payment Time Limits Law was as follows: 'Where the recovery costs incurred due to late payment in a commercial transaction exceed the amount referred to in para. 1, the creditor shall be entitled to reimbursement of those costs, including the costs of proceedings before courts, less that amount'.[80] That rule did not correctly reflect the content of Article 6 of Directive 2011/7,[81] from which it follows that the reimbursement to the creditor of the recovery costs exceeding a fixed sum of EUR 40 should be made only in a reasonable amount. The Supreme Court found, interpreting Article 10 of the Payment Time Limits Law in the original version, that this provision should be interpreted as 'taking into account Article 6 of Directive 2011/7'. This, in turn, supported the adoption of such an interpretation of Article 10 of the Law, from which it would follow that the creditor was entitled only to reimbursement of such recovery costs as could be considered 'reasonable'. Otherwise, Article 10 (2) of [the Law] of 8 March 2013, which in no way limited the compensating of the recovery costs incurred by the creditor, would be contrary to EU law.

Imposition of administrative obligations on an individual

An interesting example of the interpretation, in conformity with EU law, leading to making an individual administratively liable for law infringements, is the judgment of 6 April 2017, case III SK 15/16. It related directly to the succession of liability for the breach of the prohibition of practices violating the collective interests of consumers in the event of the acquisition of the offender by another business entity. That case related to the interpretation of the provision of the Commercial Companies Code (Article 494) on the succession of rights

79 Consolidated text: *Dz. U.* [Journal of Laws] of 2021, item 424.

80 After amendments introduced by the Law of 9 October 2015 amending the Law on Payment Time Limits in Commercial Transactions, the Act – Civil Code and certain other acts [statutes] (*Dz. U.* [Journal of Laws] of 2015 item 1830) that provision has been given the following wording: In addition to the amount, referred to in para. 1, a creditor shall be also entitled to reimbursement, in a reasonable amount, of the recovery costs exceeding that amount.

81 Directive 2011/7/EU of the European Parliament and of the Council of 16 February 2011 on combating late payment in commercial transactions Text with EEA relevance, OJ L 48, 23.2.2011, pp. 1–10.

and obligations, including administrative ones, in the event of mergers or acquisitions of commercial companies. The courts of lower instances adopted the reasoning that there was no succession of such liability in the event of an acquisition. Thus, the acquiring entity could not be held liable for the infringements committed by the acquired entity, as established by the decision of the consumer protection authority. The Supreme Court held that the acquiring company was liable for breach of the prohibition of practices violating the collective interests of consumers, which were attributed by *Prezes UOKiK* (the Head of the Polish Office of Competition and Consumer Protection, 'the Head of the UOKiK') to the acquired company in the decision adopted in the course of proceedings against the acquired company but served on, just a day after the takeover, the acquiring company. The concept of a succession of administrative liability based on Article 494 (1) and (2) of the Commercial Companies Code was supported by the judgment of the Court of Justice in case C-343/13 *Modelo Continente Hipermercados SA*,[82] according to which

> a merger by acquisition results in the transfer to the acquiring company of the obligation to pay a fine imposed by the final decision adopted after the merger by acquisition for infringements of law committed by the acquired company before that merger.

That judgment was interpreted too narrowly by the court of the second instance. The CJEU, guided by the broadly understood principle of protection of third parties, found that the principle of universal succession (the transfer to the acquiring company of all the assets and liabilities of the company being acquired) means to transfer to the acquiring company of the acquired company's liability for law infringements, which on the date of acquisition, have not been established by a decision of a competent authority yet. In the judgment mentioned previously, the CJEU interpreted Article 19 (1) of Directive 78/855,[83] which was repealed. However, Article 19 of Directive 2011/35,[84] in force now, contains the same rule. Therefore, the Supreme Court thought that the judgment of the CJEU in C-343/13 *Modelo Continente Hipermercados SA* remains valid also under the latter directive. Considering the binding nature of the interpretation made in the preliminary ruling and other cases,[85] the Supreme Court ruled that that judgment determines the direction of interpretation of Article 494 of the Commercial Companies Code. Since it is apparent, from

82 EU:C:2016:444.

83 Third Council Directive 78/855/EEC of 9 October 1978 based on Article 54 (3) (g) of the Treaty concerning mergers of public limited liability companies, OJ L 295, 20.10.1978, pp. 36–43.

84 Directive 2011/35/EU of the European Parliament and of the Council of 5 April 2011 concerning mergers of public limited liability companies Text with EEA relevance, OJ L 110, 29.4.2011, pp. 1–11.

85 See case C-8/08, *T-Mobile*, EU:C:2009:343.

that judgment, that the universal succession also includes liability for the law infringement subject to a fine, which has not been established by a decision adopted before an acquisition, even more, an obligation determined in the decision adopted before such an acquisition is the obligation falling within the scope of application of Article 494 (1) and (2) of the Commercial Companies Code (regulating in general terms succesion of rights and obligation in the event of merger or takeover).

Ensuring effectiveness by the modification of the rights of a party and the procedural obligations of the court

Consistent interpretation generally serves as a tool to increase the effectiveness of EU law without the need for a national legislator's intervention. National courts usually interpret, in conformity with EU law, national provisions of material and rarely used procedural law. However, sometimes consistent interpretation is used to enhance the effectiveness of EU law by modifying how the national courts should act when executing their judicial duties and imposing civil sanctions upon individuals. The *von Colson and Kamann* case is the earliest example. In the case-law of the Supreme Court, this category includes the judgment of 7 February 2019, case I PK 242/17. It was adopted therein that the obligation on the Member States to protect 'pregnant workers' and 'workers who have recently given birth' against the consequences of unlawful dismissal requires the court to treat a claim for work reinstatement as also including a claim for admission to work, when a worker, acting in a mistaken belief caused by her employer that her employment relationship had ended, claimed the reinstatement only (Article 10 (3) of the Council Directive 92/85 read in conjunction with Article 45 (1) of the Labour Code). In cases of that kind, without the reference to EU law and the interpretation in conformity with EU law, the action for work reinstatement would have been dismissed since an employee who was mistakenly convinced that the employer had terminated her employment contract should have brought an action for admission to work. On the other hand, applying the interpretation in conformity with EU law has modified the content of a claim that a pregnant worker may raise. The Supreme Court has pointed out that Article 10 of Directive 92/85 makes a clear distinction between the preventive protection against the dismissal of a pregnant woman and the reparation protection against the consequences of the dismissal. The correct transposition of that provision requires the Member States to ensure this double protection. Therefore, it is not enough to introduce only the rules prohibiting the termination of employment relationships, which the Polish legislator has done. In addition, it is necessary to ensure the effective restoration of the rights, which pregnant workers have been deprived of, which, in turn, requires the appropriate interpretation and the application of the general provisions on employee claims in the event of unlawful termination of employment. According to the Supreme Court, in a situation when, from the point of view of the law (due to the prohibition of termination of the employment relationship with a pregnant woman), the employment relationship (*de iure*) is still in progress, but there is *de facto* deprivation of employee rights (as a result of the mistaken belief that the employment relationship has ended), the Labour code is obliged to grant the protection required by EU law based on a legal remedy brought by the worker, if it is of a reparation nature, aimed at removing the effects of the employer's unlawful actions, and that is the nature of a claim for work reinstatement. However, the effectiveness of the reparation protection may not be made dependent on the selection of a suitable remedy under national law when there is no certainty in this regard at the moment of submitting [thereof] (it is not clear what claim is due).

Conclusions

The Supreme Court has treated the consistent interpretation of national law as a principle, not an exception. The selection of the judgments of the Supreme Court on the consistent interpretation of national law confirms the primary importance of that interpretation in ensuring the effectiveness of EU law in national legal orders. The wide use of consistent interpretation by the Supreme Court can be explained by the limited limitations placed upon its application by national courts and by the ECJ in proceedings between individuals.

Most of the cases reported in this monograph, in which the Supreme Court referred to consistent interpretation, concerned private parties and interpretation or application of private law falling within the scope of EU directives. Since directives are precluded from producing a direct effect in horizontal relations and hence, national courts may not, in proceedings between private parties, use the principle of primacy of EU law against national provisions incompatible with EU law, the consistent interpretation has been used by the Supreme Court primarily as a practical instrument to ensure the compatibility of national law with EU law at the stage of application of national law (normative compliance), in particular, when the textual interpretation of Polish law, or the existing line of case-law, would lead the Supreme Court to the reconstruction of a legal norm that would be incompatible with EU law, or would not ensure the full effectiveness to EU law.[86] The consistent interpretation of national law also served the Supreme Court to respect the principle of the uniform application of EU law in the Member States. This is evident in all those cases in which the provisions of Polish law implementing EU Directives were applied only after the prior selection of such an interpretative option, which would implement the normative standard that the Court

86 See in particular cases III PZP 6/12; I PZP 4/08; III PK 50/18.

of Justice had already established in its case-law.[87] Other examples supporting that thesis are cases in which the Supreme Court decided to depart from its previous case-law.[88]

As has already been stated previously, the principle of consistent interpretation is used by the Supreme Court in vertical and horizontal relations, both to the benefit and detriment of individuals. It should be noted that the application of the interpretation, in conformity with EU law to the detriment of individuals, whether in vertical or horizontal relations, is relatively rare. Such an interpretation is applied when there are additional reasons for doing so. The main reason is the judgment of the Court of Justice, containing the required interpretation of EU law, issued in reply to a preliminary reference referred by the Supreme Court.[89]

The Supreme Court has rarely allowed the consistent interpretation of Polish law to lead to the textual interpretation of national law that would, at first glance, seem to be *contra legem*. While national doctrine and case-law allow for, sometimes, a very courageous legal interpretation, even in criminal proceedings,[90] the practice of the Supreme Court shows far-reaching caution, motivated by respect for the principle of legal certainty, when derogating from the results of the textual interpretation in disputes between individuals. Such caution can be seen when such a derogation would change the distribution of rights and obligations resulting from the precise wording of Polish law provisions[91] or enable an administrative authority to impose a financial penalty.[92] However, such a derogation is acceptable, even to the detriment of an individual, if the recourse to the consistent interpretation takes place in cases (issues) not related to EU substantive law and does not, on its own, alter the rights and obligations of individuals, as established by the national legislature. The best example of this approach is case III UZP 3/17. The Supreme Court held the derogation from the results of the textual interpretation of procedural rules to be admissible because such a derogation would not lead either to the imposition of an obligation (not envisaged in national legislation but stemming from EU directives) upon the individual concerned nor would it deprive an individual of a right (privilege) granted to him by national legislation contrary to EU law.

From the practical point of view of discharging the obligations of national courts, resulting from the institution of interpretation in conformity with EU

87 See in particular cases III PK 18/06; III SK 27/08; III SK 15/16.

88 See in particular the resolution of the panel of seven judges of the SC of 21 January 2009, case II PZP 13/08 concerning the inadmissibility of the criteria of the retirement age as the sole reason for the termination of the employment contract by an employer, but also III UZP 3/17.

89 See in particular case III SK 28/13.

90 See case-law referred to in resolution of the SC of 21 January 2016, case III SZP 5/15.

91 See in particular case I PK 41/18.

92 See in particular case III SK 52/10.

law, consistent interpretation is easily achievable when the provisions of Polish law implementing a directive reproduce the wording of its provisions. In such a case, interpreting them in a way consistent with the interpretation of the directive made by the CJEU is not prevented. The obstacles resulting from adjusting the wording of the provisions implementing the directives to the conceptual network of the Polish language of the legal texts and legal terminology are eliminated. This is indicated, in particular, by the resolution of the Supreme Court of 19 November 2010, case III CZP 79/10. All attempts to introduce legal definitions by the national legislator may prevent the interpretation of laws in conformity with EU law.[93]

Literature

Baran M., *Stosowanie z urzędu prawa UE przez sądy krajowe* [Application of EU law by national courts ex officio], Wolters Kluwer Polska, 2014.

Kowalik-Bańczyk K., Badanie z urzędu naruszenia prawa wspólnotowego przy rozpoznawaniu skargi kasacyjnej przez Sąd Najwyższy – glosa do wyroku SN z dnia 18 December 2006, II PK 17/06 [Examination Ex Officio of Infringement of EU Law When Examining the Appeal on the Point of Law by the Supreme Court – Case Note to the Judgement of the Supreme Court of 18th December 2006, II PK 17/06], *Europejski Przegląd Sądowy*, 2009, no. 4, pp. 43–48.

Sołtys A., *Obowiązek wykładni prawa krajowego zgodnie z prawem unijnym jako instrument zapewniania efektywności prawa Unii Europejskiej* [The Obligation to Interpret National Law in Conformity with Eu Law as an Instrument to Ensure Effectiveness of EU Law], Wolters Kluwer Polska, 2015.

93 Resolution of the SC of 13 May 2010, case III SZP 2/10; judgment of the SC of 5 December 2006, case II PK 18/06.

6 The principle of consistent interpretation in the case-law of the administrative courts

Monika Szwarc

Introduction

The aim of this part of the study is to present the ways in which administrative courts comply with the obligation to interpret national law in conformity with EU law. The considerations discussed next follow the structure already adopted in the section devoted to the principle of consistent interpretation in the case-law of the Supreme Court. Thus, firstly, the general reception of the principle of consistent interpretation by administrative courts and its structural elements will be outlined. Secondly, the sources of the standards for consistent interpretation and the limits connected to it will be presented. Lastly, the consequences of consistent interpretation for administrative courts and for individuals will be discussed.

Reception of the principle of consistent interpretation

The analysis of the case-law of administrative courts in the years 2004–2022 leads to the conclusion that those courts, from the moment of the accession of Poland to the European Union, have accepted, without hesitation, their obligation of consistent interpretation in such a form and to the extent that results from the case-law of the CJEU. Administrative courts refer, in their adjudication, to the 'classical' judgments in cases *von Colson*,[1] *Marleasing*,[2] and *Pfeiffer*.[3] When referring thereto, the SAC recognises that the obligation of consistent interpretation means the obligation to interpret national law in the light of the wording and purpose of a directive (or any other legal act), to ensure that Community rules are binding in national law.[4] In addition, the principle of consistent interpretation requires national courts to interpret

1 Case 14/83, *Von Colson and Kamann*, EU:C:1984:153.

2 Case 106/89, *Marleasing*, EU:C:1990:395.

3 Joint cases C-397/01 to C-403/01 *Pfeiffer and others*, EU:C:2004:584.

4 Starting with judgment of the SAC of 30 January 2007, case I FSK 478/06, and further many others, for example, judgments of the SAC of 3 April 2007 in cases: I FSK 523/06, I FSK 462/06, I FSK 518/06, I FSK 519/06, I FSK 522/06, I FSK 175/06, I FSK 520/06, I FSK

DOI: 10.4324/9781003376019-8

national provisions 'as far as possible' with EU law, which means they are required to do everything within the scope of their competences, taking into account all provisions of national law and applying the methods of interpretation recognised in the national order, to ensure the full effectiveness of the directive under consideration and to make a decision consistent with the objectives pursued by it.[5]

On many occasions, the SAC also emphasised that a competent court, which interprets national law, should presume that the national law-maker intended to implement a given directive properly and so the textual interpretation of national law is always a starting point. When it is not enough to reach consistent interpretation, however, the reference to the function and purpose of the national provision is required (contextual and teleological interpretation). The main purpose of a contextual interpretation is to ensure compatibility between the provisions belonging to different legal orders (i.e., Polish law and EU law) and to inspire an authority applying national law to choose such a result of interpretation, which ensures the greatest possible effectiveness of EU law. Consequently, a national court should interpret existing national law in such a way as to take into account the content and purpose of a provision of EU law. On the other hand, a teleological interpretation of Union law requires taking into account to a greater extent the purposes of specific legal solutions rather than the literal wording of the provisions containing them.[6]

Administrative courts, referring primarily to the judgment of the Court of Justice in *von Colson* find that the principle of sincere cooperation (*ex* Article 10 TEC, now Article 4 (3) TEU)[7] and the principle of effectiveness of EU law are the source of the obligation of interpretation in conformity with EU law.[8] The SAC respects the obligation of consistent interpretation as the leading tool to resolve a conflict between a national and EU provision and recognises the reference to the principle of primacy and the refusal to apply national provisions as a last resort. The SAC assumes that the effectiveness of EU law should be ensured, in the first place, through the interpretation of national law in conformity with EU law, and should it be necessary to choose the interpretation method, priority should be given to such an interpretation that will guarantee the useful effect of EU legislation provisions. On the other hand, when a conflict between EU and national rules cannot be remedied by

---

521/06; judgment of the SAC of 27 May 2009, case I FSK 358/08, and many other judgments later on.

5 Judgment of the SAC of 19 September 2019, case II OSK 2034/19.

6 For example, judgment of the SAC of 27 May 2009, case I FSK 358/08.

7 For example, judgment of the SAC of 17 March 2008, case II GSK 464/07: Article 10 TEC, which lays down the obligation for a Member State to take all necessary measures to comply with the obligations under Community law, is to be regarded as the source of obligation to interpret national law in in a manner consistent with Community law.

8 For example, judgment of the SAC of 14 January 2010, case II FSK 2018/09.

consistent interpretation, a national court, in accordance with the principles of primacy and direct effect of EU law, is obliged to refuse to apply a provision of national law that is contrary to EU provision.[9]

The model methodology of consistent interpretation explained by the SAC is as follows. In a situation when a national court encounters doubts concerning a given national provision(s), it is obligated to interpret it in order to make it consistent with EU law. Therefore, when verifying the legality of a given administrative decision or tax interpretation, a national administrative court must verify whether EU law provision has been properly implemented into national law, with due account of CJEU's ruling *von Colson*. The obligation of consistent interpretation means, for a national court obligation, to interpret national provision in a manner taking account of wording and purpose of a relevant EU law provision. This is a requirement of teleological interpretation, which requires the taking account of objectives of legal regulations rather than their literal wording.[10]

Structural elements of the principle of consistent interpretation

As a result of the *von Colson* judgment, it is commonly accepted that the obligation of consistent interpretation is addressed to administrative courts in the first place. At the same time, administrative courts have repeatedly confirmed that this obligation also rests with public administration authorities. Let us recall, at this point, that these are the authorities issuing administrative decisions, which, in turn, are subject to judicial review before administrative courts. This means that respecting EU law is primarily the responsibility of administrative authorities, as they are the bodies reconstructing the standard for deciding a given case. The role of administrative courts is exclusively to review the legality of those decisions, and thus, also to review whether the standard for deciding a given case, that has been adopted by an administrative authority, is in compliance with EU law, as well as, if necessary, to develop such a standard and refer the case back to an administrative authority for re-consideration.

The necessity for administrative courts to explicitly invoke, in their adjudicating practice, the obligation of consistent interpretation for administrative authorities was mostly provoked by the standpoint of those authorities which had repeatedly taken the view that they are obliged to apply exclusively national law, whilst ignoring the fact that the issue concerned in a given case, fell within the scope of EU law and there were discrepancies between the provisions of national law and EU law. The basis for accepting that obligation for administrative authorities, at the level of judicial application of law in Poland,

9 Judgments of the SAC: of 14 January 2010, case II FSK 2018/09; of 16 March 2011, case I FSK 1588/10.

10 Judgment of the SAC of 9 June 2017, case I FSK 1317/15.

is the judgment of the Court of Justice in Case *Fratelli Costanzo*.[11] In case-law of the SAC, in addition to the reference to that judgment, the arguments in favour of imposing an obligation to interpret in conformity with EU law are as follows:

1) It results from the case-law of the CJEU that courts are just one of the categories of national authorities obliged to apply EU law.
2) Administrative authorities in Member States have competences in many areas to issue administrative acts or to take other actions, which are governed in whole or in part by EU law.
3) Administrative acts, as well as other actions of administrative authorities, are subject to judicial review, and the imposition of an obligation to apply EU law on courts only, without such an obligation in respect of administrative authorities, would lead in advance to adopting a double standard for law application and would cause a situation of uncertainty.[12] The position expressed by the SAC is widely accepted by voivodeship administrative courts.

Administrative courts correctly accept that the obligation of consistent interpretation has a very extensive scope, since it covers all provisions of national law and, at the same time, arises in all 'EU cases'.[13] This methodology has been explained in one of the SAC rulings where it is stated that, when interpreting a national provision in conformity with EU provisions, the first one should be compared with the standard resulting from the latter. The conformity with Union law means conformity with the rules resulting from the established standard of that law, which is statutory law (primary and secondary), the objectives of Union law expressed in the Treaties, as well as the preambles, protocols, and annexes to an act applicable in a given case. When constructing the standard of EU law, applicable for consistent interpretation, the case-law of the CJEU should be taken into account (*inter alia*, on the basis of Article 267 TFEU) as far as it contains interpretation of EU law.[14] What is more, it is recognised that the principle of interpreting national law in conformity with

11 Case C-103/88, *Fratelli Costanzo*, EU:C:1989:256; see, for example, judgments of the SAC: of 2 April 2009, case I FSK 4/08; of 11 March 2010, case I FSK 61/09; of 1 December 2011, case I FSK 1565/11; and more recently of 12 October 2016 in cases: I FSK 1989/15, I FSK 2044/15, I FSK 2069/15, I FSK 2070/15, and I FSK 2071/15.

12 Judgment of the SAC of 2 April 2009, case I FSK 4/08, citing S. Biernat, Wykładnia prawa krajowego zgodnie z prawem Wspólnot Europejskich [Interpretation of National Law in Conformity with Law of the European Community], in: C. Mik (ed.), *Implementacja prawa integracji europejskiej w krajowych porządkach prawnych* [Implementation of Law of European Integration into National Legal Orders], TNOIK, 1998, p. 131.

13 For information on how administrative courts interpret this concept, see Chapter 3.

14 Judgment of the SAC of 2 April 2009, case I FSK 4/08.

EU law is intended both to unify all legislation in a given State and to ensure that EU law is duly effective.[15]

Taking these into consideration, two contexts of consistent interpretation can be distinguished: 1) interpretation in order to ensure that terms used in national provisions implementing EU law are interpreted in a way consistent with the terms applied in a given EU legal act and 2) interpretation in order to resolve a conflict between a provision of national law and a provision of EU law. The analyses of the case-law of administrative courts lead to the conclusion that the use of consistent interpretation prevails in the first of the situations presented, that is, to ensure interpretation consistent with terms used in EU provisions.

Interpretation in order to ensure consistent interpretation of terms used in national provisions implementing EU law

Such a function of consistent interpretation is widely represented in the established case-law of administrative courts, in particular, in the disputes of individuals with tax authorities on the grounds of Polish laws transposing the provisions of EU Directives into national law. Several examples of such an application of interpretation in conformity with EU law are presented subsequently.

Cases concerning an exemption from tax on goods and services of the public administration authority

In one of the proceedings connected to the topic discussed previously, the dispute between a taxpayer and a tax authority concerned the question as to whether the fee for the use of stops and stations, charged by the Association of Municipalities (taxpayer of VAT) from the carriers carrying out the commercial passenger transport, was subject to value added tax at a rate of 23%, or whether it was eligible for the exemption under Article 15 (6) on the Law on Tax on Goods and Services. According to the taxpayer, it had been exempt. This was not approved by the tax authority. The VAC held that, since Article 15 (6) of the Law on Tax on Goods and Services transposed Article 4 (5) of Directive 77/388 when resolving that dispute, it was necessary to take due account of the provision of the Directive and its interpretation by the Court of Justice. Referring to the judgments of the Court of Justice in cases: *Comune di Carpaneto Piacentino*,[16] *Commission v. Netherlands*,[17] *Isle of Wight Council*,[18] the VAC recalled that the exemption was possible if two conditions were met:

15 Judgment of the SAC of 22 January 2020, case I GSK 2015/19.
16 Case C-4/89, *Comune di Carpaneto Piacentino*, EU:C:1990:204.
17 Case C-408/97, *Commission v. Netherlands*, EU:C:2000:427.
18 Case C-288/07, *Isle of Wight Council*, EU:C:2008:505.

the activity was carried out by a body governed by public law and had to be carried out in order to exercise public authority. Consequently, due to the fact that under the circumstances presented in that case both conditions had been met, the VAC found that the Association of Municipalities was entitled to tax exemption.[19] This line of reasoning has been confirmed in a vast number of cases. The SAC confirmed that the municipality had not been subject to VAT taxation when it carried out tasks in the field of education, including organising the catering for children in a kindergarten and their stay and studying after 13:00,[20] as well as in the field of organisation of school canteens, children's and youth's leisure, participation of children and young people in artistic performances and swimming classes, as well as participation of children and young people in international exchanges.[21]

Another instance of consistent interpretation is in the case-law concerning Article 15 (2) of the VAT Law, which implemented Article 9 (1) of Directive 2006/112. The SAC, when asked to rule on whether 'municipal budgetary entities' should be recognised as VAT-taxable persons, applied consistent interpretation. With reference to the rulings of the CJEU, the SAC held that municipal budgetary entities were not VAT-taxable persons.[22] That view was subsequently confirmed by the Court of Justice, which, as a result of a question submitted by another adjudicating panel of the SAC,[23] found that

> bodies governed by public law, such as the municipal budgetary entities at issue in the main proceedings, cannot be regarded as taxable persons for the purposes of value added tax in so far as they do not satisfy the criterion of independence set out in that provision.[24]

19 Judgment of the VAC in Cracow of 21 January 2014, case I SA/Kr 1677/13; confirmed by the SAC in judgment of 2 July 2015, case I FSK 821/14.

20 Judgment of the SAC of 9 June 2017, case I FSK 1317/15.

21 Judgment of the SAC of 9 June 2017, case I FSK 1271/15, approved in R. Mastalski, Podatkowe prawo, podatek od towarów i usług, podatnik podatku VAT, organ władzy publicznej, realizacja przez gminę zadań w zakresie edukacji. Glosa do wyroku NSA z dnia 9 czerwca 2017 r., I FSK 1271/15 [Commentary to the SAC Judgment of 9 June 2017, I FSK 1271/15], *Orzecznictwo Sądów Polskich*, 2018, no. 7–8, pp. 224–238.

22 Resolution of seven judges of the SAC of 24 June 2013, case I FPS 1/13.

23 Order of the SAC of 21 October 2015, case I FSK 311/12.

24 Case C-276/14, *Gmina Wrocław*, EU:C:2015:635, for discussion, see further D. Dominik-Ogińska, Gmina Wroclaw, Treatment of a Municipal Budgetary Entity as a Taxable Person. Criterion of Independence. Court of Justice, *Highlights & Insights on European Taxation*, 2015, no. 11, pp. 58–65; A.-L. Mosbrucker, Qualité d'assujetti à la TVA, *Europe*, 2015 Novembre Comm. no. 11 pp. 37–38; T. Küffner, Keine Unternehmereigenschaft einer wirtschaftlich tätigen haushaltsgebundenen kommunalen Einrichtung einer Gemeinde wegen fehlender Selbständigkeit, *Umsatzsteuer-Rundschau*, 2015, pp. 834–835; F. Klenk, Können einzelne Betriebe von Personen des öffentlichen Rechts Unternehmer sein? – Folgerungen aus dem EuGH-Urteil Gmina Wrocław, *Umsatzsteuer-Rundschau*, 2016, pp. 180–183.

In the course of another proceedings, the SAC had referred the questions for a preliminary ruling, which resulted in the order *Gmina Wrocław*.[25] The subject of the interpretation were the provisions of Directive 2006/112 (which replaced Directive 77/388 as of 1.01.2007) in the context of a dispute between a municipality and a tax administration authority concerning taxation for VAT purposes of the municipality activities of selling property, acquired by the operation of law or under a free title, in particular, by inheritance or donation, including real estate or bringing thereof in the form of an in-kind contribution to commercial law companies. The Court of Justice confirmed, in its order, that in order to resolve that problem, it was necessary to determine whether the activities of the municipality fell within the scope of 'carrying out an economic activity'. The SAC set aside the VAC judgment on the ground that it had not taken due account of the EU law elements. The SAC indicated to the VAC the correct law standard that should be applicable when reconsidering the legality of an individual interpretation issued by the Ministry of Finance, and found that it was necessary to determine whether the municipality activities at issue constituted 'carrying out an economic activity' in the meaning of Article 9 (1) of Directive 2006/112 (and the Court of Justice case-law) and whether they could be exempted under Article 13 (1) of that Directive (and the respective case-law of the Court of Justice). The assumption that had been taken by the VAC in the first instance, according to which a sufficient argument in favour of arising of the tax liability was the fact that the municipality was generally speaking a taxable person for VAT purposes, was wrong.[26]

The SAC, in another judgment, when interpreting Article 15 (6) of the Law on Tax on Goods and Services in conformity with EU law, also held that trading by the municipality in real estate that had been acquired by means of the so-called municipalisation of State property was to be considered as an economic activity (in the meaning of the Law on Tax on Goods and Services), even if the municipality, in terms of trading in that real estate, did not undertake activities similar to a real estate trader.[27]

Interpretation of the term 'capital company' for the purposes of exemption from tax

Administrative courts also adjudicated disputes between private entities and tax administration authorities relating to the classification, provided for in Polish law, of a limited joint-stock partnership for the purposes of taxation with tax on civil law transactions. A limited joint-stock partnership, under Polish law, has a mixed partnership and joint-stock company nature, which caused doubts as to

25 Case C-72/13, *Gmina Wrocław*, EU:C:2014:197.
26 Judgment of the SAC of 5 December 2014, case I FSK 1547/14.
27 Judgment of the SAC of 31 January 2019, case I FSK 1588/16.

whether it should be treated as a partnership (and then any acts of increasing of contributions would be subject to tax on legal transactions) or as a joint-stock company (and then the acts of increasing the share capital would be exempt from that tax). In order to resolve that issue, the VAC in Cracow had referred questions for a preliminary ruling to the Court of Justice. As a result of which the Court found that a limited joint-stock partnership was a capital company in the meaning of Directive 2008/7.[28] Consequently, when constructing the basis for resolving the dispute of the company with a tax administration authority, the VAC held that a joint-stock partnership was a capital company. Therefore, it exercised the exemption covered by the Law on Civil Law Transactions, in all situations provided for in Article 2 (6) of that Act.[29]

Partial tax deduction and establishing the proportion of turnover, taking into account real estate acquired

Another vast body of the administrative courts' case-law concerns disputes relating to the possibility, for the purposes of determining a partial tax refund, of taking into account the value of sales of real estate (lands, buildings, perpetual usufruct right). The municipalities (as tax payers) argued that the turnover from the sale of real estate should not be taken into account when calculating that proportion, if that real estate could be classified as fixed assets to the taxable person. Such a position had not always been approved by tax administrative authorities and, in such cases, the administrative courts had to correct administrative decisions. The view on that matter, adopted in administrative courts, is based on the assumption that Article 90 (5) of the Law on Tax on Goods and Services is the transposition of Article 174 (2) (b) of Directive 2006/112. The reconstruction of the EU law standard includes also the interpretation of Article 19 (2) of Directive 77/388 (preceding Article 174 of Directive 2006/112) delivered by the Court of Justice in case *Nordania Finans*,[30] according to which:

> By adopting the provisions of Article 19(2) of the Sixth Directive . . . the Community legislature thus intended to exclude from the calculation of the proportion, the turnover attributable to the sale of goods where that sale is of an unusual nature in relation to the normal activities of the taxable person concerned and does not therefore require the use of goods or services for mixed use in a way that is proportionate to the turnover which it generates.

28 Case C-357/13, *Drukarnia Multipress*, EU:C:2015:253.
29 Judgment of the VAC in Cracow of 17 November 2015, case I SA/Kr 1540/15; in the same vein judgments of SAC: of 9 March 2016, case II FSK 4006/13, of 19 April 2016, case II FSK 987/14.
30 Case C-98/07, *Nordania Finans*, EU:C:2008:144.

> the notion of 'capital goods used by the taxable person for the purposes of his business' within the meaning of Article 19(2) of the Sixth Directive cannot include capital goods the sale of which is, for the taxable person concerned, in the nature of a normal business activity.

As a result, the interpretation of joined Article 90 (3) and (5) of the Law on Tax on Goods and Services, with due account of conclusions from the wording of Article 174 (2) (a) of Directive 112, enabled the SAC to come to the conclusion that the term 'used for the purposes of the taxable person's business activity', concerning the supply of goods classified by a taxable person as fixed assets, should be understood as municipal property land, as well as the right to release land for perpetual usufruct, which was not the subject of a normal business activity of the taxable person in the meaning of Article 15 (2) of the Law on Tax on Goods and Services.[31]

Interpretation of the term 'payment' for the purposes of VAT in the context of financial services provided by banks

Consistent interpretation of the term 'payment', as used in the VAT Law, has become the subject matter of case-law of administrative courts in the context of financial services provided by banks.[32] In one of its judgments, the SAC found that this term was an equivalent of 'consideration' that had been used firstly in Article 11 (A) (1) (a) of Directive 77/388, and currently in Article 73 of Directive 2006/112/EC. Based on the interpretation of Articles 74–77 of Directive 2006/112/EC, the SAC concluded that the taxable amount for VAT purposes shall be a subjective value, that is, it should reflect the consideration due to a supplier for the transaction in question. It is irrelevant whether the consideration for the transaction in question has been paid to the taxable person by the customer or by a third party.[33] In addition, it has referred to the judgment of the Court of Justice in *Commissioners of Customs & Excise a First National Bank of Chicago*,[34] from which it results that 'in foreign exchange transactions in which no fees or commission are calculated with regard to certain specific transactions, the taxable amount is the [gross] result of the transactions of the supplier of services over a given period of time'. As a result, the aforementioned provision states that the taxable amount is established with reference to the provision of services and, therefore, constitutes the

31 For example, judgment of the SAC of 27 May 2015, case I FSK 117/14, and many others later on.

32 In simple terms, it may be assumed that the tax authority found that the taxable amount was the value of the entire financial service, for example, a treasury bill and the profit, while the bank assumed that the taxable amount was only the discount, that is, the amount 'earned' by the bank.

33 Judgment of the SAC of 30 September 2010, case I FSK 1402/09.

34 Case C-172/96, *Commissioners of Customs & Excise v. First National Bank of Chicago*, EU:C:1998:354.

consideration of the supplier received or due to be received from the customer for those transactions. The Court of Justice emphasised that

> [i]n this regard, the spread representing the difference between the bid price and the offer price is only the notional price which the Bank would obtain if it were to conclude, at the same instant and on similar conditions, two corresponding purchase and sale transactions for the same amounts and the same currencies.

Taking these into consideration, the SAC has assumed that money that is the subject of trade as part of the services referred to in the request for interpretation is not subject to taxation and that the trade does not, in itself, constitute services in the meaning of the Law [statute], since the specificity of the banking services is the fact that money is the subject thereof. The SAC has also correctly found that the entire benefit, understood as the entire consideration, an added value that accompanies the service, is the taxable amount in accordance with Article 29 (1) of the VAT Law. What constitutes the actual benefit of the Bank is the profit, the margin achieved by the Bank.[35]

A similar line of argument had been applied by the SAC in its interpretation of the term 'payment' in the context of currency exchange intermediation service. It held that in currency trading transactions where no fees or commission were calculated, the taxable amount was the result completed (the gross profit), taking into account the purchase price of currencies by the taxable person from the customer in a given period.[36]

Interpretation of the term 'private pleasure craft and private pleasure-flying' for the purposes of exemption from excise duty

In administrative courts, the disputes between private entities and tax administration authorities, relating to the exclusion of the right to exercise the exemption from the excise duty in the case of the use of fuels for private pleasure craft and private pleasure-flying in the meaning of Article 32 (1) (2) of the Excise Duty Law, were decided as well. The SAC identified, as a standard of EU law, the term 'private pleasure-flying' within the meaning of Article 14 of Directive 2003/96/EC and as interpreted by the Court of Justice in cases *Systeme Helmholz*[37] and *Haltergemeinschaft*.[38] The Court of Justice held, therein, that the tax exemption for energy products supplied for use as fuel for the purpose of air navigation other than in private pleasure-flying, provided for under Article 14 of Directive 2003/96/EC, could not apply to a company if it hired or chartered an aircraft belonging to it together with fuel to the companies, whose air

35 Judgment of the SAC of 30 September 2010, case I FSK 1402/09.

36 Judgments of the SAC of 21 January 2010 in cases: I FSK 1846/08 and I FSK 1847/08.

37 Case C-79/10, *Systeme Helmholz GmbH v. Hauptzollamt Nürnberg*, EU:C:2011:797.

38 Case C-250/10, *Haltergemeinschaft LBL GbR v. Hauptzollamt Düsseldorf*, EU:C:2011:862.

navigation operations were not directly used for the supply, by that company, of an air service for consideration. On these grounds, the SAC found that, although the wording used in national Law [statute] was different from that of the provision of Directive 2003/96/EC, it, nevertheless, had to be recognised that both the EU and national legislators aimed at 'increasing the competitiveness in the air services market'. Moreover, the definition of 'private pleasure craft' and 'private pleasure-flying' covered by the national Law corresponds to the definition of 'private pleasure-flying' included in Article 14 (1) (b) of Directive 2003/96/EC. As a result, the SAC accepted the position of the tax administrative authority, confirmed also by the court of the first instance, that

> fuel purchased by the company for an aircraft that is used to transport its own employees, as part of its business activity, is not exempt from excise duty referred to in Article 32 (1) (1) read in conjunction with (2) of the Excise Tax Law.[39]

Interpretation in order to resolve a conflict between a provision of national law and a provision of EU law

Administrative courts accept the position adopted by the Court of Justice that, in the event of a conflict between a rule of national law and a rule of EU law, the interpretation of national law in conformity with EU law is essential.[40] Some examples of how consistent interpretation enabled the court to resolve such a conflict in particular proceedings are presented subsequently.

The possibility of depriving a taxable person of the right to reduce the output tax

Shortly after the accession, administrative courts dealt with the issue of the admissibility of depriving a taxable person, by the tax authority, of the possibility of reducing their output tax by the input tax resulting from the invoices issued by an entity who had not been registered as a VAT taxable person and who did not submit returns in respect of that tax. Such a refusal was based on the provision of the Law on Tax on Goods and Services, according to which, when reducing the output tax, it was unacceptable to take into account the invoices issued by an unauthorised entity. The entity in question, not registered as a taxable person for VAT purposes, was deemed to be such an entity (*ex* Article 88 3A (1) (a) of the Law on Tax on Goods and Services applicable at that time). The reasoning of administrative courts is presented in Table 6.1, Consistent interpretation of national legislation with Directive 77/388, starting

39 Judgment of the SAC of 22 January 2020, case I GSK 2015/19 (earlier in the same vein judgments of the SAC of 7 September 2017 in cases: I GSK 1225/15 and I GSK 1233/15).

40 For example, judgment of the SAC of 26 April 2013, case II FSK 1521/11.

Table 6.1 Consistent interpretation of national legislation with Directive 77/388

<table>
<tr><td>The provision of EU law</td><td>Directive 77/388/EC

Article 2 The following shall be subject to value-added tax:

1. the supply of goods or services effected for consideration within the territory of the country by a taxable person acting as such;
2. the importation of goods.

Articles 17 (1) and (2)

Origin and scope of the right to deduct

The right to deduct shall arise at the time when the deductible tax becomes chargeable.
In so far as the goods and services are used for the purposes of his taxable transactions, the taxable person shall be entitled to deduct from the tax which he is liable to pay:

(a) value added tax due or paid in respect of goods or services supplied or to be supplied to him by another taxable person;
(b) value added tax due or paid in respect of imported goods;
(c) value added tax due under Articles 5 (7) (a) and 6 (3).

Article 22 (8)

8. Without prejudice to the provisions to be adopted pursuant to Article 17 (4), Member States may impose other obligations which they deem necessary for the correct levying and collection of the tax and for the prevention of fraud.</td></tr>
<tr><td>The provision of Polish law</td><td>Article 86 (1)

To the extent in which goods and services are used for the purposes of taxable transactions, the taxable person referred to in Article 15, shall be entitled to deduct from the amount of the output tax, the amount of the input tax.

Article 88 (3a) (1) (a)

Invoices and customs documents shall not be the grounds for reduction in the output tax and a refund of the tax difference or the refund of the input tax if:

1) the sale has been documented with invoices or correcting invoices:

a) issued by an entity that does not exist or is not authorised to issue invoices or correcting invoices,</td></tr>
<tr><td>Interpretation prior to accession</td><td>Article 88 (3A) (1) (a) – enables the tax authorities to refuse to reduce the output tax in a situation, when the sale has been documented with invoices or correcting invoices issued by an entity not registered in the VAT taxable persons register – it was treated as an entity not entitled to deduct VAT</td></tr>
</table>

(*Continued*)

Table 6.1 (Continued)

Interpretation after the accession to EU	In principle, the rules included in Article 88 (3a) (1) (a) of the VAT Law, in so far as it prevents abuse of the right to deduct, is in compliance with VI Directive. In order to apply Article 88 (3a) (1) (a) of the VAT Law, it is necessary, in addition to establishing that an invoice comes from an entity not authorised to issue it, to ***state that it follows from overall objective circumstances that the taxable person, when purchasing goods from the person not authorised to issue the invoice, at least could have foreseen that the transaction was an abuse (fraud).***

with the EU provision, domestic provision, and followed by the comparison of the interpretation of national law before and after consistent interpretation (before and after the accession).

One of the voivodeship courts, when considering the admissibility of depriving the taxable person of such a right (to reduce the output tax in a situation, such as this provided for in the Polish law), took into account the principle of tax neutrality (resulting from the then Articles 2 and 17 (2) of Directive 77/388) on the one hand, and the admissibility of imposing, by Member States, obligations aimed at avoiding tax fraud (on the basis of the then Article 22 (8) of Directive 77/388). In order to determine whether a provision of Polish Law, which had been the basis for refusing the right to a reduction in the output tax, was compatible with Directive 77/388, the VAC referred to case-law of the Court of Justice on combating abuse of law, including the judgments *Halifax*,[41] *Kefalas*,[42] *Diamantis*,[43] and *Fini*.[44] The VAC also took into account the ruling of the Court of Justice *Axel Kittel*,[45] according to which Article 17 of Directive 77/388

> precludes a rule of national law under which the fact that the contract of sale is void – by reason of a civil law provision which renders that contract incurably void as contrary to public policy for unlawful basis of the contract attributable to the seller – causes that taxable person to lose the right to deduct the value added tax he has paid. It is irrelevant in this respect whether the fact that the contract is void is due to fraudulent evasion of value added tax or to other fraud.
>
> By contrast, where it is ascertained, having regard to objective factors, that the supply is to a taxable person who knew or should have known

41 Case C-255/02, *Halifax*, EU:C:2006:121.
42 Case C-367/96, *Kefalas*, EU:C:1998:222.
43 Case C-373/97, *Diamantis*, EU:C:2000:150.
44 Case C-32/03, *Fini*, EU:C:2005:128.
45 Cases C-439/04, *Axel Kittel* and C-440/04, *Recolta Recycling*, EU:C:2006:446.

that, by the purchase, he was participating in a transaction related to the fraudulent evasion of value added tax, it is for the national court to refuse to that taxable person an entitlement to the right to deduct.

The VAC held that the provision of the Polish Law (Article 88 (3a) (1) (a) of the Law on Tax on Goods and Services), in so far as it counteracted abuse of the right to deduct, was compatible with Directive 77/388. However, at the same time, the VAC found that for the application of this provision of the VAT Law, it was necessary, in addition to determining that the invoice came from an entity not authorised to issue it, to ascertain – on the basis of the overall objective circumstances – that the taxable person, when purchasing goods from the entity not authorised to issue the invoice, at least could have foreseen that the transaction was an abuse (fraud). What is more, according to the VAC, it was necessary for the tax authority to record in its decision that such a reasoning had been completed. Otherwise, the decision had to be annulled as unlawful, failure to present the facts of the case and the proper assessment thereof taking into account the purpose of the provision of Article 88 (3a) (1) (a) of the VAT Law, read in conjunction with the provisions of Directive 77/388.[46] Such a ruling was upheld by the SAC, which found that, in principle, the rules included in Article 88 (3a) (1) (a) of the Law on Tax on Goods and Services, in so far as they prevented the abuse of the right to deduct, complied with the Sixth Directive. The application of the rules provided for in Article 88 (3a) (1) (a) of the Law on Tax on Goods and Services was admissible but had to be preceded by ascertaining – on the basis of the overall objective circumstances of a given case – that the taxable person could have foreseen that the transaction was intended to obtain a tax advantage. Such a standpoint was based on the fact that a taxable person could not be deprived of the right to deduct tax, resulting from invoices issued by another taxable person, on the mere fact that he had been regarded as an 'inactive' VAT taxable person. Where it was established, on the basis of objective circumstances, that a supply had been made to a taxable person who knew, or should have known, that by purchasing goods he was involved in the transaction used to commit the fraud in the value-added tax, it was for the national court to determine whether it was impossible to exercise the right to deduct.[47]

The possibility of applying the estimated value of turnover for tax purposes (Article 32 of the Law on Tax on Goods and Services)

The reasoning of the SAC is presented in Table 6.2, starting with the EU provision, domestic provision, and followed by a comparison of the interpretation of national law before and after consistent interpretation.

46 Judgment of the VAC in Gdańsk of 7 August 2007, case I SA/Gd 532/07.

47 Judgments of the SAC: of 29 January 2009, case I FSK 1822/07; of 29 January 2009, case I FSK 1821/07; of 20 May 2009, case I FSK 1915/07; of 3 June 2009, case I FSK 544/08.

Table 6.2 Consistent interpretation of national legislation with Article 80 of Directive 2006/112

<table>
<tr><td>The provision of EU law</td><td>Directive 2006/112

Article 80

1. In order to prevent tax evasion or avoidance, Member States may in any of the following cases take measures to ensure that, in respect of the supply of goods or services involving family or other close personal ties, management, ownership, membership, financial or legal ties as defined by the Member State, the taxable amount is to be the open market value:

(a) where the consideration is lower than the open market value and the recipient of the supply does not have a full right of deduction under Articles 167 to 171 and Articles 173 to 177;
(b) where the consideration is lower than the open market value and the supplier does not have a full right of deduction under Articles 167 to 171 and Articles 173 to 177 and the supply is subject to an exemption under Articles 132, 135, 136, 371, 375, 376, 377, 378 (2), 379 (2) or Articles 380 to 390;
(c) where the consideration is higher than the open market value and the supplier does not have a full right of deduction under Articles 167 to 171 and Articles 173 to 177.

For the purposes of the first subpara., legal ties may include the relationship between an employer and employee or the employee's family, or any other closely connected persons.

2. Where Member States exercise the option provided for in para. 1, they may restrict the categories of suppliers or recipients to whom the measures shall apply.
3. Member States shall inform the VAT Committee of national legislative measures adopted pursuant to para. 1 in so far as these are not measures authorised by the Council prior to 13 August 2006 in accordance with Article 27 (1) to (4) of Directive 77/388/EEC, and which are continued under para. 1 of this Article.</td></tr>
<tr><td>Polish legislation</td><td>Article 32

1. Where there is a link between a customer and a supplier of goods or services, referred to in 2, and where the consideration is:

1) lower than the market value, and the person acquiring goods or services [customer], in accordance with Articles 86, 88 and 90 as well as with legislative measures issued under Article 92 (1) (2) and (3), has not a full right to reduce the amount of the output tax by the amount of the input tax;
2) lower than the market value, and the supplier of goods or services, in accordance with Articles 86, 88 and 90 as well as with legislative measures issued under Article 92 (1) (2) and (3), has not a full right to reduce the amount of the output tax by the amount of the input tax, and the supply of goods or services is exempt from tax;</td></tr>
</table>

	3) higher than the market value, and the supplier of goods or services, in accordance with Articles 86, 88 and 90 as well as with legislative measures issued under Article 92 (1) (2) and (3), has not a full right to reduce the amount of the output tax by the amount of the input tax – the tax authority shall assess the amount of the turnover on the basis of the market value reduced by the amount of the tax, if it turns out that this link had an impact on the determination of consideration for the supply of goods or services. 2. There is a link referred to in (1), where there are family ties, or those resulting from adoption, capital, property or employment relationships between contracting parties or persons performing managerial, supervisory or control functions at contracting parties. That link also exists when any of these persons combines the managerial, supervisory or control functions at contracting parties. . . . 4. The capital link, referred to in (2), is understood as a situation, where one of the persons or one of the contracting parties has a voting right of at least 5% of all voting rights or has directly or indirectly such a right.
Interpretation adopted by a tax administration authority	Article 32 of the Law on Tax on Goods and Services is applicable to transactions concluded by entities forming a tax capital group in the meaning of the Law of 15 February 1992 on Corporate Income Tax.
The interpretation in conformity with EU law taking into account the purpose of Article 80 (1) Directive 2006/112	The taxable amount may be assessed on the basis of Article 32 of the Law on Tax on Goods and Services if there is a link referred to in (2) between the parties, and in addition, one of the situations listed in (1)–(3) has taken place. The occurrence of any of the above mentioned situations in the case at issue had not been considered at all and for that reason, the authority could not conclude that Article 32 of the Law on Tax on Goods and Services was applicable therein. However, for the purposes of the legal classification of a future event presented by the Applicant, the criterion of the purpose referred to in Article 80 of Directive 112 is essential. Since it is necessary to answer the question, whether the settlement of the transaction prices under PGK may be considered as an activity aimed at tax evasion or avoidance. According to the SAC that question must be answered in the negative.

When adjudicating the dispute between the capital group of companies and the tax authority, the SAC held that, since Article 32 of the Law on Tax on Goods and Services was an equivalent of Article 80 of Directive 112, it had to be determined whether the provision of the Directive had been correctly transposed to Polish law. It found that the taxable amount might be established on the basis of the market value only if several conditions were met. First of all, the taxable amount should be established on that basis only in order to prevent tax evasion or tax avoidance and only in the cases listed in Article 80 (1) (a)-(c) of Directive 112, when the links referred to in that provision occurred. In other words, the following must occur cumulatively: meeting the objective, that is, the prevention of tax evasion or avoidance, one of the instances listed in Article 80 (1) (a)–(c), and the occurrence of the links laid down in that provision. The absence of one of those elements excluded the applicability of Article 80 of Directive 112.

The comparison of the EU standard, reconstructed on the ground of Article 80 of Directive 112 with the wording of Article 32 of Law on Tax on Goods and Services, led the SAC to the conclusion that the latter provision had not been properly implemented to Polish Law. The SAC considered that the textual interpretation was not sufficient in that case. It was necessary to apply a teleological interpretation. This was due to the fact that only with the application of a teleological interpretation could the result intended by the rule of Article 80 of Directive 112 be achieved. According to the SAC, the Polish legislator omitted the objective of the application of Article 80 of the Directive (in order to prevent tax evasion or avoidance) and, at the same time, the provision of the Law was drafted in such a way that it might suggest that it was not necessary to meet the conditions laid down in that sentence cumulatively (the occurrence of the link referred to in (2) and one of the situations listed in (1)–(3) of that provision). Whereas, in the opinion of the SAC, pursuant to Article 80 of Directive 112, these conditions should be fulfilled cumulatively, that is, the taxable amount could be assessed under Article 32 of the Law on Tax on Goods and Services, if there was a link referred to in (2) between the parties, and, in addition, one of the situations listed in (1)–(3) occured. The occurrence of any of those situations, in the case at issue, was not considered at all and, for that reason alone, the tax administrative authority could not conclude that Article 32 of the Law on Tax on Goods and Services was applicable therein. Therefore, in order to assess the future event, that is, the settlement of transaction prices within the capital group, the criterion of the purpose laid down in Article 80 of the Directive should be of key importance.[48]

Interpretation of the term 'the first occupation' – to remedy non-compliance

The reasoning of the SAC is presented in Table 6.3, starting with the EU provision, domestic provision, and followed by the comparison of the interpretation of national law before and after consistent interpretation.

48 Judgment of the SAC of 28 November 2011, case I FSK 155/11.

Table 6.3 Consistent interpretation of national legislation with Article 12 of Directive 2006/112

EU law provision	Directive 2006/112/EC Article 12 1. Member States may regard as a taxable person anyone who carries out, on an occasional basis, a transaction relating to the activities referred to in the second subpara. of Article 9 (1) and in particular one of the following transactions: (a) the supply, before first occupation, of a building or parts of a building and of the land on which the building stands; . . . 2. For the purposes of para. 1 (a), 'building' shall mean any structure fixed to or in the ground. Article 135 1 Member States shall exempt the following transactions: (j) the supply of a building or parts thereof, and of the land on which it stands, other than the supply referred to in point (a) of Article 12 (1);
Polish law provision	Article 2 (14) of the VAT Law[49] For the purposes of the following provisions: 14) **first occupation**, shall mean **release for use** of buildings, civil engineering works or their parts, **in performance of taxable activities**, to the first customer or user, following their: a) erection, or b) upgrade, if the expenditure incurred for the upgrade, as defined in the regulations on income tax, constituted at least 30% of the initial value; Article 43 (1) (10) of the VAT Law The following are exempt from tax: 10) the supply of buildings, civil engineering works or parts thereof, except where: a) the supply is made within the framework of the first occupation or prior to the first occupation, b) the period between the first occupation and the supply of the building, civil engineering works or parts thereof was less than two years;
Interpretation in conformity with EU law taking into account Article 12 (1) (a) of Directive 2006/112	The first occupation – in the meaning of Article 2 (14) (a) – shall be understood as the use by the first customer or user of buildings, civil engineering works or their parts, following their erection.

49 Version applicable at the date of the case, April 2012; it has been changed after the CJEU judgment, see subsequently.

The SAC also settled the dispute, in the context of the right to the VAT exemption, as regards the interpretation of the term 'first occupation', the condition adopted in the Polish VAT Law, allowing the exemption. The clarification of that issue was crucial in the case concerned, since in Directive 2006/112, that term has been applied. However, it was neither defined therein nor were any additional conditions defining it introduced. The SAC, when analysing that term in the context of Directive 2006/112, took into account 1) the obligation to interpret strictly the exceptions to the general rule, that VAT is charged on every supply of goods and services for consideration by a taxable person, but at the same time 2) the need to interpret the terms applied in the Directive in accordance with the objectives pursued by those exemptions, and satisfying the requirements of the principle of tax neutrality, on which the common VAT system is based; and 3) the need to interpret autonomously the term 'first occupation' used in Directive 2006/112. It also referred to case-law of the Court of Justice relating to the exemption itself, including the judgments in Cases *J.J. Komen en Zonen Beheer Heerhugowaard BV, Caixa d'Estalvis and Pensions de Barcelona*,[50] *Don Bosco Onroerend Goed BV*,[51] *Gemeente's-Hertogenbosch*,[52] where the Court of Justice *ad casu* was deciding on the understanding of the term 'first occupation' in the meaning, firstly, of Directive 77/388 and, subsequently, Directive 2006/112.

On these grounds, the SAC found that the definition of 'first occupation' included in Directive 112 was autonomous and, therefore, it was not necessary to define it in the VAT Law, except for the instances provided for in Article 12 (2) the second sentence of Directive 112, that is, the 'conversion' of a building. The comparison of the definition 'the first occupation' resulting from the VAT Law and Directive 112 led the SAC to the conclusion that the Polish Legislator had narrowed the previous definition in comparison with the EU definition. Whereas, textual, contextual, and teleological interpretation of Directive 112 indicated clearly that the aforementioned term should be understood broadly as 'the first occupation of a building, use'. Therefore, the definition provided for in Article 2 (14) of the VAT Law should be read in this way.

In this case, in order to ensure the effectiveness of Directive 2006/112, the SAC has found partial non-compliance of Article 2 (14) (a) of the VAT Law with Article 12 (1) (a) and 2 of Directive 112, as well as Article 135 (1) (j) of Directive 112, that is, in so far as the condition 'in performance of taxable activities' has been used in the Polish Law. The application of interpretation of Article 2 (14) (a) of the VAT Law, in conformity with EU law,

50 Case C-139/12, *J.J. Komen en Zonen Beheer Heerhugowaard BV, Caixa d'Estalvis and Pensions de Barcelona*, EU:C:2014:174.

51 Case C-461/08, *Don Bosco Onroerend Goed BV*, EU:C:2009:722.

52 Case C-92/13, *Gemeente's-Hertogenbosch*, EU:C:2014:2188.

has allowed the court to correct the content, as follows: the term 'first occupation', shall be understood as the use, by the first customer or user, of buildings, civil engineering works, or parts thereof, following their erection.[53]

The compliance of the definition of 'the first occupation', included in VAT Law, was subsequently the subject matter of the judgment of the Court of Justice in *Kozuba*,[54] as a result of the request of the SAC.[55] The Court of Justice held:

> Articles 12(1)(a) and 135(1)(j) of Council Directive 2006/112/EC must be interpreted as precluding a national law, such as that at issue in the main proceedings, which makes the VAT exemption on the supply of buildings subject to the condition that the first occupation thereof arises in the context of a taxable transaction. The same provisions must be interpreted as not precluding such a national law from making that exemption subject to the condition, in the case of the 'upgrade' of an existing building, that the costs incurred have not exceeded 30% of the initial value thereof, provided that that concept of 'upgrade' is interpreted in the same way as that of 'conversion' in Article 12(2) of Directive 2006/112, namely as meaning that the building concerned must have been subject to substantial modifications intended to modify the use or alter considerably the conditions of occupation.

As a result of the judgment of the Court of Justice, the VAT Law has been amended[56] in such a way that the condition at issue has been removed from the definition of 'the first occupation'. The position of the Court of Justice is also accepted by administrative courts. The SAC considered that, in the absence of a definition of the 'first occupation' in Polish Law, the term should be provided with a colloquial meaning and it should be assumed that any form of use, of the buildings, civil engineering works, or their parts meets that condition.[57]

53 Judgment of the SAC of 14 May 2015, case I FSK 382/14.

54 Case C-308/16, *Kozuba*, EU:C:2017:869, for discussion, see further H. Nieskens, Steuerbefreiung für Lieferung von Gebäuden – Begriff des Erstbezugs, *EU-Umsatz-Steuerberater*, 2018, pp. 20–21; M. Wilk, Dostawa budynków i budowli na gruncie VAT a pierwsze zasiedlenie w świetle wyroku Trybunału Sprawiedliwości z 16 listopada 2017 r., C-308/16, Kozuba Premium Selection sp. z o.o. przeciwko Dyrektorowi Izby Skarbowej w Warszawie [The Supply of the Building on the in the Context of VAT and First Occupation – in the Light of the Judgment of the CJEU in C-308/16 Kozuba Premium Selection], *Przegląd Podatkowy*, 2018, no. 2, pp. 40–46.

55 Order of the SAC of 23 February 2016, case I FSK 1573/14.

56 By Law of 4 July 2019, *Dziennik Ustaw* [Journal of Laws] 2019.1520

57 Judgments of the SAC: of 10 August 2018, case I FSK 1208/15; of 19 September 2019, case I FSK 1294/17.

Sources of the interpretative standard for consistent interpretation

Administrative courts, when reconstructing the standard for consistent interpretation, primarily refer to the judgments of the Court of Justice, issued either under the procedure of preliminary rulings at the request of the courts of other Member States, or under the action procedure of 258 TFEU. They, themselves, also refer the questions for a preliminary ruling to the CJEU.

The standard for consistent interpretation derived from the preliminary rulings in Polish cases

The standard for the interpretation, in conformity with EU law, is included in preliminary rulings issued in response to the questions referred by the courts, which are to adjudicate in the main proceedings. Administrative courts, since 1 May 2004, have referred to the Court of Justice 99 requests for preliminary rulings.[58] From the statistics alone, it can be concluded that administrative courts are looking for the standard of EU law interpretation by also referring the questions for preliminary ruling to the Court of Justice. When the CJEU delivers a preliminary ruling, the administrative court that addressed the questions accepts that the interpretation, made by the Court of Justice, in a given case is binding for it. Similarly to the practice of the Supreme Court administrative courts hardly ever articulate the principle of binding all national courts with the interpretation of EU law made by the Court of Justice.[59] Nevertheless, the approach applied by those courts confirms not only a formal approach but also the actual recognition of that principle.

As already presented earlier, the SAC has applied for the interpretation of Article 9 (1) of Directive 2006/112 and the tax exemption for the actions of the State authority included therein, in the context of the application thereof to the activities of the municipality.[60] The Court of Justice had issued, in response, an order under the *act éclairé* procedure,[61] which was subsequently applied by the SAC to develop the EU law standard as the basis for adjudicating the case.[62] The preliminary ruling of the Court of Justice, issued upon the request of the SAC,[63] was also the basis for resolving the disputes relating to the classification of a limited joint-stock partnership (determining whether to

58 The status as of 1 October 2022; all available in Polish at www.nsa.gov.pl/pytania-prejudycjalne-wsa-i-nsa.php.

59 Judgment of the SAC of 27 June 2013, case I FSK 720/13: 'There is no doubt, that the ruling of the Court of Justice on the interpretation of EU law is binding on the court which has referred the question for a preliminary ruling. . . . That binding covers not only the court which has referred the question, but also all national courts hearing the case in question'.

60 Order of the SAC of 17 August 2012, case I FSK 1612/11.

61 Case C-72/13, *Gmina Wrocław*, EU:C:2014:197.

62 Judgment of the SAC of 5 December 2014, case I FSK 1547/14.

63 Order of the SAC of 17 August 2012, case I FSK 1612/11.

treat it as a 'capital company' in the meaning of Directive 2008/7) for the purposes of applying the exemption from tax on civil law transactions.[64]

Other examples are those cases before administrative courts where doubts have arisen as to the interpretation of the term 'fixed establishment' in the meaning of Article 44 of Directive 2006/112 and Article 11 (1) of Council Implementing Regulation (EU) No. 282/2011, laying down the implementing measures for Directive 2006/112/EC. In 2012, the SAC referred to the Court of Justice the requests for a preliminary ruling relating to the interpretation of the term 'fixed establishment' in the context of the facts of the case at issue, where services supplied by a Polish company (established in Poland) to a Cypriot company (established in another EU Member State), in circumstances where the Cypriot company carried out its economic activity by making use of the Polish company's infrastructure.[65] When deciding as to whether, in such a situation, the fixed establishment within the meaning of Article 44 of the VAT Directive was in Poland (Polish company's establishment), the Court of Justice held that, in order to answer this question, it was necessary to determine 'that establishment is characterised by a sufficient degree of permanence and a suitable structure in terms of human and technical resources to enable it to receive the services supplied to it and use them for its business'.[66] At the same time, the Court of Justice referred the decision on that issue to a national court. As a result, the SAC, in its judgment, established a correct interpretation of Article 28b of the VAT Law with a due account of the CJEU's ruling, annulled the decisions of tax authorities in the case at issue (and the VAC judgment that accepted their position). When constructing a standard for deciding the case, to be applied by an administrative authority, the SAC held that in order to determine whether the services provided by the applicant to a Cypriot company are, under Article 19 (1) and (4) read in conjunction with Article 28b (2) of the VAT Law, subject to taxation in the territory of Poland at the VAT rate of 22%, it was necessary to establish that the Cypriot company had in Poland at least a structure, char-

64 Case C-357/13, *Drukarnia Multipress*, EU:C:2015:253, and its application in judgment of the VAC in Cracow of 17 November 2015, case I SA/Kr 1540/15; judgments of the SAC: of 9 March 2016, case II FSK 4006/13, of 19 April 2016, case II FSK 987/14.

65 Order of the SAC of 25 October 2012, case I FSK 1993/11.

66 Case C-605/12, *Welmory*, EU:C:2014:2298, for discussion, see further: S. Heinrichshofen, Feste Niederlassung i.S.v. Art. 44 MwStSystRL, *EU-Umsatz-Steuerberater*, 2014, pp. 70–71; F. Richter, Welmory sp. z o.o. (Elmory) v. Dyrektor Izby Skarbowej w Gdansku, *Revue générale de fiscalité luxembourgeoise*, 2015, pp. 64–65; N. Jovanovic, M. Merkx, Welmory: A Recipe for VAT Avoidance?, *EC Tax Review*, 2015, pp. 202–209; J. Kollmann, L. Turcan, D. Turić, K. Spies, Kann eine Webseite eine 'feste Niederlassung' begründen?, *Ecolex*, 2015, pp. 812–813; M. Machalski, Analiza pojęcia stałego miejsca prowadzenia działalności gospodarczej, z uwzględnieniem praktyki organów podatkowych po wyroku TSUE ws. C-605/12 (Welmory) – zarys problemu [The Analysis of 'Fixed Establishment' with Due Regard of Tax Authorities' Practice After the Judgment of the CJEU in C-605/12 Welmory], *Przegląd Ustawodawstwa Gospodarczego*, 2019, no. 3, pp. 154–159.

acterised by a sufficient degree of permanence, suitable in terms of human and technical resources to enable it to receive the services supplied by the Polish company and use them for its own business purposes, namely managing the electronic auctions system in question as well as issuing and selling 'bids'. Regarding the question whether the Cypriot company had 'human and technical resources' in Poland, the SAC stated that such a business, as carried out by the Cypriot company, required at least a suitable structure, in particular, human and technical resources, such as IT equipment, servers, and suitable software.[67]

In 2018, the VAC in Wrocław had doubts as to the interpretation of that term in the context of a company that had its establishment outside the EU and only that its subsidiary was established in Poland,[68] for the purposes of determining whether the applicant company was entitled to apply a preferential rate of taxation. The interpretation of the aforementioned EU provisions, formulated by the Court of Justice, according to which: 'the existence, in the territory of a Member State, of a fixed establishment of a company established in a non-Member State may not be inferred by a supplier of services from the mere fact that that company has a subsidiary there' and at the same time, 'supplier is not required to inquire, for the purposes of such an assessment, into contractual relationships between the two entities'[69] was used to interpret Article 28b of the VAT Law (transposing Article 44 of Directive 2006/112) in compliance with Directive 2006/112. Consequently, the VAC held that tax authorities had deprived the Applicant of the right to apply a preferential tax rate by imposing on them an obligation, not arising from legislation, to inquire into relationships between a customer and third parties.[70] Thus, the tax authority deciding the case was obligated to duly take into account the judgment of the Court of Justice and the VAC guidelines.

It is also worth emphasising that the interpretation of EU law in the preliminary ruling issued by the Court of Justice in one 'Polish' case is accepted by other administrative courts, ruling on the cases under the same legal basis. For example, the judgment of the Court of Justice in case *Magoora*,[71] relating

67 Judgment of the SAC of 20 March 2017, case I FSK 1884/14.

68 Order of the VAC in Wrocław of 6 June 2018, case I SA/Wr 286/18.

69 Case C-547/18, *Dong Yang*, EU:C:2020:350, for discussion, see further K. Lasiński-Sulecki, Czego nowego dowiedzieliśmy się o stałym miejscu prowadzenia działalności gospodarczej?: Wyrok TS, C-547/18, Dong Yang Electronics Sp. Z o.o. przeciwko Dyrektorowi Izby Administracji Skarbowej we Wrocławiu [What New Can We Find Out About Fixed Establishment?: Judgment of the CJEU, C-547/18, Dong Yang Electronics], *Przegląd Podatkowy*, 2020, no. 9, pp. 13–19.

70 Judgment of the VAC of 10 September 2020, case I SA/Wr 286/18.

71 Case C-414/07, *Magoora*, EU:C:2008:766, for discussion, see further I. Hofstätter, Einschränkung des Vorsteuerabzugs auf den Kauf von Kraftstoffen, *European Law Reporter*, 2009, pp. 109–111; S. Heinrichshofen, Einschränkung des Vorsteuerabzugs, *EU-Umsatz-Steuerberater*, 2009, pp. 5–6; A. Bartosiewicz, R. Kubacki, Odliczenie podatku od

to the interpretation included in Directive 77/388 of the *stand-still* clause, has been referred to in 1099 judgments of administrative courts, including 242 rulings of the SAC. Another very important decision of the Court of Justice is the ruling in the joint cases *Fortuna, Grand and Forta*,[72] where the Court had ruled on the interpretation of a provision of Directive 98/34/EC in the context of the Polish Gambling Law, was referred to in 12,881 rulings in total, including 3,169 rulings of the SAC.

The standard for the interpretation derived from preliminary rulings of the Court of Justice in cases other than Polish ones

Administrative courts reconstruct the standard for consistent interpretation additionally using extensive references to the judgments of the Court of Justice, issued under the preliminary ruling procedure, or under the action procedure in cases other than Polish ones, which are a source of a standard for interpretation of EU laws applicable in a case to be decided by a court concerned. It results from the examples discussed earlier that administrative courts have made a reference to the preliminary rulings for the purpose of reconstructing the scope of the VAT exemption for public authorities (in particular, municipalities or associations of municipalities),[73] the term 'consideration' in the meaning of Directive 77/388 and Directive 2006/112 (in the context of financial services and currency exchange provided by the bank),[74] the term 'pleasure-flying' in the meaning of Directive 2003/96,[75] and the term 'first occupation' for the purposes of applying the VAT exemption.[76]

---

samochodów osobowych i paliwa do nich – glosa do wyroku ETS z 22 December 2008 r. w sprawie C-414/07 Magoora przeciwko Dyrektorowi Izby Skarbowej w Krakowie [Commentary on Judgment of the CJEU C-414/07 Magoora], *Europejski Przegląd Sądowy*, 2009, no. 9, pp. 47–55.

72 Joined cases C-213/11 *Fortuna*, C-214/11 *Grand*, C-217/11 *Forta sp. z o.o.*, EU:C:212:495; for discussion, see further: S. Roset, Notion de « règle technique », *Europe*, 2012 Octobre Comm. no. 10, p. 30; D. Miąsik, Sąd Najwyższy – Postanowienie Sądu Najwyższego z dnia 28 listopada 2013 r. (sygn. akt I KZP 15/13) [Commentary to the Order of the Supreme Court of 28 November 2013, I KZP 15/13], *Zeszyty Naukowe Sądownictwa Administracyjnego*, 2014, no. 1, pp. 122–133; A. Krzywoń, Glosa do postanowienia Sądu Najwyższego z dnia 28 listopada 2013 r. (sygn. akt I KZP 15/13) [Commentary to the Order of the Supreme Court of 28 November 2013, I KSP 15/13], *Zeszyty Naukowe Sądownictwa Administracyjnego*, 2014, no. 1, pp. 163–168.

73 Judgment of the VAC in Cracow of 21 January 2014, case I SA/Kr 1677/13; confirmed by the SAC in judgment of 2 July 2015, case I FSK 821/14; also judgments of the SAC of 9 July 2017 in cases: I FSK 1317/15 and I FSK 1271/15.

74 Judgments of the SAC: of 30 September 2010, case I FSK 1402/09; of 21 January 2010, case I FSK 1846/08.

75 Judgments of the SAC: of 7 September 2017, case I GSK 1225/15; of 7 September 2017, case I GSK 1233/15; of 22 January 2020, case I GSK 2015/19.

76 Judgment of the SAC of 14 May 2015, case I FSK 382/14.

Limits of consistent interpretation

In the declarative sphere, administrative courts accept the limitations of consistent interpretation resulting from established case-law that

> the obligation on a national court to refer to the content of a directive when interpreting and applying the relevant rules of domestic law is limited by general principles of law, . . . and that obligation cannot serve as the basis for an interpretation of national law *contra legem*.[77]

Those two limitations of consistent interpretation are referred to by administrative courts, in particular the SAC,[78] listing among the general principles of law (following case-law of the Court of Justice) the principle of legal certainty and the principle of non-retroactivity.[79] In addition, the administrative courts, in many rulings, provide that there is no obligation of interpretation if it was to lead to a denial or rejection of national law, thus, to interpretation *contra legem*.[80] The analysis of the judicial practice reveals that there are still some challenges before administrative courts in terms of understanding and application of the *contra legem* exception.

This can be illustrated by the case-law of the administrative courts adjudicating in disputes of taxable persons with the tax authority relating to the VAT taxation of the transfer of goods in the context of the competition organised by the applicant company. In one of such cases, the company claimed that tax was not due, whilst the tax authority considered that such a transaction was charged with VAT. The VAC held that the provision of Article 7 (2) and (3) of the Law on Tax on Goods and Services made a reference to the content of Article 5 (6) of Directive 77/388, from which it resulted, that also the following was considered to be the supply of goods: the application of goods forming part of the business assets 1) for the private use of a taxable person, 2) for the private use of taxable person's staff, 3) the disposal thereof free of charge, and 4) their application for purposes other than those of the taxable person's business. According to the VAC, Article 5 (6) of VI Directive 77/388 covered each disposal of goods free of charge, both for the purposes other than the economic activity carried out and for the purposes of that activity, whereas in the provision of Polish Law the *ratione materiae* of taxable activities was limited to the transfer for the purposes other than those related to the business

77 Case 80/86, *Kolpinghuis Nijmegen*, EU:C:1987:431; case C-212/04, *Adeneler*, EU:C:2006:443; case C-282/10, *Dominguez*, EU:C:2012:33.

78 For example, judgments of the SAC of 8 October 2014, case I FSK 1512/13; of 14 May 2015, case I FSK 382/14.

79 For example, judgments of the SAC: of 29 March 2018, case I FSK 1069/15; of 4 April 2015, case I FSK 1872/14; of 2 July 2019, case I FSK 119/17.

80 For example, judgment of the SAC: of 8 January 2009, case I FSK 1798/07; of 5 February 2009, case I FSK 1880/07; of 27 May 2009, case I FSK 358/08; of 8 May 2009, case I FSK 1509/08.

carried out by the taxable person, without taking account of the transfer, free of charge, of the goods for the purposes related to the business.[81] Facing such a discrepancy between the EU provision and Polish provision, the VAC decided to interpret the latter in a way consistent with the preceding in order to ensure the effectiveness of EU law in this case. Such consistent interpretation resulted, however, in subjecting a taxable person to the tax liability that had not resulted *prima facie* from the provisions of Polish Law.

In the cassation proceedings, the SAC admittedly found that, although the literal wording of the then Article 7 (2) of the VAT Law deviated from the content of Article 5 (6) of Directive 77/388, it, nevertheless, had doubts as to the consequences of that inconsistency for a given case and, therefore, submitted a question of law to the enlarged panel of the SAC (seven judges). The judges found that

> there are no obstacles – following consistent interpretation of provisions of Article 7 (2) and (3) of the VAT Law in their version applicable from 1 May 2004 to 31 May 2005 – to establish their understanding in accordance with the interpretation and purpose of Article 5 (6) of the VI [Directive] 77/388.

Consequently, it was accepted that the supply of goods should also be understood as the transfer, by a taxable person, free of charge, of the goods belonging to their business for the purposes related to that business if the taxable person was entitled to reduce the output tax by the amount of the input tax in relation to the acquisition of these goods.[82] The SAC had not referred, in this case, to the *contra legem* interpretation (as a limit to consistent interpretation) nor had it doubts that consistent interpretation adopted was leading to the imposition of the tax liability on the taxable person.[83]

Article 7 of the VAT Law had been modified as of 1.06.2005, which was a ground for another, quite different from the previous discussion, line of case-law of administrative courts in terms of the limits of consistent interpretation. Adjudicating on the ground of the modified Polish provision, the VAC in Warsaw decided to rely on the grammatical (literal) reading of the relevant Article 7 (2) of the VAT Law and to conclude that its interpretation, in conformity with Article 5 (6) of Directive 77/388, was inadmissible due to the fact that it would lead to the interpretation *contra legem*.[84] Such a position was confirmed

81 Judgment of the VAC in Bydgoszcz of 23 November 2005, case I SA/Bd 473/05, which referred to case C-48/97, *Kuwait Petroleum*/GB/Ltd, EU:C:1999:203.

82 Resolution of seven judges of the SAC of 28 May 2007, case I FPS 5/06.

83 The standpoint of the SAC in case I FPS 5/06 is still applied in the case-law, see, for example, judgment of the SAC of 26 of May 2021, case I FSK 1027/18, and other 78 rulings in the database.

84 Judgment of the VAC in Warsaw of 5 October 2007, case III SA/Wa 1255/07; earlier in this vein judgment of VAC in Wrocław of 3 April 2007, case I SA/Wr 152/07.

by the SAC when it found that referring to other methods of interpretation (available in Polish legal theory), is unacceptable, because a grammatical interpretation of national provisions, namely Article 7 (2) and (3) of the VAT Law, led to a clear result. On the one hand, the SAC noticed that grammatical interpretation of the Polish provision led to the narrowing of the *ratione materiae* of tax liability in comparison with Article 5 (6) of Directive 77/388 and, as a result, it was not compatible with the latter. On the other, it concluded that consistent interpretation of the Polish provision, in order to ensure *effet utile* of EU law, was not possible. It held that teleological interpretation of the aforementioned provisions of the VAT Law would lead to an extension of their *ratione materiae*, as reconstructed with the use of the grammatical interpretation. According to the SAC, consistent interpretation was not allowed when it would lead to the results contrary to the effects of the grammatical (textual, literal) interpretation since that could lead to the unacceptable interpretation *contra legem*. That, in turn, would amount to allowing the national court, without the proper transposition by the State of a particular provision of the Directive to national law, to impose, via the interpretation applied, an obligation, on a citizen, resulting from that Directive, contrary to national rules. In addition, as the SAC concluded, an interpretation of national law leading to the imposition, on the taxable person, of the obligations not expressed directly in national law, cannot be applied.[85]

Furthermore, in order to give reasons of such a conclusion, the SAC referred to the principle of statutory exclusivity in tax matters, provided for in the Constitution of the Republic of Poland (Article 217), requiring a clear and understandable, for addressees, definition of that scope in a tax provision of the statutory law. In its opinion, an interpretation of national law, which would lead to the imposition, on the taxable person, of the obligations not expressed directly in national law, would be incompatible with the aforementioned principle. The subject matter of the taxation (transactions giving rise to a tax liability) cannot be presumed and determined on the basis of the application of a teleological or consistent [in conformity with Community law] interpretation, leading to the extension of the tax liability to those transactions, which in the light of the wording of the interpreted provisions, are not covered by such an obligation. The SAC stated that the interpretation of provisions of Article 7 (2) and (3) of the Law on Tax on Goods and Services, allowing, in accordance with Article 5 (6) of the Sixth Directive (Article 16 of Directive 2006/112/EC) for the taxation of the goods transferred for business purposes, had to be declared as an inadmissible interpretation *contra legem*, infringing Article 217 and Article 2 of the Constitution. The administrative court, in addition to the EU court, responsible for interpreting the provisions of tax law in conformity with Community law, should, as far as possible, strive to achieve the (legal,

85 Judgment of the SAC of 13 May 2008, case I FSK 600/07; confirmed in judgments of the SAC: of 25 June 2008, case I FSK 743/07, and of 23 March 2009, case I FPS 6/08.

economic, social) situation required by the Directive. However, the results of that interpretation, by extending the scope of the tax liability beyond the limits defined by the provisions of national tax laws [statutes], might not infringe the principles resulting from the applicable provisions of the Constitution to the detriment of the taxable persons. For those reasons, the SAC found that the transfer by the taxable person, free of charge, of the goods belonging to his business for the purposes relating to that business did not constitute a supply of goods in the light of Article 7 (2) and (3) of the Law on Tax of Goods and Services in the version, applicable since 1 June 2005, even if the taxable person was entitled to the reduction of the output tax by the amount of the input tax due to the acquisition of those goods.[86]

This line of judgments of the SAC, as initiated by the rulings in cases I FSK 600/07 and I FPS 6/08, deserves two general remarks. Firstly, it has confirmed the approach of administrative courts regarding the limits of consistent interpretation, which rely very often on the literal (textual, grammatical) method of interpretation of Polish provisions, treating as subsidiary other methods of interpretation as available in the Polish legal theory. Such an approach, unfortunately, has been petrified in administrative courts due to the fact that the presented judgment is widely referred to in case-law (in the context of the *contra legem* limitation of consistent interpretation). It seems that the modification of such an approach into one taking due account of other methods of interpretation (stemming from domestic legal theory) is a great challenge for administrative courts. It has already been expressed and supported in the legal writing that a literal (textual, grammatical) interpretation shall not be treated as a primary one and that all other methods as only subsidiary; in addition, the limits of consistent interpretation in the *contra legem* results shall not be understood as results of a literal interpretation only.[87] It is worth explaining that, in Polish legal theory (in particular the theory of interpretation), priority had been given to the grammatical interpretation, reflected by the principle *interpretation cessat in claris.* The situation has changed already, as the latest theories of interpretation question this principle. Still, in the case-law of administrative courts, the priority of grammatical interpretation is well established, and it seems more time is necessary to adjust their position on this point. Still, this is not an easy issue and is discussed in the legal writing.[88]

86 Judgment of the SAC of 13 May 2008, case I FSK 600/07; confirmed in judgments of the SAC: of 25 June 2008, case I FSK 743/07 and of 23 March 2009, case I FPS 6/08.

87 A. Sołtys, *Obowiązek wykładni prawa krajowego zgodnie z prawem unijnym jako instrument zapewniania efektywności prawa Unii Europejskiej* [The Obligation to Interpret National Law in Conformity with EU Law as an Instrument to Ensure Effectiveness of EU Law], Wolters Kluwer Polska, 2015, pp. 544–547.

88 See further R. Wiatrowski, *Wykładnia prounijna Naczelnego Sądu Administracyjnego w zakresie przepisów dotyczących podatku od towarów i usług* [The Consistent Interpretation of Rules Regarding VAT by the Supreme Administrative Court], Wolters Kluwer Polska, 2021, pp. 121–125.

Secondly, the SAC, in its judgments in cases I FSK 600/07 and I FPS 6/08, somehow equated *contra legem* limit of consistent interpretation with the prohibition of imposing an obligation on an individual as a result of consistent interpretation. Such a position seems not to have any grounds in the case-law of the Court of Justice, which has consequently held that consistent interpretation may not lead to 'effect of determining or aggravating the liability in criminal law of persons who act in contravention of the provisions of that directive'.[89] The consistent interpretation is not excluded in other cases, when it would result in aggravation of a situation of an individual in a particular proceeding, in particular in imposing an obligation.[90] It is worth adding that such a position of administrative courts reflects a more general issue of the proper distinction between consistent interpretation and direct effect of EU law as two different tools to ensure *effet utile* of EU law. It seems in this context that SAC, when examining the possibility of imposing an obligation on an individual, equated the results of direct effect (when the imposition of such an obligation, directly on the basis of an EU Directive provision, is prohibited) with the results of consistent interpretation (when such an imposition would be admissible). Again, it is worth noticing that the discussion on the possibility of aggravation of the situation of an individual is still present in legal writing.[91]

In this context, it is also worth noticing that administrative courts have problems with the imposition of an obligation on individuals only when the consistent interpretation is used as a tool to resolve a conflict between a national provision and EU law. Such doubts and limits are not considered when consistent interpretation is used as a tool to ensure that terms used in national provisions adopted to transpose EU law are interpreted in a way consistent with the terms applied in a given EU legal act. The following analyses confirm such a conclusion.

Consequences of the consistent interpretation

The results of consistent interpretation by an administrative court may relate to the functioning of administrative courts or a legal situation of an individual (the entity's complaining about the actions of an administrative authority).

89 Case 80/86, Kolpinghuis Nijmegen, EU:C:1987:431.

90 Again for further reading, see A. Sołtys, *Obowiązek wykładni prawa krajowego zgodnie z prawem unijnym jako instrument zapewniania efektywności prawa Unii Europejskiej* [The Obligation to Interpret National Law in Conformity with EU Law as an Instrument to Ensure Effectiveness of EU Law], Wolters Kluwer Polska, 2015, pp. 387–392; R. Wiatrowski, *Wykładnia prounijna Naczelnego Sądu Administracyjnego w zakresie przepisów dotyczących podatku od towarów i usług* [The Consistent Interpretation of Rules Regarding VAT by the Supreme Administrative Court], Wolters Kluwer Polska, 2021, p. 97.

91 A. Sołtys does not exclude such possibility, R. Wiatrowski presents arguments on the basis of VAT cases, pp. 134–140.

Consequences from the perspective of administrative courts

An example of consistent interpretation leading to changing the interpretation applied by the SAC, so far, is the change in approach to VAT taxation of leasing services and insurance services. In the resolution of the seven judges, the SAC held that (in the legal situation applicable in 2006) the entity providing leasing services should include, in the taxable amount of those services, the costs of insuring the leased item, since the insurance service together with the leasing service constitute a comprehensive service, subject to taxation at the relevant rate.[92] At the same time, one of the adjudicating panels of the SAC referred to the Court of Justice the preliminary questions on whether the leasing insurance and the leasing service should be treated together or as distinct services subject to separate taxation.[93] The Court of Justice decided, in the *BGŻ* judgment, that, essentially, those services should be treated separately, but 'where the lessor insures the leased item itself and re-invoices the exact cost of the insurance to the lessee, such a transaction constitutes . . . an insurance transaction within the meaning of Article 135(1)(a) of Council Directive 2006/112/EC'.[94]

Consequences from the perspective of individuals

The application of the interpretation, in conformity with EU law, may, in particular, lead to a change in the scope of an application of a provision. It is also worth noting that these may be administrative decisions or tax interpretations. However, this is not important from the point of view of determining what the consequences of interpretation in conformity with EU law are. Thus, the application of consistent interpretation in the course of the judicial review of the administrative authorities' rulings (administrative decisions) may result in 1) conclusion that an individual is not under obligation of an administrative nature (e.g., no tax liabilities); 2) conclusion that an individual is under obligation of an administrative nature (e.g., tax liabilities).

The determination of the absence of obligations of an administrative nature

Firstly, finding that an entity concerned is not subject to tax liability may result from the recognition of the fact that the entity concerned is not a taxable person at all, for example, for VAT purposes. An example of such a result is

92 Resolution of seven judges of the SAC of 8 November 2010, case I FPS 3/10.

93 Order of the SAC of 7 April 2011, case I FSK 460/10.

94 Case C-224/11, *BGŻ*, EU:C:2013:15; for discussion, see further A.-L. Mosbrucker, Exonération de TVA. La refacturation des prestations d'assurance portant sur un bien fourni en crédit-bail est exonérée de TVA, *Europe,* 2013 Mars Comm. no. 3 p. 34; W. Peperkorn, Einstufung einer Versicherungsleistung im Zusammenhang mit einer Leasingleistung als eigenständige steuerbefreite Leistung, *European Law Reporter*, 2013, pp. 157–163.

the aforementioned case of recognising that municipal budgetary entities are not VAT-taxable persons. Administrative courts have adopted such a position as the result of the interpretation of Article 15 (1) and (2) of the VAT Law in the light of the interpretation of Article 9 (1) of the Directive 2006/112 made by the Court of Justice in the *Gmina Wrocław* judgment.[95] The administrative courts consistently accepted that the municipal budgetary entities were not VAT-taxable persons.[96] Similarly, in the case-law of administrative courts mentioned before, relating to the activities taken by the associations of municipalities or by municipalities, consistent interpretation led to the conclusion that the municipality or the association of municipalities, when taking certain activities (e.g., collecting fees from carriers for using stops and stations, performing tasks in the area of education, such as organising catering for children in the kindergarten and organising canteens) was not a VAT-taxable person, and therefore, those activities were not taxable.[97]

Secondly, the exclusion of the existence of tax liability may result from the adoption of the legal classification of given services provided by a taxable person (e.g., a registered VAT-taxable person) or the legal classification of the activities taken by an entity (regardless of whether it is a taxable person or not). The example in this category of rulings, where consistent interpretation has been used, is the case, in which the SAC was hearing the dispute between a company and a tax administration authority relating to VAT on engineering services. That dispute concerned the legal classification of the services provided by that company affecting the place of taxation of such services. Kronospan Mielec, a company with its registered office in Poland, provided, for a customer established in Cyprus, services in the field of technical investigations and analyses and carried out research and development work in the fields of natural sciences and technology. These services encompassed the investigation and measurement of emissions, including the conduct of investigations relating to emissions of carbon dioxide (CO_2) and trading in CO_2 emissions, the preparation and checking of documentation in relation to such work, and the analysis of potential sources of pollution linked to the manufacture of goods consisting mainly of wood. This work

95 Case C-276/14, EU:C:2015:635; for discussion see further D. Dominik-Ogińska, Gmina Wroclaw, Treatment of a Municipal Budgetary Entity as a Taxable Person. Criterion of Independence. Court of Justice, *Highlights & Insights on European Taxation*, 2015, no. 11, pp. 58–65; A.-L. Mosbrucker, Qualité d'assujetti à la TVA, *Europe*, 2015 Novembre Comm. no. 11, pp. 37–38; T. Küffner, Keine Unternehmereigenschaft einer wirtschaftlich tätigen haushaltsgebundenen kommunalen Einrichtung einer Gemeinde wegen fehlender Selbständigkeit, *Umsatzsteuer-Rundschau*, 2015, pp. 834–835; F. Klenk, Können einzelne Betriebe von Personen des öffentlichen Rechts Unternehmer sein? – Folgerungen aus dem EuGH-Urteil Gmina Wrocław, *Umsatzsteuer-Rundschau*, 2016, pp. 180–183.

96 For example, judgment of the SAC of 30 October 2018, case I FSK 2008/15.

97 Judgment of the VAC in Cracow of 21 January 2014, case I SA/Kr 1677/13; judgments of the SAC of 9 June 2017, cases: I FSK 1317/15 and I FSK 1271/15; recently also judgment of the SAC of 25 February 2021, case I FSK 1899/18.

is carried out with the objective of acquiring new knowledge and new technological know-how aimed at the production of new substances, products, and systems and the application of new technological procedures to production processes. If those services were considered 'services of engineers' in the meaning of Article 9 (2) (e), the third indent of Directive 77/388, they would not be taxable in Poland since, according to the aforementioned provision of the Directive, they should be taxable in the State of the [customer] (in this case in Cyprus). That was the position taken by the applicant company. On the other hand, if those services were considered 'scientific' services in the meaning of Article 9 (2) (c), the first intend, as claimed by the tax administration authority, then the company would be taxable in Poland, in accordance with the rule laid down in that provision, according to which the services are taxable at the place, where those services are carried out. In order to resolve doubts in relation to the interpretation of the provisions of Directive 77/388, the SAC referred a preliminary question to the Court of Justice,[98] as a result of which the CJ classified the services at issue as 'services of engineers'.[99] The SAC applied such an interpretation and held that the services at issue should be classified as services of engineers. Thus, the place where the services are supplied shall be the place where the recipient of the service has established its business, has a fixed establishment to which the service is supplied or, in the absence of such a place, the place where it has its permanent address or normal residence, pursuant to Article 27 (4) (3) read in conjunction with (3) of the VAT Law in the version applicable until 31 December 2009.[100] As a result of consistent interpretation, the applicant company was not subject to the obligation to pay VAT on the territory of Poland.

Yet, in another case, the consistent interpretation led to the conclusion that a private person is not liable to pay VAT at all, since the sale made by him or her is not a taxable transaction. The dispute between a private person and the tax administration authority, related to the issue of charging VAT on selling by a private person of parts of land, which earlier had been used for the purposes of an agricultural activity but after the modification of the urban management plan could be used for a holiday home development. The plots were sold to natural persons on an occasional and non-organised basis. According to the persons selling plots of land, it was the sale of private property, and, therefore, the sale of such immovable property could not be treated as economic activity in the meaning of the VAT Law (and thus not subject to VAT). The tax administration authority presented the opposite opinion. When the SAC in the cassation proceedings referred for clarification on this issue,[101]

98 Order of the SAC of 23 April 2009, case I FSK 185/08.
99 Case C-222/09, *Kronospan Mielec*, EU:C:2010:593.
100 Judgment of 15 December 2010, case I FSK 1503/10.
101 Order of the SAC of 9 March 2010, case I FSK 2039/08.

the Court of Justice provided extensive explanations on the classification of a taxable person for value-added tax purposes in the meaning of Article 9 (1) of Directive 2006/112. It indicated in which situation such a person could not be considered a taxable person (within the scope of the management of the private property of that person), and when he or she should be recognised as such (taking active steps, for the purpose of concluding those sales, to market property by mobilising resources similar to those deployed by a producer, a trader, or a person supplying services within the meaning of the second sub-para. of Article 9 (1) of Directive 2006/112). The SAC, applying the standard for interpretation included in the judgment of the Court of Justice, found that it was important to assess the facts at issue and to determine whether an applicant, in order to sell land, 1) took active steps to market property by mobilising resources similar to those deployed by a producer, a trader, or a person supplying services within the meaning of Article 15 (2) of the VAT Law (transposing Article 9 (1) of Directive 2006/112), which results in the need to consider that he/she was an entity carrying out 'economic activity' in the meaning of that provision, thus, as a taxable person for the purposes of the value-added tax, or if 2) the sale occurred within the scope of the management of the private property [of that person]. The SAC also pointed out that the professionalisation of the immoveable property sale could be evidenced by taking such activities as land development, delimitation of internal roads, and marketing activities undertaken to sell plots of land, going beyond the usual forms of advertising, in addition to obtaining a decision on the conditions of land development before the sale, or requesting for the preparation of the spatial development plan for the area being sold, in particular, in a situation where the seller has already been a taxable person for the purposes of the construction and development of other such services of the similar nature.[102] Such interpretation of Polish legal provisions, transposing Article 9 (1) and (12) of Directive 2006/112, resulted in considering the applicants not to be liable to pay value-added tax.

Thirdly, consistent interpretation may lead to covering a given individual with tax exemption or exclusion. An example, in this respect, is the issue of recognising a limited joint-stock partnership as a capital company within the meaning of Directive 2008/7/EC that was mentioned before. As a result of applying consistent interpretation and, thus, providing the term 'capital company', adopted for the purposes of applying the Law on the Tax on Civil Law Transactions, the possibility of exercising the exemption from that taxation in the event of carrying out, by the company, one of the transactions provided for in that Law, was recognised.[103]

102 Judgment of the SAC of 15 December 2011, case I FSK 1695/11.

103 Judgment of the VAC in Cracow of 17 November 2015, case I SA/Kr 1540/15; in the same vein judgments of the SAC: of 9 March 2016, case II FSK 4006/13, of 19 April 2016, case II FSK 987/14.

Interpretation leading to the imposition of an obligation of administrative nature

The interpretation can also lead to the imposition of an obligation of administrative nature on the individual.

Firstly, such imposition may be the result of the recognition of an entity as a taxable person. An example, in this regard, could be the consistent interpretation of Article 15 (1) and (2) of the VAT Law, taking into consideration Article 9 (1) of Directive 2006/112 and its CJ interpretation by SAC in the judgment, in which it was assumed that the municipality should be treated as a taxable person, when it traded in immovable property acquired through the so-called municipalisation of the State property, even if the municipality, as regards of trading in that immovable property, did not take activities similar to an entity trading in real estate.[104] Consequently, in such cases, the tax liability is imposed on the municipality.

Secondly, an obligation imposed on an individual may result from recognising the fact that certain services are subject to taxation or transactions are subject to taxation. For example, the SAC was dealing with the issue of considering whether a transfer of ownership of immovable property belonging to a taxable person for value-added tax purposes to the Public Treasury of a Member State, where the same person simultaneously represented the expropriating authority and the municipality that is the subject of the expropriation and where the latter continues the practical management of the relevant property, was to be considered as a transaction subject to value-added tax, even if the payment of compensation has been made only by means of an internal accounting transfer within the budget of the municipality. As a result of a question referred by SAC,[105] the Court of Justice confirmed such an interpretation of Article 2 (1) (a) and Article 14 (2) (a) of Directive 2006/112. The application of the provision of the Polish Law implementing the provisions of Directive 2006/112 led to the conclusion that the transaction concluded by the VAT-taxable person was liable to VAT.[106]

The SAC, in another case, found that the transfer by a limited company to one of its shareholders, of the ownership of immovable property, made as consideration for the buy-back, by that limited company, under a mechanism for the redemption of shares provided for in national legislation, of shares held in its share capital by that shareholder, constituted a supply of goods for consideration subject to value added tax.[107] In this case, the SAC accepted the interpretation of Polish Law consistent with the interpretation of Article 2 (1)(a) of Directive 2006/112 adopted by the CJ, which held that such a transaction was 'a supply of goods for consideration subject to value added tax, provided

104 Judgment of the SAC of 31 January 2019, case I FSK 1588/16.
105 Order of the SAC of 14 September 2016, case I FSK 1857/13.
106 Judgment of the SAC of 16 May 2019, case I FSK 1857/13.
107 Judgment of the SAC of 20 February 2019, case I FSK 1048/15.

that that immovable property is used in the economic activity of that limited company'.[108] Consequently, adopting consistent interpretation led to recognising that there was tax liability on the part of the taxable person.

Recently, the Court of Justice declared that the transformation of the right of perpetual usufruct into full immovable property ownership rights provided for by national legislation against payment of a fee constitutes a supply of goods within the meaning of Article 14 (2) of Directive 2006/112 and that where the transformation of the right of perpetual usufruct into full immovable property ownership rights provided for by national legislation takes place against payment of a fee to the municipality which owns the property, enabling it to obtain income, therefrom, on a continuing basis that municipality, subject to the verifications to be made by the referring court, acts as a taxable person within the meaning of Article 9 (1) of that directive (and not as a public authority for the purposes of Article 13 (1) of that directive)[109] As a consequence, VAC in Wrocław (which asked for preliminary ruling in this case) decided that in a dispute between the municipality and tax administration authority, the first one was obliged to pay the tax due.[110]

Thirdly, consistent interpretation may lead to the exclusion of the right to exercise a tax exemption. One of the cases before the SAC related to the possibility of making use of the tax exemption provided for in the provision of the VAT Law, implementing Article 132 (1) (f) of Directive 2006/112, according to which Member States shall exempt

> the supply of services by independent groups of persons, who are carrying on an activity which is exempt from VAT or in relation to which they are not taxable persons, for the purpose of rendering their members the services directly necessary for the exercise of that activity, where those groups merely claim from their members exact reimbursement of their share of the joint expenses, provided that such exemption is not likely to cause distortion of competition.

The applicant company, active in the area of insurance and pension protection services in Europe, claimed that it could exercise that VAT exemption in a situation when it established a series of shared-services centres in a number of Member States. It was intended that those centres would provide the services which were directly necessary for carrying on the activity of insurance by the entities in that group, in particular services in the area of human resources,

108 Case C-421/17, *Polfarmex*, EU:C:2018:432; for discussion, see further H. Nieskens, Rückkauf von Aktien als Gegenleistung für eine Grundstücksübertragung, *EU-Umsatz-Steuerberater* 2018, no. 3, pp. 77–79; F. Grube, Friederike, Grundstücksübertragung von Aktiengesellschaft an Aktionär gegen Rückkauf seiner Aktien als steuerbare Lieferung – EuGH, Urt. v. 13.6.2018 – C-421/17, Polfarmex, *Mehrwertsteuerrecht*, 2018, pp. 649–652.

109 Case C-604/19, *Gmina Wrocław*, EU:C:2021:132.

110 Judgment of the VAC in Wrocław of 13 May 2021, case I SA/Wr 295/19.

financial and accounting services, information technology services, administrative services, customer services, and services connected with the creation of new products.

The Minister of Finance was of the opposite opinion and issued a tax interpretation that was later challenged to the administrative court. The SAC, hearing the case in the cassation proceedings, referred to the Court of Justice the preliminary questions, as regards the interpretation of the aforementioned provision of the Directive. However, the Court of Justice found that, in the situation such as that at issue before the administrative court, Article 132 (1)(f) of Directive 2006/112 had not been applicable at all. According to the CJ,

> the exemption provided for in that provision relates only to independent groups of persons whose members carry on an activity in the public interest referred to in Article 132 of that directive and that, therefore, the services supplied by independent groups of persons whose members carry on an economic activity in the area of insurance, which does not constitute such an activity in the public interest, are not entitled to that exemption.[111] Therefore, in that case, the consequence of the interpretation in conformity with EU law was the finding that the Company that had applied for a tax interpretation was not entitled to the exemption provided for in the provision of the VAT Law, implementing Article 132 (1)(f).[112]

111 Case C-605/15, *Aviva*, EU:C:2017:718; for discussion, see further H. Jacobs, Dienstleistungen, die selbständige Zusammenschlüsse von Personen an ihre Mitglieder erbringen – bestimmte, dem Gemeinwohl dienende Tätigkeiten – Anwendbarkeit auf das Versicherungswesen, *Umsatzsteuer-Rundschau*, 2017, pp. 804–805; R. Ismer, S. Piotrowski, Steuerbefreiung für Dienstleistungen selbständiger Zusammenschlüsse für ihre Mitglieder (Kostenteilungsgemeinschaft), *Mehrwertsteuerrecht*, 2017, pp. 834–836; T. Schneider, Umsatzsteuerbefreiung für Cost-Sharing Groups – Was bleibt nach den Entscheidungen des EuGH vom 21.9.2017?, *Betriebs-Berater*, 2017, pp. 2519–2524; O. Courjon, Comme un ouragan qui s'abat sur la finance . . . la CJUE a tout emporté !, *La Semaine Juridique – entreprise et affaires*, 2017, no. 41, pp. 52–54; A. Erdbrügger, Der EuGH versagt dem Finanzsektor die Umsatzsteuerbefreiung für Kostenteilungsgemeinschaften – Welche Auswirkungen ergeben sich für deutsche Banken und Versicherungen?, *Umsatzsteuer-Rundschau*, 2018, pp. 301–306; K. Lasiński-Sulecki, Zakres przedmiotowy zwolnienia usług świadczonych przez niezależne grupy osób – po wyrokach DNB Banka i Aviva [The Ratione Persone of Exemption of Services Provided by Independent Groups of Persons – After Judgments in DNB Banka and Aviva], *Przegląd Podatkowy*, 2018, no. 4, pp. 14–21; P. Pailler, Cour de justice, 4e ch., 21 septembre 2017, Minister Finansow c/ Aviva, aff. C-605/15, ECLI:EU:C:2017:718 – Cour de justice, 4e ch., 21 septembre 2017, « DNB Banka » AS c/ Valsts ienemumu dienests, aff. C-326/15, ECLI:EU:C:2017:719 – Cour de justice, 4e ch., 21 septembre 2017, Commission c/ RFA, aff. C-616/15, ECLI:EU:C:2017:721, case-law de la CJUE 2017, Bruylant, Bruxelles. Décisions et commentaires 2018, pp. 798–814.

112 The SAC in the judgment found the interpretation of the MF to be correct, although in fact it was based on a different argument, judgment of 11 December 2018, case I FSK 906/14.

In addition, in a number of rulings issued by administrative courts, a consistent interpretation of the following terms 'private pleasure craft and private pleasure-flying' used in the Excise Duty Law had been applied for the purposes of tax exemption. The adoption of consistent interpretation of Article 32 (1) (1) and (2) of that Law, in the light of Article 14 (1) (b) of Directive 2003/96 in numerous rulings was the reason for recognising that fuel purchased by the company for an aircraft, used to transport its own employees in the course of its business, was not exempted from the excise duty (provided for in the aforementioned provisions of the Excise Duty Law.[113]

Conclusions

The analysis of the case-law of the administrative courts, in the years 2004 to 2021, leads to the conclusion that those courts, since the moment of the accession of Poland to the European Union, have accepted, without hesitation, their obligation of consistent interpretation in such a form and to the extent that results from the case-law of the Court of Justice of the European Union (CJEU).

The Supreme Administrative Court respects the obligation of consistent interpretation and recognises the reference to the principle of primacy and the refusal to apply national provisions as a last resort. The SAC assumes that the effectiveness of EU law should be ensured, in the first place, using the interpretation of national law in conformity with EU law and, should it be necessary to choose the interpretation method, priority should be given to such an interpretation that will guarantee the useful effect of EU legislation provisions. Conversely, when a conflict between the EU and national rules cannot be remedied by consistent interpretation, a national court, in accordance with the principles of primacy (supremacy) and direct effect of EU law, is obliged to refuse to apply a provision of national law that is contrary to an EU provision more favourable to an individual.[114]

Administrative courts correctly accept that the obligation of consistent interpretation has a very extensive scope since it covers all the provisions of national law and, at the same time, arises in all 'EU cases'. As the SAC ruled in one of their judgments,

> The consistent interpretation can be applied, where the issue concerned is governed by [EU] law (the [EU] case). When interpreting a national provision in conformity with EU provision the first one should be compared with the standard resulting from the latter. The conformity with

113 Judgment of the SAC of 22 January 2020, case I GSK 2015/19 (earlier in this vein judgments of SAC of 7 September 2017 in cases: I GSK 1225/15 and I GSK 1233/15).

114 Judgments of the SAC: of 14 January 2010, case II FSK 2018/09; of 16 March 2011, case I FSK 1588/10.

> [EU] law means the conformity with: the rules resulting from the established standard of that law, which is statutory law (primary and secondary), the objectives of [EU] law expressed in the Treaties, as well as – the preambles, protocols and annexes to an act applicable in a given case. When constructing the standard for [EU] law, account should be also taken of the CJEU's case-law, that creates understanding of rules concerned and develops the general principles. When reconstructing the meaning of such a standard, account should be taken of the CJEU's case-law (inter alia, on the basis of Article 234 TEC) as far as it contains the interpretation of EU law.[115]

What is more, it is recognised, in the SAC case-law, that the principle of interpreting national law, in conformity with EU law, is intended both to unify all legislation in a given State and to ensure that EU law is duly effective.[116]

In comparison with the case-law of the Supreme Court, there is a significant difference in the choice of the method of the resolution of a conflict between a national provision and EU law. As was stated earlier, the wide use of consistent interpretation by the Supreme Court can be explained by the limitations placed upon its application in proceedings between individuals. As most of the cases, resolved by the Supreme Court, concern disputes between private parties, consistent interpretation remains the primary way to ensure *effet utile* of EU law. Whereas cases resolved by administrative courts concern unique disputes between individuals and administrative bodies, which enables them to ensure *effet utile* of EU law with the use of principles of primacy and direct effect.

The administrative courts correctly accept that the obligation of consistent interpretation has a very extensive scope, since it covers all provisions of national law and, at the same time, arises in all 'EU cases'. As the SAC ruled in one of the judgments

> The consistent interpretation can be applied, where the issue concerned is governed by [EU] law (the [EU] case). The conformity with Union law means conformity with the rules resulting from the established standard of that law, which is statutory law (primary and secondary), the objectives of Union law expressed in the Treaties, as well as the preambles, protocols, and annexes to an act applicable in a given case. When constructing the standard of EU law, applicable for consistent interpretation, the case-law of the CJEU should be taken into account (*inter alia*, on the basis of Article 267 TFEU) as far as it contains interpretation of EU law.[117]

115 Judgment of the SAC of 2 April 2009, case I FSK 4/08.
116 Judgment of the SAC of 22 January 2020, case I GSK 2015/19.
117 Judgment of the SAC of 2 April 2009, case I FSK 4/08.

What is more, it is recognised, in the SAC case-law, that the principle of interpreting national law in conformity with EU law is intended both to unify all legislation in a given State and to ensure that EU law is duly effective.[118]

Taking these into consideration, two contexts of consistent interpretation can be distinguished: 1) interpretation in order to ensure that the terms used in national provisions adopted to transpose EU law are interpreted in a way that is consistent with the terms applied in a given EU legal act, and 2) interpretation in order to resolve a conflict between a provision of national law and a provision of EU law. The analyses of case-law of administrative courts lead to the conclusion that the use of consistent interpretation prevails in the first of the situations presented, that is, to ensure the full effectiveness of the provisions of EU law.

In the declarative sphere, administrative courts accept the limitations of consistent interpretation resulting from established case-law that

> the obligation on a national court to refer to the content of a directive when interpreting and applying the relevant rules of domestic law is limited by general principles of law, . . . and that obligation cannot serve as the basis for an interpretation of national law *contra legem*.[119]

Those two limitations of consistent interpretation are referred to by administrative courts, in particular the SAC,[120] listing, among the general principles of law (following case-law of the Court of Justice), the principle of legal certainty and the principle of non-retroactivity.[121] In addition, the administrative courts in many rulings provide that 'there is no obligation of interpretation, if it was to lead to a denial or rejection of national law, thus, to interpretation *contra legem*'.[122]

The analysis of the judicial practice reveals that there are still some challenges before administrative courts in terms of the understanding and application of the *contra legem* exception, when consistent interpretation is a tool to resolve a conflict between a provision of national law and a provision of EU law. Administrative courts currently rely mostly on the literal (textual, grammatical) method of interpretation of Polish provisions, ignoring other methods of interpretation, available in the Polish legal theory. Such an approach,

118 Judgment of the SAC of 22 January 2020, case I GSK 2015/19.

119 Case 80/86, *Kolpinghuis Nijmegen*, EU:C:1987:431; case C-212/04, *Adeneler*, EU:C:2006:443; case C-282/10, *Dominguez*, EU:C:2012:33.

120 For example, judgments of the SAC of 8 October 2014, case I FSK 1512/13; of 14 May 2015, case I FSK 382/14.

121 For example, judgments of the SAC: of 29 March 2018, case I FSK 1069/15; of 4 April 2015, case I FSK 1872/14; of 2 July 2019, case I FSK 119/17.

122 For example, judgment of the SAC: of 8 January 2009, case I FSK 1798/07; of 5 February 2009, case I FSK 1880/07; of 27 May 2009, I FSK 358/08; of 8 May 2009, I FSK 1509/08.

unfortunately, has been petrified in administrative courts as the presented judgment is widely referred to in case-law (in the context of the *contra legem* limitation of consistent interpretation). This issue has, however, been thoroughly analysed in Polish literature, in terms of the interrelation of consistent interpretation (obligation stemming from the EU law), and national methods of interpretation (stemming from the domestic legal theory). It has already been stated that a literal (textual, grammatical) interpretation shall not be a primary one (whereas all other methods shall be only subsidiary) and that the limits of consistent interpretation in the *contra legem* results shall not be understood as the results of a literal interpretation only.[123]

Secondly, the SAC in the aforementioned judgment somehow equated *contra legem* limit of consistent interpretation with the prohibition of imposing an obligation on an individual as a result of consistent interpretation. Such a position seems not to have any grounds in the case-law of the Court of Justice, which consequently held that consistent interpretation may not lead to 'effect of determining or aggravating the liability in criminal law of persons who act in contravention of the provisions of that directive'.[124] The consistent interpretation is not excluded in other cases, when it would result in the aggravation of a situation of an individual in a specific proceeding, in particular in imposing an obligation.[125]

At the same time, administrative courts do not have any problems with imposing obligations (in particular tax liability) as a result of consistent interpretation, as a tool for interpretation, in order to ensure that terms, used in national provisions adopted to transpose EU law, are interpreted in a way consistent with the terms applied in a given EU legal act.

Literature

Bartosiewicz A., Kubacki R., Glosa do wyroku TK z 7 listopada 2007 r., K 18/06, *Europejski Przegląd Sądowy*, 2008, no. 11, pp. 42–49.

Bartosiewicz A., Kubacki R., Odliczenie podatku od samochodów osobowych i paliwa do nich – glosa do wyroku ETS z 22.12.2008 r. w sprawie C-414/07 Magoora przeciwko Dyrektorowi Izby Skarbowej w Krakowie [Commentary on Judgment of the CJEU C-414/07 Magoora], *Europejski Przegląd Sądowy*, 2009, no. 9, pp. 47–55.

Biernat S., Wykładnia prawa krajowego w zgodzie z prawem Wspólnoty Europejskiej [Interpretation of National Law in Conformity with Law of the European Community], in C. Mik (ed.), *Implementacja prawa integracji europejskiej w krajowych*

123 A. Sołtys, *Obowiązek wykładni prawa krajowego zgodnie z prawem unijnym jako instrument zapewniania efektywności prawa Unii Europejskiej* [The Obligation to Interpret National Law in Conformity with EU Law as an Instrument to Ensure Effectiveness of EU Law], Warszawa Wolters Kluwer Polska, 2015, pp. 544–547.

124 Case 80/86 Kolpinghuis Nijmegen, EU:C:1987:431.

125 Again for further reading, see A. Sołtys, *Obowiązek wykładni prawa krajowego zgodnie z prawem unijnym jako instrument zapewniania efektywności prawa Unii Europejskiej* [The Obligation to Interpret National Law in Conformity with EU Law as an Instrument to Ensure Effectiveness of EU Law], Wolters Kluwer Polska, 2015, pp. 387–392.

porządkach prawnych [Implementation of Law of European Integration into National Legal Orders], TNOIK, 1998.

Courjon O., Comme un ouragan qui s'abat sur la finance . . . la CJUE a tout emporté !, *La Semaine Juridique – entreprise et affaires*, 2017, no. 41, pp. 52–54.

Dominik-Ogińska D., Gmina Wroclaw, Treatment of a Municipal Budgetary Entity as a Taxable Person. Criterion of Independence, Court of Justice, *Highlights & Insights on European Taxation*, 2015, no. 11, pp. 58–65.

Erdbrügger A., Der EuGH versagt dem Finanzsektor die Umsatzsteuerbefreiung für Kostenteilungsgemeinschaften – Welche Auswirkungen ergeben sich für deutsche Banken und Versicherungen?, *Umsatzsteuer-Rundschau*, 2018, pp. 301–306.

Grube F., Grundstücksübertragung von Aktiengesellschaft an Aktionär gegen Rückkauf seiner Aktien als steuerbare Lieferung – EuGH, Urt. v. 13.6.2018 – C-421/17, Polfarmex, *Mehrwertsteuerrecht*, 2018, pp. 649–652.

Heinrichshofen S., Einschränkung des Vorsteuerabzugs, *EU-Umsatz-Steuerberater*, 2009, pp. 5–6.

Heinrichshofen S., Feste Niederlassung i.S.v. Art. 44 MwStSystRL, *EU-Umsatz-Steuerberater*, 2014, pp. 70–71.

Hofstätter I., Einschränkung des Vorsteuerabzugs auf den Kauf von Kraftstoffen, *European Law Reporter*, 2009, pp. 109–111.

Ismer R., Piotrowski S., Steuerbefreiung für Dienstleistungen selbständiger Zusammenschlüsse für ihre Mitglieder (Kostenteilungsgemeinschaft), *Mehrwertsteuerrecht*, 2017, pp. 834–836.

Jacobs H., Dienstleistungen, die selbständige Zusammenschlüsse von Personen an ihre Mitglieder erbringen – bestimmte, dem Gemeinwohl dienende Tätigkeiten – Anwendbarkeit auf das Versicherungswesen, *Umsatzsteuer-Rundschau*, 2017, pp. 804–805.

Jovanovic N., Merkx M., Welmory, A Recipe for VAT Avoidance? *EC Tax Review*, 2015, pp. 202–209.

Klenk F., Können einzelne Betriebe von Personen des öffentlichen Rechts Unternehmer sein? – Folgerungen aus dem EuGH-Urteil Gmina Wrocław, *Umsatzsteuer-Rundschau*, 2016, pp. 180–183.

Kollmann J., Turcan L., Turić D., Spies K., Kann eine Webseite eine 'feste Niederlassung' begründen? *Ecolex*, 2015, pp. 812–813.

Krzywoń A., Glosa do postanowienia Sądu Najwyższego z dnia 28 listopada 2013 r. (sygn. akt I KZP 15/13) [Commentary to the Order of the Supreme Court of 28 November 2013, I KSP 15/13], *Zeszyty Naukowe Sądownictwa Administracyjnego*, 2014, no. 1, pp. 163–168.

Krzywoń A., Glosa do wyroku TK z dnia 13 października 2010 r., Kp 1/09, *Przegląd Sejmowy*, 2011, no. 5, pp. 133–143.

Küffner T., Keine Unternehmereigenschaft einer wirtschaftlich tätigen haushaltsgebundenen kommunalen Einrichtung einer Gemeinde wegen fehlender Selbständigkeit, *Umsatzsteuer-Rundschau*, 2015, pp. 834–835.

Lasiński-Sulecki K., Czego nowego dowiedzieliśmy się o stałym miejscu prowadzenia działalności gospodarczej?: Wyrok TS, C-547/18, Dong Yang Electronics Sp. z o.o. przeciwko Dyrektorowi Izby Administracji Skarbowej we Wrocławiu [What New Can We Find Out About Fixed Establishment?: Judgment of the CJEU, C-547/18, Dong Yang Electronics], *Przegląd Podatkowy*, 2020, no. 9, pp. 13–19.

Lasiński-Sulecki K., Zakres przedmiotowy zwolnienia usług świadczonych przez niezależne grupy osób – po wyrokach DNB Banka i Aviva [The Ratione Persone of Exemption of Services Provided by Independent Groups of Persons – After Judgments in DNB Banka and Aviva], *Przegląd Podatkowy*, 2018, no. 4, pp. 14–21.

Machalski M., Analiza pojęcia stałego miejsca prowadzenia działalności gospodarczej, z uwzględnieniem praktyki organów podatkowych po wyroku TSUE ws. C-605/12 (Welmory) – zarys problemu [The Analysis of 'Fixed Establishment' with Due Regard of Tax Authorities' Practice After the Judgment of the CJEU in C-605/12 Welmory], *Przegląd Ustawodawstwa Gospodarczego*, 2019, no. 3, pp. 154–159.

Mastalski R., Glosa do wyroku NSA z dnia 9 czerwca 2017 r., I FSK 1271/15 [Commentary to the SAC Judgment of 9 June 2017, I FSK 1271/15], *Orzecznictwo Sądów Polskich*, 2018, no. 7–8, pp. 224–238.

Miąsik D., Sąd Najwyższy – Postanowienie Sądu Najwyższego z dnia 28 listopada 2013 r. (sygn. akt I KZP 15/13) [Commentary to the Order of the Supreme Court of 28 November 2013, I KSP 15/13], *Zeszyty Naukowe Sądownictwa Administracyjnego*, 2014, no. 1, pp. 122–133.

Mosbrucker A.-L., Exonération de TVA. La refacturation des prestations d'assurance portant sur un bien fourni en crédit-bail est exonérée de TVA, *Europe*, 2013 Mars Comm., no. 3, p. 34.

Mosbrucker A.-L., Qualité d'assujetti à la TVA, *Europe*, 2015 Novembre Comm., no. 11, pp. 37–38.

Nieskens H., Rückkauf von Aktien als Gegenleistung für eine Grundstücksübertragung, *EU-Umsatz-Steuerberater*, 2018, no. 3, pp. 77–79.

Nieskens H., Steuerbefreiung für Lieferung von Gebäuden – Begriff des Erstbezugs, *EU-Umsatz-Steuerberater*, 2018, pp. 20–21.

Pailler P., Cour de justice, 4e ch., 21 septembre 2017, Minister Finansow c/ Aviva, aff. C-605/15, ECLI:EU:C:2017:718 – Cour de justice, 4e ch., 21 septembre 2017, « DNB Banka » AS c/ Valsts ienemumu dienests, aff. C-326/15, ECLI:EU:C:2017:719 – Cour de justice, 4e ch., 21 septembre 2017, Commission c/ RFA, aff. C-616/15, ECLI: EU:C:2017:721, case-law de la CJUE 2017, Bruylant, Bruxelles. Décisions et commentaires, 2018, pp. 798–814.

Peperkorn W., Einstufung einer Versicherungsleistung im Zusammenhang mit einer Leasingleistung als eigenständige steuerbefreite Leistung, *European Law Reporter*, 2013, pp. 157–163.

Richter F., Welmory sp. z o.o. (Elmory) v. Dyrektor Izby Skarbowej w Gdansku, *Revue générale de fiscalité luxembourgeoise*, 2015, pp. 64–65.

Roset S., Notion de « règle technique », *Europe*, 2012 Octobre Comm. no. 10, p. 30.

Schneider T., Umsatzsteuerbefreiung für Cost-Sharing Groups – Was bleibt nach den Entscheidungen des EuGH vom 21.9.2017?, *Betriebs-Berater*, 2017, pp. 2519–2524.

Sołtys A., *Obowiązek wykładni prawa krajowego zgodnie z prawem unijnym jako instrument zapewniania efektywności prawa Unii Europejskiej* [The Obligation to Interpret National Law in Conformity with EU Law as an Instrument to Ensure Effectiveness of EU Law], Wolters Kluwer Polska, 2015.

Wiatrowski R., *Wykładnia prounijna Naczelnego Sądu Administracyjnego w zakresie przepisów dotyczących podatku od towarów i usług* [The Consistent Interpretation of Rules Regarding VAT by the Supreme Administrative Court], Wolters Kluwer Polska, 2021.

Wilk M., Dostawa budynków i budowli na gruncie VAT a pierwsze zasiedlenie w świetle wyroku Trybunału Sprawiedliwości z 16.11.2017 r., C-308/16, Kozuba Premium Selection sp. z o.o. przeciwko Dyrektorowi Izby Skarbowej w Warszawie [The Supply of the Building on the in the Context of VAT and First Occupation – in the Light of the Judgment of the CJEU in C-308/16 Kozuba Premium Selection], *Przegląd Podatkowy*, 2018, no. 2, pp. 40–46.

7 The principle of consistent interpretation in the case-law of the Constitutional Tribunal

Monika Domańska

Introduction

Polish law distributes the competencies to remove hierarchical inconsistencies from the legal system to various authorities and provides for different procedures, which are the basis for a range of rulings, for example, *erga omnes* rulings in the case of the Constitutional Tribunal or *inter partes* rulings, as far as the ordinary courts or administrative courts are concerned.

Taking these into consideration, it has to be emphasised that the competencies of the Constitutional Tribunal and the courts are partly complementary and partly overlapping in the context of examining the compliance of provisions (applied in respective cases) with higher rank rules. As a result of the accession of Poland to the European Union, the problem of (in)coherence of such a review system has, additionally, been intensified.

The accession of Poland to the EU was the ground for numerous doubts as to the relations between the Constitution of the Republic of Poland and EU law, in particular in the context of any possible conflict of rules and how they should be resolved. Although the Constitution of the Republic of Poland provides in Article 8 (1) that it is the supreme law of the Republic of Poland, however, Poland, by concluding accession treaties, assumed an obligation to comply with the entire EU law, in which the principle of the primacy over the national law of Member States is applicable. Thus, from the very beginning, the main problem, in this dimension, was the sphere of competence of the Constitutional Tribunal to interpret the EU law in the procedure of constitutional review of national law.[1]

1 Put differently, pluralism imposes upon both national and European legal order some obligation of mutual accommodation which requires some constitutional tolerance, see M. Poiares Maduro, Three Claims of Constitutional Pluralism, in: M. Avbelj, J. Komárek (eds.), *Constitutional Pluralism in the European Union and Beyond*, Hart Publishing, 2012, p. 82; see also F.C. Mayer, M. Wendel, Multilevel Constitutionalism and Constitutional Pluralism, in: M. Avbelj, J. Komárek (eds.), *Constitutional Pluralism in the European Union and Beyond*, Hart Publishing, 2012, pp. 138–139; J.H.H. Weiler, In Defence of the Status Quo: Europe's Constitutional Sonderweg, in: J.H.H. Weiler, M. Wind (eds.), *European Constitutionalism Beyond the State*, Cambridge University Press, 2003, pp. 18–20.

DOI: 10.4324/9781003376019-9

The Polish Constitutional Tribunal referred to the scope of its competencies, relating to the issue of examining the conformity of Polish law with EU law, as early as the judgment in case P 37/05,[2] in which the question of law was submitted as regards the compatibility of a provision of the Polish Act of 23 January 2004, the Excise Tax Law,[3] with the Treaty establishing the European Community. Ultimately, the CT decided to discontinue the proceedings on the grounds of inadmissibility of issuing a ruling. However, the Tribunal found, on the grounds that

> the exercise of competence to examine the compliance of a Law with international agreements was justified, . . . only if there were no other ways to remove the resulting conflict (e.g., if a rule of an international agreement was not a directly applicable rule), or that was of importance considering legal certainty (e.g., if the scope of application of an international rule overlapped completely with the scope of application of a statutory rule, and as a result, the latter would become normatively 'empty').
>
> Preference should be given to the removal of conflict between national and international rules at the level of application of the law by national courts. Putting the purely doctrinal considerations aside, the mechanism of removing the conflicts of rules at the level of the application of the courts is more operative and flexible than the constitutional review exercised by the Constitutional Tribunal and, from the systemic side, is justified by the fact that, usually, the rules of international law have a narrower scope of application than the national statutory law, whether in the temporal, material or personal aspects.[4]

It is worth noting that exercising the competencies of the CT in the area of consistent interpretation of Polish law with EU law is carried out under the circumstances of the conflict of rules, which should be understood as the situation resulting from the law system, under which 'compliance with or application of one rule leads inevitably to an infringement of the other or may result in such an infringement'.[5] Given the existing (and still progressing) complexity of the legal matter resulting from the co-applicability of the national and EU

2 Judgment of the CT of 19 December 2006, case P 37/05.

3 *Dz.U.* [Journal of Laws] No. 29, item 257 as amended.

4 This position is the confirmation that the Constitutional Tribunal limited partially its competences to examine the consistency of national law with EU law, in so far as they overlapped with the same powers of the courts. However, at the same time it held, that 'in view of the wording of Article 8 (1) of the Constitution, the Tribunal is obliged to such understanding of its position that, in essentials matters for the constitutional and systemic dimension, it will preserve the position of the 'court of the last word'.

5 H. Kelsen, Derogation, in: H. Kelsen, R. Marcic, H. Schambeck (eds.), *Die Wiener Rechtstheoretische Schule*, Wien, 1968, p. ii (1429).

legal systems in a Member State, the likelihood of such conflicts is constantly increasing and the analysis aimed at resolving the conflict of rules becomes even more complex, insofar as respective right is protected by more than one legal instrument. Several sources of protection of that right lead to a situation where *ratione personae*, *ratione materiae* (and even the territorial scope) usually do not coincide. What is more, the values and principles of the national law system may impose restrictions on the exercise of certain rights. On the other hand, the interpretation of rules by the Constitutional Tribunal is performed with particular emphasis on the values of a particular legal system. This means that the same principles or concepts may gain different meanings and significance in a different constitutional axiological environment. This reservation is also the main reason for the change in the direction of the jurisprudence of the CT in EU matters after 2015.

Implementation of the obligation of consistent interpretation by the Constitutional Tribunal

Source of the obligation

The membership of Poland in the EU has had a significant impact on the range of sources of law used by the Constitutional Tribunal in its review procedure of the constitutionality of norms. This applies to both the norm under review (i.e., the reviewed norm) and the reference norm (i.e., the reviewing norm). In turn, the content of Article 267 TFEU fundamentally limits the interpretative freedom of the Constitutional Tribunal concerning EU law and thus affects the scope of possibilities to remove collisions between the Polish Constitution and EU law. Whilst the Constitutional Tribunal has a wide range of competencies concerning establishing a consistent interpretation of Polish law within the framework of its review of the constitutionality of national law, the possibility to interpret EU law in a way that is consistent with the Polish constitution is limited.

However, the analysis should begin by emphasising that, even in the pre-accession period, the Tribunal repeatedly applied the rules resulting from the obligation to interpret national law in conformity with EU law, stressing the significance of this obligation both under the provisions of the Constitution, that is, Articles 9 and 91, and the articles of the Europe Agreement concluded by Poland (so in the judgment no. K 2/02).[6] The legitimacy of following the rules of the obligation of consistent interpretation has been linked by the Tribunal to the principle of favouring the process of European

6 'The case-law of the Constitutional Tribunal has already expressed the view several times that in a situation where Poland is bound by an association agreement, obliging Poland to adapt national law to Community law, efforts should be made to interpret the law (in the areas subject to adaptation) in accordance with the European standard', Judgment of the CT of 28 January 2003, case K 2/02.

integration. Although, at that time, the obligation to apply consistent interpretation had not yet been sanctioned by treaty provisions, the CT sought to ensure that the content of Polish legislation complied with the norms applicable in a united Europe, applying the principles arising from the ***acquis communautaire*** of the EU law. A clear example of the application of this instrument is also the judgment in case K 24/04,[7] in which it was emphasised that it is necessary to attempt to interpret the constitutional norms in such a way as to enable the influence of the organs of the Polish State, including the Parliament, on the enactment of EU law to be integrated into the existing constitutional framework of the Republic of Poland'. In the context of implementing the 'EU-law-friendly interpretation', the CT has focused more on the compatibility of the axiology of the EU and national law systems and the search for a common normative context at this level fulfilling this level the future obligation of a consistent interpretation. Crucial arguments of the CT were references to the shared constitutional values of Poland and the EU.

In the post-accession period, the obligation to apply consistent interpretation has been explicitly linked by the Constitutional Tribunal to both Articles 9 and 91 para. 1 of the Constitution and the provisions contained in its preamble (emphasising the identity of the values contained therein and the values guiding the functioning of the EU), in addition to Treaty provisions, in particular, the former Article 10 TEC.[8] The content of Article 234 of the EC Treaty (now Article 267 of the TFEU) identified the scope of norms subject to interpretation by the CJEU and those which were beyond the competence of the CJEU. In its judgment, delivered in case Kp 3/08,[9] the CT recognised that

> by ratifying the Treaty of Accession, the Republic of Poland approved the division of functions within the system of institutions of the European Communities and the European Union. The attribution to the Court of Justice of the European Communities of powers to interpret Community (Union) law and ensure its uniformity remains part of this division.

The Tribunal confirmed that the CJEU is an authorised observer of the correct understanding of the Treaties but it is not the only one. The interpretation of Union law, delivered by the CJEU, should be performed within the scope of competence and functions conferred thereupon by the Member

7 Judgment of the CT of 12 January 2005, case K 24/04.
8 Judgment of the CT of 2 July 2007, case K 41/05; judgment of the CT of 7 November 2007, case K 18/06; judgment of the CT of 24 November 2010, case K 32/09.
9 Judgment of the CT of 18 February 2009, case Kp 3/08.

States and should respect the principle of mutual loyalty of EU and Member States authorities.[10]

Since the judgment of the CT, in K 18/06, the principle of interpreting domestic law in a 'Europe-friendly' manner is phrased in the case-law of the Polish Constitutional Tribunal. The CT has developed a constitutional principle of EU-friendly interpretation of legislation, and it accepts that it can rely on Union law and the judgments handed down by the CJEU in interpreting the Polish constitution.[11] The CT accepted, in the case-law, that the obligation to interpret national law, in conformity with EU law, constitutes one of the foundations for the cohesion of the legal systems of the Member States with EU law. In the judgment of the Constitutional Tribunal in case SK 45/09,[12] it was emphasised that it would be difficult to assume that EU law would contain norms fully overlapping with the norms of Polish law.

> This is due to the differences in the way EU law is made, with the participation of all Member States, as well as the different nature of the two legal orders being compared (on the one hand, the law of the State, on the other, the law of an international organization.

The CT, referring to its earlier ruling (judgment of 11 May 2005, K 18/04, the Accession Treaty), stated that the subsystems of legal regulations, originating from different legislative centres, should co-exist based on mutually friendly interpretation and cooperative co-application and contradictions should be eliminated using interpretation respecting the relative autonomy of European and national law.[13] The CT emphasised that its competence to assess the constitutionality of an EU regulation should be treated as independent but at the same time as subsidiary to the jurisdiction of the CJEU.[14]

10 K. Wójtowicz, *Constitutional Courts and the European Union Law*, Wydawnictwo Sejmowe 2014, p. 90.

11 Judgment of the CT of 7 November 2007, case K 18/06; A. Bartosiewicz, R. Kubacki, Glosa do wyroku TK z 7 listopada 2007 r., K 18/06 [Commentary on the CT judgment of 7 November 2007, K 18/06], *Europejski Przegląd Sądowy* 2008, no. 11, pp. 42–49.

12 Judgment of the CT of 16 November 2011, case SK 45/09.

13 'The European Constitution, thus, is one legal system, composed of two complementary constitutional layers, the European and the national, which are closely interwoven and interdependent, one cannot be read and fully understood without regard to the other' – I. Pernice, Multilevel Constitutionalism in the European Union, *WHI Papers*, 2002, 5, p. 4. Polish doctrine – instead of many – see A. Sołtys, Cechy i charakter prawa unijnego oraz problem jego konstytucjonalizacji [Features and nature of EU law and the problem of its constitutionalization], in: S. Biernat (ed), *System Prawa Unii Europejskiej* [The EU Law System], C.H. Beck, 2020, pp. 237–289.

14 It is impossible to ignore the doctrinal view – expressed against the background of the above ruling – that the CT, by stressing the importance of the formula concerning 'cooperative

The cognition of the Constitutional Tribunal to consistent interpretation in the procedure for review of constitutionality of legal norms

The subjective scope of the obligation to apply consistent interpretation, from the point of view of the competence of the Constitutional Tribunal, is closely related to the issue of the so-called 'constitutional dialogue', in which the Constitutional Tribunal and the CJEU are involved. The interaction of these bodies, which creates a multicentric model of legal interpretation, should be carried out under conditions of mutual loyalty and openness to the co-existing legal systems. In the opinion of the Constitutional Tribunal, such dialogue is conditioned and possible due to the axiological consistency of the legal orders, that is, national law and EU law. In judgment K 32/09 (concerning the Lisbon Treaty), it was clearly stated that the values expressed in the Constitution of the Republic of Poland and the Lisbon Treaty determine the axiological identity of Poland and the European Union.

In this context, it is important, from the perspective of the effectiveness of the obligation to apply consistent interpretation,[15] as to the ways in which the CT understands the role played by the CJEU in ensuring the uniformity and effectiveness of EU law in the broadest sense. In the *Accession Treaty* judgment (K 18/04), the CT did not accept the pleas submitted to it concerning the incompatibility of Article 234 EC with the Polish Constitution. The position of the Tribunal was based, among other things, on the argument that the CJEU has exclusive jurisdiction to rule on the interpretation and validity of the EU law. According to the Constitutional Tribunal, the interpretation made by the CJEU should remain within the scope of the functions and competencies delegated by the Member States to the Communities (now the EU). Furthermore, it 'should correlate with the principle of subsidiarity, which determines the actions of the Community institutions and the Member States'.

Similarly, the way in which the Constitutional Tribunal expressed itself in judgment no. Kp 3/08[16] indicates that Poland has accepted the division of functions within the EU bodies, and an element of this division remains the

application', sent an 'invitation' of sorts to the CJEU to take more account of the Polish contribution to the European constitutional heritage and, at the same time, promised to respect Luxembourg's case-law on condition that the offer was accepted. K. Wojtyczek, Trybunał konstytucyjny w europejskim systemie konstytucyjnym [Constitutional Tribunal in the European constitutional system], *Przegląd Sejmowy*, 2009, no. 4, p. 191.

15 Relation of the principle of consistent interpretation to other principles of EU law, see D. Miąsik, *Zasady i prawa podstawowe. System Prawa Unii Europejskiej* [Principles and fundamental rights. System of EU Law], C.H. Beck, 2022, pp. 36–37.

16 Judgment of the CT of 18 February 2009, case Kp 3/08; B. Nita, Jurysdykcja TS w trzecim filarze UE. Glosa do wyroku TK z dnia 18 lutego 2009 r., Kp 3/08 [Jurisdiction of the Court of Justice in the third pillar of the EU. Commentary on the CT judgment of 18 February 2009, Kp 3/08], *Europejski Przegląd Sądowy*, 2010, no. 7, pp. 47–54; A. Grzelak, Glosa do wyroku TK z dnia 18 lutego 2009 r., Kp 3/08 [Commentary on the CT judgment of 18 February 2009, Kp 3/08], *Przegląd Sejmowy*, 2009, no. 4, pp. 205–215.

assignment of the interpretation of Community law and concern for its uniformity to the Court of Justice in Luxembourg. This obligation arises from international agreements ratified in conformity with (and based on) the Constitution, of which Article 234 TEC (now 267 TFEU) remains an element, in addition to the fact that the CJEU has jurisdiction to answer preliminary questions and give binding interpretations of acts of Community law.

The subjective scope, of the obligation to apply the consistent interpretation of the law, is, thus, closely linked to the material scope of that obligation and, in extreme cases, can lead to a potential conflict with regard to the assessment of the scope of application of EU law, which in turn affects the determination of the scope of the competence of the two Courts in a given case. As already noted, from an EU law perspective, the scope of application of EU law in cases of doubtful interpretation is decided by the CJEU. On the other hand, the Polish Constitutional Tribunal takes the view that the Polish Constitution guarantees it the position of a 'court of last resort'.

The essence of the constitutional dialogue, between national constitutional courts and the CJEU, also concerns the acceptance (or not) by a national constitutional court of the view that it is a court of the last instance within the meaning of Article 267 TFEU (under Article 234 EC) and, therefore, that it fulfils the conditions for making a preliminary reference to the CJEU. In this context, the position of the CT, in which it acknowledged the admissibility of referring questions for a preliminary ruling to the CJEU, is relevant to this analysis. This issue deserves emphasis, with regard to this position, invariably maintained over the years, and is currently undergoing a certain deformation, which is connected with a change in the view of the current composition of the Constitutional Tribunal as regards the scope of competencies delegated by the Republic of Poland to the European Union, and which has a direct impact on the application of Article 267 TFEU by the Constitutional Tribunal.

Referring to the established line of case-law, one should cite the position of the Constitutional Tribunal, expressed in case K 18/04 (The Accession Treaty), in which it was held that in a situation in which the CT decides to submit a preliminary question to the Court of Justice concerning the validity or content of an act of EU law, it should do so in a case in which, adjudicating on its compliance with the Constitution, it should apply EU law. This position was reflected in case K 61/13,[17] in which the Constitutional Tribunal referred to the CJEU as its first question for a preliminary ruling on the validity of EU law.[18] The Constitutional Tribunal argued that the national legislation was

17 Order of the CT of 7 July 2015, case K 61/13.

18 1) Is item 6 of Annex III to Council Directive 2006/112/EC of 28 November 2006 on the common system of value added tax (OJ 2006 L 347, p. 1. L EU L 347, 11 December 2006, p. 1, as amended), as amended by Council Directive 2009/47/EC of 5 May 2009 amending Directive 2006/112/EC as regards reduced rates of value added tax (OJ L 347, 11 December 2006, p. 1, as amended). L EU L 116, 9 May 2009, p. 18) is invalid because an essential procedural requirement that the European Parliament be consulted was infringed during the

challenged in the proceedings before implementing the provisions of Directive 2006/112/EC. The need to comply with EU law made it necessary for Poland to apply the norm VAT rate to the supply of books sent electronically. The basic rate differed from the reduced rate that applied to books on media. For this reason, the CJEU decided that the outcome of the case pending before the Constitutional Tribunal depended on the content of the ruling of the CJEU. On the grounds for the question referred, the CJEU also noted that, according to the case-law of the CJEU,

> where a national court enters into a dispute concerning European Union law and considers that a national provision is not only contrary to European Union law but is also unconstitutional, the fact that the declaration that a national law is unconstitutional is made by way of an action which must be brought before The CT does not deprive that court of the power, or of the obligation under Article 267 TFEU, to refer questions to the CJEU about the interpretation or validity of European Union law.[19]

The change in the position of the Constitutional Tribunal, regarding the effectiveness, expected by the EU order of the instrument of the question for a preliminary ruling, in addition to other means of protecting EU law available to the Constitutional Tribunal, was visible during the examination by the CT of the case P 7/20.[20] The position expressed in this judgment is the beginning of a new line of case-law.[21] The decision in case P 7/20 goes far beyond an

---

legislative process? Is Article 98 para. 1 of Directive 2006/112/EC, cited at 1, in conjunction with point 6 of Annex III thereto, invalid because it infringes the principle of fiscal neutrality, inasmuch as it excludes the application of reduced rates of taxation to books published in digital form and other electronic publications? By judgment of 7 March 2017 (reference C-390/15), the CJEU stated that 'an examination of the questions referred for a preliminary ruling has not revealed any element capable of affecting the validity' of the provisions of EU law invoked. Eventually, as a result of the withdrawal of the application by the applicant, the Constitutional Tribunal discontinued the proceedings (decision of 17 May 2017, case K 61/13).

19 Joint cases C-188/10 *Aziz Melki* and C-189/10 *Selim Abdeli*, EU:C:2010:363, para. 45.

20 Judgment of the CT of 14 July 2021.

21 It has to be underlined that this analysis of the case-law of Polish Constitutional Tribunal does not aim at a serious systemic crisis concerning the rule of law principle in Poland, which formally began at the end of 2015. For detailed analysis, see: M. Taborowski, *Mechanizmy ochrony praworządności państw członkowskich w prawie Unii Europejskiej. Studium przebudzenia systemu ponadnarodowego* [Mechanisms of protection of the rule of law of Member States in EU law. A study of the awakening of the supranational system], Wolters Kluwer Polska, 2019, p. 484. See also Report on the activities of Polish authorities after the rulings of the CJEU in case C-204/21 and in case C-791/19, Report on the activities of Polish authorities after the rulings of the CJEU in case C-204/21 and in case C-791/19 with attachments – Stowarzyszenie Sędziów Polskich Iustitia; W. Sadurski, Polish Constitutional Tribunal under PiS: From an Activist Court, to a Paralysed Tribunal, to a Governmental Enabler, *Hague Journal on the Rule Law*, 2019, no. 11, p. 63; E. Łętowska, A. Wiewiórowska-Domagalska, A

incidental deviation from the established line of case-law. The totality of the circumstances surrounding the judgment in question is all the more noteworthy and will be cited in extenso. It is important to note that the Supreme Court initiated the entire set of the preliminary questions of the dispute to the CJEU, which resulted in the judgment of 19 November 2019, in the joined cases C-585/18, C-624/18, and C-625/18,[22] which were considered the question of the independence of the National Council of the Judiciary and the Disciplinary Chamber of the Supreme Court.[23] In the light of the issues raised, the CJEU considered that it could not, *prima facie*, be ruled out that the national legislation at issue breached the obligation under the second sentence of Article 19 (1) TEU, ensuring that all judgments given in disciplinary proceedings concerning judges are subject to review by a body which meets the requirements of independence. By contrast, in the context of satisfying the condition of urgency, the CJEU assessed whether the application of the national provisions at issue was likely to cause severe and irreparable damage to the functioning of the legal order of the Union. There was concern that the functioning of this body could adversely affect the independence of the judges of the Supreme Court and the judges of the ordinary courts. The Tribunal also considered that the balance of interests involved militates in favour of ordering the interim measures requested by the Commission. The effect of ordering the measures requested may be to 'temporarily suspend the activities of the Disciplinary Chamber pending final judgment'. The ruling of the CJEU, on the suspension of national legislation concerning the functioning of one of the chambers of a Member State's constitutional authority, was precedent-setting. The following

'Good' Change in the Polish Constitutional Tribunal?, *Osteuropa Recht*, 2016, no. 1, p. 79; M. Szuleka et al., *The Constitutional Crisis in Poland*, Helsinki Foundation for Human Rights 2016, <www.hfhr.pl/wp-content/uploads/2016/09/HFHR_The-constitutional-crisis-in-Poland-2015–2016.pdf>, M. Wiącek, Constitutional Crisis in Poland 2015–2016 in the Light of the Rule of Law Principle, in: A. von Bogdandy et al. (eds.), *Defending Checks and Balances in EU Member States*, Beiträge zum ausländischen öffentlichen Recht und Völkerrecht (Veröffentlichungen des Max-Planck-Instituts für ausländisches öffentliches Recht und Völkerrecht), Springer, 2021; M. Matczak, *The Rule of Law in Poland: A Sorry Spectacle*, verfassungsblog, https://verfassungsblog.de/the-rule-of-law-in-poland-a-sorry-spectacle/.

22 Joined cases: *A.K. v. National Council of the Judiciary* (C-585/18) and *CP* (C-624/18) and *DO* (C-625/18) *v. Supreme Court*, EU:C:2019:982. See U. Karpenstein, R. Sangi, Polexit vom Rechtsstaat?, *Europäische Zeitschrift für Wirtschaftsrecht*, 2020, pp. 140–143; M. Leloup, M. Krajewski, M. Ziółkowski, EU judicial independence decentralized: A.K., *CML Review*, 2020, pp. 1107–1138; M. Leloup, An Uncertain First Step in the Field of Judicial Self-Government. CJEU 19 November 2019, joined cases C-585/15, C-624/18 and C-625/18, A.K., CP and DO, *European Constitutional Law Review*, 2020, 16, no. I, pp. 145–169.

23 Following the decision referred to, the Supreme Court issued judgments on 5 December 2019 (case III PO 7/18) and 15 January 2020 (case III PO 8/18 and case III PO 9/18), in which it stated that the Disciplinary Chamber does not constitute an independent and impartial court due to the circumstances of its establishment, its scope of competence and composition, and the participation of the National Council of the Judiciary in its new composition in the constitution of the Chamber.

day, the Disciplinary Chamber submitted a legal question to the CT in which it alleged that the second sentence of Article 4 (1) TEU, in conjunction with Article 279 TFEU, was unconstitutional to the extent that these provisions result in 'the obligation of an EU Member State to implement provisional measures relating to the form and functioning of the constitutional organs of its judicial power'. The Constitutional Tribunal, in a judgment of 14 July 2021, P 7/20, ruled that the second sentence of Article 4 (3) TEU, in conjunction with Article 279 TFEU, to the extent that the CJEU imposes *ultra vires* obligations on the Republic of Poland, as a Member State of the European Union, by issuing provisional measures relating to the system and jurisdiction of Polish courts and the procedure before Polish courts, is incompatible with Article 2 (principle of legal certainty), Article 7 (principle of legalism), Article 8 para. 1 (principle of supremacy of the Constitution), and Article 90 para. 1 (delegation of state competence to an international organisation) in conjunction with Article 4 para. 1 (principle of sovereignty) of the Constitution of the Republic of Poland and to that extent is not covered by the principles of primacy and direct application in Article 91 para. 1–3 of the Constitution.

The statement of the Constitutional Tribunal, in case P 7/20, remains in apparent opposition to the judgment of the CJEU of 19 November 2019 in C-585/18 *A.K.*, in addition to the fact that this demonstrates a new model of interpretation of Article 91 of the Constitution, which is the legal basis for the validity, as well as direct application and primacy (in case of conflict) of an international agreement in the Polish legal order. This ruling is also an expression of the position of the CT that within the framework of 'its constitutional powers and to protect the Polish constitutional identity', it has the right and obligation to examine the compatibility with the Constitution in the mode of *ultra vires* review not only of the norms of primary EU law but also of derived law and auxiliary law. When conducting a review of the norms established by the CJEU (decision of the CJEU of 8 April 2020, C-791/19 R imposing interim measures on Poland),[24] the CT argued that, in the case of the norms issued by the CJEU, the cognition of the CJEU does not include the review of the compliance with the Constitution of the CJEU case-law falling within the competence delegated[25] whilst respecting the Polish constitutional identity

24 EU:C:2020:277. See L. Pech, Protecting Polish Judges from Poland's Disciplinary 'Star Chamber': Commission v. Poland (Interim proceedings), *CMLRev.*, 2021, pp. 137–162; A. Ziętek-Capiga, Zawieszenie funkcjonowania Izby Dyscyplinarnej Sądu Najwyższego [The Suspension of the Disciplinary Chamber of Pilish Supreme Court], *Praca i Zabezpieczenie Społeczne*, 2020, no. 6, pp. 43–45.

25 The Tribunal notes that different understandings of the very concept of competence are not excluded, all the more so as the languages spoken by the peoples of Europe often use a similar or linguistically recognised designator, which is by no means identical. Therefore, it cannot be ruled out that bodies, institutions, other organisational units of the EU, and in particular the CJEU, will apply a different interpretation of the limits of competences delegated by the Republic of Poland on the basis and within the limits of the Constitution.

and the principles of subsidiarity and proportionality. However, if the CJEU exceeds the limits of the conferred powers and the said principles or enters arbitrarily into the area of constitutional identity, a tribunal review of such normative activity of the CJEU is not excluded as regards its compliance with the Constitution. Leaving the constitutionality of any legal norms binding in Poland outside the review of the CT would mean consenting to the resignation from its sovereignty in the legal aspect.

Regarding the doubts as to whether the answer to the question posed by the Supreme Court falls within the competence of the CT or the CJEU, it was noted that the procedure, under Article 267 TFEU, was, justifiably, not followed. This question directly concerns the competence of the CT, as it is exclusively competent to assess the compliance of a normative act with the Constitution of the Republic of Poland. The principle that a national court or tribunal should refer a question to the CJEU for a preliminary ruling, only where it is necessary to do so and only where European Union law is involved, also applies in this situation. Therefore, it is necessary to establish a link between the dispute before the court and the rules of European Union law whose interpretation is sought, consisting of the fact that that interpretation is strictly necessary for the decision to be given by the referring court. In the present case, however, neither the requesting court nor the CT is faced with the issue of the interpretation of EU law. In the case of the waiver of immunity of a judge whom the public prosecutor intends to charge with an offence against road safety (such is the subject matter of the leading case in the disciplinary proceedings before the Supreme Court), there is no link whatsoever with EU law.

The Constitutional Tribunal decided, in this case, that the question posed by the Supreme Court does not concern the interpretation of EU law, as this is clear to the inquiring court, nor does it concern the conflict of this law with the provisions of Polish statutes but rather the extent to which the norms of EU law that are intended to be applied are consistent with the Constitution. In other words, the questioning court doubted whether the norms, set out in the interim measure of the CJEU in the context of the principle of loyalty, were compatible with the provisions of Basic Law. In the process of applying the law, a court cannot decide on its own whether an act is unconstitutional. Nor is it possible to declare Union law norms invalid on their own. In this state of affairs, as the Constitutional Tribunal emphasised, the questioning court had no other choice but to address a legal question to the CT to resolve the existing doubts.

The CT further noted that, in the scope under consideration, the material competence of the Constitutional Tribunal had not been questioned either in the case-law to date, or in the doctrine of law. Article 188 of the Constitution is invoked as the basis for this jurisdiction, and it should be assumed that Union Treaties fall within the concept of international agreements concluded by Poland. Therefore, excluded from the cognition of the Constitutional

Tribunal is the review of the compliance of the derived law of the EU with the primary law of this organisation. However, there are no obstacles to the exercise by the CT of the review of the compliance of the derived and primary EU law with the Constitution of the Republic of Poland. In the opinion of the CT, determining the normative meaning of a provision of EU law is one thing, and comparing the content of laws and international agreements with the provisions of the Constitution and the consequences set out in Article 190 para. 1 of the Constitution is another. The activities performed in the two areas mentioned are not mutually exclusive and by no means interfere with each other.

The judgment of the Constitutional Tribunal discussed earlier and its reasoning raised many doubts in the doctrine of both Polish and EU law.[26] However, the line of considerations adopted in that judgment was, in its essential aspect, confirmed in the judgment of the Constitutional Tribunal in case K 3/21[27] (in which a full panel of judges of the CT ruled). In that case, the CT ruled that

> 1. Article 1(3) TEU in so far as the EU, constituted by equal and sovereign States and forming an 'ever closer union among the peoples of Europe' whose integration, carried out based on EU law and through its interpretation by the CJEU, reached a 'new stage' in which: (a) the organs of the European Union act beyond the limits of the competencies delegated by the Republic of Poland in the Treaties, (b) the Constitution is not the supreme law of the Republic of Poland, having priority of validity and application, (c) the Republic of Poland cannot function as a sovereign and democratic state – is incompatible with Article 2 (the rule of law), Article 8 (principle of supremacy of the Constitution) and Article 90 para. 1 (transfer of state competencies to an international organisation) Of the Constitution of the Republic of Poland.

26 Instead of many, see J. Barcz, A. Grzelak, R. Szyndlauer (eds.), *Problem praworządności w Polsce w świetle orzecznictwa Trybunału Sprawiedliwości UE (2018–2020)* [The problem of the rule of law in Poland in the light case law of the Court of Justice of the EU (2018-2020)], Dom Wydawniczy Elipsa, 2021; M. Kawczyńska, Środki tymczasowe stosowane w postępowaniach przed Trybunałem Sprawiedliwości ze szczególnym uwzględnieniem środków podjętych w sprawach dotyczących Polski [Interim measures in proceedings before the Court of Justice of the EU, with particular reference to the measures taken in the cases concerning Poland], in: J. Barcz, A. Grzelak, R. Szyndlauer (eds.), *Problem praworządności w Polsce w świetle orzecznictwa Trybunału Sprawiedliwości UE (2018–2020)* [The problem of the rule of law in Poland in the light case law of the Court of Justice of the EU (2018-2020)], Dom Wydawniczy Elipsa, 2021, s. 670; T. Lawson, 'Non-Existent'. The Polish Constitutional Tribunal in a State of Denial of the ECtHR Xero Flor Judgment – Verfassungsblog; J. Jaraczewski, Polexit or Judicial Dialogue? CJEU and Polish Constitutional Tribunal in July 2021 – Verfassungsblog; A. Wójcik, *Constitutional Tribunal Ruled: CJEU Interim Orders Do Not Apply in Poland*, https://ruleoflaw.pl/constitutional-tribunal-ruled-CJEUeu-interim-orders-do-not-apply-in-poland/; O. Polański, *Poland: Another Episode of 'Rule of Law Backsliding' – Judgment P 7/20 and a Threat to the Integrity of the EU Legal Order (eui.eu)*; M. Szwed, The Polish Constitutional Tribunal Crisis from the Perspective of the European Convention on Human Rights. ECtHR 7 May 2021, No. 4907/18, Xero Flor w Polsce sp. z o.o. v Poland, *European Constitutional Law Review*, 2022, 18, no. 1, pp. 132–154.

27 Judgment of the CT of 7 October 2021, case K 3/21.

2. Article 19(1), second subpara. of TEU, insofar as to ensure adequate legal protection in areas governed by European Union law, it confers on national courts (ordinary courts, administrative courts, military courts, and the Supreme Court of Justice) competence to a) bypass the provisions of the Constitution in the course of adjudication – is inconsistent with Article 2 (the rule of law), Article 7 (principle of the rule of law), Article 8 para. 1 (principle of supremacy of the Constitution), Article 90 para. 1 (transfer of powers of the State to an international organization) and Article 178 para. 1 (principle of independence of judges) and Article 190(1) of the Constitution, b) adjudication based on laws that are no longer in force, have been repealed by the Sejm, or have been deemed unconstitutional by the Constitutional Tribunal, is inconsistent with Article 2 (principle of the rule of law), Article 7 (principle of the rule of law) and Article 8 para. 1 (principle of the supremacy of the Constitution), Article 90 para. 1 (transfer of powers from the state to an international organization), Article 178 para. 1 (principle of the independence of judges) and Article 190 para. 1 (universal validity and finality of decisions of the Constitutional Tribunal) of the Constitution.

3. Article 19(1), second subpara., and Article 2 of the TEU – insofar as, for the purpose of ensuring effective legal protection in the areas covered by EU law and ensuring the independence of judges – they grant domestic courts (common courts, administrative courts, military courts, and the Supreme Court) the competence to: a) review the legality of the procedure for appointing a judge, including the review of the legality of the act in which the President of the Republic appoints a judge – are inconsistent with Article 2 (principle of the rule of law), Article 8(1) (principle of supremacy of the Constitution), Article 90(1) (transfer of state powers to an international organization) and Article 179 (procedure for the appointment of judges) in conjunction with Article 144(3)(17) (President's prerogative to appoint judges) of the Constitution; b) review the legality of the National Council of the Judiciary's resolution to refer a request to the President of the Republic to appoint a judge – are inconsistent with Article 2, Article 8(1), Article 90(1) and Article 186(1) (tasks of the National Council of the Judiciary) of the Constitution; c) determine the defectiveness of the process of appointing a judge and, as a result, to refuse to regard a person appointed to a judicial office in accordance with Article 179 of the Constitution as a judge – are inconsistent with Article 2, Article 8(1), Article 90(1) and Article 179 in conjunction with Article 144(3)(17) of the Constitution.

The judgment discussed earlier has not yet been substantiated, but the announcement of its verdict has triggered a wave of criticism in the doctrine.[28]

28 Instead of many, see M. Lasek-Markey, *Poland's Constitutional Tribunal on the Status of EU Law: The Polish Government Got All the Answers It Needed from a Court it Controls*, https://

All the challenged provisions concern fundamental issues from the point of view of the functioning of the Polish state in EU structures. The allegations made by the Prime Minister against them, however, questioned not so much the content of these provisions as their specific understanding adopted in the case-law of the CJEU. Thus, the applicant *de facto* demanded a constitutional review of the interpretation of EU law provided by the CJEU. From the perspective of the obligation to apply consistent interpretation, it is the EU Court that is authorised to make binding and final interpretations of provisions of EU law (which has already been emphasised in the earlier case-law of the CT, for example, judgments of 11 May 2005, K 18/04; 16 November 2010, SK 45/09). It is apparent, from the oral reasons for this judgment presented by a panel of the CT, that the Tribunal, whilst noting the incompatibility of the provisions mentioned earlier of the Treaties with constitutional norms, in no way attempted to remove such a conflict through the application of appropriate methods of interpretation. The press release on this issue explained,

> The Constitutional Tribunal does not interpret EU law on its own. The Constitutional Court respects the exclusivity of the Court of Justice of the European Union in this area. The thought process of the Polish Constitutional Tribunal consists solely in determining the content of these norms and verifying their compliance with the Constitution.

---

europeanlawblog.eu/2021/10/21/polands-constitutional-tribunal-on-the-status-of-eu-law-the-polish-government-got-all-the-answers-it-needed-from-a-court-it-controls/; P. Bogdanowicz, *Legal Opinion on the Legal Consequences of the Constitutional Tribunal Ruling in Case K 3/21 on the Incompatibility of the Provisions of the Treaty on European Union with the Constitution of the Republic of Poland in Light of European Union Law*, www.batory.org.pl/wp-content/uploads/2021/11/P.Bogndanowicz_Legal.opinion.on_.the_.legal_.consequences.of_.the_.Polish.Constitutional.Tribunal.ruling.in_.caseK3_.21.pdf; S. Biernat, E. Łętowska, *This Was Not Just Another Ultra Vires Judgment!: Commentary to the Statement of Retired Judges of the Constitutional Tribunal, VerfBlog*, 27 October 2021 r., https://verfassungsblog.de/this-was-not-just-another-ultra-vires-judgment/; M. Florczak-Wątor Monika, (Nie)skuteczność wyroku Trybunału Konstytucyjnego z 7.10.2021 r., K 3/21. Ocena znaczenia orzeczenia z perspektywy prawa konstytucyjnego [(In) Effectiveness of Constitutional Tribunal Judgment of 7 October 2021, K 3/21. Assessment of the Judgment's Significance from a Constitutional Law Perspective], *Europejski Przegląd Sądowy*, 2021, no. 12, pp. 4–11; N. Półtorak, Kilka uwag o skutkach wyroku Trybunału Konstytucyjnego w sprawie K 3/21 dla stosowania prawa unijnego przez polskie sądy [Some Remarks on the Implications of the Decision of the Polish Constitutional Tribunal in Case K 3/21 for the Application of EU Law by Polish Courts], *Europejski Przegląd Sądowy*, 2021, 12, pp. 12–18; W. Wróbel, Skutki rozstrzygnięcia w sprawie K 3/21 w perspektywie Sądu Najwyższego i sądów powszechnych [Effects of the Judgment in Case K 3/21 from the Perspective of the Polish Supreme Court and Ordinary Courts], *EPS* 2021, 12, pp. 19–26; A. Wyrozumska, Wyroki Trybunału Konstytucyjnego w sprawach K 3/21 oraz K 6/21 w świetle prawa międzynarodowego [Judgments of the Polish Constitutional Tribunal in Cases K 3/21 and K 6/21 in the Light of International Law], *EPS* 2021, no. 12, pp. 27–38; J. Łacny, Pieniądze nerwem wojny? – czyli o możliwych skutkach finansowych wyroku Trybunału Konstytucyjnego w sprawie K 3/21 z 7.10.2021 *r.* [The compliance of the Treaty of Accession with the Constitution. Comments on the CT judgment of 11 May 2005, K 18/04], *Europejski Przegląd Sądowy*, 2021, no. 12, pp. 39–50.

This approach to the CT cannot be sustained. When examining the constitutionality of legal provisions, the CT is obliged to reconstruct their normative content by way of interpretation, hence the omission of 'independent interpretation' of these provisions does not fall within the paradigm of constitutional review of the law. In the case of the commented judgment of the Constitutional Tribunal, there is no doubt that the resolved problems concerned the interpretation of the provisions and not their literal wording. Thus, the scope of the decision in the present case is, in fact, exclusively concerned with EU law, to which the obligation contained both directly in Article 267 TFEU and expressed in the earlier case-law of the CT should be connected.

The context of the arguments presented earlier leads to the conclusion that the CT continues the development of this new anti-EU line of case-law by the Tribunal. The CT has changed its position on the scope of the effectiveness of the CJEU's preliminary rulings in the area of the legal system in Poland, and thus also on the issue of the division of jurisdiction between the CT and the CJEU, and on the effectiveness of the measure which is the consistent interpretation of the law.[29]

It is clearly noticeable that the CT departs from the previously presented common 'axiological identity' of the national constitutional order and the EU legal system, and thus departs from the dialogue with the CJEU due to the different axiology of principles, values, and rights in force in these legal systems. Such a clear questioning of the axiological foundations of the EU expressed in Art. 2 and Art. 19 (1) of the TEU and the jurisprudence of the

29 Another case deserves attention, namely – K 7/18 – the outcome of which may have far-reaching consequences for the issue of the validity of the acquis communautaire in Poland. The Public Prosecutor General challenged, among other things, the constitutionality of Article 267 TFEU, understood as authorising the national court to ask a question for a preliminary ruling in a situation where the decision of the CJEU does not relate to the subject matter of the case which the referring court is called upon to decide. He also sought a declaration that Article 267 TFEU is unconstitutional to the extent that it allows a national court to make a preliminary reference for a preliminary ruling on the interpretation of the Treaties or EU acts in matters concerning the system, shape, and organisation of the judiciary and proceedings before the judicial authorities of a Member State. According to the Public Prosecutor General, Article 267 TFEU gives a court of an EU state the freedom to 'determine competencies contrary to the Constitution of the Republic of Poland' and allows the court to interfere in the competencies of other constitutional bodies. This case is still pending. Nevertheless, it should be noted that the case is anchored in a Supreme Court decision in which, examining one of the social security cases – involving, but not explicitly referring to, judges over 65 – the SC asked the CJEU for an interpretation of EU law, which was to allow an answer as to whether the 'new' provisions of the SC Act of December 2017 are compatible with EU law, that is, whether these provisions violate the principle of irremovability of judges (by lowering their retirement age from 70 to 65) and the principle of the rule of law, as well as the prohibition of age discrimination. According to the arguments put forward by the Supreme Court, if this contradiction were to arise, there would be a risk that the judgments of the Supreme Court would be challenged. At the same time, the Supreme Court applied the so-called safeguard under the Polish Code of Civil Procedure, that is, suspended the application of these provisions of the Act on the Supreme Court – pending the response of the CJEU (however, these provisions were still applied by the National Council of the Judiciary and the President of the Republic of Poland).

CJEU constitutes an unprecedented conflict between the CT and the CJEU and a break in the dialogue between these courts. The CT's arguments that it was resolving the existing, real, and irremovable contradiction between constitutional standards and EU regulations caused it to break with its previous position that in Poland exist legal subsystems based on mutually friendly interpretations and cooperative application.

The material scope of consistent interpretation carried out by the Constitutional Tribunal

The analysis of the obligation to apply the consistent interpretation of the law by the Constitutional Tribunal requires a clear delineation of its material framework. The provisions of EU law appear, in the case-law of the CT, as a model of interpretation, a model of review, and the object of review. In each of these cases, a rule of EU law shall be interpreted using the same model methods that are used to give effect to the obligation to apply the consistent interpretation of the law in the judicial process of applying the law. However, due to the fact that the implementation of the obligation to apply consistent interpretation by the Constitutional Tribunal involves somewhat different tasks than those attributed to ordinary courts, as the very methodology of 'resolving cases' (exercising constitutional review) is different, one should share the view, expressed in the doctrine, that the necessary stages in the implementation by the Constitutional Tribunal of its duty to interpret domestic law in conformity with EU law, where EU law appears as a review criterion, are the following: 1) identification of the norm of domestic law which is the object of review and which provision of the Constitution is the review norm; 2) what is the normative EU context of the object of review, that is, whether the norm of domestic law is subject to the regulatory scope of EU law; 3) identification of the EU norm of interpretation, that is, interpretation of the norm of EU law (with the application of EU methods of interpretation developed mainly in the case-law of the CJEU); and 4) *sensu stricto* interpretation – interpretation of the norm of domestic law in accordance with the established norm resulting from EU law.[30]

The determination of the relevance of a provision of the European Union law, as a norm of interpretation for a provision of national law that is subject to constitutional review, takes place via an explicit reference by the Constitutional Tribunal regarding the wording of the provision of the EU law in the context of which the Constitutional Tribunal exercises its duty of consistent interpretation. A clear example is the judgment P 40/13,[31] in which the Tribunal indicated that, due to the EU character of the case, Article 108 para. 1 of the VAT Act implements Article 203 of Directive 2006/112, it was obliged to render a

30 A. Sołtys, Wykładnia prawa UE w orzecznictwie TK [Interpretation of EU law in the jurisprudence of the Constitutional Tribunal], in: L. Leszczyński (ed.), *System Prawa Unii Europejskiej. Wykładnia prawa Unii Europejskiej* [System of EU Law. Interpretation of European Union law], vol. 3, C.H. Beck, 2019, p. 519.

31 Judgment of the CT of 21 April 2015, case P 40/13.

consistent interpretation of Article 108 of the Polish Act in the light of the said provision of the Directive. Thus, a provision of the Directive was interpreted to establish a detailed benchmark for the consistent interpretation of a national provision. Such a position was in line with the previously adopted view of the Constitutional Tribunal (K 41/05),[32] according to which:

> the implementation of the secondary law of the European Communities is a requirement stemming from Article 9 of the Constitution. However, its implementation does not automatically and in every case ensure material compliance of the provisions of this secondary law and the acts implementing it into national law with the norms of the Constitution. The fundamental constitutional function of The Constitutional Tribunal is to examine the compatibility of normative acts with the Constitution, and this obligation also applies when the allegation of unconstitutionality concerns the scope of the act which serves to implement Community law.

A similar example, contained in the justification of the judgment, is an explicit reference to EU secondary law as a benchmark for the consistent interpretation of national law, is the judgment of the CT in the 'biofuels' case K 33/03[33]

> the present case cannot be considered in isolation from EU regulations concerning biofuels in the broad sense. Directive 2003/30/EC of 8 May 2003 on the promotion of the use of biofuels or other renewable fuels for transport is of primary importance here.

Determining the EU review norm for a provision of national law (a norm of EU law is a reviewing norm in relation to a norm of national law), as it results from the case-law of the CT, is not an easy task for entities addressing a specific question to the CT.[34] This concerns cases in which international agreements and EU law treaties have been indicated as models of reference for reviewing a national norm contained in the laws or other acts with precisely those EU provisions. The complexity of this issue was also the reason for the dissenting opinions of the panel of the CT in case no. Kp 1/09.[35]

32 Judgment of the CT of 2 July 2007, case K 41/05 (review of constitutionality of the Anti-Money Laundering Act).

33 Judgment of the CT of 21 April 2004, case K 33/03.

34 Cases in which the CT issued a decision on discontinuance of proceedings and treaties and international agreements were the standard for examining the compliance of acts and other legal acts: of 20 October 2009, case SK 15/08; of 26 November 2007, case U 4/07, or of 19 December 2006, case P 37/05, in which the CT emphasised that the case involved the need to interpret a provision of the EC Treaty and a judgment issued by the Constitutional Tribunal would be an act of interference in the scope of competence of the CJEU.

35 Judgment of the CT of 13 October 2010, case Kp 1/09.

An example of the first situation is the judgment in case K 33/12,[36] in which the Constitutional Tribunal had to review the provisions of the Act on the ratification of the European Council Decision 2011/199/EU,[37] with Article 48 (6) TEU indicated as one of the review norms. According to the entity requesting the review, the Polish act was incompatible with Article 48 (6) TEU, as the decision which this act implemented was issued without legal basis, which resulted in introducing into the national legal order provisions established in a manner contrary to EU law. The Tribunal found that there was no adequate relationship between the Polish act implementing the EU decision and the norm of review, that is, Article 48 (6) TEU, which could justify the derivation of a common ground for assessing the compliance of the challenged domestic regulation with the norm of review thus established. To justify its position, the Constitutional Tribunal also quoted a broader context of EU law, referring to, among other things, Article 136 (3) TFEU and the so-called Fiscal Compact. In conclusion, the CT found that the Polish Act does not lead to a transfer of competencies of state authorities (Article 90, para. 1 of the Constitution of the Republic of Poland) and is therefore not inconsistent with the Constitution (Article 90 in conjunction with Article 120, sentence 1 *in fine* of the Constitution). However, in the justification of the judgment, the CT indicated that Article 48 (6) TEU is an admissible norm for reviewing the constitutionality of laws in proceedings before the CT, particularly laws ratifying international agreements. The Tribunal also made it clear that it does not have the authority to rule on the validity of EU acts and that this is not a matter for its review.

As a distinguished example of the second situation, the basis for the judgment Kp 1/09, one should cite the problem of the reviewing of the compliance of the Act on the organisation of the fish market with the provisions of the Constitution but with significant consideration of the EU context of the issue under consideration. Although the main norms of the review were the provisions of the Constitution, relating to the possibility of limiting the freedom of economic activity (Article 22 of the Constitution) and the principle of determinacy (Article 2 of the Constitution), controversy arose as to the constitutionality of authorising the competent minister for fisheries to determine 'another place of first sale' of fish species specified in the Act. The Tribunal questioned the compatibility of such authorisation with the Constitution, justifying that all significant formal requirements limiting economic freedom should be explicitly included in an act with the rank of a statute, while

36 Judgment of the CT of 26 June 2013, case K 33/12. M. Nowakowski, Glosa do wyroku TK z dnia 26 czerwca 2013 r., K 33/12 [Commentary on the CT judgment of 26 June 2013, K 33/12], *Ius.Novum* 2015, no. 4, pp. 154–168.

37 The Act ratified into domestic law European Council Decision 2011/199/EU of 25 March 2011 amending Article 136 of the Treaty on the Functioning of the European Union with regard to a stability mechanism for Member States whose currency is Euro (Official Journal of the European Union L No. 91, p. 1).

making extensive reference to arguments stemming from EU law. It emphasised, among other things, that competence for the conduct of the Common Fisheries Policy lies exclusively with EU bodies and that the basic piece of EU legislation, on the review of compliance with the rules of the Common Fisheries Policy, is the (then) Council Regulation 1224/2009, establishing a Community review system for ensuring compliance with the rules of the Common Fisheries Policy. However, the Constitutional Tribunal found that invoking this regulation would lead to the indication that it is a norm for review, which it deemed inadmissible in the light of the norms in force. It pointed out that the assessment of the constitutionality of the contested Polish provision was carried out based on its compliance with the Constitution. At the same time, the Constitutional Tribunal does not have the competence to examine the compliance of acts of Polish law with acts of law enacted by EU authorities.[38]

As already highlighted, five dissenting opinions were submitted to the judgment by the judges sitting in the composition. They emphasised, first of all, that the issue in the case was not to determine the compatibility of Polish law with EU law or vice versa but to use EU law in such a way as to correctly determine the content and scope of legal norms determining the admissibility of limitations to constitutional, economic freedom and requirements for statutory norms. It was pointed out that the content of national implementing regulations may be determined not only by the provisions of national laws but also by EU regulations which are directly effective in national legal systems.

Thus, although EU law was not the norm of review for the national norm, in this case, it could (and should) be used as a norm of interpretation either for the national norm under review or the norm of review.

Worth noting, in addition, is the CT judgment of 30 October 2019.[39] In this case, the asking court questioned a provision of the Code of Administrative Procedure, which stipulates that the time limit for acting (in a court trial) is met only if the letter is delivered to a Polish post office (i.e., to an operator designated in the act regulating postal law), in the context of, among other things, Articles 21 and 45 of the Treaty on the Functioning of the European Union. The CT found the doubt raised to be well-founded. The operative part of the decision stressed that the Polish provision is, in addition to the provisions of the Constitution, incompatible with Article 21 TFEU. It stated that the relevant characteristic in the present case is that the participant in the proceedings is resident in the territory of the European Union, where there is free movement of goods, services, capital, and persons coming from the EU Member States. In the opinion of the CT, if the EU Treaty guarantees to an individual the freedom of movement and residence on the freely chosen territory of an EU Member State, as well as protects

38 A. Krzywoń, Glosa do wyroku TK z dnia 13 października 2010 r., Kp 1/09 [Commentary on the CT judgment of 13 October 2010, Kp 1/09], *Przegląd Sejmowy*, 2011, no. 5, pp. 133–143.
39 Judgment of the CT of 30 October 2019, case P 1/18.

against discrimination on the grounds of nationality, then the requirement to effectively send a letter through only the Polish postal service violates the said freedoms. In the judgment mentioned previously, the CT decided on the procedural guarantees of the parties to administrative proceedings by interpreting the national provisions through the prism of the treaty guarantees enjoyed by EU citizens.

These considerations should be supplemented with reference to the judgment of the CT in case P 13/19,[40] which provided an answer to the legal question submitted to the Constitutional Tribunal by the Supreme Court concerning the question of whether, based on the provisions of the Polish Code of Civil Procedure, adjudication by a court on an application for exclusion of a judge on the grounds of raising the issue of the defectiveness of his or her appointment by the President of the Republic of Poland on the motion of the National Council of the Judiciary is consistent with the Constitution, as well as with Article 6 (1) ECHR and Article 47 of the Charter of Fundamental Rights (CFR). The Constitutional Tribunal found that the invoked provision of the Code of Civil Procedure was inconsistent with Article 179 of the Constitution (which provides for the President of the Republic of Poland's prerogative to appoint judges on the motion of the National Council of the Judiciary for an indefinite period). The Constitutional Tribunal did not refer at all (neither in the justification of the judgment nor the operative part) to the review models presented in the question, which were based on the ECHR and the CFR. It seems that this ruling should be included in the emerging line of case-law of the Constitutional Tribunal, which overemphasises the priority review of norms with the Constitution, leaving on the margin of consideration (or completely ignoring it) the interpretation of national norms with the norm found in EU law or other international agreements, even though the coexistence of different legal subsystems originating from different legislative centres is still recognised.[41]

In the case-law of the CT, there are judgments in which EU law appears as the subject of the review, the norm of EU law is the reviewed norm. This line of case-law is characterised by the fact that the Tribunal interprets EU law due to the need to review the compatibility of international agreements, including EU treaties, with the Constitution. These rulings have already been mentioned in the analysis carried out and included, above all, the judgment of 11 May 2005, K 18/04 (the Treaty of Accession)[42] and the judgment of 24 November

40 Judgment of the CT of 02 June 2020, case P 13/19.

41 Some remarks concerning the judgment, see A. Grabowski, B. Naleziński, Konstytucyjne prawo do niezawisłego i bezstronnego sądu w państwie pozornie praworządnym [The Constitutional Right to the Independent and Impartial Court in a Pretendedly Rule of Law State], *Państwo i Prawo*, 2020, no. 10, pp. 25–47.

42 Instead of many, see R. Kwiecień, Zgodność traktatu akcesyjnego z Konstytucją. Glosa do wyroku TK z dnia 11 maja 2005 r., K 18/04 [The compliance of the Treaty of Accession with the Constitution. Comments on the CT judgment of 11 May 2005, K 18/04], *Europejski Przegląd Sądowy*, 2005, no. 1, pp. 40–45; K. Wójtowicz, Traktat akcesyjny – wyrok z dnia 11 maja 2005 r., K 18/04 [The Accession Treaty - Judgment of 11 May 2005, K 18/04], in:

2010, K 32/09 (the Treaty of Lisbon).[43] In these judgments, the Constitutional Tribunal found no grounds to state that (provisions of) the Accession Treaty or the Lisbon Treaty are inconsistent with the Polish Constitution. The justifications for these judgments focus largely on the principles concerning the conditions for a country, such as Poland, to become a member of the integration process and a community such as the EU. The issues of the relationship between domestic law and Community (EU) law, the place of the Constitution of the Republic of Poland in the multicentric system of law, the relation of these systems to one another, as well as the common set of principles, values, and fundamental rights, common for the states belonging to the EU, that is, the axiological identity of the created community of states, were the main scope of deliberations conducted by the Constitutional Tribunal.

This group of rulings also includes the judgment of the Constitutional Tribunal in the case SK 45/09,[44] which clearly emphasises that the starting point for the required analysis is the assumption that EU law will not always contain norms that entirely overlap with the norms of Polish law. The Tribunal emphasised that its competence to assess the constitutionality of an EU regulation with the Constitution should be treated as independent but at the same time as subsidiary to the jurisdiction of the CJEU. In the cited case, the constitutionality of the provision of Article 41, second sentence, of Council Regulation (EC) No 44/2001 of 22 December 2000 on jurisdiction and the recognition and enforcement of judgments in civil and commercial matters were assessed by the Constitutional Tribunal,[45] holding that it complies with

---

M. Derlatka, L. Garlicki, M. Wiącek (eds.), *Na straży państwa prawa. Trzydzieści lat orzecznictwa Trybunału Konstytucyjnego* [Upholding the rule of law. Thirty years jurisprudence of the Constitutional Tribunal], Wolters Kluwer, 2016, LEX/el. 2017; W. Czapliński, *Znaczenie Orzecznictwa Trybunału Sprawiedliwości Unii Europejskiej w procesie rozwoju prawa europejskiego* [The importance of the case law of the Court of Justice of the European Union in the process of development of EU law], Scholar, 2021, p. 240; A. Dubicka, Konstytucyjność przystąpienia Polski do Unii Europejskiej (w świetle wyroku TK) [Constitutionality of Poland's accession to the European Union (in the light of the Constitutional Tribunal's decision], *Państwo i Prawo*, 2007, no. 6, pp. 35–48; M. Safjan, Niezależność Trybunału Konstytucyjnego i suwerenność konstytucyjna RP [Independence of the Constitutional Tribunal and constitutional sovereignty of the Republic of Poland], *Państwo i Prawo*, 2006, no. 6, pp. 3–17; K. Wójtowicz, Glosa do wyroku TK z dnia 11 maja 2005 r., K 18/04 [Commentary to the CT judgment of 11 May 2005, K 18/04], *Przegląd Sejmowy*, 2005, no. 6, pp. 190–196; J. Barcz, Glosa do wyroku TK z dnia 11 maja 2005 r., K 18/04 [Commentary to the CT judgment of 11 May 2005, K 18/04], *Kwartalnik Prawa Publicznego*, 2005, no. 4, pp. 169; S. Biernat, Glosa do wyroku TK z dnia 11 maja 2005 r., K 18/04 [Commentary to the CT judgment of 11 May 2005, K 18/04], *Kwartalnik Prawa Publicznego*, 2005, no. 4, pp. 185.

43 K. Wójtowicz, Zachowanie tożsamości konstytucyjnej państwa polskiego w ramach UE – uwagi na tle wyroku TK z 24.11.2010 r. (K 32/09) [Preservation of the constitutional identity of the Polish state within the EU - remarks on the background of the judgment of the CT of 24 November 2010 (K 32/09)], *Europejski Przegląd Sądowy*, 2011, no. 11, pp. 4–11; E. Dąbrowska, Judgment of 24 November 2010 Ref. No. K 32/09 Concerning the Treaty of Lisbon (application submitted by a group of Senators), *Polish Yearbook of International Law*, 2010, pp. 304–314.

44 Judgment of 16 November 2011, case SK 45/09.

45 OJ L 12, 16.1.2001, pp. 1–23.

Article 45 para. 1 (right to a court) and Article 32 para. 1 (principle of equality) in conjunction with Article 45 para. 1 of the Constitution (right to a fair and public hearing of a case without delay by a competent, impartial, and independent court). In other words, the Constitutional Tribunal did not find a violation of the constitutional right to a court by these regulations, finding that they serve legitimate substantive purposes and are not arbitrary by nature.

Concerning the ruling discussed earlier, it should be added that, by Article 79 para. 1 of the Constitution, individuals may complain in a constitutional complaint about the compliance of a statute or other normative act with the Constitution (acts based on which a court decides about their freedoms or rights). According to the case-law of the Constitutional Tribunal, 'normative acts' refer not only to acts issued by national authorities but also, after fulfilling certain requirements, to legal acts issued by institutions of international organisations. In the view of the Constitutional Tribunal, the legal acts listed in Article 288 TFEU may be regarded as normative acts within the meaning of Article 79 para. 1 of the Constitution. With regard to the possibility of reviewing the compatibility of EU secondary legislation with the Constitution, the Tribunal, at the same time, emphasises the need to exercise due care and due diligence, given the principle of sincere cooperation established by Article 4 (3) TEU. The Tribunal exercises its competence to review secondary Union law (normative acts) only when the Constitution expressly allows it (i.e., in the context of a constitutional complaint or in response to a question posed by the court deciding the case). The Tribunal has no jurisdiction to declare a normative act, issued by the institutions of the Union, invalid. However, like other courts in the Member States, where it has doubts as to the assessment of the content of the norms of acts of secondary Union law, it may refer a question to the CJEU for a preliminary ruling, under Article 267 TFEU, seeking to interpret or assess the validity of specific provisions.

In the judgment in case P 7/20,[46] the Constitutional Tribunal indicated that a court might challenge, by way of a legal question, any 'normative act', that is, an act expressing general and abstract patterns of conduct, regardless of the legal form in which and by which entity it was issued. The only condition for an act to be subject to review is normative. The Court continued that the question at issue in the case is the scope compatibility with the Constitution of a rule ordering the Republic of Poland to enforce interim measures ordered by the CJEU concerning the system of courts, their jurisdiction, and the procedure before the courts. In this way, the Constitutional Tribunal reviewed the general and abstract norms derived from the second sentence of Article 4 (3) TEU in conjunction with Article 279 TFEU with the provisions of the Constitution constituting, in this case, the norm of review for EU provisions.

46 Judgment of the CT of 14 July 2021, case P 7/20, in which it held that the second sentence of Article 4 (3) TEU in conjunction with Article 279 TFEU is inconsistent with Articles 2, 7, 8 para. 1 and 90 para. 1 in conjunction with Article 4 para. 1 of the Constitution and to that extent is not covered by the principles of primacy and direct applicability set out in Article 91 para. 1–3 of the Constitution.

The direction of considerations adopted in this judgment was in its essential aspect, confirmed in the judgment of the Constitutional Tribunal in case K 3/21.[47]

Content and limits of the obligation of consistent interpretation

The content and limits of the obligation to apply consistent interpretation, such as the obligation itself, have no explicit treaty basis and have been shaped by the CJEU case-law. The authorities of a Member State, including the Constitutional Tribunal, shall exercise their powers of interpretation by applying the interpretative methods recognised by the national order, thereby giving full effect to the Union norm and achieving its aim. The injunction arising from the CJEU case-law to interpret EU law 'in the light of the content and purpose' of the EU provision should be carried out 'as far as possible'. For the Constitutional Tribunal, this means that it is obliged to choose the method of interpretation that most fully realises the result of the EU norm by eliminating those interpretative results that do not meet the criterion of compatibility with EU law. Legal and constitutional pluralism requires an expansion of the scope of legal arguments to be employed by courts and an increased focus on systemic and teleological reasoning resulting in increasing contextualisation of judicial reasoning.[48] The new legal challenges before the courts do not require a construction of new judicial techniques but rather a recognition that law is a dynamic structure and requires the reflexive methodology of adjudication.[49]

Interpretative directives corresponding to the obligation of 'interpretation friendly to European law' were already recognised and applied by the Constitutional Tribunal in the pre-accession period (as extensively discussed earlier). In judgment K 2/02,[50] the CT made it clear that

> the interpretation friendly to European law in the construction of the norm of constitutionality involves two directives for such an interpretation: firstly, the interpretation favourable to European law may be undertaken on condition (and only then) that Polish law does not show a different approach to the problem (strategy of solving it) in the period preceding formal accession – secondly when there are several possibilities

47 Judgment of the CT of 7 October 2021, case K 3/21.

48 P. Maduro, Courts and Pluralism: Essay on a Theory of Judicial Adjudication in the Context of Legal and Constitutional Pluralism, in: J.L. Dunoff, J.P. Trachtman (eds.), *Ruling the World? Constitutionalism, International Law, and Global Governance*, Cambridge University Press, 2009, pp. 356, 361. Quotation after I. Skomerska-Muchowska, The Dialogue of CEE Constitutional Courts in the Era of Constitutional Pluralism, in: A. Wyrozumska (ed.), *Transnational Judicial Dialogue on International Law in Central and Eastern Europe*, Wydawnictwo Uniwersytetu Łódzkiego, 2017, p. 111.

49 I. Skomerska-Muchowska, The Dialogue of CEE Constitutional Courts in the Era of Constitutional Pluralism, in: A. Wyrozumska (ed.), *Transnational Judicial Dialogue on International Law in Central and Eastern Europe*, Wydawnictwo Uniwersytetu Łódzkiego, 2017, p. 111.

50 Judgment of the CT of 28 January 2003, case K 2/02.

of interpretation, one should choose the one which is closest to the approach of the *acquis communautaire.*

It should be stressed that the boundaries of the consistent interpretation, in an approach that is representative of the judgments of common courts and which is taken from the case-law of the CJEU, are not an explicit subject of consideration by the CT but are rather conducted on the margins of the reconstruction of the EU benchmark. Both for the norm, which is the norm of interpretation, the norm of the review, or the object of review. Thus, the *Lisbon Treaty* judgment K 32/09 is noteworthy because the CT presented an absolute position on the question of respecting the limits of the obligation to apply consistent interpretation:

> deciding on the application must take into account both the principle of preserving sovereignty in the process of European integration and the principle of favouring the process of European integration and cooperation between States. . . . From the point of view of this principle, in reconstructing the norm by which constitutionality is to be assessed, use should be made not only of the text of the Constitution itself but – in so far as this text refers to terms, concepts, and principles known to European law – reference should be made to these meanings. . . . Under no circumstances may an interpretation favourable to European law lead to results which are contrary to the clear wording of the constitutional norms and impossible to reconcile with the minimum guarantee functions performed by the Constitution.

In the justification of the judgment discussed earlier, the Constitutional Tribunal referred to the case K 18/04, on *the Treaty of Accession,* in which it had already noted that

> the norms of the Constitution in the area of individual rights and freedoms set a minimum and impassable threshold which cannot be lowered or questioned as a result of the introduction of Community regulations. In this respect, the Constitution fulfils its guarantee role, from the point of view of protecting the rights and freedoms set out therein, and this is about all entities active in the sphere of its application.

Therefore, the Constitutional Tribunal does not recognise the possibility of questioning the validity of a constitutional norm by the mere fact of introducing into the system of European law a Community regulation that is contrary to it.

The judgments discussed earlier have been commented on in many ways, referring to the specificity of the limits of the consistent interpretation formulated by the Constitutional Tribunal.[51] It should be noted that the position of

51 M. De Visser, *Constitutional Review in Europe: A Comparative Analysis*, Hart Publishing, 2013, pp. 260–262.

the CT justifies the expectation that the limits of consistent interpretation in the jurisdiction of the CT are established not only by reference to the linguistic meaning of the constitutional norms being interpreted but also by taking into account the guarantee functions of these regulations. In the light of the foregoing, it may be assumed that the interpretation *contra legem* as a criterion for determining the limit of the obligation to interpret the norms in conformity with the Constitution is such an interpretation that would be contrary to the minimum guarantee functions realised by the Constitution.[52]

Another ruling that should be recalled in the analysed context is the judgment of the CT of 7 November 2007.[53] The Tribunal tied the obligation of consistent interpretation in respect of the principles of EU law. It stated that direct taxation falls within the competence of the Member States of the European Union but that they should exercise this competence in accordance with Community law. Given the previous discussion, it found that the CT respected the principle of interpreting national law in a manner friendly to Community law, which finds support in Article 91 para. 1 of the Constitution, and according to this principle. Nonetheless, from the principle of loyal cooperation (expressed at the time in Article 10 EC), the CT concluded that all state authorities, including administrative authorities, are obliged to interpret and apply national law in such a way as to ensure the full effectiveness of the rights guaranteed by Community provisions. Since joining the EU, Poland has been obliged to comply with the rules of interpretation arising from the *acquis communautaire*.

A similar convention of argumentation can be found in judgment no. K 41/05,[54] in which the constitutionality of provisions of the Act on Counteracting Money Laundering was assessed, in which the CT referred to the argument, stemming from the case-law of the CJEU, that the EU law requires, under Article 6 (1) TEU, in the EU the observance of a general principle – the right to a fair trial, shaped in Article 6 ECHR. The central part of the consideration of the CT is the assessment of the principle of a fair trial and its impact on the previous findings.

In the case-law of the Constitutional Tribunal, references to EU law are repeatedly found, which is an ‘indirect’ way of influencing the determining of the content of a norm of national law. This is a way of ‘confirming’ the accepted interpretation of a provision of national law and reinforcing the line of argument as to the extent to which it is consistent with an obligation to interpret the provision in question in conformity with EU law. The practice of the CT delivers examples that the CT notes explicitly, albeit in an *obiter dictum*, that relevant provisions of domestic law were consistent with these

52 See A. Sołtys, *Obowiązek wykładni prawa krajowego zgodnie z prawem unijnym jako instrument zapewniania efektywności prawa Unii Europejskiej* [The Obligation to Interpret National Law in Conformity with EU Law as am Instrument to Ensure Effectiveness of EU Law], Wolters Kluwer Polska, 2015, p. 691.

53 Judgment of the CT of 7 November 2007, case K 18/06.

54 Judgment of the CT of 2 July 2007, case K 41/05.

European standards. Illustrative of the methodology discussed earlier for interpreting national law are the decisions of the Constitutional Tribunal in the cases: U 5/12 (review of the physical parameters of radiological equipment),[55] P 11/12 (requirement to reside in Poland as a condition for granting and exercising the right to a social pension),[56] P 8/08 (postal order as an exclusive service of the public operator),[57] P 1/11 (co-financing from a regional operational program),[58] U 4/12 (ritual slaughter),[59] P 32/12 (tax and criminal sanction for the same act),[60] P 2/14 (reinstatement of a customs officer),[61] and Kp 2/15 (protection of historical monuments).[62]

From the point of view of the content and limits of the obligation of consistent interpretation, it should be stressed that the CT recognised an autonomous EU legal order, as a part of international legal order based on Polish internal principles, as an element of Polish legal order. In particular, the norms of the Constitution concerning individual rights and freedoms indicate a minimum and unsurpassable threshold, which may not be lowered due to EU provisions. The Court also noticed that a result of consistent interpretation may not lead to results contradicting the explicit wording of constitutional norms (SK 26/08, K 32/09, SK 45/09).

Comparative reasoning in EU cases

Sometimes the CT examine the decisions of foreign courts in order to seek guidance on the interpretation of domestic law or to determine the standard of protection of certain rights. The Constitutional Tribunal usually uses comparative argumentation, carefully considering both the circumstances of the case at hand and the level of approximation of referred legal system, with the Polish legal system.[63] In case K 38/07[64] the CT held that comparative reasoning, including reference to EU law and other international law, may be used, however, subject to various preconditions:

> there are particular circumstances in which one may resort to non-linguistic methods of legal interpretation. . . . The role of those methods is subsidiary to linguistic and logical interpretation, however, even if by means of that

55 Judgment of the CT of 30 July 2013, case U 5/12.
56 Judgment of the CT of 25 June 2013, case P 11/12.
57 Judgment of the CT of 25 January 2011, case P 8/08.
58 Judgment of the CT of 12 December 2011, case P 1/11.
59 Judgment of the CT of 27 November 2012, case U 4/12.
60 Judgment of the CT of 21 October 2015, case P 32/12.
61 Judgment of the CT of 6 April 2016, case P 2/14.
62 Judgment of the CT of 25 May 2016, case Kp 2/15.
63 On the methodology of the CT of reference to comparative materials by the Constitutional Tribunal, see A. Paprocka, Argument komparatystyczny w orzecznictwie Trybunału Konstytucyjnego [Comparative argument in the jurisprudence of the Constitutional Tribunal], *Państwo i Prawo*, 2017, no. 7, pp. 37–54.
64 Judgment of the CT of 3 July 2008, case K 38/07.

> method a text is found to be synonymous, its interpreter may sometimes 'go beyond' its determined meaning. However, a strong axiological substantiation is required which will mainly invoke constitutional values.[65]

The reference to foreign courts takes place especially in 'important' cases, to find inspiration for the determination of the content of reviewing the issue, for example, democratic standards, international human rights, or other interests.[66] The CT, most frequently, refers to decisions issued by the Federal Constitutional Court of Germany[67] but also to other counterparts of the 'old' EU. This referral is used to justify its own position within the pluralistic system as the highest courts of national constitutional orders.

In *Lisbon Treaty* case (K 32/09), the CT, very carefully, analysed the judgments of other European Constitutional Courts (143/2010, the Hungarian Constitutional Court; 2007-560, the DC French Constitutional Council; 2 BvE 2/08, the German Federal Constitutional Court; Pl. US 19/08, the Czech Constitutional Court; 2008-35-01, and the Latvian Constitutional Court) and stated that

> case-law the constitutional courts of the Member States share, as a vital part of European constitutional traditions, the view that the constitution is of fundamental significance as it reflects and guarantees the state's sovereignty at the present stage of European integration, and also that the constitutional judiciary plays a unique role as regards the protection of the constitutional identity of the European Union.

It is quite important to notice that the CT in cases P 7/20[68] and K 3/21[69] also made a detailed reference to the jurisdiction of the constitutional courts of, i.e., Germany, Czech Republic, France, and Spain. According to the CT, its judgment fits within this line of judgments questioning the supremacy of

65 I. Skomerska-Muchowska, The Dialog of CEE Constitutional Courts in the Era of Constitutional Pluralism, in: A. Wyrozumska (ed.), *Transnational Judicial Dialog on International Law in Central and Eastern Europe*, Wydawnictwo Uniwersytetu Łódzkiego, 2017, p. 141. The author underlines that the CT treated, in the same way, the ECtHR case-law and that of foreign courts as an emanation of a universal standard in the field of human rights protection. J. Krzemińska, Courts as Comparatists: References to Foreign Law in the Case-law of the Polish Constitutional Court, *Jean Monnet Working Paper*, 2012, no. 5, p. 49, www.jeanmonnetprogram.org.

66 P. Chybalski, Aprobata i krytyka stosowania wykładni komparatystycznej w orzecznictwie konstytucyjnym [Approval and Critique of the Use of Comparative Interpretation in Constitutional Adjudication], *Państwo i Prawo*, 2022, no. 4, pp. 27–45.

67 As suggested by A.F. Tatham, it should be explained by historical and legal cultures affinities, linguistic ability and intellectual stimulus, constitution and constitutional jurisdictional formation in the post-Communist era, and resulting influences on courts' decisions. A.F. Tatham, *Central European Constitutional Courts in the Face of EU Membership: The Influence of German Model in Hungary and Poland*, Martinus Nijhoff Publishers, 2013, p. 5.

68 Judgment of the CT of 14 July 2021.

69 Judgment of the CT of 7 October 2021.

the EU law and allowing for the judicial control of EU ultra vires acts. This argumentation was criticised and recognised as entirely unfounded when one takes into account the context, merits, and effects of the constitutional conflicts as invoked by the Constitutional Court.[70]

In case K 23/11 (Data Retention Directive), the CT broadly analysed the case-law of the ECHR, the case-law of the CJEU, and other constitutional courts of Member States (13627, The Supreme Administrative Court of Bulgaria; 1258, The Romanian Constitutional Court; Pl. US 24/10, Pl. US 10/2014, The Slovakian Constitutional Court; G 47/2012, G 62/2012, G 70/2012, G 71/2012, The Austrian Constitutional Court). The referral to those judgments created a 'dialogue' that determined not only a way of understanding the right to privacy as guaranteed by European and national law but also the scope of justified limitation in similar situations.

The effect of consistent interpretation of national law in the case-law of the Constitutional Tribunal

As noted previously, the obligation to apply consistent interpretation carried out by the Constitutional Tribunal, within the framework of constitutional review, may concern three basic configurations in which EU law is the norm of interpretation, the object of review, and the norm of review. Each of the review patterns carried out may lead to a change in the interpretation of the reviewed norm and a change in its scope of application. In both cases, the CT seeks to ensure the compatibility of national law with EU law, thus fulfilling its obligation to ensure the effectiveness of EU law.

In the context of the implementation of the obligation to apply consistent interpretation resulting in a change in the existing interpretation of national law, for the complete illustration of this reasoning, it is necessary to refer to judgment K 41/05[71] concerning the protection of professional secrecy of persons providing legal assistance. In this case, the Tribunal made a detailed

70 A. Sołtys stated:

> Firstly, most of them remained in the declaratory stage. Notwithstanding the claim to the supremacy of a national constitution over EU law made by the constitutional courts, in concrete cases they managed to avoid a real conflict between the national constitutions and EU law. Secondly, for the reasons indicated above (context, merits, and the effects of the constitutional conflicts), the cases where there was a real conflict between the Court of Justice and the apex courts of Member States cannot be compared with the dispute between the Polish Constitutional Court and the Court of Justice. Generally, the conflicting judgments of the apex courts in other Member States concerned strictly-defined contentious issues that arose in the interpretations of the domestic constitution and EU law, mainly in particular areas of substantive law.

A. Sołtys, The Court of Justice of the European Union in the Case Law of the Polish Constitutional Court: The Current Breakdown in View of Polish Constitutional Jurisprudence Pre-2016, *Hague Journal on the Rule of Law*, 2022, 15, pp. 40–41, https://link.springer.com/article/10.1007/s40803-022-00186-6

71 Judgment of the CT of 2 July 2007, case K 41/05.

consideration of the EU context of the case and its impact on determining the content of the national law rule. First of all, it stressed that 'the scope of professional activities' to which the said obligations would be connected was not unambiguously defined in the Act, in particular the services whose provision would absolutely oblige one to breach the secrecy of communications with clients (cf. Article 2a (5) of Directive 91/308/EEC as amended by Directive 2001/97/EC and Article 2 para. 1 (3) (b) of Directive 2005/60/EC), the Constitutional Tribunal recognises the possibility and necessity of interpreting the Anti-Money Laundering Act in a way that, on the one hand, meets the requirements of EU law and, on the other hand, makes it possible to conclude that the challenged provisions are consistent with the Constitution. In this connection, the CT reminded that legislation (domestic legislation) should be interpreted in a favourable (friendly) manner to EU law, deriving this injunction from Articles 9 and 91 para. 1 of the Constitution and from the obligation of loyal cooperation arising from Article 10 of the EC Treaty, which presupposes that the bodies applying the law in the countries of the EU will interpret domestic law in accordance with European law, even that which is not itself directly applicable. In the next place, the Constitutional Tribunal stated that:

> taking into account the findings made in the present case, and above all taking into account: a) the framework, reconstructed in the present case, of the constitutional guarantee of protection of the secrecy of communications relating to the peculiar relationship between a person seeking legal assistance and a person exercising a profession of public trust providing that assistance, including in particular in connection with legal proceedings; b) the purpose for which the AML Act was enacted (namely to implement Directive 91/308/EEC, as amended by Directive 2001/97/EC), which determines the manner in which its provisions are to be interpreted; c) the position taken by the CJEU in case C-305/05 (which determines the manner in which not only Directive 91/308/EEC, as amended by Directive 2001/97/EC, which was directly referred to by the Constitutional Tribunal but also the subsequent Directive 2005/60/EC, which regulates this sphere of issues, is to be understood); d) the fact that the Member States are under an obligation not only to interpret national law in conformity with Community law, but also to take care to ensure that they do not rely on an interpretation of secondary legislation which would be in conflict with the fundamental rights protected by the Community legal order or with the other general principles of Community law; e) the content of Directive 2005/60/EC, which now regulates the prevention of the use of the financial system for the purpose of money laundering and terrorist financing and lays down the obligations arising therefrom, including in particular recital 48, which states that:
>
> > "This Directive respects the fundamental rights and observes the principles recognised in particular by the Charter of Fundamental Rights of the European Union. Nothing in this Directive should be interpreted or

> implemented in a manner inconsistent with the European Convention on Human Rights."

> The Constitutional Tribunal finds it inadmissible to interpret the questioned provisions of the AML Act in such a way that the obligation to collect and transmit information would refer to lawyers exercising professions of public trust and confidence to the extent that they provide legal assistance consisting of determining the legal situation of a client or otherwise related to prepared, initiated (conducted) or completed court proceedings.

In other words, the CT has ruled out the possibility that the national provisions at issue could be interpreted as imposing a specific obligation under that law on legal aid practitioners and has thus limited their scope of application.

Since the enactment of the Polish Constitution (1997), it has been amended only twice. The amendment, which was introduced in 2006, was directly related to the membership of Poland of the EU and referred to the provision prohibiting the extradition of Polish citizens, Article 55 para. 1 of the Constitution. The Constitution was amended to give effect to Council Framework Decision 2002/584 on the European Arrest Warrant.[72] The primary reason that influenced the decision on the need to amend Article 55 para. 1 of the Constitution was the judgment of the CT on the European Arrest Warrant (EAW).[73] The provision in question was very lapidary and stated that 'the extradition of a Polish citizen is prohibited'. The Tribunal held that Article 607t §1 of the Polish Code of Criminal Procedure, insofar as it extended permission to surrender a Polish national to an EU Member State, was incompatible with Article 55 para. 1 of the Constitution. The Tribunal analysed whether there was a difference between extradition within the meaning of Article 55 para. 1 of the Constitution and surrender (transfer) as provided for in the Framework Decision on the EAW. Ultimately, the Constitutional Tribunal held that the fundamental basis for extradition is the surrender of an accused or convicted person for the purpose of further prosecution or execution of the sentence imposed on him. The surrender of a person prosecuted under an EAW, on the other hand, has essentially the same purpose. Thus, the Constitutional Tribunal recognised the EAW as a particular form of extradition. The Tribunal stressed that, in view of the obligations of Poland as a Member of the EU, it was essential that the applicable law be amended in such a way as to ensure full implementation of the Framework Decision on the EAW (Table 7.1).

The Constitutional Tribunal stated that, under Article 607p § 1 para. 5 of the Code of Criminal Procedure, it should be possible to refuse to execute an EAW in cases where it is evident to the court, ruling on the execution of the warrant, that the person to whom the warrant relates has not committed

72 Council Framework Decision of 13 June 2002 on the European arrest warrant and the surrender procedures between Member States (2002/584/JHA), OJ L 190, 18.7.2002, pp. 1–20.

73 Judgment of the CT of 27 April 2005, case P 1/05.

Table 7.1 Consistent interpretation of national legislation with Framework Decision 2002/584

The original content of Article 55 of the Constitution	The current content of Article 55 of the Constitution – after the amendment introduced by Article 1 of the Act of 8 September 2006 amending the Constitution of the Republic of Poland (Dz.U.06.200.1471), entered into force on 7 November 2006.
1. The extradition of a Polish citizen is prohibited.	1. The extradition of a Polish citizen shall be prohibited, except in cases specified in paras. 2 and 3.
2. The extradition of a person suspected of committing a non-violent offence for political reasons is prohibited. 3. A court shall decide on the admissibility of extradition.	2. Extradition of a Polish citizen may be granted upon a request made by a foreign state or an international judicial body if such a possibility stems from an international treaty ratified by Poland or a statute implementing a legal instrument enacted by an international organisation of which the Republic of Poland is a member, provided that the act covered by request for extradition: (1) was committed outside the territory of the Republic of Poland, and (2) constituted an offence under the law in force in the Republic of Poland or would have constituted an offence under the law in force in the Republic of Poland if it had been committed within the territory of the Republic of Poland, both at the time of its commitment and at the time of the making of the request.
	3. Compliance with the conditions specified in para. 2 subparas. 1 and 2 shall not be required if an extradition request is made by an international judicial body established under an international treaty ratified by Poland in connection with a crime of genocide, crime against humanity, a war crime or a crime of aggression, covered by the jurisdiction of that body.
	4. The extradition of a person suspected of the commission of a crime for political reasons but without the use of force shall be forbidden, so as extradition, which would violate the rights and freedoms of persons and citizens.
	5. The courts shall adjudicate on the admissibility of extradition.

the alleged act which the warrant relates. In the case of surrender to another EU Member State, on the basis of an EAW, the level of confidence in the legitimacy of the request for surrender should be higher than in the case of surrender on the basis of a 'classic' extradition request to another state, which is not necessarily linked to the, at least minimal, level of guarantees provided by the ECHR.[74] This concession was granted, however, on the basis of the Constitutional of Poland. According to M. Safjan, 'in this judgment an ideal balance between, on the one hand, the requirements stemming from the clear constitutional rule which forbade extradition of a Polish citizen and, on the other hand, the requirements of the European framework decision on EAW, was struck' and that is why two goals were achieved – sustained supremacy of Constitution and the effectiveness of the EU law.[75]

In spite of clarifying the unconstitutionality of the matter, the CT considered that the obligation of the consistent interpretation of the constitutional provision was not a relevant tool in the current situation since the obligation was limited by the CJEU itself, as it may not worsen an individual's condition, especially as regards the sphere of criminal liability.[76]

Another example of a judgment of the Constitutional Tribunal, which assessed the compliance of Polish regulations with the provisions of EU law and, consequently, stated the necessity to change the scope of application of national regulations, is judgment K 13/08.[77] The Constitutional Tribunal found that specific provisions of the implementing regulation concerning the number of fines for fisheries infringements are incompatible with the principle of legal certainty guaranteed by Article 2 of the Constitution. These penalties resulted from the application of Commission Regulation No 804/2007 of 9 July 2007, establishing a prohibition of cod fishing in the Baltic Sea by vessels flying the Polish flag. As a result of the Constitutional Tribunal ruling, the Ministry of Agriculture has cancelled fines imposed on Polish fishermen for illegal cod fishing.

Conclusions

The analysis of the case-law of the Constitutional Tribunal, in which the obligation to apply consistent interpretation was exercised, leads us to summarise the main directions of the examination of the compatibility of the confronted

74 K. Kowalik-Bańczyk, Should We Polish It Up? The Polish Constitutional Tribunal and the Idea of Supremacy of EU Law, *German Law Journal*, 2005, no. 6, p. 1355.

75 M. Safjan, Central & Eastern European Constitutional Courts Facing New Challenges – Ten Years of Experience, in: M. Bobek (ed.), *Central European Judges Under the European Influence. The Transformation Power of the EU Revisited*, Hart Publishing, 2015, p. 375.

76 G. Martinico, O. Pollicino, *The Interaction between Europe's Legal Systems. Judicial Dialogue and the Creation of Supranational Laws*, Edward Elgar, 2012, pp. 212–213.

77 Judgment of the CT of 7 July 2009, case K 13/08.

norms by the Constitutional Tribunal. Under the first reference, it should be noted that EU law can act as a benchmark for interpretation by the Constitutional Tribunal. In such a case, the CT may establish the contradiction of the object of review with EU law (the consistent interpretation does not remove the contradiction) and then examine the review model (constitutional norm) in such a way as to eliminate the provision that is contrary to EU law from the national legal order. Furthermore, the Constitutional Tribunal may establish that the object of review (a norm of national law simultaneously implementing the objectives of the EU regulation) is consistent with the EU law and then interpret the review model (constitutional norm) in such a way as to maintain the object of review as a norm binding in the national legal order.

In the case-law of the Constitutional Tribunal, such a configuration is also accepted, in which the EU law is the review model and the object of review. In the first case, the EU law norm is the benchmark for reviewing national law. In the second case, EU law is examined for its compatibility with the Constitution. In all types of conducted reviews of constitutionality, the Constitutional Tribunal applies methods of interpretation of law recognised in national law, taking into account the content, scope, and limits of the obligation to apply pro-EU interpretation, also specified in the case-law of the CJEU.

Since the beginning of the membership of Poland of the EU (and even in its earlier case-law), the Constitutional Tribunal has assumed that the consistent interpretation of the norm of review (constitutional norm) should be made in the context of the maximum assurance (maintenance of guarantees) of the realisation of constitutional objectives, principles, and values, that is, the maintenance of axiological guarantees contained in the Constitution with the maximum respect for state sovereignty in the perspective of the membership of Poland of the EU.

In principle, however, the Constitutional Tribunal recognises that the principle of mutually friendly interpretation and cooperative co-application should be taken as the basis for the coexistence of legal subsystems originating from different legislative centres.

Since the accession of Poland to the EU, the CT has examined the decisions of foreign courts (from the other Member States) in order to obtain guidance on the interpretation of domestic law or to determine the standard of protection of certain rights.

The Polish Constitutional Tribunal intentionally entered into a judicial dialogue with the CJEU by referring a question to the CJEU for a preliminary ruling (K 61/13) and acting as a court responsible for the effective application of the EU provisions as it is interpreted in the case-law of the CJEU.

Regarding the consequences of the constitutionality review, carried out by the Constitutional Tribunal, taking into account the consistent interpretation, the judgment in cases P 7/20 and K 3/21 shall be treated as a new line of the case-law for the CT, which forms a part of the 'rule of law crisis' in Poland. This new jurisprudence invokes 'old' case-law of the TC as crucial argument, but 'new' cases give to the same words (principles, values, provisions) whole different definitions and quite different significance in this new constitutional axiological environment. It has to be underlined that, in principle, a judgment, made by the Constitutional Tribunal, eliminates a norm specified in the operative part of the judgment as violating the hierarchical legal order in Poland. However, these effect relates to norms established by the national legislator.

Literature

Barcz J., Glosa do wyroku TK z dnia 11 maja 2005 r. (zgodność Traktatu akcesyjnego z Konstytucją RP) K 18/04 [Commentary on the CT judgment of 11 May 2005 (conformity of the Treaty of Accession with the Constitution of the Republic of Poland) K 18/04], *Kwartalnik Prawa Publicznego*, 2005, no. 4, pp. 169–184.

Barcz J., Grzelak A., Szyndlauer R. (eds.), *Problem praworządności w Polsce w świetle orzecznictwa Trybunału Sprawiedliwości UE (2018–2020)* [The problem of the rule of law in Poland in the light case law of the Court of Justice of the EU (2018–2020)], Dom Wydawniczy Elipsa, 2021.

Bartosiewicz A., Kubacki R., Glosa do wyroku TK z 7 listopada 2007 r., K 18/06 [Commentary on the CT judgment of 7 November 2007, K 18/06], *Europejski Przegląd Sądowy*, 2008, no. 11, pp. 42–49.

Biernat S., Glosa do wyroku TK z dnia 11 maja 2005 r., K 18/04 [Commentary on the CT judgment of 11 May 2005, K 18/04], *Kwartalnik Prawa Publicznego*, 2005, no. 4, pp. 185–206.

Biernat S., Łętowska E., *This Was Not Just Another Ultra Vires Judgment!: Commentary to the Statement of Retired Judges of the Constitutional Tribunal*, VerfBlog, 27.10.2021, https://verfassungsblog.de/this-was-not-just-another-ultra-vires-judgment/

Bogdanowicz P., *Legal Opinion on the Legal Consequences of the Constitutional Tribunal Ruling in Case K 3/21 on the Incompatibility of the Provisions of the Treaty on European Union with the Constitution of the Republic of Poland in Light of European Union Law*, www.batory.org.pl/wp-content/uploads/2021/11/P.Bogndanowicz_Legal.opinion.on_.the_.legal_.consequences.of_.the_.Polish.Constitutional.Tribunal.ruling.in_.caseK3_.21.pdf

Chybalski P., Aprobata i krytyka stosowania wykładni komparatystycznej w orzecznictwie konstytucyjnym [Approval and Critique of the Use of Comparative Interpretation in Constitutional Adjudication], *Państwo i Prawo*, 2022, no. 4, pp. 27–45.

Craig P., Directives, Direct Effect and the Construction of National Legislation, *European Law Review*, 1997, 22, no. 6, pp. 519–538.

Czapliński W., *Znaczenie orzecznictwa Trybunału Sprawiedliwości Unii Europejskiej w procesie rozwoju prawa europejskiego* [The importance of the case law of the Court of Justice of the European Union in the process of development of EU law], Scholar, 2021.

Dąbrowska E., Judgment of 24 November 2010 Ref. No. K 32/09 concerning the Treaty of Lisbon (application submitted by a group of Senators), *Polish Yearbook of International Law*, 2010, no. 1, pp. 304–314.

De Visser M., *Constitutional Review in Europe: A Comparative Analysis*, Hart Publishing, 2013.

Dubicka A., Konstytucyjność przystąpienia Polski do Unii Europejskiej (w świetle wyroku TK) [Constitutionality of Poland's accession to the European Union (in the light of the Constitutional Tribunal's decision], *Państwo i Prawo*, 2007, no. 6, pp. 35–48.

Florczak-Wątor M., (Nie)skuteczność wyroku Trybunału Konstytucyjnego z 7.10.2021 r., K 3/21. Ocena znaczenia orzeczenia z perspektywy prawa konstytucyjnego [(In)Effectiveness of Constitutional Tribunal Judgment of 7 October 2021, K 3/21. Assessment of the Judgment's Significance from a Constitutional Law Perspective], *Europejski Przegląd Sądowy*, 2021, no. 12, pp. 4–11.

Grabowski A., Naleziński B., Konstytucyjne prawo do niezawisłego i bezstronnego sądu w państwie pozornie praworządnym [The Constitutional Right to the Independent and Impartial Court in a Pretendedly Rule of Law State], *Państwo i Prawo*, 2020, no. 10, pp. 25–47.

Grzelak A., Glosa do wyroku TK z dnia 18 lutego 2009 r., Kp 3/08 [Commentary on the CT judgment of 18 February 2009, Kp 3/08], *Przegląd Sejmowy*, 2009, no. 4, pp. 205–215.

Jaraczewski J., *Polexit or Judicial Dialogue*? CJEU and Polish Constitutional Tribunal in July 2021, Polexit or judicial dialogue? – Verfassungsblog, 19.07.2021, https://verfassungsblog.de/polexit-or-judicial-dialogue/

Karpenstein R., Sangi, Polexit vom Rechtsstaat, *Europäische Zeitschrift für Wirtschaftsrecht*, 2020, pp. 140.

Kawczyńska M., Środki tymczasowe stosowane w postępowaniach przed Trybunałem Sprawiedliwości ze szczególnym uwzględnieniem środków podjętych w sprawach dotyczących Polski [Interim measures in proceedings before the Court of Justice of the EU, with particular reference to the measures taken in the cases concerning Poland], in J. Barcz, A. Grzelak, R. Szyndlauer (eds.), *Problem praworządności w Polsce w świetle orzecznictwa Trybunału Sprawiedliwości UE (2018 2020)* [The problem of the rule of law in Poland in the light case law of the Court of Justice of the EU (2018-2020)], Dom Wydawniczy Elipsa, 2021.

Kowalik-Bańczyk K., Prowspólnotowa wykładnia prawa krajowego [The principle of conform interpretation of national law], *Europejski Przegląd Sądowy*, 2005, no. 3, pp. 9–18.

Kowalik-Bańczyk K., Should We Polish It Up? The Polish Constitutional Tribunal and the Idea of Supremacy of EU Law, *German Law Journal*, 2005, no. 6, pp. 1355–1366.

Krzemińska J., Courts as Comparatists: References to Foreign Law in the Case-law of the Polish Constitutional Court, *Jean Monnet Working Paper*, 2012, no. 5, www.jeanmonnetprogram.org.

Krzywoń A., Glosa do wyroku TK z dnia 13 października 2010 r., Kp 1/09 [Commentary on the CT judgment of 13 October 2010, Kp 1/09], *Przegląd Sejmowy*, 2011, no. 5, pp. 133–143.

Kwiecień R., Zgodność traktatu akcesyjnego z Konstytucją. Glosa do wyroku TK z dnia 11 maja 2005 r., K 18/04 [The compliance of the Treaty of Accession with the Constitution. Comments on the CT judgment of 11 May 2005, K 18/04], *Europejski Przegląd Sądowy*, 2005, no. 1, pp. 40–45.

Łacny J., Pieniądze nerwem wojny? – czyli o możliwych skutkach finansowych wyroku Trybunału Konstytucyjnego w sprawie K 3/21 z 7.10.2021 r. [Is Money the Soul of War? Or on the Possible Financial Consequences of the Constitutional Tribunal's Judgment in case K 3/21 of 7.10.2021], *Europejski Przegląd Sądowy*, 2021, no. 12, pp. 39–50.

Lasek-Markey M., *Poland's Constitutional Tribunal on the Status of EU Law: The Polish Government Got All the Answers it Needed from a Court it Controls*, https://europeanlawblog.eu/2021/10/21/polands-constitutional-tribunal-on-the-status-of-eu-law-the-polish-government-got-all-the-answers-it-needed-from-a-court-it-controls/

Lawson T., *'Non-Existent'. The Polish Constitutional Tribunal in a State of Denial of the ECtHR Xero Flor Judgment*, 'Non-Existent' – Verfassungsblog, 18.06.2021, https://verfassungsblog.de/non-existent/

Leloup M., An Uncertain First Step in the Field of Judicial Self-Government. CJEU 19 November 2019, Joined Cases C-585/15, C-624/18 and C-625/18, A.K., CP and DO, *European Constitutional Law Review*, 2020, 16, no. 1, pp. 145–169.

Leloup M., Krajewski M., Ziółkowski M., EU Judicial Independence Decentralized: A.K., *CMLRev.*, 2020, pp. 1107–1138.

Łętowska E., Wiewiórowska-Domagalska A., A 'Good' Change in the Polish Constitutional Tribunal? *Osteuropa Recht*, 2018, no. 1, pp. 79–93.

Maduro P., Courts and Pluralism: Essay on a Theory of Judicial Adjudication in the Context of Legal and Constitutional Pluralism, in J.L. Dunoff, J.P. Trachtman (eds.), *Ruling the World? Constitutionalism, International Law, and Global Governance*, Cambridge University Press, 2009.

Martinico G., Pollicino O., The Interaction between Europe's Legal Systems, in *Judicial Dialogue and the Creation of Supranational Laws*, Edward Elgar, 2012.

Matczak M., The Rule of Law in Poland: A Sorry Spectacle, *Verfassungsblog*, https://verfassungsblog.de/the-rule-of-law-in-poland-a-sorry-spectacle/

Mayer, F.C., Wendel M., Multilevel Constitutionalism and Constitutional Pluralism, in: M. Avbelj, J. Komárek (eds.), *Constitutional Pluralism in the European Union and Beyond*, Hart Publishing, 2012.

Miąsik D., Szwarc M., Primacy and Direct Effect – Still Together: Popławski II, *CMLRev.*, 2021, pp. 571–590.

Miąsik D., *Zasady i prawa podstawowe. System Prawa Unii Europejskiej* [Principles and fundamental rights. System of EU Law], CH Beck, 2022, s. 36–37.

Nita B., Jurysdykcja TS w trzecim filarze UE. Glosa do wyroku TK z dnia 18 lutego 2009 r., Kp 3/08 [Jurisdiction of the Court of Justice in the third pillar of the EU. Commentary on the CT judgment of 18 February 2009, Kp 3/08], *Europejski Przegląd Sądowy*, 2010, no. 7, pp. 47–54.

Nowakowski M., Glosa do wyroku TK z dnia 26 czerwca 2013 r., K 33/12 [Commentary on the CT judgment of 26 June 2013, K 33/12], *Ius Novum*, 2015, no. 4, pp. 154–168.

Paprocka A., Argument komparatystyczny w orzecznictwie Trybunału Konstytucyjnego [Comparative argument in the jurisprudence of the Constitutional Tribunal], *Państwo i Prawo*, 2017, no. 7, pp. 37–54.

Pech L., Protecting Polish Judges from Poland's Disciplinary 'Star Chamber': Commission v. Poland (Interim proceedings), *CMLRev.*, 2021, pp. 137–162.

Pernice I., *Multilevel Constitutionalism in the European Union*, WHI Paper 5/02 whipaper0502.pdf (hu-berlin.de)

Poiares Maduro M., Three Claims of Constitutional Pluralism, in M. Avbelj, J. Komárek (eds.), *Constitutional Pluralism in the European Union and Beyond*, Hart Publishing, 2012.

Polański O., *Poland: Another Episode of 'Rule of Law Backsliding' – Judgment P 7/20 and a Threat to the Integrity of the EU Legal Order*, https://hdl.handle.net/1814/74056 (eui.eu).

Półtorak N., *European Union Rights in National Courts*, Kluwer Law International, 2015.

Półtorak N., Kilka uwag o skutkach wyroku Trybunału Konstytucyjnego w sprawie K 3/21 dla stosowania prawa unijnego przez polskie sądy [Some Remarks on the Implications of the Decision of the Polish Constitutional Tribunal in Case K 3/21 for the Application of EU Law by Polish Courts], *Europejski Przegląd Sądowy*, 2021, no. 12, pp. 12–18.

Report on the Activities of Polish Authorities after the Rulings of the Court of Justice of the EU of July 14, 2021 in case C-204/21 and of July 15, 2021 in case

C-791/19, Report on the Activities of Polish Authorities after the Rulings of the Court of Justice of the EU of July 14, 2021 in case C-204/21 and of July 15, 2021 in case C-791/19 with attachments – Stowarzyszenie Sędziów Polskich Iustitia.

Sadurski W., Polish Constitutional Tribunal under PiS: From an Activist Court, to a Paralysed Tribunal, to a Governmental Enabler, *Hague Journal on the Rule Law*, 2019, no. 11, pp. 63–84.

Safjan M., Central & Eastern European Constitutional Courts Facing New Challenges – Ten Years of Experience, in M. Bobek (ed.), *Central European Judges Under the European Influence. The Transformation Power of the EU Revisited*, Hart Publishing, 2015.

Safjan M., Niezależność Trybunału Konstytucyjnego i suwerenność konstytucyjna RP [Independence of the Constitutional Tribunal and constitutional sovereignty of the Republic of Poland], *Państwo i Prawo*, 2006, no. 6, pp. 3–17.

Skomerska-Muchowska I., The Dialogue of CEE Constitutional Courts in the Era of Constitutional Pluralism, in A. Wyrozumska (ed.), *Transnational Judicial Dialogue on International Law in Central and Eastern Europe*, Wydawnictwo Uniwersytetu Łódzkiego, 2017.

Skouris V., Effet Utile Versus Legal Certainty: The Case-law of the Court of Justice on the Direct Effect of Directives, *European Business Law Review*, 2006, 17, no. 2, pp. 241–255.

Sołtys A., Cechy i charakter prawa unijnego oraz problem jego konstytucjonalizacji [Features and nature of EU law and the problem of its constitutionalization], in S. Biernat (ed.), *System Prawa Unii Europejskiej* [System of EU Law], C.H. Beck, 2020, pp. 237–289.

Sołtys A., *Obowiązek wykładni prawa krajowego zgodnie z prawem unijnym jako instrument zapewniania efektywności prawa Unii Europejskiej* [The Obligation to Interpret National Law in Conformity with EU Law as an Instrument to Ensure Effectiveness of EU Law], Wolters Kluwer Polska, 2015.

Sołtys A., The Court of Justice of the European Union in the Case Law of the Polish Constitutional Court: The Current Breakdown in View of Polish Constitutional Jurisprudence Pre-2016, *Hague Journal on the Rule of Law*, 2022, 15, p. 19–49, https://link.springer.com/article/10.1007/s40803-022-00186-6

Sołtys A., Wykładnia prawa UE w orzecznictwie TK [Interpretation of EU law in the jurisprudence of the Constitutional Tribunal], in L. Leszczyński (ed.), *System Prawa Unii Europejskiej. Wykładnia prawa Unii Europejskiej* [System of EU law. Interpretation of European Union law], vol. 3, CH Beck, 2019.

Szuleka M., *The Constitutional Crisis in Poland*, Helsinki Foundation for Human Rights, 2016, www.hfhr.pl/wp-content/uploads/2016/09/HFHR_The-constitutional-crisis-in-Poland-2015-2016.pdf

Szwed M., The Polish Constitutional Tribunal Crisis from the Perspective of the European Convention on Human Rights. ECtHR 7 May 2021, No. 4907/18, Xero Flor w Polsce sp. z o.o. v Poland, *European Constitutional Law Review*, 2022, no. 1, pp. 132–154.

Taborowski M., *Mechanizmy ochrony praworządności państw członkowskich w prawie Unii Europejskiej. Studium przebudzenia systemu ponadnarodowego* [Mechanisms of protection of the rule of law of Member States in EU law. A study of the awakening of the supranational system], Wolters Kluwer Polska, 2019.

Tatham A.F., *Central European Constitutional Courts in the Face of EU Membership: The Influence of German Model in Hungary and Poland*, Martinus Nijhoff Publishers, 2013.

Weiler J.H.H., In Defence of the Status Quo: Europe's Constitutional Sonderweg, in J.H.H. Weiler, M. Wind (eds.), *European Constitutionalism Beyond the State*, Cambridge University Press, 2003.

Wiącek M., Constitutional Crisis in Poland 2015–2016 in the Light of the Rule of Law Principle, in A. von Bogdandy et al. (eds.), *Defending Checks and Balances in EU Member States, Beiträge zum ausländischen öffentlichen Recht und Völkerrecht (Veröffentlichungen des Max-Planck-Instituts für ausländisches öffentliches Recht und Völkerrecht)*, Springer, 2021.

Wójcik A., *Constitutional Tribunal Ruled: CJEU Interim Orders Do Not Apply in Poland*, https://ruleoflaw.pl/constitutional-tribunal-ruled-CJEUeu-interim-orders-do-not-apply-in-poland/

Wójtowicz K., *Constitutional Courts and the European Union Law*, Wydawnictwo Sejmowe, 2014, p. 220, http://www.bibliotekacyfrowa.pl/Content/63576/Constitutional_courts.pdf

Wójtowicz K., Glosa do wyroku TK z dnia 11 maja 2005 r., K 18/04 [Commentary on the CT judgment of 11 May 2005, K 18/04], *Przegląd Sejmowy*, 2005, no. 6, pp. 190–196.

Wójtowicz K., Traktat akcesyjny – wyrok z dnia 11 maja 2005 r., K 18/04 [The Accession Treaty – Judgment of 11 May 2005, K 18/04], in M. Derlatka, L. Garlicki, M. Wiącek (eds.), *Na straży państwa prawa. Trzydzieści lat orzecznictwa Trybunału Konstytucyjnego* [Upholding the rule of law. Thirty years jurisprudence of the Constitutional Tribunal], Wolters Kluwer Polska, 2016.

Wojtyczek K., Trybunał konstytucyjny w europejskim systemie konstytucyjnym [Constitutional Tribunal in the European constitutional system], *Przegląd Sejmowy*, 2009, no. 4, pp. 177–192.

Wójtowicz K., Zachowanie tożsamości konstytucyjnej państwa polskiego w ramach UE – uwagi na tle wyroku TK z 24.11.2010 r. (K 32/09) [Maintaining the constitutional identity of the Polish state within the EU – remarks against the background of Constitutional Tribunal's judgment of 24 November 2010 (K 32/09)], *Europejski Przegląd Sądowy*, 2011, no. 11, pp. 4–11.

Wróbel A., Pośredni skutek dyrektyw, czyli wykładnia prawa państwa członkowskiego zgodnie z prawem wspólnotowym [Indirect Effect of Directives – Interpretation of Member State's Law in Conformity with Community Law], in A. Wróbel (ed.), *Stosowanie prawa Unii Europejskiej przez sądy. Tom I* [Application of EU Law by Courts], Wolters Kluwer, 2005.

Wróbel W., Skutki rozstrzygnięcia w sprawie K 3/21 w perspektywie Sądu Najwyższego i sądów powszechnych [Effects of the Judgment in Case K 3/21 from the Perspective of the Polish Supreme Court and Ordinary Courts], *Europejski Przegląd Sądowy*, 2021, no. 12, pp. 19–26.

Wyrozumska A., Wyroki Trybunału Konstytucyjnego w sprawach K 3/21 oraz K 6/21 w świetle prawa międzynarodowego [Judgments of the Polish Constitutional Tribunal in Cases K 3/21 and K 6/21 in the Light of International Law], *Europejski Przegląd Sądowy*, 2021, no. 12, pp. 27–38.

Ziętek-Capiga A., Zawieszenie funkcjonowania Izby Dyscyplinarnej Sądu Najwyższego [The suspension of the Disciplinary Chamber of Pilish Supreme Court], *Praca i Zabezpieczenie Społeczne*, 2020, no. 6, pp. 43–45.

Part III

The principles of primacy and direct effect of EU law in the case-law of Polish courts

The principles of primacy and direct effect define the legal system of EU law as a system that is independent of international and national legal systems.[1] The principle of direct effect of EU law, as declared by the CJEU in *Van Gend en Loos*, means that a provision of Union law, which is clear and unconditional, may create the rights of individuals which national courts must protect.[2] The principle of primacy, since the ruling of the CJEU in *Costa v. ENEL*, is understood in a way that 'the law stemming from the Treaty, an independent source of law, could not, because of its special and original nature, be overridden by domestic legal provisions, however framed, without being deprived of its character as Community law and without the legal basis of the Community itself being called into question', which results in the limitation of sovereign rights of Member States as they are prohibited from adopting acts incompatible with EU law.[3]

The previous statements were concretised further by the CJEU in *Simmenthal*,[4] when it ruled that:

1) the direct effect of EU law provisions means that they are a direct source of rights and duties for all those affected thereby, whether they concern Member States or individuals who are parties in legal relationships under Community law and that any national court whose task it is as an organ of a Member State to protect, in a case within its jurisdiction, the rights conferred upon individuals by Community law;[5]
2) the relationship between the provisions of the Treaty and the directly applicable measures of the institutions, on the one hand, and the National

1 Cases: C-61/11, *El Dridi*, EU:C:2011:268, para. 61; C–752/18, *Deutsche Umwelthilfe*, EU:C:2019:1114, para. 42; C-556/17, *Torubarov*, EU:C:2019:626, para. 73.
2 Case 26/62, *Van Gend en Loos*, EU:C:1963:1.
3 Case 6/64, *Costa v. ENEL*, EU:C:1964:66.
4 Case 106/77, *Simmenthal*, EU:C:1978:49.
5 Case 106/77, *Simmenthal*, paras. 14–16.

DOI: 10.4324/9781003376019-10

Law of the Member States, on the other, is such that those provisions and measures that, not only by their entry into force render automatically inapplicable any conflicting provision of current national law but also, insofar as they are an integral part of, and take precedence in, the legal order applicable in the territory of each of the Member States, also preclude the valid adoption of new national legislative measures to the extent to which they would be incompatible with Community provisions;[6] and

3) every national court must, in a case within its jurisdiction, apply Community Law in its entirety and protect the rights which the latter confers on individuals and must accordingly set aside any provision of national law which may conflict with it, whether prior or subsequent to the Community rule.[7]

The meaning of the principles of primacy and direct effect provided earlier has been accepted for the considerations in this volume. As both principles have been thoroughly discussed in the literature,[8] let us then recall the most important aspects of direct effect and primacy from the perspective of a national court.

It is commonly accepted that EU law provisions are directly effective, if they can act as a direct source of legally cognisable rights and obligations before national courts.[9] These provisions may be invoked[10] or relied on[11] by individuals in proceedings before national courts. Thus, the perspective of an individual focuses on the capability of EU law to create judicially enforceable rights or obligations that an individual may exert from the Member State or

6 Case 106/77 *Simmenthal*, EU:C:1978:49, para. 17.

7 Case 106/77 *Simmenthal*, EU:C:1978:49, para. 21.

8 P. Graig, G. de Burca, *EU Law: Text, Cases, and Materials*, Oxford University Press, 2020; R. Schutze, *European Constitutional Law*, Oxford University Press, 2021; K. Bradley, Direct Effect, Primacy and the Nature of the Legal Order, in: P. Craig, G. de Burca (eds.), *The Evolution of EU Law*, Oxford University Press, 2021; M. Dougan, Primacy and the Remedy of Dissapplication, *CMLRev.*, 2019, pp. 1459–1508; in Polish literature in particular: A. Wróbel, Zasady ogólne (podstawowe) prawa Unii Europejskiej. Tom I, wydanie 2 [The general principles of EU law. Vol. 1. Second edition], in: A. Wróbel (ed.), *Stosowanie prawa Unii Europejskiej przez sądy* [Application of EU Law by Courts], Wolters Kluwer Polska, 2010, pp. 89–156; M. Domańska, *Implementacja dyrektyw unijnych przez sądy krajowe* [Implementation of EU Directives by National Courts], Wolters Kluwer Polska, 2014; D. Miąsik, *Zasady i prawa podstawowe. System Prawa Unii Europejskiej*, T. 2 [The Principles and Fundamental Rights. System of EU Law. Vol. 2], C.H. Beck, 2022, pp. 91–116–157.

9 M. Dougan, General Report. National Courts and the Enforcement of EU Law, in: M. Botman, J. Langer (eds.), *National Courts and the Enforcement of EU Law: The Pivotal Role of National Courts in the EU Legal Order*. The XXIX FIDE Congress in the Hague 2020 Congress Publications vol. 1, Eleven International Publishing, 2020, p. 31.

10 Case C-176/12, *Association de médiation sociale*, EU:C:2014:2, para. 47–49; case C-316/13, *Fenoll*, EU:C:2015:200, para. 48; case C-569/16 and C-570/16, *Bauer et al.*, EU:C:2018:871, para. 79.

11 Case C-356/05, *Farell I*, EU:C:2007:229, para. 37–39; case C-237/07, *Janecek*, EU:C:2008:447, para. 36; case C-135/10, *SCF*, EU:C:2012:140, para. 43; case C-282/10, *Dominguez*, para. 32; case C-425/12, *Portgas*, para. 19–21.

from another individual. The perspective of national courts is different in that it focuses on the possibility (or rather the duty) of a national court to apply, directly, the provisions of EU law when deciding a case on the merits of or even a single contentious issue that falls within the scope of the application of EU law. For this reason, whereas from the point of view of an individual it is about the possibility of invoking EU provisions before national courts, from the point of view of national courts, it is about the capability of EU law to create binding norms that must be applied by national courts.

A provision of EU law may be considered directly effective when two conditions are met. Firstly, it must be sufficiently precise and unconditional.[12] Secondly, the provision under consideration must be contained in a source of EU law that is capable of producing a direct effect. Some sources of EU law can produce a direct effect without any restrictions other than the wording of their provisions, while other sources can be directly effective only in certain circumstances (directives) or do not produce a direct effect at all, since the Member States had excluded such a capability in the founding treaties (framework decisions).[13]

The direct effect is about the duty of national courts to apply directly EU law when adjudicating an 'EU case'. However, this principle is silent as to what a national court should do when it encounters a legal situation in which there is a collision between a provision of national law and a directly effective provision(s) of EU law. This is the domain of the principle of primacy under which, in case of a conflict between EU law and national law, EU law must prevail. Whilst the primacy of EU law entails several specific duties for all Member States and their authorities, for a national court the most important aspect of the primacy of EU law concerns its duty to decide, in a particular case, on decentralised manner (for single proceedings), whether there is an actual conflict of provisions belonging to two legal orders and if so, to grant EU law the priority (precedence) of application (as was already explained earlier).[14] Primacy operates when, having failed to interpret national law in conformity with EU law, a national court finds that there is any inconsistency between the two sets of provisions applicable to the fact of the case or the contentious issue. The principle of primacy dictates that the EU provision should take precedence.

Following the formulation of both principles, EU law could be used in national proceedings as a shield or as a sword. The so-called offensive use of EU law (as a 'sword')[15] concerns a situation in which the directly effective

12 Case C-282/10, *Dominguez*, EU:C:2012:33, para. 33; in some rulings the CJEU still applies three conditions: 'clear, precise and unconditional', see case C-573/17, *Popławski II*, EU:C:2019:530, para. 64.

13 See further: D. Miąsik, M. Szwarc, Primacy and Direct Effect – Still Together: Popławski II, *CMLRev.*, 2021, pp. 571–590.

14 Case 106/77, *Simmenthal*, EU:C:1978:49, para. 24.

15 For example, opinion of AG Mazak in case C-411/05, *Félix Palacios de la Villa*, EU:C:2007:106, para. 124.

provision of EU law constitutes a source of a right or obligation that can be executed by another party to the proceedings, either a Member State or an individual and has not been provided for in national law (e.g., a worker claims that his dismissal was discriminatory because of their age). On the contrary, the defensive (or 'exclusionary' or 'shield')[16] use of directly effective provisions of EU law covers a situation in which a party to the proceedings tries, by recourse to EU law, to avoid the negative consequences resulting from the application of provisions of national law that are incompatible with EU law (e.g., undertaking sued for unfair competition tort claims that national legislation prohibiting certain marketing activity violates the Treaty).

Whilst it may have seemed in the past that primacy and direct effect can be applied separately, in *Popławski II*, the CJEU finally ruled that national courts are obliged to respect the primacy of EU law only when they have established a collision between national legal norms and norms derived from the directly effective provisions of EU law. If a provision of EU law does not pass the direct effect test, or when a provision of EU law comes from a source of EU law that is not capable of producing a direct effect at all (framework decisions), or in most situations (directives in disputes between individuals), then a national court is not bound by the duty to disapply provisions of national law. The position taken by the CJEU in *Popławski II* makes the use of consistent interpretation even more important for the effectiveness of EU law. In *Popławski II*, the Court explicitly precluded 'exclusionary' effects of those EU norms that are derived from provisions contained in such sources of EU law, whose direct effect was limited by the Court itself or excluded by the contracting Member States.[17] This reduces the scope of application of the primacy of EU law.

In judicial practice, by disapplying those provisions of national law that lead to the reconstruction of a legal norm, inconsistent with a norm of EU origin, a national court will be able to formulate the legal basis of adjudication, which will not contain national provisions incompatible with EU law. Three situations can be distinguished in this context.

In the first one, a national court would disapply all substantive provisions of national law that were supposed to form a legal basis of its decision (substitution effect). These provisions will be supplemented by the directly effective provisions of EU law and grant rights or impose obligations upon Member States or individuals. In the second one, which happens much more often, a national court will disapply only some of the provisions of national law (exclusionary effect). The remedy of disapplication will be used against those provisions of national law that make a national court unable to decode from national law a legal norm that would be compatible with an

16 For example, opinion of AG Saggio, joint cases C-240/98 to C-244/98, *Océano Grupo Editorial SA*, EU:C:1999:620, para. 37–38.

17 Case C-573/17, *Popławski II*, para. 61.

EU norm. By doing that, a national court will create a 'new' legal base for its decision that will consist purely of other national provisions that allow a national court to deliver a judgment that will be based on the application of national norms compatible with EU norms.[18] The third situation encompasses cases when a national court adjudicates on a legal base composed of national provisions and EU provisions combined (exclusion and substitution combined), as, for example, in discrimination cases in which an individual discriminated (contrary to EU law) must be awarded the same rights granted to a privileged individual.

This part presents the case-law of Polish courts, which exemplifies that they apply the primacy and direct effect in all possible contexts, as explained earlier.

18 As to the working of exclusionary effect, see Editorial comments: Horizontal direct effect – A law of diminishing coherence?, *CMLRev.*, 2006, pp. 3–5. The concept could result in depriving individuals of rights granted to them by the national 'incompatible' legislation, see reservations to the concept of exclusionary effect as summarised by P. Craig, G. de Burca, *EU Law. Text, Cases and Materials*, Oxford University Press, 2008, pp. 302–303, and P. Craig, The Legal Effect of Directives: Policy, Rules and Exceptions, *European Law Review*, 2009, 34, no. 3, pp. 349–377.

8 The principles of primacy and direct effect in the case-law of the Supreme Court

Dawid Miąsik

Introduction

Compared with the interpretation of Polish law in conformity with EU law, the case-law of the Supreme Court provides only a few examples of references to the principles of direct effect and primacy of EU law. From the point of view of pure statistics, the *Simmenthal* judgment has been referred to only in 20 cases. As many as 12 of those rulings were the preliminary references of the Chamber of Labour and Social Security in matters concerning the independence of the judiciary, intended to formulate a common, EU-wide standard of protection of the rule of law in the Member States that could be applied by national courts that have found themselves under hostile takeover by the legislative or executive powers.[1] Among the rulings mentioned earlier, the *Simmenthal* rule (the refusal to apply a provision of national law incompatible with EU law) has been used seven times,[2] once the interpretation in conformity with EU law has been made due to the limitations in the application of the principle of the primacy of EU law because of the lack of direct effect of Directives,[3] and twice a national provision has not been found inconsistent with EU law.[4] In the case-law of the Civil Chamber of the Supreme Court, the principle of primacy has been directly referred to only once.[5] In the case-law of the Criminal Chamber of the Supreme Court, the principle of primacy of EU law has been referred to twice.[6]

1 See the reasoning of the preliminary reference in C-508/19, para. 12–16, available on the curia.eu.
2 Judgments of the SC: of 14 June 2012, case I PK 230/11; of 4 December 2018, case I PK 181/17; of 8 December 2020, case II PK 35/19; of 5 December 2019, case III PO 7/18; order of the SC of 15 January.2020 r., case III PO 8/18.
3 Order of the panel of seven judges of the SC of 29 August 2019, case III UZP 3/17.
4 Judgment of the SC of 8 October 2014, case III SK 85/13; order of the panel of seven judges of the SC of 9 September 2020, case III UZP 4/18.
5 Order of the SC of 8 April 2010, case III CZP 3/10.
6 Order of 27 November 2014, case II KK 55/14; resolution of the panel of seven judges of the SC of 19 January 2017, case I KZP 17/16.

DOI: 10.4324/9781003376019-11

Reception of the principles of primacy and direct effect

Both principles have been approved in case-law developed so far, by the Supreme Court. However, it should be noted that there is a certain dissonance as to the source of being bound by them and thus, the nature of both principles. On the one hand, there are cases in which a reference is made referring to Article 91 (3) of the Constitution of the Republic of Poland as the legal source allowing Polish courts to apply the principle of primacy of EU law. That approach was used in one of the first EU cases resolved by the Supreme Court, namely in the judgment of 10 February 2006, case III CSK 112/05 (discussed in more detail subsequently). It was also repeated later. For example, in the resolution of the panel of seven judges of the SC of 19 January 2017, case I KZP 17/16, the consequences of the conflict between Polish law and EU law were analysed in the light of the principle of direct applicability of EU law, which is embedded in Article 91 (3) of the RP Constitution. Such an approach suggests that both EU law principles, referred to in this chapter, are the principles governed by the national Constitution and may be treated as the principles binding upon Polish courts only and exclusively to the extent governed by the RP Constitution and the rulings of the Constitutional Tribunal. On the other hand, in numerous judgments of the Supreme Court, the principles of direct effect and primacy of EU law are treated as legal principles characteristic of EU law as an autonomous legal system. In such cases, the principle of primacy is applied as a principle of EU law without reference to the national constitutional provisions accepting this principle.[7] That dissonance can be noticed between the case-law of the Civil Chamber and the Criminal Chamber of the Supreme Court (emphasising the constitutional embedding of both principles) versus the case-law of the Chamber of Labour and Social Security (treating both principles as autonomous principles of the EU legal order mandatorily binding in the legal order of the State which has voluntarily accessed the European Union).

In addition, it should be noted that in the initial period of membership of Poland in the EU, compliance with the principle of primacy sometimes faced resistance at the stage of the proceedings before the courts of lower instances, which in certain cases ruled directly, that it was not possible to disapply the provisions of national law, even if it was inconsistent with EU law, until the legislature or a judgment introducing suitable amendments was issued by the constitutional court finding a particular normative measure to be unconstitutional.[8] The reluctance to

7 Judgment of the SC of 4 January 2008 case I UK 182/07; see, for example, judgments described in the historical part of the grounds for the judgment of the SC of 10 February 2006, case III CSK 112/05, and in the historical part of the grounds for the judgment of the SC of 4 August 2009, case I PK 64/09.

8 See the judgment of the court of the second instance described in the historical part of the grounds for the judgment of the SC of 8 December 2009, case I BU 6/09: 'Consequently, the Court of Appeal held that as long as Article 5 of the Law of 29 May 1974 is not repealed

refuse to apply the provisions of national law, inconsistent with EU law, is evident in those cases in which, in order to avoid conflicts pertaining to the interpretation of laws, reference was made to the understanding of national law in conformity with EU law without presenting the interpretative reasoning, which led the adjudicating court to ensure compliance between the content of a rule of national law and EU law.[9]

For the completeness of the argumentation and to demonstrate what problems may be expected in the future with the application of both principles of EU law in Poland, resulting from the rule of law crisis, the following should be mentioned. This is about the position expressed in the statements of the recently established Chambers of the Supreme Court, whose status is assessed by the Court of Justice.[10] In the resolution of the Chamber of the Extraordinary Control and Public Affairs of 8 January 2020, case I NOZP 3/19, the principle of primacy of EU law was formally accepted (item 18). Still, only to the extent delimited by the Constitution of the Republic of Poland (item 18) and the competences conferred on the Union (Para. 19 and 20) with the conclusion: 'the application of EU law must not lead to the results contrary to the express wording of the constitutional rules and impossible to be reconciled with the minimum guarantee functions performed by the RP Constitution' (Para. 21). That position was shared in the judgment of the Disciplinary Chamber of 30 January 2020, case II DSK 5/19. Thus, the conditionality of the principle of primacy of EU law was emphasised, and the jurisdiction was reserved for the Constitutional Tribunal of the Republic of Poland to finally decide whether the principle of primacy in a given case would oblige the Supreme Court to refuse to apply the provisions of Polish law, contrary to EU law. Since 2017, the Polish Constitutional Court has found unconstitutional only those rules of which non-compliance with the Constitution is suitable for the political authorities. In this situation, it can be assumed, with the probability closer to certainty, that, in the event of normative measures consistent with the political will of the governing majority but contrary to EU law and requiring the application of the principle of primacy, the use of the latter by the court will be treated as an infringement of the Constitution of the Republic of Poland, either by the constitutional court ruling in response to the request of the political authority or by a disciplinary body which is not a court in the meaning of EU law.

On the other hand, in the decision of the Disciplinary Chamber of 9 May 2019, case II DSI 37/18, it was found that a national court was obliged to refuse to apply a provision of national law because it was inconsistent with EU law only if

---

by the legislator or declared unconstitutional by the Constitutional Tribunal, it continues to function in legal transactions and is subject to the application by State or judicial authorities'.

9 See the position of the courts of lower instances in the judgment of 18 November 2020, case III PK 53/19.

10 Case C-585/18, *A.K. and Others*, EU:C:2019:982; case C-487/19, *proceedings brought by W.Ż.*, EU:C:2021:798.

it had referred to the Court of Justice for a preliminary ruling and from the judgment of the CJ resulted 'an interpretative ruling on non-compliance of national law with EU law'. In turn, that position suggests that, contrary to the principle of uniform interpretation and the application of EU law in the Member States, in the future case-law of the Chambers of the Supreme Court, it is possible not to comply with the interpretation of the EU law given by the Court of Justice in the preliminary rulings unless the adjudicating panel of the court has referred a question for a preliminary ruling in the case under consideration.

The content of the principles of primacy and direct effect

The principles of direct effect and the primacy of EU law are treated and applied by the Supreme Court and the ordinary courts as the practical instrument enabling the issuance of rulings based on the legal basis compatible with Union law. The principle of direct effect is treated as specifying, in whole or part, the content of the normative basis for the ruling to be taken by the national court. On the other hand, the principle of primacy of EU law is treated as an instrument that allows the national court to remove from the legal basis of the ruling such provisions (the elements of a legal rule) of national law, which would lead to the reconstruction and application of a legal norm, contrary to EU law and, thus, to issue an incorrect judgment from the point of view of EU law. Thus, the principle of direct effect relates to the possibility of a court applying a provision (rule) of EU law in given proceedings when issuing a final ruling or deciding on an incidental issue (judgment of the SC of 18 November 2020, case III PK 53/19). Whereas, the principle of primacy serves to form the legal basis of the ruling without taking into account national provisions contrary to EU law (order of the panel of seven judges of the SC of 29 August 2019, case III UZP 3/17).

Both principles are directly related in terms of how they function. The national courts are obliged to respect the principle of primacy only in case of a conflict between the rules of national law and the rules of EU law resulting from the directly effective provisions of EU law. In the case of the provisions of EU law which, due to their content, are not directly effective or which are contained in a source of law that has no direct effect or produces it to a limited extent (e.g., directives), the only way to remedy any possible conflict between national law and EU law is the interpretation of national law in conformity with EU law.

In this respect, in the case-law of the Supreme Court, inevitable volatility could be observed resulting from the focus on ensuring the greatest possible effectiveness of EU law. Initially, in the case-law of the Supreme Court, the principle of the primacy of EU law was combined only with the provisions that fulfilled the direct effect test. In the judgment of the SC of 4 January 2008, case I UK 182/07,[11] it was recognised that if a provision of EU law was directly effective,

11 See P. Brzeziński, *Relacje między zasadą pierwszeństwa a zasadą efektywności. Glosa do wyroku SN z dnia 4 stycznia 2008 r., I UK 182/07*, [Relationship Between the Principle of Primacy and the Principle Of Effectiveness of EU Law. Case Note to theJudgement of the Supreme Court of 4th January 2008, I UK 182/07], *Europejski Przegląd Sądowy*, 2010, no. 1, p. 50 and ff.

it might be relied on 'to exclude the application of any provision of national law incompatible with that provision'. Subsequently, case-law began to use the principle of primacy in isolation from the principle of direct effect. An example is the judgment of the SC of 4 August 2009, case I PK 64/09. It was adopted therein that the provision of Article 6 (1) (1) of the Law of 13 July 2006 on the protection of employee claims in the event of the insolvency of the employer[12] was incompatible with Article 8a of Directive 80/987,[13] imposing on the Member States the obligation to 'undertake necessary measures' to ensure that, in the event of the insolvency of an employer, employing workers in at least two the Member States, 'decisions taken in the context of insolvency . . . are taken into account when determining the employer's state of insolvency within the meaning of this Directive'. Subsequently, the concept of a close link between the principle of direct effect and the principle of primacy was returned to the refusal to apply national provisions only in the event of a conflict with a directly effective provision of EU law.[14] Finally, an attempt was made to clarify the relationship between the principle of direct effect and the principle of primacy in case III UZP 3/17, in which a question had been referred for a preliminary ruling, discussed in more detail in the chapter on consistent interpretation. After the CJEU replied that the application of a provision of the national code of civil procedure might not be refused on the grounds of incompatibility with Article 7 (1) of Directive 67/67 with a procedural effect detrimental to an individual, the Supreme Court confined itself to the application of the principle of interpretation in conformity with EU law[15] (whilst, initially, the Supreme Court argued in its reference that such an interpretation was not possible).

A distinction has to be drawn between the issues of the addressees of the obligations resulting from the principles of direct effect and primacy and the *ratione personae* of applying those principles. That personal scope results from the restrictions on the ability of EU law provisions to produce a direct effect, depending on the source of the EU law in which they have been included. The case-law of the Supreme Court respects the position of the CJEU as regards the restrictions on applying the principle of direct effect in the case of specific sources of law. In the case of Directives, it was allowed to use the principle of direct effect for the benefit of an individual in employment matters for the

12 *Dz. U.* [Journal of Laws] of 2006 No. 158, item 1121 as amended.

13 Council Directive 80/987/EEC of 20 October 1980 on the approximation of the laws of the Member States relating to the protection of employees in the event of the insolvency of their employer, OJ L 283, 28.10.1980, pp. 23–27 with amendments; Article 8a was added by Directive 2002/74/EC of the European Parliament and of the Council of 23 September 2002 amending Council Directive 80/987/EEC on the approximation of the laws of the Member States relating to the protection of employees in the event of the insolvency of their employer (Text with EEA relevance), OJ L 270, 8.10.2002, pp. 10–13.

14 Judgments of the SC: of 14 June 2012, case I PK 230/11; of 19 October 2012, case III SK 3/12; of 24 June 2015, case III SK 59/12.

15 See the preliminary reference made in order of the panel of seven judges of the SC of 19 July 2017, case III UZP 3/17, and order of the panel of seven judges of the SC of 29 August 2019, case III UZP 3/17, adopted following the judgment of CJEU in C-545/17, *Pawlak*, EU:C:2019:260.

benefit of an employee against the employer, that is, the court (judgment of the SC of 18 November 2020, case III PK 53/19). It was found that where the party to the proceedings was an emanation of a Member State acting as an employer in employment matters, an employee 'is entitled to rely on, in the proceedings before the labour courts, on the rights conferred on him/her under EU Directives'. In such a situation, the employee of a public employer may 'not only assert the rights under EU Directives, and which are not provided for in national law or to which he/she is entitled to under national law to a narrower extent'. Still, he/she may also

> rely on the provisions of EU Directives to exclude the application of provisions of national law contrary to them and to replace those provisions with other provisions of national law, consistent with EU law or directly effective provisions of EU law, in particular, contained in Directives.

The same treatment was given, for the purposes of applying Directive 2001/23,[16] to the national park with the status of a state organisational unit, which had acquired an undertaking in the form of an auxiliary enterprise although operating in the structure of the public administration authorities, at the same time having the status of an undertaking engaged in economic activities in the meaning of Directive 2001/23 and not being independently a public administration authority.[17]

When one of the parties involved in the civil proceedings is an entity, which may be treated as an emanation of a Member State, then if a national regulation is found to be in contradiction with the EU Directive

> the common [ordinary] court is obliged first to remove, from the initially considered legal basis of the ruling the national provisions inconsistent with EU law and then to decide the case based on the legal rule interpreted from other provisions of national law consistent with EU law or, depending on the type of inconsistencies and the structure of national provisions, based on a legal rule interpreted from the provisions of national law used in conjunction with the provisions of an EU Directive.

When the Supreme Court finds that national law is incompatible with the provisions of EU law, which are not directly effective or which cannot be applied with direct effect, in the absence of the possibility of interpretation in conformity with EU law, it will decline to use the *Simmenthal* rule. An example

16 Council Directive 2001/23/EC of 12 March 2001 on the approximation of the laws of the Member States relating to the safeguarding of employees' rights in the event of transfers of undertakings, businesses or parts of undertakings or businesses, OJ L 82, 22.03.2001, pp. 16–20.

17 Judgment of the SC of 14 June 2012, case I PK 230/11.

of clearly illustrating the operation of the principles under consideration is the judgment of the SC of 8 May 2019, case I PK 41/18. The case was between an employee, employed under a fixed-term contract, and an employer, a joint-stock company, as regards the legality of the dismissal from work. It was disputed whether, when terminating a fixed-term employment contract, an employer had to comply with the same rigour (formal requirements), applicable in the termination of employment contracts for an indefinite period. The Supreme Court held that Article 30 (4) of the Labour Code was clear – the obligation to provide the reason for termination applied only to a contract for an indefinite period. That meant that it was impossible to interpret it in its conformity with EU law in such a way that its result would also extend the application of that provision to fixed-term contracts. Despite the fact that the implementation of Directive 99/70[18] was defective and hence Article 30 (4) of the Labour Code was incompatible with Directive 99/70, the cassation appeal [on the point of law] was dismissed on the grounds of the fact that the employer did not have the status of an emanation of a Member State.[19]

Functions of the principles of primacy and direct effect

The function of both principles amounts to, in the light of established CJEU case-law, ensuring the effectiveness of EU law by enabling the Supreme Court to issue a ruling that will be consistent with EU law in a situation where using the interpretation in conformity with EU law, it will not be possible to derive, from Polish law, [itself] a legal rule consistent with EU law. That function has been implemented in different ways, which can be grouped into the cases of using both principles in a manner consisting of 1) omission of a provision of substantive law, 2) omission of a provision of procedural law, 3) omission of a sy3stemic [structural] law provision on the jurisdiction, 4) taking account of the EU law rules in the process of application of a national procedural provision, and 5) omission of a provision constituting a criminal law rule.

In the model approach, the principle of direct effect and the principle of primacy affect the set of substantive law provisions which ultimately constitute the legal basis for the resolution of the case (an incidental issue). Therefore, it is not surprising that, in the established practice, the provisions of national law exclude, in a manner contrary to EU law, the effectiveness of the exclusive right to intellectual property (the judgment of the SC of 10 February 2006, case III CSK 112/05) or depriving specific categories of employees of the protection against the insolvency of the employer (judgments of the SC

18 Council Directive 1999/70/EC of 28 June 1999 concerning the framework agreement on fixed-term work concluded by ETUC, UNICE and CEEP, OJ L 175, 10.07.1999, pp. 43–48.

19 With reference, in particular, to case C-321/05, *Kofoed*, EU:C:2007:408, para. 42.

of 10 January 2019, case I PK 177/18 and of 4 December 2018, case I PK 181/17) were disregarded. However, it happens that, to ensure the effectiveness of EU law, it is necessary to omit those national provisions which are not substantive law provisions.

An example of the omission of a procedural provision is the judgment of the Supreme Court of 8 December 2020, case II PK 35/19. It was held, therein, that the Supreme Court was obliged to disregard Article 398(20) of the Code of Civil Procedure, according to which the Supreme Court itself was bound by the interpretation of the law it had made in its earlier ruling, delivered in the same case (if the judgment of Court of the second instance is set aside for re-examination and a further appeal in cassation [on the point of law] against the new ruling of the Court of the second instance is submitted), when the interpretation of the provisions of EU law, that had been made in the previous judgment in cassation [on the point of law] of the Supreme Court, occurred to be inconsistent with the interpretation of the same provisions adopted in the later ruling of the Court of Justice of the European Union.

A classic example of ensuring the effectiveness of EU law (and specifically the right to a fair trial under Article 47 CFR) is the disregarding of, in the judgment of the Supreme Court of 5 December 2019, case III PO 7/18, the provisions providing for the jurisdiction of the Disciplinary Chamber of the Supreme Court, as not being a court in the meaning of EU law, to hear an appeal of a judge against the resolution of the National Council of Judiciary by the Chamber of the Supreme Court meeting the criteria of a court in the meaning of Article 47 CFR and Article 19 (1) TEU.[20]

Sometimes, the assessment of the compatibility of national legislation with EU law is a prerequisite for applying a national law provision. Such a situation occurs when it is necessary to verify, using a normative standard resulting from the directly effective rules of EU law, whether a hypothesis of a legal norm resulting from a provision of national law has been met. An example of a ruling falling into this category is case II UK 504/17.[21] It raised the allegation of invalidity of the proceedings because a party involved in the proceedings had been deprived of the rights of defence as regards being represented by a

20 'Therefore, finally, a national provision Article 27 (1) (3) read in conjunction with Article 37(1) and (1a) and Article 111 (1) of the Law on the Supreme Court (in the original version) and Article 49 of the Act of 25 July 2002 – Law on the Organisation of Administrative Courts, which entitle(d) to hear the dispute, a body that is not the embodiment of the characteristics under Article 47 CFR, depriving the appellant of an effective remedy in the meaning of Article 9 (1) of Directive 2000/78, must be disregarded on the basis referred to in Article 4 (3) TEU, and the national court must refrain from applying thereof, so that this dispute could be heard by the court, which satisfies the above requirements and which would have jurisdiction in the area concerned, if that provision had not prevented it, thus, in principle, the court which had jurisdiction to do so in accordance with the provisions applicable before the introduction of a legislative amendment conferring that jurisdiction on an authority which does not meet the abovementioned requirements'.

21 Judgment of the SC of 10 April 2019, case II UK 504/17.

professional legal representative. In that case, the applicant claimed that the representative had not been entitled to appear before the Polish courts.[22] The Supreme Court held that a declaration of invalidity of the proceedings due to the defective representation of the party in the proceedings would be contrary to Article 56 TFEU, since the party had been represented before ordinary [common] courts by a Polish lawyer running their law firm in Germany and providing legal services in Poland under the freedom to provide services.

The consequence of the incompatibility of the national legislation with directly effective provisions of EU law may also be the inability to apply the provisions shaping the elements of a rule of criminal law, which leads to the exclusion of the criminality of a given behaviour, most often due to the absence of unlawfulness of that behaviour (repealed by EU law). For example, in the resolution of the panel of seven judges of the SC of 19 January 2017, case I KZP 17/16, it was held that the requirement of EU law to disapply a national technical provision, whose draft had not been notified to the European Commission, resulting from Directive 98/34/EC,[23] excluded applicability, in a criminal office case under Article 107 (1) of the Fiscal Penal Code, the provision of Article 14 (1) of the Law of 19 November 2009 r. on gambling[24] in its original version.

Personal scope of the application of the principles of primacy and direct effect

About the addressees of the obligations arising from both principles of EU law under consideration, the established case-law has confirmed that national courts and national administrative authorities are both bound by the principles of the direct effect and primacy of EU law. For example, in the resolution of 15 January 2013, case III SZP 1/12, it was held that the President of *the Urząd Regulacji Energetyki* (Energy Regulatory Office, ERO) might not issue a decision that would be based on the provisions of Polish law, considered to be inconsistent with EU law, in the proceedings upon the action of the European Commission. Not only can such provisions not, according to the Supreme Court, constitute a legal basis for the issuance of a decision, but, what is more, it is unacceptable for the entrepreneur (in this case, an energy undertaking) to suffer the negative consequences of applying to it the provisions, contrary to EU law, of another area, or in other proceedings. That case concerned the calculation of compensation for stranded costs in the energy

22 A Polish lawyer appeared before a Polish court, who under the freedom of establishment conducted a law firm in Germany. That lawyer had not been entered into the list of foreign lawyers providing legal services in the territory of Poland.

23 Directive 98/34/EC of the European Parliament and of the Council of 22 June 1998 laying down a procedure for the provision of information in the field of technical standards and regulations, OJ L 208, 21.7.1998, pp. 37–48.

24 Journal of Laws of 2015, item 612.

sector based on a calculation based on electricity sales prices, taking into account the excise duty, the structure of which was considered contrary to EU law in the proceedings upon the Commission's action against Poland.[25] The calculation adopted by the ERO based on Polish tax rules incompatible with EU directives resulted in a significantly lower value of the stranded costs to be reimbursed by the state in comparison to prices of electricity calculated without the excise tax that the EC successfully challenged before the ECJ.[26]

On the other hand, in the judgment of 4 December 2018, case I PK 181/17, the principles at issue were required to be respected not only by the courts but also by the Guaranteed Employee Benefits Fund established under Directive 2008/94, which is a State special-purpose fund with legal personality. For this reason, the Fund was treated as an emanation of the Member State against which the direct effect of the Directive operates.[27] The same approach was applied in case III PK 53/19 (discussed earlier in the chapter on consistent interpretation) in respect of a court of ordinary jurisdiction acting in the capacity of an employee in a case brought against it by an employer claiming the right to parental leave under Directive 96/34.

Determination of the direct effect of EU law provisions

In the current practice of the Supreme Court, the general approach is to look for a decision of the ECJ as to the direct effect of a specific provision of EU law. Therefore, the Supreme Court refers to that principle when there has already been the ECJ case-law confirming that the provision in question has a direct effect. In cases such as these, not only are preliminary rulings relevant. An order of the ECJ can also be a source of a judicial qualification of a provision of EU law as directly effective.[28] Attention is drawn to the fact that the Supreme Court does not refer to the problem of direct effect at all when applying the provisions of EU Regulations on the coordination of social security systems (which prevail in its judicial practice) and the Regulations in the area of cooperation of courts in civil matters as their direct effect is obvious.

A rare example of the determining by the Supreme Court, under its own ruling alone, that a provision of EU law is directly effective, is the judgment of the SC of 18 November 2020, case III PK 53/19. This judgment assigned such a characteristic to Article 33 (2) CFR. That provision was found

25 Case C-475/07, *Commission v. the Republic of Poland*, EU:C:2009:86.

26 Ibidem.

27 See also judgments of the SC: of 18 August 2010, case II PK 228/09, and of 18 December 2006, case II PK 17/06; resolution of the SC of 13 March 2008, case I PZP 11/07; order of the SC of 13 October 2009, case II PZP 10/09.

28 For example, with reference to Article 1 (c) and Article 3 (1) of Directive 2001/23, the Supreme Court made a reference to the order of CJEU C-297/03, *Sozialhilfeverband Rohrbach*, EU:C:2005:315 – see judgment of the SC of 14 June 2012, case I PK 230/11.

to be clear, precise, and unconditional regarding the right of every worker to maternity and parental leave. That qualification was made in the case brought by an employee of one of the courts, to whom the public employer (the court) refused to grant the right to maternity leave for the father and the parental leave since the mother of the employee's child had neither the status of an employee nor of an employer because she had resigned from her post to provide permanent care for a disabled *child*. The attribution of direct effect to Article 33 (2) CFR was based on the case-law of the CJ concerning Article 31 (2) CFR. That provision is formulated in a very similar way to Article 33 (2) CFR. At the same time, probably due to the content of the Polish-British protocol to avoid controversy as regards the application of the directly effective provision of CFR as the exclusive legal basis for the ruling, that provision was applied in conjunction with Article 4 and Article 9 of Directive 2006/54,[29] following the interpretation of EU law adopted in the judgment of the Court of Justice of 16 July 2015 in case C-222/14 *Maïstrellis*.[30]

Determination of incompatibility of national law with EU law

Similarly, as is the case of determining whether a provision of EU law is directly effective, in the case of applying the principle of primacy, the Supreme Court usually finds that Polish law is contrary to EU law after having established an EU normative standard, based on the case-law of the CJEU. For example, in the judgment of 4 December 2018, case I PK 181/17, the Supreme Court held that 'the exclusion from the personal scope of the Law . . . of the legal persons subject to the obligation to be entered in the register of associations, other social and professional organizations, foundations . . . that were also entered into the register of entrepreneurs carrying out economic activity, infringes Directive 2008/94/EC', since, from the established case-law of the CJ, it clearly resulted that 'the scope of the exemptions contained in the Directive is exhaustive, and must be interpreted strictly'. The same was done in the judgment of the SC of 10 January 2019 r., case I PK 177/18, in which the application of the provision, excluding from the protection the employees of a foundation engaged in economic activity, was refused. On the other hand, in the judgment of the SC of 18 November 2020, case III PK 53/19, it was held that the refusal to grant father-employee maternity and then parental leave was an expression of unlawful discrimination against the father-employee on the grounds of sex, if such a refusal was based on the sole basis that Article 180 (5)

29 Directive 2006/54/EC of the European Parliament and of the Council of 5 July 2006 on the implementation of the principle of equal opportunities and equal treatment of men and women in matters of employment and occupation (recast), OJ L 204, 26.07.2006, pp. 23–36.

30 EU:C:2015:473.

of the Labour Code provides that the condition for granting a maternity leave for the father is that the mother has the status of an employee or another title of insurance for illness or maternity. It follows clearly, from Article 9 of Directive 2006/54 (listing the examples of the prohibited discrimination), that this Polish provision is discriminatory based on gender as it sets different conditions for granting benefits or restricts such benefits to workers of one or other of the gender. Such a legal assessment of the rule, resulting from Article 180 (5) of the Labour Code, was supported by the judgment of the CJEU in case C-222/14 *Maïstrellis*,[31] in which the CJEU interpreted the conditions of the parental leave but also assessed the compatibility of national legislation with EU law in that respect, not from the perspective of the EU provisions on the parental leave themselves but from the perspective of the breach of the prohibition of discrimination on the grounds of gender in employment (para. 42 and para. 46–50). In such a situation, the finding of the Polish court that national legislation differentiates the right to use maternity leave or parental leave by the father, depending on the employment or insurance status of the mother and whereas there are no similar rules in the case of mothers' rights to those leaves, implies discrimination on the grounds of gender prohibited by EU law in employment relations.

From time to time, the Supreme Court, when finding incompatibility between Polish law and EU law, refers to the *acte clair* doctrine. For example, in the judgment of 4 December 2018, case I PK 181/17, it was accepted that it was clear from the wording of Directive 2008/94[32] that 'the subject related [personal] exclusion due to the type of an employer (an association with the status of an entrepreneur) does not correspond to the enumerated authorization contained in Article 12 of Directive 2008/94', since that provision allows to limit the subject related scope of the Directive 'to avoid abuses' and taking into account the relationship between an employee and an employer ('special links' and 'common interests'), and not in a general way, in relation to all employers falling within a specific category (e.g., associations and foundations engaged in economic activity).

The incompatibility of national law with EU law may be established by the Supreme Court both based on the analysis of preliminary rulings of the CJEU and the rulings issued in the proceedings brought by the Commission against a Member State. In the latter case, finding the inconsistency between a provision of national law and EU law, based on the judgment of the CJEU, issued under the proceedings of Article 258 TFEU, is not sufficient to refuse the application of a provision of the Law. The same applies to the action of the European Commission against the Republic of Poland under Article 258

31 EU:C:2015:473.

32 Directive 2008/94/EC of the European Parliament and of the Council of 22 October 2008 on the protection of employees in the event of the insolvency of their employer, OJ L 283, 28.10.2008, pp. 36–42.

TFEU.[33] In the judgment, in case III SK 3/12 (upon the undertaking's appeal against the decision of the President of *Urząd Komunikacji Elektronicznej* (the Office of Electronic Communications)), the Supreme Court, setting aside the judgment of the Court of the second instance and, taking into the account that, contrary to the position of the Court of Appeal, it did not follow from the judgment of the Court of Justice of the European Union of 13 November 2008, C-227/07 *Commission v. the Republic of Poland*[34] that the imposition of the obligation to interconnect the networks, under Article 5 (1) of Directive 2002/19,[35] was limited only to the cases where one of the parties was an entity having a significant market power and a regulatory obligation to provide telecommunications access. In its ruling, the Court of Justice did not admit the action of the Commission in that regard because the statement of reasons for the plea had been too vague and that the burden of proof had not been resolved. Thus, this legal issue remained unresolved, and it was not clear whether the interpretation of Article 5 (1) of Directive 2002/19 should be made in a manner consistent with the interpretation adopted by the Commission. Therefore, we could not discuss the incompatibility of Article 28 (1) of the Telecommunications Law with the provisions of Directive 2002/19. Next, the Supreme Court pointed out that a national court could refuse to apply provisions of the domestic telecommunications law on the grounds of incompatibility with Directive 2002/19 only if Article 5 (1) of Directive 2002/19 was considered as directly effective. For this reason, a distinction must be made between the scope and results of the review of the compatibility of national law with EU law under the procedure of Article 258 TFEU and the consequences of such a review in proceedings before national courts. While in the proceedings upon the action of the EC, the CJEU may find that a State has infringed its obligations under TFEU; irrespective of whether the provisions of EU law giving rise to those obligations were directly effective, a national court hearing the EU case may refuse to apply the provisions of national law because they are contrary to a provision of a Directive only if that provision of the Directive passes the test of direct effect.

Suppose the CJEU finds that a Member State has breached its obligations under the Treaty as the result of the failure to implement or there has been a defective implementation of provisions of EU secondary law, which are directly effective. In that case, such a ruling will be treated as a precedent deciding on the conflict between national law and EU law and the justification of the application, by the national court, of the *Simmenthal* rule in its entirety. For example, in the resolution of the SC of 15 January 2013, case III SZP 1/12,

33 Judgment of the SC of 19 October 2012, case III SK 3/12.

34 EU:C:2008:620.

35 Directive 2002/19/EC of the European Parliament and of the Council of 7 March 2002 on access to, and interconnection of, electronic communications networks and associated facilities (Access Directive), OJ L 108, 24.4.2002, pp. 7–20.

it was assumed that the excise duty should not be included in the costs of generating 1 MWh of electricity by a given generator, referred to in Article 46 (5) of the Law. The Supreme Court inferred from case C-475/07 *Commission v. the Republic of Poland* that the President of the URE, as an authority of a Member State, should apply Polish law in administrative proceedings in a manner compatible with Directive 2003/96. In that case, that application would consist of setting the reference price at a lower level (without excise duty), which consequently meant that the unit cost of generating 1 MWh of electricity at the electricity undertaking was higher than that reference price. Thus, it was entitled to support, which would cover gas-stranded costs. It followed, for the III SZP 1/12, that where excise duty was included in the average price of electricity on a competitive market announced by the President of *Urząd Regulacji Energetyki* (the Energy Sector Regulatory Authority), under Article 23 (1) (18) (b) of the Energy Law,[36] the value of that duty should have been disregarded by the very same Office for the application of Article 46 (5) of the Law of 29 June 2007, on the principles of covering costs incurred by generators about the early termination of long-term costs for the sale of power and electricity,[37] since, by imposing this excise duty on electricity, Poland breached directly effective provisions of Directive 2003/96.

Another example of using the judgments delivered in infringement actions are judgments of 4 December 2018, case I PK 181/17,[38] and of 10 February 2006, case III CSK 112/05.[39]

The results of the application of the principles of primacy and direct effect

It follows, from the statements of the Supreme Court on the practical effects of the application of both principles in question, that,

> the conflict of national law with EU law may lead to the replacement of national provisions with the EU law provisions or the exclusion of a rule of national law by a directly effective rule of the European Union law.

According to the Supreme Court's statement, applying the principle of primacy and direct effect can produce either an exclusionary effect or a substitution effect. The exclusionary effect means it is impossible to apply the provision(s) of national law contrary to EU law. The case is then decided on the basis of

36 The Act of 10 April 1997 – the Energy Law, consolidated text: on the basis of: *Dz. U.*[Journal of Laws] of 2021 item 716 as amended.

37 *Dz. U.*[Journal of Laws] No. 130, item 905 as amended.

38 With references to C-22/87, *Commission v. Italy*, EU:C:1989:45, and C-68/88, *Commission v. Greece*, EU:C:1989:339.

39 With references to case C-235/89, *Commision v. Italy*, EU:C:1992:73, and case C-30/90, *Commision v. UK*, EU:C:1992:74.

other provisions of national law (compatible with EU law). The substitution effect consists of forming the legal basis of a judicial decision entirely from the directly effective provisions of EU law. However, in the Supreme Court's judicial practice, the substitution effect is quite often only partial as the legal basis for resolving the case consists of national provisions compatible with EU law and directly effective provisions of EU law. It can be treated as an option of the replacement effect, mentioned before in case I KZP 17/16. In addition to the effects mentioned earlier, the result of the application of the principles of primacy and direct effect may supplement the legal basis of the ruling consisting of the provisions of national law with the provisions of EU law, whose application will enable the national court to formulate a legal rule (which is the basis for the ruling) compatible with EU law (the so-called *Jonkman* formula).

It should be emphasised that, in the established practice, it has always been determined whether the provision of Polish law referred to in the grounds for the appeal in cassation [on the point of law] is consistent with the provision of EU law or a general principle of EU law.[40] In addition, it was uniformly assumed that the effect of finding an incompatibility between Polish law and EU law is 'the impossibility of applying that provision by Polish courts'. Thus, although there is a conflict between a rule of national law and a rule of EU law, in practical terms, there is no refusal to apply a rule of national law but the refusal to apply the provisions of national law from which, at the stage of making a judicial decision on the application of the law, a rule (or an element of a rule) contrary to EU law would be interpreted.

A classic example of applying the principle of primacy is the judgment of the SC of 10 February 2006, case III CSK 112/05. It has been held therein that 'Article 4 (6) of the Act of 30 October 1992 amending the Law on the Invention and the Law on the Patent Office of the Republic of Poland,[41] reproduced in Box 8.1, Primacy and direct effect of Article 34 TFEU, is a measure having equivalent effect to quantitative restrictions on imports prohibited by the then Article 28 of the Treaty establishing the European Community. Article 4 (6) of the afore-mentioned Law [statute], as creating such a measure, 'could not be applied since the date of the accession of Poland to the European Union in the area of Community law'.

Article 4 of that Law created, in the Polish legal system, an exclusive right with the content corresponding to the right from the patent. The aim was to protect the rights to chemical and pharmaceutical inventions of foreign companies, which, during the communist period, could not benefit from patent protection in the territory of Poland due to the exclusion of the possibility of granting patent protection to them. It should be emphasised that the exclusive right introduced in Article 4 of the Law given earlier was, as such, compatible with EU law. The non-compliance was limited only to the rules resulting from

40 Judgment of the SC of 10 February 2006, case III CSK 112/05.
41 *Dz. U.*[Journal of Laws] of 1993, No. 4, item 14 as amended.

Box 8.1 Primacy and direct effect of Article 34 TFEU

Article 4.

1 Until 30 December 1992 patents shall not be granted for foodstuffs, pharmaceuticals, and chemical compounds.
2 Under the conditions laid down in paragraphs 3–8 a patent holder in one of the States belonging to the International Union for the Protection of Industrial Property for foodstuffs, pharmaceuticals and chemical compounds may temporarily get the right for the exclusive manufacturing and sale of those products on the territory of the Republic of Poland.
3 The Patent Office will grant the exclusive right, referred to in paragraph 2, if:

1) before the date laid down in paragraph 1 the patent holder obtained the first consent to market a product in any State and within six months of obtaining it will apply for permission to sell the product in Poland, at the same time submitting an application for granting the right to the Patent Office,
2) a product meets the requirements of admission to marketing in Poland,
3) on the date of submitting in the State of the original registration, the invention complied with the conditions laid down in Article 10–12 of the Law on Invention,
4) until the date of submitting the application, referred to in item 1, the product has not been sold in Poland,
5) manufacturing the product in Poland is aimed at satisfying the needs of the Polish market and is economically justified,

4 The time-limit referred to in paragraph 3 item 1, is not recoverable.
5 To obtain and exercise the right, referred to in paragraph 2, the provisions of the Law on Invention shall apply accordingly.
6 It shall not constitute an infringement of the right, referred to in paragraph 2, to sell the same products by third parties before the entitled party undertakes the production to the extent, that satisfies the needs of the Polish market.
7 The right to exclusively manufacture and sell the product shall expire at the latest on the date until which protection has been granted in the country of the original registration but may not exceed 20 years.
8 The Council of Ministers shall determine, by way of a Regulation, the amount of the one-off fee for the application referred to in paragraph 3 item 1, and the periodic fees charged in relation to the protection granted.

Article 4 (6) of the Law. It follows from that provision that the effectiveness of an exclusive right to manufacture, and the sale of products containing a particular active substance, depends on undertaking the manufacturing of it in the territory of Poland. Only after the commencement of such a production, the right holder could effectively demand the cessation of sales, on the Polish market, of the products manufactured in violation of their right. Article 4 (6) of the Law encouraged domestic production, at the expense of meeting demand with imports from the other Member States. The incompatibility of Article 4 (6) of the Law with Article 28 TEC meant that 'since 1 May 2004, it has become impossible to make the provisional protection granted under Article 4 of the amending Law dependent on the commencement of production in Poland'. Consequently, the action brought by the holder of an exclusive right (equivalent to a patent) could not be dismissed because they had not commenced, in breach of Article 4 (6) of the Law, production in Poland in the required economic dimension. This provision, making the effectiveness of the rightsholder's right dependent on undertaking such actions, could not be considered when reconstructing the normative basis for the ruling. Without the reference to the principle of primacy of EU law, the action brought by the holder of the exclusive right, under Article 4 of the Law, who had not commenced the production in the territory of Poland, would have been dismissed. On the other hand, the use of the principle of primacy enabled the Supreme Court to find that Article 4 (6) of the Law should not be applied by the court of the second instance as a legal basis for dismissing an action for infringement of the exclusive right to intellectual property. As a result, the judgment of the court of a lower instance should be set aside, and, subsequently, the action of the right holder against the infringer should be upheld.

In the same way, both principles mentioned earlier have been used in case I PK 230/11.[42] First, it was assumed that, in accordance with the EU normative standard, the transfer by a state organisational unit of a business operating in the area of public administration constitutes an undertaking engaged in economic activities in the meaning of Article 1 (1) (c) of Directive 2001/23 and retaining identity after the transfer, is the transfer of the business to another employer in the meaning of Article 3 (1) of that Directive. Both the provisions mentioned earlier had been considered as directly effective by the CJ. Consequently, it was necessary to disregard the provisions of the special Law [statute] excluding the effect in the form of a transfer of the business to the new employer.[43] That decision allowed for applying Article 23 (1) (1) of the Labour Code and resolving the case on the basis of the National Law provisions.

42 Judgments of the SC of 14 June 2012, case I PK 230/11.

43 Article 100 of the Law of 27 August 2009 – the Provisions introducing the Public Finance Law, *Dz.U.* [Journal of Laws] No. 157, item 1241 as amended.

In the judgment of 4 December 2018, case I PK 181/17, it was found that the court should disregard Article 2 (2) of the Law of 13 January 2006, on the protection of employee claims in the event of the insolvency of the business,[44] as incompatible with Article 1 (2) and Article 12 of Directive 2008/94,[45] to the extent that it provides that bankruptcy does not occur in respect of an employer who is an association entered in the register of entrepreneurs.

Another example of the refusal to apply a provision of national law incompatible with EU law is the judgment of the SC in case II PK 18/06.[46] The Supreme Court held that the interpretation of Article 6 (4) and (6) of the Law on the Protection of Employee Claims in the event of the Employer's Insolvency (hereinafter Insolvency Protection Law) – within the scope of the term 'date of employer's insolvency' and 'in conjunction with the definition of the employer's insolvency contained in Article 3 of the Insolvency Protection Law, and the determination of the date of arising that insolvency, as referred to in paragraph 2a thereof, as the date on which the court's ruling rejecting the petition for the employer's insolvency becomes final' – was incompatible with Article 2 (1), Article 3 (2), and Article 4 (2) of Directive 80/987. Therefore, only a particular understanding of Articles 6 (4) and (6) of the Insolvency Protection Law was contrary to EU law. What is more, that contradiction existed only if the account was taken of Article 3 (2a) of the Insolvency Protection Law when applying that provision. That provision defined the date of insolvency of a business by referring to the date of a particular judgment of the insolvency court becoming final. The refusal to apply concerned *de facto*, not Article 6 (4) and (6) of the Insolvency Protection Law but Article 3 (2a) of the Insolvency Protection Law. That provision had to be, usually, (without taking into consideration Directive 80/987), referred to by Polish courts when applying Article 6 (4) and (6). As a result of finding non-compliance of Article 3 (2a) of the Insolvency Protection Law with Article 3 (2) of Directive 80/987, the expression 'the date of arising the employer's insolvency' under Article 6 (4) and (6) of the Insolvency Protection Law should be assigned a meaning corresponding to that resulting from Article 3 (2) of Directive and the case-law of CJEU. To make consistent interpretation of Polish law possible, the Supreme Court, in its judgment of 5 December 2006, case II PK 18/06, first had to disapply a provision of national law that contained a legal definition of the 'date of insolvency of an employer'. This disapplication allowed the SC to use the principle of interpretation of Polish law in conformity with EU law of other provisions of the Insolvency Protection Law that used the phrase 'date of employer's insolvency'. Since the SC omitted the Polish provision defining when such insolvency occurred, it could interpret

44 Consolidated text: *Dz.U.* [Journal of Laws] of 2018, item 1433.

45 Directive 2008/94/EC of the European Parliament and of the Council of 22 October 2008 on the protection of employees in the event of the insolvency of their employer (Codified version) (Text with EEA relevance), OJ L 283, 28.10.2008, pp. 36–42.

46 Judgment of the SC of 5 December 2006, case II PK 18/06.

that phrase in a manner compatible with the interpretation of Directive 80/987 adopted by the CJEU as, without Article 3 (2a) of the Insolvency Protection Law, that phrase was vague enough to accommodate the meaning required by the effectiveness of EU law.

The mere refusal to apply a provision of national law because it is contrary to EU law does not always lead to the provision of effectiveness to EU law. Therefore, another option for compliance with the requirements arising from the principle of direct effect and the principle of primacy is to refuse to decide the case exclusively on the legal basis, based solely on the provisions of national law and supplementing the legal basis of the ruling with a directly effective provision of EU law. In such a case, the Supreme Court refers to the so-called *Jonkman* formula, according to which, where the prohibition of discrimination under the EU Directive is found, in the case with the participation of a Member State's emanation, a national court will grant the discriminated person the rights provided for by national law to persons, who under national law, have been favoured. The Supreme Court accepts that the corollary of the directly effective provisions of EU law prohibiting discrimination on the grounds of gender is the right of their addressee to be non-discriminated and to enjoy the benefits provided for in the Polish legal system, the access to which they would be deprived of if the discriminatory national provisions were applied against them.

For example, in the judgment of the SC of 18 November 2020, case III PK 53/19 (discussed in more detail in the section on the interpretation in conformity with EU law), the disregard for the national law provision, Article 180 (5) of the Labour Code, as contrary to the prohibition of discrimination against workers on the grounds of gender, does not lead to ensuring the situation of compliance of national law with EU law and issuing a ruling corresponding to the normative standard resulting from the EU standard. Such an omission would not confer on the applicant the maternity or parental leave requested by them. It was necessary to supplement the legal basis of the ruling, consisting of the provision of national law incompatible with EU law (Article 180 (5) of the Labour Code), with the directly effective provision of EU law (Article 4 and Article 9 of Directive 2006/54 read in conjunction with Article 33 (2) CFR), which enabled a party to remedy the effects of that contradiction by the granting of, to the applying employee, a right he had applied for and which he had been deprived of by a national law provision. Thus, the legal basis for resolving the case, enabling the interpretation of a legal rule compatible with EU law, consisted of the national law provision and the EU law provision applied cumulatively (Article 180 (5) of the Labour Code used in conjunction with Article 4 and Article 9 of Directive 2006/54 read in conjunction with Article 33 (2) CFR).

In the judgment of 4 January 2008, case I UK 182/07, the Supreme Court held that 'exclusion by the provisions of Polish law male conductors from the statutory pension scheme at the lower age solely on the grounds of sex' was incompatible with Article 4 of Directive 79/7.[47] The Supreme Court found reasonable the plea alleging the infringement of the provision of § 12 (1) (1) (d) of the Regulation of the Polish Council of Ministers of 1983[48] by its application (provisions are reproduced in Box 8.2, Primacy and direct effect of Directive 79/7). Due to the incompatibility mentioned earlier with Article 4 of Directive 79/7, that provision could not be the legal basis for the decision of the pension authority on the refusal to grant the right to a pension followed by the judgment, dismissing an appeal, and the judgment dismissing the appeal of the insured. Disapplication of the provision of § 12 (1) (1) (d) of the Regulation of 1983 would not resolve the legal problem which arose in this case since the incompatibility with EU law consisted of the discriminatory deprivation of a specific category of workers of the right to a pension at a lower age. The provision, presented later, contained a rule, from which it resulted that workers engaged in creative or artistic activities could retire at a lower age (early retirement) than the so-called general retirement age. The age for early retirement has been set differently for respective professions and separately for women and men working in those professions (which is allowed by EU law). Only for female actors and female conductors (the provision is presented in Box 8.2) the law provided for the right to retire at a reduced age. This provision neither mentioned male conductors nor male actors as workers entitled to benefit from reduced retirement age.

Box 8.2 Primacy and direct effect of Directive 79/7

§ 12. 1. An employee performing a creative or artistic activity within the meaning of the provisions on pension provision for authors and their families acquires the right to a pension if he meets the following conditions cumulatively

1) has reached the retirement age for:

    a) dancer, acrobat, gymnast, equilibrist, stuntman – 40 years for women and 45 years for men,
    b) solist vocalist, musician playing with wind instruments, trainer of predatory animals – 45 years for women and 50 years of men,
    c) choir artist, juggler, circus comedian, puppet theatre actor – 50 years for women and 55 years for men,
    d) actresses, [female] conductor- 55 years,

47 Council Directive 79/7/EEC of 19 December 1978 on the progressive implementation of the principle of equal treatment for men and women in matters of social security, OJ L 6, 10.1.1979, pp. 24–25.

48 The Regulation of the Council of Ministers of 7 February 1983 on the retirement age for workers employed under special conditions or of special character (*Dz.U.* [Journal of Laws] No. 8, item 43 as amended).

e) musician playing string, percussion and keyboard instruments, cinematographer, photographer – 55 years for women and 60 years for men,

2) reached the retirement age during employment or within 5 years of employment termination,
3) has the required period of employment, including at least 15 years of creative or artistic activity.

Therefore, the Supreme Court made a reference to the *Jonkman*[49] rule assuming, that

> until the introduction of the relevant legislative amendments resulting from this judgment, including the amendment to the provision of § 12 (1) (1) (d) of the Regulation of 1983, in matters relating to retirement at a lower age, the provisions on female conductors should be applied directly to male conductors.

Therefore, the result of finding the incompatibility of national law with EU law, in this case, is the refusal to apply, § 12 (1)(1) (d) of the Resolution of 1983 as the independent legal basis for rejecting the insured's claim and then applying Article 4 of Directive 79/7 in conjunction with § 12 (1) (1) (d), of the Resolution of 1983, to grant to a male with the profession of a conductor, the right to a pension at a lower age, if he meets the conditions provided for in the provisions of the Regulation for female conductors. The mere reference to the principle of primacy of EU law and the disapplication of the provision mentioned earlier of Regulation of 1983 would not lead to issuing a ruling compatible with EU law.

An essential contribution to developing the use of the principle of primacy and direct effect by national courts comes from the judgment of the Supreme Court of 5 December 2019, case III PO 7/18, issued after the ECJ's judgment in C-585/18. The Supreme Court, Chamber of Labour Law and Social Security, not only disapplied national statutory provision granting the competence to hear this particular case to the Disciplinary Chamber of the Supreme Court. It also omitted a provision of the Supreme Court Act under which the adjudicating panel of the adequately established Supreme Court was to be bound by a resolution adopted by the 'illegal' Disciplinary Chamber. Then, after the disapplication of both provisions of Polish statutory legislation (principle of primacy), the adjudicating panel of the Supreme Court considered itself to be the proper court to hear the case (direct effect of Article 47 CFR and Article 19 (1) TEU). It then revoked the unlawful resolution of the National Council

49 Joint cases C-231/06 to C-233/06, *Jonkman*, EU:C:2007:373, para. 39.

for the Judiciary, which resulted in an illegal (under Directive 2000/78) discharge from the office of a judge of the Supreme Administrative Court and was challenged by that judge, who brought an appeal against that resolution to the Labour Law and Social Security Chamber of the Supreme Court, which under law in force before April 2018 heard such appeals (instead of bringing it to the Disciplinary Chamber that was made competent to hear such appeals in April 2018).

Conclusions

The review of the rulings of the Supreme Court, relating to the principles of primacy and direct effect, highlights, once more, the primary importance of the principle of the interpretation of national law in conformity with EU law in ensuring the effectiveness of EU law. Apart from the cases adjudicated based on the provisions of Regulations and Treaties, the use of the principles of direct effect and primacy has always been preceded by an attempt to interpret national provisions in conformity with EU law, which were to constitute the legal basis for the ruling to be issued. The Supreme Court referred to the principles of primacy and direct effect only when it was impossible to interpret Polish law in conformity with EU law.[50] The main reason for such an approach is the limitations imposed on the direct effect of directives and hence the primacy of EU law in case of conflicts between directives and national legislation in judicial proceedings between individuals.

Attention is drawn to the fact that, as far as such EU cases are concerned, which are covered by the directly applicable Regulations on the EU coordination of social security systems and judicial cooperation in civil matters, there are no references to both principles in question, due to the lack of any reservations as to the direct effect of the provisions contained therein. Such references occur in matters falling within the scope of the primary law (including the CFR)[51] and Directives.[52] The Supreme Court respects, in its case-law, a close link between the principle of primacy and the principle of direct effect. Even in the judgments preceding the CJEU judgment in the case C-573/17 *Popławski II*,[53] the Supreme Court had refused to apply Polish provisions only if they were contrary to a provision of EU law capable of producing a direct effect. The contribution of the Supreme Court in the development of both principles of EU law, using preliminary references, may seem not to be that significant since the interactions between both principles, which, inter alia, were the subject matter of the reference in the case C-545/17 *Pawlak*, have

50 See, for example, cases I UK 182/07; III PK 53/19.
51 See, for example, case III PK 53/19.
52 See, for example, case I UK 182/07.
53 EU:C:2019:530.

been resolved by the CJ in other rulings delivered just after the question had been referred.[54]

The Supreme Court determines the direct effect of the provisions of EU law on the basis of the *acte eclaire* doctrine: either due to the CJEU judgment finding explicitly that the provision of EU law, whose application is being considered by the Supreme Court is or is not directly effective, or by comparing the content of the EU law provision, on whose effectiveness the CJ has not commented on yet, with the similarly formulated provision that has already received such an assessment by the CJ (e.g., compare Article 33 (2) CFR with Article 31 (2) CFR).[55]

From the perspective of applying both principles in the practice of the Supreme Court, the most important is the exclusionary effect of the principle of primacy. The substitution effect, in the form of replacing a national provision incompatible with a provision of EU law, seems to be rarely used. One of the best examples was provided by III PO 7/18, III PO 8/18, and III PO 9/18, where Article 47 CFR and Article 19 (1) TEU were used to disapply the statutory provision granting the competence to hear this particular case in the Disciplinary Chamber of the Supreme Court. On that occasion, both provisions served as the legal base, together with other, not disapplied, national provisions of the Supreme Court Act, allowing the adjudicating panel of the Supreme Court to hold itself competent to hear the case. It seems that the Supreme Court did not take the approach envisaged by the ECJ itself in C-585/18 *A.K.* When ruling on the practical aspects of the principle of primacy in that judgment, the ECJ held that

> the principle of the primacy of EU law must be interpreted as requiring the referring court to disapply the provision of national law which reserves jurisdiction to hear and rule on the cases in the main proceedings to the abovementioned chamber, so that those cases may be examined by a court which meets the abovementioned requirements of independence and impartiality and which, were it not for that provision, would have jurisdiction in the relevant field.

This phrase could be understood as empowering the Supreme Court, not only to disapply the provisions of the Supreme Court Act of 2017 in force that reserves jurisdiction in some instances to the Disciplinary Chamber but also those final provisions of this Act that derogated the previous Supreme Court Act of 2002, under which, the cases in which preliminary references had been submitted to the ECJ fell within the jurisdiction of the Labour, Social Security, and (then) Public Affairs Chamber of the Supreme Court (thus restoring the

54 See, especially case C-122/17, *Smith*, EU:C:2018:631, para. 49; case C-193/17, *Cresco Investigation*, EU:C:2019:43, para. 73.

55 See, for example, III PK 53/19.

original jurisdiction of the adjudicating panel of the Supreme Court, composed of judges of the Labour and Social Security Chamber, who had been deprived of the power to adjudicate in these cases).

However, the use of both EU law principles in the Supreme Court's jurisprudence is about to change. With the growing number of newly appointed judges (with the participation of the National Council for the Judiciary failing to meet standards established in C-585/18, *A.K. and others*), the recourse to the principle of primacy is very unlikely in issues and cases concerning the independence of the judiciary and the right to a fair trial before a duly established court. As some of the examples have shown in this chapter, new judges follow the 'new' anti-EU jurisprudence of the Constitutional Court that has declared a lack of EU competence on the issues of independence of the judiciary.

Literature

Brzeziński P., Relacje między zasadą pierwszeństwa a zasadą efektywności. Glosa do wyroku SN z dnia 4 stycznia 2008 r., I UK 182/07 [Relationship Between the Principle of Primacy and the Principle Of Effectiveness of EU Law. Case Note to the Judgement of the Supreme Court of 4th January 2008, I UK 182/07], *Europejski Przegląd Sądowy*, 2010, no. 1, pp. 50–54.

9 The principles of primacy and direct effect of EU law in the case-law of the administrative courts

Monika Szwarc

Introduction

The purpose of this part of the study is to present how administrative courts, as EU courts in functional terms, fulfil their obligation to apply the principles of primacy and direct effect of EU law. That issue will be presented on the basis of the selection of judgments of voivodeship administrative courts (VAC) and the Supreme Administrative Court (SAC). Similarly to other parts of the study, in the first place, it will be presented how administrative courts have made the reception of the sources of an obligation to respect the principles of direct effect and primacy, the elements of their legal structure, *ratione personae* and *ratione materiae*, and their functions. Next, the generalised effects of applying the direct effect and primacy on the substance of a national rule and the consequences of its application in resolving various categories of cases will be discussed.

Reception of the principles of primacy and direct effect

In the case-law of administrative courts, the references to the judgments of the Court of Justice in the cases *Van Gend en Loos*,[1] *Costa v. ENEL*,[2] and *Simmenthal*[3] prevail. Already, in the early case-law of the SAC, including an EU element, it was emphasised that, in the event of incompatibility between a provision of national law and a provision of Community law, a court of a Member State should issue a judgment on the basis of the provision of Community law and refuse to apply a provision of national law. In that case, incompatibility of the rule (of national law) is understood as a situation in which it is not possible to fulfil, at the same time, the rules belonging to both legal systems in question, having at least partially, a common scope of application.[4]

1 Case 26/62, *Van Gend en Loos*, EU:C:1963:1.
2 Case 6/64, *Costa v. ENEL*, EU:C:1964:66.
3 Case 106/77, *Simmenthal*, EU:C:1978:49.
4 See a large group of judgments of the SAC of 3 April 2007 in cases: I FSK 523/06; I FSK 462/06; I FSK 518/06; I FSK 519/06; I FSK 522/06; I FSK 175/06; I FSK 520/06; I FSK 521/06.

DOI: 10.4324/9781003376019-12

Later on, the SAC indicated that the principle of primacy is treated as one of so-called structural principles (*principes structurels*), which requires national authorities to refuse the application of, in a particular case, the provision of a national law, when it is contrary to the provision of EU law.[5]

Since that decision of the SAC, administrative courts have consistently held that, in the event of a conflict between EU and national rules, which cannot be remedied by consistent interpretation, a national court, in accordance with the principles of primacy (supremacy) and direct effect of EU law, is obliged to refuse to apply a provision of national law which is, contrary to EU law, more favourable to an individual.[6] It is also worth emphasising that, for Polish courts, a standard, important in the context of the principle of primacy, is also the judgment of the Court of Justice in the *Filipiak*[7] case. Referring to that ruling, administrative courts generally accept that the principle of primacy of Union law obliges a national court to apply that law and to refrain from applying provisions of national law that are in conflict, irrespective of the judgment of the national constitutional court, which defers losing the binding force of those provisions, which have been held unconstitutional. They also accept that the examination of the compatibility of national law with EU law is based on the decentralised review standard, where it is a requirement for each court, ruling on an individual case, to consider the conflict between the rules of national law with Community law[8] (instead of a centralised review exercised by a constitutional court). It was also emphasised in the case-law that administrative courts are obliged to review the activities of public administration in a way that makes it possible to eliminate decisions that are incompatible with EU law. It is for this reason that the national court, which is responsible within its competences for the application of EU law, is obliged to ensure the full effectiveness of those rules, by non-application of conflicting provisions of national law.[9] From the perspective of the procedure before administrative courts, it is assumed that an infringement of EU provisions (of primary or secondary EU law) by an administrative authority in the process of issuing of an administrative decision results in a substantial, legal defect of this decision, which is the basis of declaring such decision invalid.[10] The same has been explained in a detailed manner also in the context of a situation in which an administrative decision was adopted on the basis of national provision, which itself infringes EU law. In such a case, an administrative decision

5 Judgment of the SAC of 24 March 2009, case I FSK 1367/07.

6 For example, judgment of the SAC of 16 March 2011, I FSK 1588/10.

7 Case C-314/08, *Filipiak*, EU:C:2009:719; presented *in extenso* later on.

8 For example, judgment of the SAC of 15 February 2010, case I OSK 672/09.

9 Judgement of the SAC of 12 March 2020, case II GSK 3028/17.

10 Explained further by M. Kamiński, Konstruowanie wzorca legalności decyzji administracyjnej na podstawie prawa UE przez polskie sądy administracyjne, cz. I [Reconstructing by Polish administrative courts of the standard of legality for administrative decision pursuant to EU law, part I], *Europejski Przegląd Sądowy*, 2011, no. 4, pp. 22–27, at 26.

is legally defective, as a result of non-conformity of national provision, which was the legal basis for such a decision.[11]

In addition, in the case-law of administrative courts, the guidelines on how to proceed in the event of a refusal to apply a national law provision (due to incompatibility with EU law) can be found. Then, such a legal vacuum (resulting from non-application of a national law provision) has to be filled either by direct substitution with an EU rule in lieu of a disapplied rule of national law or by other rules of national law, which must be constructed by an authority applying law. Whereas, the rules of a Directive provide for the basis for determining the field, where such an authority can operate.[12]

In one of the most recent judgments which is significant, primarily, in relation to the crisis of the rule of law and judicial independence in Poland, the SAC recalled that the principle of primacy operates in the sphere of application of law and not its validity, thus, in the horizontal, content-based, and not a hierarchical perspective of the conflict between national and EU law rules. What is more, the SAC derives from the *Simmenthal* judgment that the competence for derogation of internal law rule that it is not compatible with a Community law rule, is the exclusive area of constitutional orders of Member States, and the purpose of that principle is to guarantee the effectiveness and uniformity in the application of EU law rules, which is a natural fulfilment of the Treaty on the functioning of the EU obligations.[13]

The principles of primacy and direct effect are treated, by administrative courts, in such a way that they are anchored in the national Basic Law, namely in Article 91 (3) of the Constitution of the Republic of Poland, according to which 'If an agreement, ratified by the Republic of Poland, establishing an international organization so provides, the laws established by it shall be applied directly and have precedence in the event of a conflict of laws'.[14] In some

11 M. Kamiński, Konstruowanie wzorca legalności decyzji administracyjnej na podstawie prawa UE przez polskie sądy administracyjne, cz. II [Reconstructing by Polish administrative courts of the standard of legality for administrative decision pursuant to EU law, part II], *Europejski Przegląd Sądowy*, 2011, no. 5, pp. 22–27.

12 For example, judgment of the SAC of 29 September 2011, case II FSK 601/10.

13 Judgment of the SAC of 6 May 2021, case II GOK 2/18.

14 Official translation of the Constitution of the Republic of Poland available at https://www.sejm.gov.pl/prawo/konst/angielski/kon1.htm [access 1.10.2022]. One of the first judgments where Article 91(3) was referred to in judgment of the VAC of 6 March 2007, case III SA/Wa 254/07 (case *Brzeziński*, which is presented later in this chapter); judgment of the VAC in Poznań of 4 January 2010, case I SA/Po 1006/09 (case *Filipiak*, which is presented later in this chapter); and in judgments of the SAC: of 10 March 2006, case I FSK 705/05 and of 13 September 2006, case II FSK 1133/05; later see for example, judgments of the SAC: of 11 March 2006, case I FSK 61/09; of 27 February 2007, case I OSK 570/06; of 13 March 2007, case I OSK 627/06; of 17 July 2007, case I OSK 1193/06; of 22 April 2008, case II GSK 70/08; of 29 September 2011, case II FSK 601/10; of 1 March 2012, case II GSK 295/11; of 8 April 2016, case II GSK 2429/14; of 12 October 2016, case II OSK 3262/14; Order of 19 February 2018, case II OSK 1346/16; judgment of the VAC in

judgments, administrative courts see the source of a refusal to apply national law, contrary to EU law, also in other provisions of the Constitution of the Republic of Poland, namely, Article 9 from which it results, that the Republic of Poland shall respect international law binding upon it. Article 91 (1) of the Constitution, according to which a ratified international agreement, '[a]fter promulgation thereof in the Journal of Laws of the Republic of Poland (*Dziennik Ustaw*), shall constitute part of the domestic legal order and shall be applied directly, unless its application depends on the enactment of a statute'[15] and Article 91 (2), which provides that '[a]n international agreement ratified upon prior consent granted by statute shall have precedence over statutes if such an agreement cannot be reconciled with the provisions of such statutes' (also by interpretation).[16]

Content of the principles of primacy and direct effect

As regards the provisions of the respective sources of EU secondary law, administrative courts adopt, predominantly, the terminology of the TFEU (Article 288) and case-law of the Court of Justice. For that reason, where a Regulation is applicable to the case concerned, the courts use the term 'direct application'. In that respect, the courts refer to Article, now 288 (2) TFEU (*ex* Article 249 (2) TEC), from which 'the principle of direct applicability' results *expressiss verbis*.[17] The acceptance of such a nature of the Regulation is, firstly, the recognition that if the provisions of the Regulation are applicable in a given case, in principle, they meet the requirements of direct application and may give rise to obligations[18] and that an EU Regulation as a source of generally applicable law and part of the national legal order is directly applicable.[19] Secondly, the rule is that the Regulation neither requires any transformation act adopted by a given Member State nor the promulgation in accordance with the provisions of national law, and the essence of direct application is that the legal basis for deciding a case pending before a public authority (a court, a public administration authority) of a Member State is a provision of an EU Regulation, and not a provision of national law.[20] Thirdly, direct application means that a Regulation enters into force and produces an

Szczecin of 14 May 2015, case I SA/Sz 1474/14; judgment of the VAC in Poznań of 7 April 2010, case III SA/Po 123/10.

15 Referred to for example in judgments of the SAC: of 27 February 2007, case I OSK 570/06; of 17 July 2007, case I OSK 1193/06.

16 Judgment of the SAC of 26 April 2013, case II FSK 1521/11.

17 Judgments of the SAC: of 27 February 2007, case I OSK 570/06; of 17 July 2007, case I OSK 1193/06.

18 Judgments of the SAC: of 13 March 2007, case I OSK 627/06; of 22 April 2008, case II GSK 70/08.

19 Judgment of the SAC of 1 March 2012, case II GSK 295/11.

20 Judgment of the SAC of 8 April 2016, case II GSK 2429/14.

effect in favour of encumbering legal entities without requiring any actions to transform it into national law. Therefore, the Member States cannot take any action, which would affect the Union nature of the Regulation provisions and the effects on an individual resulting therefrom.[21] It follows that, including the rules of EU law with the binding force in national legislation, it is therefore unnecessary and even unacceptable. It may lead to doubts as to their binding force in the absence of a reference to the provisions of EU law.[22]

Regarding the principle of direct effect of the provisions of Directives, it should be noticed that it has been reproduced into the administrative courts case-law, first of all, through the judgment of the Court of Justice in the *Becker* case.[23] Following that ruling, administrative courts decided that a provision of a Directive can be directly effective if it is unconditional in addition to being clear and precise, that is, if it is possible to determine, by means of interpretation, the circle of individuals deriving rights from it, the substance of their rights, and the circle of obliged entities, that is State authorities.[24] The SAC, in one of its judgments, referring to the established case-law of the Court of Justice, held that in relations between an individual and a State, a provision of a Directive is directly effective and could be the basis for a ruling of a national court, if the time limit for its implementation into the national legal order had expired or it had been implemented after that time limit or contrary to its content and, what is more, when its wording was clear, precise, and unconditional. In other words, according to the SAC, the directly effective provisions of EU law, including obviously provisions of Directives are those which enable the reconstruction of an unambiguous legal rule on their basis. The same adjudicating panel has found that an act of EU law, whose provisions are directly effective, could and should be a review standard for the operation of public administration from the point of view of its legality, including, in terms of its compliance with EU law. That is the fulfilment of an obligation, imposed on administrative courts, to apply EU law. Thus, if a provision of a Directive is clear, precise, and unconditional, it is recognised, by the SAC, as 'the basis for the reconstruction of a legal rule', which, in a given case, determines the right of an individual (e.g., terms and conditions for the tax refund).[25] In some judgments, administrative courts also define the unconditionality of the provision of EU law, finding, that it is such a provision, which 'establishes an obligation, whose performance is neither reserved by any condition nor requires for its effectiveness or enforceability, the adoption of any additional measure by authorities of the EU or Member States'.[26] On the other hand, it is possible to find judicial statements from which it results that there

21 Judgment of the SAC of 12 October 2016, case II OSK 3262/14.

22 Judgments of the SAC: of 27 February 2007, case I OSK 570/06; of 17 July 2007, case I OSK 1193/06.

23 Case 8/81, *Becker*, EU:C:1982:7.

24 Judgment of the SAC of 14 January 2010, case II FSK 2018/09.

25 For example, judgment of the SAC of 5 December 2013, case I GSK 280/12.

26 Judgment of the SAC of 16 November 2015, case I FSK 759/14.

can be no direct effect of a given provision if the Member State and the EU bodies have a margin of discretion for its application or if the provision of the Directive does not explicitly state the obligation of the Member State.[27]

Functions of the principles of primacy and direct effect

Administrative courts have accepted, in line with the position of the CJEU, that the function of both principles is to ensure the effectiveness of EU law in a situation where it is not possible through consistent interpretation.[28] This function is performed in administrative courts in various ways, which (similarly as in the chapter on case-law of the Supreme Court) can be grouped into cases of using both principles in a way consisting in:

1) non-application of a provision of substantive law;
2) non-application of a provision of procedural law;
3) taking into account a provision of EU law in the process of applying national substantive law.

Non-application of a national provision of substantive law

In the first group distinguished, when a provision of EU law serves to disregard national substantive law, numerous rulings of administrative courts relate to tax matters, in particular, those in which Directives establish the standard of EU law.

One of the first rulings of the Court of Justice, resulting from the questions referred for a preliminary ruling by a Polish court,[29] is the *Sosnowska* judgment in which it was held that:

> Article 18(4) of the Sixth VAT Directive and the principle of proportionality preclude national legislation, such as that at issue in the main proceedings, which, in order to allow the investigations required to prevent tax evasion and avoidance, extends from 60 to 180 days, as from the date of submission of the taxable person's VAT return, the period available to the national tax office for repayment of excess VAT to a category of taxable persons unless those persons lodge a security deposit to a value of PLN 250 000.[30]

27 For example, if a provision of a Directive is optional, which the States may but not have to use, judgment of the SAC of 17 September 2019, case I GSK 286/17.

28 For example, judgments of the SAC: of 14 January 2010, case II FSK 2018/09; of 16 March 2011, case I FSK 1588/10; of 20 November 2013, case I FSK 1749/13.

29 Order of the VAC in Wrocław of 22 December 2006, case I SA/Wr 1238/06.

30 Case C-25/07, *Sosnowska*, EU:C:2008:395; for discussion, see further: F. Huschens, Anmeldung von Vorsteuerüberhängen – Erstattungsfristen und Forderungen nach Sicherheitsleistungen, *EU-Umsatz-Steuerberater*, 2008, p. 25; S. Heinrichshofen, Verzögerte Auszahlung von Vorsteuern bei Unternehmensgründungen, *EU-Umsatz-Steuerberater*, 2008, pp. 53–54;

On this basis, the VAC found that the provision of the VAT Law, providing for in certain situations, a 180-day time limit for the refund of the excess tax (instead of 60 days) was contrary to the then Article 18 (4) of the VI VAT Directive[31] and the principles of EU law, the proportionality, and neutrality. Consequently, the VAC found that, in this case, it was necessary to refuse the application of a provision of the VAT Law imposing a 180-day time limit for the refund of excess tax and to apply the general time limit of 60 days (provided for in another provision of the national law).[32]

In addition, administrative courts examined the cases relating to the compatibility with VAT Directives of the Polish provision according to which the reduction of the amount or the refund of the difference of the tax due shall not apply to imported services purchased by the taxable person in connection with which payment of the amount due is made directly or indirectly to a person having their place of residence, registered office, or central management in a territory or country referred to in a list of so-called tax paradises. The doubts as to their compatibility with Article 17 (6) of the VI VAT Directive,[33] and Article 176 of Directive 2006/112,[34] were shared by the SAC which referred the question to the Court of Justice for a preliminary ruling.[35] The Court of Justice in the judgment C-395/09 *Oasis East* held that:

> Article 17(6) of the Sixth Directive, the provisions of which have, in essence, been reproduced in Article 176 of Directive 2006/112, must be construed as not authorising the retention of national legislation, applicable when the Sixth Directive entered into force in the Member State concerned, which excludes in general the right to deduct input VAT paid at the time of the purchase of imported services, the price of which is directly or indirectly paid to a person established in a State or territory classified as a 'tax haven' by that national legislation.[36]

D. Simon, Remboursement des excédents de TVA et lutte contre la fraude, *Europe* 2008 Octobre Comm. no. 337 pp. 36–37.

31 Sixth Council Directive 77/388/EEC of 17 May 1977 on the harmonisation of the laws of the Member States relating to turnover taxes – Common system of value added tax: uniform basis of assessment, OJ L 145, 13.7.1977, pp. 1–40.

32 Judgment of the VAC in Wrocław of 29 September 2008, case I SA/Wr 1238/06; accepted widely also in other cases, for example, judgment of the VAC in Opole of 13 July 2009, case I SA/Op 92/09; judgment of the SAC of 14 October 2010, case I FSK 1741/09 (until the provisions were modified).

33 Sixth Council Directive 77/388/EEC of 17 May 1977 on the harmonisation of the laws of the Member States relating to turnover taxes – Common system of value added tax: uniform basis of assessment, OJ L 145, 13.7.1977, pp. 1–40.

34 Council Directive 2006/112/EC of 28 November 2006 on the common system of value added tax, OJ L 347, 11.10.2006, pp. 1–118.

35 Order of the SAC of 6 August 2009, case I FSK 990/09.

36 Case C-395/09, *Oasis East sp. z o.o.*, EU:C:2010:570, para. 32; for discussion, see further: A.-L. Mosbrucker, Taxe sur la valeur ajoutée, *Europe* 2010 Novembre Comm. no. 11 pp. 32–33; D. Dominik, *Highlights & Insights on European Taxation*, 2010, no. 8, pp. 73–74; D. Dominik, *Highlights & Insights on European Taxation*, 2011, no. 1, pp. 62–63.

The consequence of finding such an incompatibility was the obligation to refuse to apply the national provision restricting the taxpayer's right to reduce the amount of tax, that is to say, to remove it from the basis for adjudicating. Consequently, the administrative court held that a taxable person was still entitled to reduce the amount of the output tax by the amount of the input tax in the case of import of management services.[37]

In another group of cases, administrative courts settled the disputes relating to the incompatibility, alleged by the individuals, of the due date of the value-added tax laid down in national legislation with Article 66 of Directive 2006/112/EC.[38] As a result of the preliminary references submitted by the SAC,[39] The Court of Justice held that

> Article 66 of [the VAT Directive] is to be interpreted as precluding national legislation which provides that, in respect of transport and shipping services, value added tax is to become chargeable on the date on which payment is received in full or in part, but no later than 30 days from the date on which those services are supplied, even where the invoice has been issued earlier and specifies a later deadline for payment.[40]

The SAC had no doubt that the judgment of the CJEU results in declaring that the Polish provision is contrary to Article 66 of Directive 2006/112. Due to the fact that consistent interpretation in that case was not possible, the SAC (relying on the judgments of the CJEU in *Costa v. ENEL* and *Simmenthal*) found that the national court was obliged to refuse the application of the national provision. Consequently, the moment at which the tax liability arose had to be determined in accordance with the general rule, applicable to all services, that is to say, at the time when the invoice was issued. In other words, the refusal to apply the national provision incompatible with EU law led to the application of another provision, specifying the moment of arising tax liability in accordance with Directive 2006/112.[41]

As the last example in this group, the SAC judgment ruling on the possibility of applying a preferential VAT rate can be mentioned in a situation where national legislation limited such a possibility to taxable persons who 'attained a minimum level of turnover in the preceding tax year, or have concluded an agreement with a person authorised to refund VAT to travellers'.

37 Judgment of the VAC in Gliwice of 29 June 2011, case III SA/Gl 699/11.

38 Council Directive 2006/112/EC of 28 November 2006 on the common system of value added tax, OJ L 347, 11.12.2006, pp. 1–118.

39 Order of the SAC of 4 January 2012, case I FSK 484/11.

40 Case C-169/12, *TNT WorldWide*, EU:C:2013:314; for discussion, see further: D. Dominik-Ogińska, *Highlights & Insights on European Taxation*, 2013 no. 8, pp. 86–87; M. Militz, Wyrok w sprawie TNT Express Worldwide – analiza skutków wyroku 'na dziś' i 'na przyszłość' [Case TNT Express Worldwide – Analysis of the Implications 'for Today' and 'for Tomorrow'], *Przegląd Podatkowy*, 2013, no. 8, pp. 12–18.

41 Judgment of the SAC of 20 November 2013, case I FSK 1749/13.

Following a question referred by the SAC for the preliminary ruling,[42] the Court of Justice found that:

> Article 131, Article 146(1)(b) and Articles 147 and 273 of Council Directive 2006/112/EC of 28 November 2006, on the common system of value added tax, must be interpreted as precluding national legislation under which, in the context of a supply of goods for export to be carried in the personal luggage of travellers, the vendor, a taxable person, must have attained a minimum level of turnover in the preceding tax year, or have concluded an agreement with a person authorised to refund VAT to travellers, where the mere failure to meet those conditions results in the definitive loss for the vendor of the exemption in relation to that supply.[43]

Following the CJ ruling given earlier, the SAC held that the administrative authorities, assessing the taxable person's right to benefit from the preferential 0% VAT rate could not refuse the applicant the status of a taxable person entitled to make, in the capacity of a seller, a direct refund of VAT to travellers, solely for the reason that he had not met the conditions for the taxable person to achieve a turnover exceeding PLN 400, 000 for the previous tax year or to conclude an agreement with an authorised entity. That condition was incompatible with EU law and, consequently, the tax authorities were required to disregard (refuse to apply) a rule of national law contrary to EU law (Article 127 (6) of the VAT [Law] at issue).[44]

In the disputes referred to earlier, the administrative courts refused to apply the provisions of the national law without having examined whether the provisions of the Directive (applicable in a given case) were directly effective or not. It is difficult to find grounds for that situation, in particular, since the courts have ensured the effectiveness of EU law and the compatibility of the rulings, the acts of law application, with EU law. However, it should be borne in mind that the reason for that situation may be the circumstance that in each of the cases referred to earlier, as a refusal to apply a national provision, there was no need to substitute, in order to reconstruct the basis for adjudicating, a national provision (contrary to EU law) for an EU provision, since there was another national provision governing a given issue (most often defining a certain 'general rule' resulting from the Directive, and consequently, the Law). In other words, the basis for the ruling could be 'supplemented' by the court with

42 Order of the SAC of 27 January 2016, case I FSK 1398/14.

43 Case C-307/16, *Pieńkowski*, EU:C:2018:124; for discussion, see further: H. Nieskens, Ausfuhrlieferung von Gegenständen im persönlichen Reisegepäck, *Umsatz-Steuerberater*, 2018, no. 2, pp. 41–42.

44 Judgment of the SAC of 10 May 2018, case I FSK 1398/18; also many other judgments in the same vein, for example, judgment of the SAC of 10 May 2018, case I FSK 1602/14.

another provision of national law, instead of that, which had been removed from the basis for the ruling as incompatible with EU law.

However, there are numerous rulings in case-law where administrative courts have taken into account the link between the refusal to apply a provision (an obligation resulting from the principle of primacy) and the direct effect of a provision of EU law constituting the standard for review. In this group of judgments, it is worth pointing out that the line of judgments, in which administrative courts ruled on the compatibility, with Directive 2003/96/EC,[45] of the provision of the Excise Duty Law, according to which one of the types of additives added to fuels was to be taxed at the highest possible tax rate, reserved for the so-called 'other motor fuels' (Article 89 (1) (14)) of the Excise Duty Law), instead of, as required by Article 2 (3) of Directive 2003/96, the rate applicable to the fuel, to which that additive was added. As a result of the findings of the Court of Justice that the aforementioned provision of the Directive does not allow the maintenance of a national provision, such as that indicated in the case, it was necessary to refuse to apply a national provision, contrary to EU law,[46] and to apply a different rate, appropriate to the fuel, to which the additives were added. However, in that case, the referring court preparing itself to disapply a national provision (if its doubts were confirmed by the CJEU) asked, in its preliminary question, whether Article 2 (3) of Directive 2003/96 satisfied the criteria of direct effectiveness[47] and it was confirmed by the CJ in the judgment. Gradually, however, this obligatory link between primacy (and obligation of non-application of a national provision) and direct effect of the EU provision, that is applicable in a given case, will win due respect in the case-law of administrative courts. It is predicted on the grounds that administrative courts continue to refer preliminary questions to the CJEU, and this Court takes due account of its recent rulings, including in case Popławski II.[48] In one of VAT cases, the Court of Justice recalled that Article 90 (1) of Directive 2006/112 fulfils the conditions for it to have direct effect and that, secondly, the principle of the primacy of EU law means that any national court, hearing a case within its jurisdiction, has, as an organ of a Member State, the obligation to disapply any provision of national law which is contrary to a provision of EU law with direct effect in the case pending before it.[49] The SAC, when adjudicating the case

45 Council Directive 2003/96/EC of 27 October 2003 restructuring the Community framework for the taxation of energy products and electricity, OJ L 283, 31.10.2003, p. 51.

46 Case C-275/14, *Jednostka Innowacyjno-wdrożeniowa*, EU:C:2015:75; judgment of the SAC of 27 October 2015, case I FSK 678/15.

47 Order of the SAC of 12 September 2013, case I FSK 454/13.

48 Case C-573/17, *Popławski II*, EU:C:2019:530, para. 61.

49 Case C-335/19, *E. sp. z o.o. sp. k.*, EU:C:2020:829, para. 51; see also A. Bartosiewicz, Wyrok Trybunału Sprawiedliwości, C-335/19, E. Sp. z o.o. Sp. k. przeciwko Ministrowi Finansów, a ograniczenie w czasie możliwości skorzystania z ulgi na złe długi [Case C-335/19 E. Sp. z o.o. Sp. k. przeciwko Ministrowi Finansów and Restricting the Time Limit to Benefit from the Exemption on 'Bad Doubts'], *Przegląd Podatkowy*, 2020, no. 12, pp. 24–28.

pending before it with due account of this ruling of the CJEU, also repeated that when a taxpayer fulfils the conditions of reduction of taxable amount envisaged in Article 90 (1) of Directive 2006/112 and does not fulfil exclusively the conditions from national provisions which are incompatible with EU law, then such a taxpayer may rely on that provision before the national courts against the State in order to obtain a reduction in the taxable amount and the competent court is obligated to refuse application of these nonconforming provisions of national law.[50]

The link between primacy and direct applicability is accepted by administrative courts in the context of the application of the Regulations, based on the wording of Article 288 subparagraph 2 TFEU. In particular, in the early period after the accession of Poland to the EU, administrative courts dealt with disputes in which doubts arose as to the compatibility of national law with the provisions of Regulations. For example, disputes arose over the issue as to who is charged with the fee for examining goods declared in the course of customs proceedings. Although, in accordance with the Polish provision applicable in 2004 those charges were borne by the person declaring the goods, pursuant to Article 63 (3) of the Community Customs Code applicable at that time,[51] those costs should be borne by the customs authorities instead. The administrative courts rightly considered that a national provision was contrary to the aforementioned provision of the EU Regulation insofar as it charged the declarant for *ex officio* examinations or analyses of goods in relation to the verification of the customs declaration, when the data provided by that entity therein turned out to be incorrect. In such a case, the national court was obliged to disregard the national provision and apply Community law, that is to say, in this case Article 69 (3) of the Community Customs Code.[52]

Non-application of a national provision of procedural law

Administrative courts discharge the obligation, resulting from the principle of primacy, to refuse the application also in relation to procedural rules, in particular, the Law on proceedings before administrative courts.

In the case-law of administrative courts, the subject matter of examination was the issue as to whether it is allowed to refuse to apply Article 133 of the Law on proceedings before administrative courts, according to which: 'the court shall issue a judgment upon the closure of the trial on the basis of files

50 Judgment of the SAC of 17 June 2021, case I FSK 2261/15.

51 Council Regulation (EEC) No 2913/92 of 12 October 1992 establishing the Community Customs Code, OJ L 302, 19.10.1992, pp. 1–50.

52 Judgments: of the VAC in Bydgoszcz of 28 March 2008, case I SA/Bd 35/08; of the VAC in Gdańsk of 10 September 2008, case III SA/Gd 154/08; of the VAC in Lublin of 23 November 2010, case III SA/Lu 170/10, confirmed in judgment of the SAC of 6 June 2012, case I GSK 658/11.

of the case' where, following the delivery of the judgment by the VAC and in the course of the cassation proceedings before the SAC, the judgment was issued by the Court of Justice, which affected the interpretation of national law (on which the VAC was based). The SAC had no doubts that, in such a case, if the CJEU ruling delivered a different interpretation of the EU provisions than that adopted in case-law of national courts (before that ruling), when those provisions were applicable to the applicant party in cassation, the CJEU ruling should be taken into account in the cassation proceedings and final judgment. In other words, the rule, resulting from Article 133 of the Law on proceedings before administrative courts (to hear the case on the basis of the factual and legal situation on the date of the adoption of the contested administrative act), in order to give full effectiveness of EU law must be disregarded in a given case, and it must be assumed that the legal situation has changed retroactively since the date of entry into force of the national legislation at issue.[53]

Another national procedural provision, which may undermine the effectiveness of EU law is Article 183 § 1, of the Law on proceedings before administrative courts, according to which '[t]he Supreme Administrative Court shall hear the case within the limits of the cassation appeal, however, it takes into account, on its own authority, invalidity of the proceedings', which is possible in instances explicitly described in the law.

The problem arises in situations when an applicant does not include claims grounded in the EU law in its appeal in cassation. The wording, of Article 183 (1), suggests that the SAC may act on its own authority (thus without pleas from an applicant) only when it considers invalidity of proceedings, but none of the possible grounds for such invalidity concerns arguments based on EU law. Thus, the SAC would have two possibilities: either disapply Article 183 (1) of the Law on proceedings before administrative courts or interpret one of the grounds for declaring invalidity of the proceedings with a view to take EU law arguments into account.

First, it is worth mentioning that the SAC had already decided, by issuing a resolution of seven judges, that Article 183 § 1, the Law on proceedings before administrative courts, is not binding in a situation when the Constitutional Tribunal issued the judgment on the unconstitutionality of a normative act in the course of administrative court proceedings, but the unconstitutional provision, under which the contested ruling had been issued, was not indicated in the grounds for cassation (plead to the SAC in the instance review). In such situations, the adjudicating chamber of the SAC should apply directly the provisions of Article 190 (1) and (4) of the Constitution and take account of the judgment of the Constitutional Tribunal without being bound by the content of Article 183 § 1.[54] The SAC argued that non-application of the rule that it

53 For example, judgments of the SAC of 13 December 2016 in cases: I GSK 304/15, I GSK 305/15 and I GSK 306/15.

54 Resolution of seven judges of the SAC of 7 December 2009, case I OPS 9/09.

is bound by the limits of the cassation appeal is justified by the exceptional procedural situation of an individual, on which he or she had no influence (meaning that he or she could not predict that the Constitutional Tribunal would declare a provision unconstitutional). In the context of this resolution of seven judges, it is claimed that also when the need to respect immediate and full effectiveness of CJEU's ruling so requires, it is necessary to undertake, by the SAC, such actions which will overstep the established scheme of operation.[55]

The analysis of the case-law may be a basis for a conclusion that the SAC in many cases rightly accepts that an administrative court cannot adopt an interpretation different from that previously adopted by the CJ and that the preliminary judgment is binding upon a national court (of each instance, provided that this court does not refer its own questions to the CJ). Whereas the SAC has not adopted a resolution on the effects of the CJEU's ruling (from which the incompatibility of a national provision results) in the cassation proceedings, similar to the resolution mentioned earlier (on the effects of the CT's ruling on the unconstitutionality of a national provision), it may be concluded that in many cases the SAC finds that it is not bound by the wording of Article 183 § 1 of the Law, on proceedings before administrative courts in a situation, when after submitting an appeal in cassation (which may be on the point of law solely) by the applicant the CJEU ruled on the interpretation of the provision of EU law transposed into the Polish legal order, on the basis of which the contested ruling had been issued, if the interpreted provision or the provision of national law transposing it, was not provided for in the grounds for cassation.[56] The SAC forwarded arguments grounded in Article 9 of the Constitution, as well as Articles 87 (1) and 91 (3). Additionally, it argued that a preliminary ruling, delivered by the CJEU, is binding to the national court (unless it decides to address its own preliminary questions to the CJEU) and that the administrative court may not adopt interpretation of EU law different to that adopted by the Court of Justice. Otherwise, such administrative courts would usurp the exclusive competence of the CJEU to interpret EU law. Due to the fact that the Court of Justice interprets the rules and principles of EU law, the binding force of such interpretation corresponds to the binding force of the EU law provisions and which administrative courts

55 Z. Kmieciak, Wykonanie przez Naczelny Sąd Administracyjny w ramach kontroli instancyjnej wyroku Trybunału Sprawiedliwości – Glosa do wyroku Naczelnego Sądu Administracyjnego z dnia 12 czerwca 2019 r., II GSK 5001/16 [Implementation of the Judgment of the CJEU by the Supreme Administrative Court in the Second Instance Proceedings (Control of the Ruling of the Court of First Instance) – Commentary on the Judgment of the SAC of 12 June 2019, II GSK 5001/16], *Orzecznictwo Sądów Polskich* 2020, no. 3, pp. 144–150, at 146.

56 See, for example, group of judgments of the SAC of 12 October 2016, in cases: I FSK 2035/15, I FSK 2034/15, I FSK 2072/15, I FSK 2071/15, I FSK 2069/15, I FSK 2044/15, I FSK 1989/15; such view is supported also in the legal writing, see B. Dauter, Komentarz do Art. 183 [Commentary on Article 183], in: B. Dauter, A. Kabat, M. Niezgódka-Medek, *Prawo o postępowaniu przed sądami administracyjnymi. Komentarz* [The Law on Proceedings before Administrative Courts. Commentary], Wolters Kluwer, 2020, p. 663.

must respect.[57] The SAC, in this case, accepted that it was bound by the principles of loyal cooperation and primacy (as tool of ensuring the *effet utile* of EU law). One must admit that the reasoning, in this example, is, however, blurred because the adjudicating chamber mixes the primacy (which requires non-application of a national provision) with the obligation of consistent interpretation (which requires application of national provision but interpreted in accordance with EU law). On the one hand, the adjudicating chamber of the SAC referred to the aforementioned ruling of the Constitutional Tribunal, where, let us remember, suggested disapplication of the procedural provision and direct application of the provisions of the Constitution. In addition, it referred to the principle of procedural autonomy of the Member States and its limits, namely non-discrimination and equivalence. On the other, concluding this reasoning the SAC stated that ***interpretation consistent with the Constitution and the EU law*** (underlined by Monika Szwarc) allows a party involved to decide that, in a situation where after submitting an appeal in cassation, the CJEU ruled on interpretation of EU provision, transposed into national legal order and when this interpreted EU provision or transposing national provision has not been invoked in the appeal, the SAC is under obligation to take this CJEU's ruling into account, ***not being bound by*** (underlined by Monika Szwarc) Article 183 § 1 of the Law on proceedings before administrative courts.[58] Therefore, it seems that it was rather the application of primacy and the obligation of non-application of a national rule stemming from it rather than the interpretation of a procedural rule in a way consistent with EU law. Nevertheless, this line of cases deserves approval as assurance of the effectiveness of EU law, in particular of CJEU's decisions.

Still, the possibility of the consistent interpretation of Article 183 (1) and (2) is also considered in the legal science. It was argued that one of the grounds for declaring the invalidity of proceedings could be applied in a situation when the CJEU delivered a ruling after the cassation procedure had been already initiated. This ground would be a situation when the party was deprived of the possibility of defending its rights, as provided in Article 183 (2) p. 5 of the Law on proceedings before administrative courts. The justification of such a proposal is reconstructed on the basis of the assumption that interpretation of the aforementioned procedural provision shall not lead to 1) differentiation of legal situation of individuals depending on the circumstances, whether infringement of their rights stems from non-conformity with the Constitution or with the EU law, and 2) to make it impossible in practice or seriously undermine exercise of the rights stemming from the EU law.[59]

57 With reference to monography by P. Dąbrowska, Skutki orzeczenia wstępnego Europejskiego Trybunału Sprawiedliwości [Effects of the Preliminary Ruling of the European Court of Justice], Dom Wydawniczy ABC, 2006, at 82, 86–88.

58 Judgment of the SAC of 12 October 2016, in case I FSK 2035/15 and other referred to in fn 50.

59 Z. Kmieciak, Wykonanie przez Naczelny Sąd Administracyjny w ramach kontroli instancyjnej wyroku Trybunału Sprawiedliwości – Glosa do wyroku Naczelnego Sądu Administracyjnego

As can be easily concluded, these assumptions are based on the principle of procedural autonomy and corresponding principles of non-discrimination and equivalence.[60]

Article 190 of the Law on proceedings before administrative courts, according to which 'interpretation of law made in a case by the Supreme Administrative Court shall bind the court to which the case has been referred' may be another obstacle to the full implementation of the principle of primacy. It is accepted, however, that this rule, that the VAC is bound by the interpretation issued by the SAC, is not absolute. The SAC found, in its case-law, that it was allowed to disapply that provision in a specific situation, that is, when the CJEU delivered the ruling, in which a different interpretation of EU law applicable in the case was made then the interpretation, which had been made by the cassation Court referring the case for reconsideration to the court of the first instance.[61] The SAC found that the principle of primacy of EU law (in particular, the CJ judgments in cases *Elczinow* and *Filipiak*) required, so that in such a situation the voivodeship administrative court, as the court of the first instance could take account of the most recent interpretation of EU law formulated by the CJEU.[62]

Another procedural provision, which may prevent assurance of the full effectiveness of EU law is Article 269 of the Law on proceedings before administrative courts, according to which

> if any panel of the administrative court hearing the case does not share the position taken in the resolution by seven judges, by a panel of the entire Chamber or by the full panel of the Supreme Administrative Court, it shall submit the arising legal issue for resolution by an appropriate panel.

This provision is interpreted in the legal writing of administrative law in such a way that resolutions of the SAC, delivering to lower administrative courts the interpretation of a given national provision *in abstracto* or *in concreto* (adopted in the course of the particular administrative court proceedings), are generally

---

z dnia 12 czerwca 2019 r., II GSK 5001/16 [Implementation of the Judgment of the CJEU by the Supreme Administrative Court in the Second Instance Proceedings (Control of the Ruling of the Court of First Instance) – Commentary on the Judgment of the SAC of 12 June 2019, II GSK 5001/16], *Orzecznictwo Sądów Polskich* 2020, no. 3, pp. 144–150, at 147.

60 Case 33/76, *REWE*, EU:C:1976:188; case 45/76, *Comet*, EU:C:1976:191.

61 Judgments of the SAC: of 12 June 2013, case I FSK 146/13; of 20 September 2013, case I FSK 1370/12.

62 Judgments of the SAC of 20 September 2013, case I FSK 1370/12; of 12 January 2017, case I GSK 280/15; accepted also in the legal writing, B. Dauter, Komentarz do Art. 190 [Commentary on Article 190] in: B. Dauter, A. Kabat, M. Niezgódka-Medek (eds.), *Prawo o postępowaniu przed sądami administracyjnymi. Komentarz* [The Law on Proceedings before Administrative Courts. Commentary], Wolters Kluwer, 2020, p. 709.

binding.[63] It results in a situation that the position, taken by the SAC in a resolution, binds indirectly all adjudicating panels of administrative courts; until this position is changed, administrative courts should respect it. Therefore, it is the procedural provision, the application of which could eventually lead to a situation where the adjudicating court was forced to disregard the case-law of the CJEU, applicable in a given case. However, in that respect, administrative courts have developed a position that makes it possible, in certain situations, to disapply Article 269 § 1 of the Law on proceedings before administrative courts. Justifying the obligation to refuse the application of Article 269 § 1 administrative courts:

- first, have accepted, that the preliminary ruling procedure (Article 267 TFEU) is a form of cooperation between the CJ and a national court, according to the competences of each of them, in addition to the fact – that the preliminary rulings are *de facto* of the precedential nature;
- secondly, it is consequently accepted that the court could not adopt an interpretation different from that that had which been previously made by the CJ due to the fact that then it would step in the exclusive competence of the CJ to interpret EU law; whereas, failure to comply with the interpretation delivered by the CJ might result in liability for damages (the *Köbler* judgment referred to);
- thirdly, have associated the obligation to respect the rulings of the CJ to the principle of primacy and efficiency: namely, 'an interpretation by the CJ, in practice, amounts to the obligation and need to apply the consistent interpretation or even a refusal to apply national law incompatible with EU law' (here: *Simmenthal*); what is more, 'the consequence of the compliance with preliminary rulings by a national court is each time . . . an obligation to ensure effective legal protection of individuals and the full effectiveness of EU law, i.e. the full implementation of the principle of the effectiveness of EU law'; consequently, referring quite generally to the principle of primacy of EU law, the courts conclude, that these are sufficient grounds for the court to disapply Article 269 of the Law on proceedings before administrative courts.[64]

The consequence of acceptance that the national court must refrain from initiating the procedure provided for in Article 269 (1) of the Law on proceedings before administrative courts was disregarding the interpretation delivered in the resolution of seven judges of the SAC, if such interpretation was

63 A. Kabat, Komentarz do Art. 269 [Commentary on Article 269], in: B. Dauter, A. Kabat, M. Niezgódka-Medek (eds.), *Prawo o postępowaniu przed sądami administracyjnymi. Komentarz* [The Law on Proceedings before Administrative Courts. Commentary], LEX, 2019.

64 All quotes in this passage are derived from the judgment of the VAC in Wrocław of 24 July 2014, case I SA/Wr 754/14.

contrary to, or inconsistent with, the subsequent case-law of the CJEU. For example, in the dispute concerning the right to deduct all input tax resulting from a VAT invoice relating to the legal services as regards both transactions subject to VAT and the transactions outside the VAT system, the VAC in Wrocław waived the application of arguments adopted in the resolution of the panel of seven judges of the SAC,[65] to adopt, for the purposes of hearing the case, subsequent case-law of the CJEU.[66]

It should be also explained that resolutions of that type may be issued in the extended panel of seven judges of the SAC 'in order to explain legal provisions whose application has caused differences in jurisprudence of administrative courts' or to solve 'legal issues raising considerable doubts in respect of a particular administrative court case' (according to Article 15 § 1 of Law on proceedings before administrative courts). Additionally, in this context, in a situation where it turned out, that the resolution which had been adopted by the extended panel of the SAC included a different interpretation[67] to that which was adopted by the CJ,[68] the ordinary adjudicating panels of the SAC (thus, composed of three judges) heard the cases in accordance with a subsequent ruling of the CJ without launching the procedure of amending the resolution of the extended panel of the SAC.[69] The adjudicating panel of the SAC in this case stated that the principle of law certainty, the need for the consistent interpretation and application of EU law, and to ensure its effectiveness require the national courts to rely, in their rulings, on the relevant ruling of the Court of Justice. In pursuing that objective, and recognising the primacy and significance of the interpretation of the provisions of the VAT Directive contained in case C-224/11 *BGŻ Leasing*, the adjudicating panel decided not to initiate the procedure provided for by Article 269 § 1 of the Law on proceedings before administrative courts, considering that referring to the enlarged panel of the SAC the legal issues arising in the present case, in addition to those in the CJ judgment, was purposeless. It added that was even more justified as it was only the Court of Justice that was entitled to interpret EU law and, in this case, VAT Directives and any possible extended panel, when interpreting Article 29 (1) and Article 30 (3) of the Law on proceedings before administrative courts, would be thus, obliged, as regards the aforementioned reference to

65 Resolution of the SAC of 24 October 2011, case I FPS 9/10.

66 Judgment of the VAC in Wrocław of 24 July 2014, case I SA/Wr 754/14, whereas in this case the operative part of the resolution was compatible with EU law, only the argumentation required modification and adaptation of the interpretation of provisions to the CJ case-law, which was emphasised by the adjudicating panel itself; the judgments of the CJEU: case C-496/11, *Portugal Telecom*, EU:C:2012:557; case C-104/12, *Becker*, EU:C:2013:99; case C-319/12, *MDDP*, EU:C:2013:778.

67 Resolution of seven judges of the SAC of 8 November 2010, case I FPS 3/10.

68 Case C-224/11, *BGŻ Leasing*, EU:C:2013:15.

69 Judgment of the SAC of 27 June 2013, case I FSK 720/13.

the principle of primacy of EU law, to do so taking into account also the interpretation included in the CJ judgment relating to the provisions of the Directive relevant to the case. The non-application of the procedure under Article 269 § 1 of the Law on proceedings before administrative courts does not amount – opined the adjudicating panel – to the disregard for the national provisions of administrative-court proceedings. On the contrary, such a solution to the problem avoids putting a subsequent panel of the SAC into a situation in which a newly adopted resolution would not, in fact, be the answer to a legal issue raising serious doubts (Article 187 § 1 of the Law on proceedings before administrative courts), which has already been resolved by the CJEU judgment, binding also upon that panel. At the same time, the panel noticed that Article 269 § 1 of the Law on proceedings before administrative courts was a procedural rule established in 2002 and therefore, for obvious reasons, could not take into consideration the role and impact of the case-law of the CJ on the interpretation of provisions of national law by administrative courts.[70] Thus, in fact, the panel of three judges of the SAC departed from the legal assessment of the extended panel of the SAC without the need to change that assessment under Article 269 of the Law on proceedings before administrative courts.

Therefore, in a situation where the interpretation of EU provisions implemented to national legislation made by the extended panel of the SAC is in contradiction to the interpretation of these provisions of an EU Directive made by CJEU, in the opinion of the panel ruling in that case, the application of the interpretation presented in the CJEU judgment does not require the need to initiate the procedure provided for in Article 269 § 1 of the Law on proceedings before administrative courts.[71] The interpretation of provisions relating to the apportionment of the amounts of input tax in respect of the taxable person's mixed expenditure, made by the Court and binding upon the national court, is sufficient to rule on the case and to ensure the implementation of the principles of effectiveness of EU law, with simultaneous obligation of ensuring effective protection of an individual as well.[72] Incidentally, however, it is interesting to note that in the same ruling the SAC limited its effects and, as a matter of consequence, of the judgment of the Court of Justice.

70 Judgments of the SAC: of 29 May 2013, case I FSK 147/13; for further discussion see also P. Wróbel, Dialog of Administrative Courts with the Court of Justice of the European Union, *Zeszyty Naukowe Sądownictwa Administracyjnego*, 2021, no. 1–2, pp. 175–195, at pp. 190–192.

71 Judgments of the SAC: of 7 October 2020, case I FSK 763/17; of 15 January 2020, case I FSK 928/16; of 15 January 2020, case I FSK 1353/16; of 17 December 2020, case I FSK 1750/16; of 22 November 2019, case I FSK 293/16; of 21 November 2019, case I FSK 1907/15; of 21 November 2019, case I FSK 1970/15; of 21 November 2019, case I FSK 2047/15; of 8 November 2019, case I FSK 258/16; of 31 October 2019, case I FSK 1071/17; of 18 October 2019, case I FSK 1718/15; of 26 September 2019, case I FSK 256/16; of 11 September 2019, case I FSK 1007/17; of 4 September 2019, case I FSK 204/16 and many others later on.

72 Judgment of the SAC of 2 July 2019, case I FSK 119/17.

In this context, it shall be explained that, back in 2011, the extended panel of seven judges of the SAC adopted resolution in which a certain interpretation of national provisions implementing corresponding Article of VAT Directive.[73] To be more specific, prior to 2016, domestic provisions on VAT contained no rules regarding the apportionment of the input VAT paid in respect of mixed expenditure.[74] On the grounds of Polish rules, the panel of seven judges of the SAC held that, in the absence of such criteria in national law, a taxable person was entitled to deduct VAT in full, including the share of the input tax connected with transactions falling outside the scope of the common system of VAT. In addition, referring, inter alia, to the principle of the legality of taxation and public levies and of the setting of tax rates, enshrined in Article 217 of the Constitution of the Republic of Poland, that particular court held that, prior to the entry into force of amendments to the Law on VAT on 1 January 2016, taxable persons could not be charged with non-compliance with the criteria established by those amendments. However, such an interpretation of national law raised doubts of the administrative courts in the first instance (VACs) as to whether it was compatible with the VAT Directive, in particular Article 168, which expressly states that the right to deduct VAT is connected solely to transactions subject to VAT. As a result of preliminary reference of VAC in Wrocław,[75] the Court of Justice ruled that Article 168 (a) of Directive 2006/112/EC precluded a national practice which permitted a taxable person to deduct, in full, the input value-added tax (VAT) charged in respect of their acquisition of goods and services for the purposes of both economic activities subject to VAT and non-economic activities, not falling within the scope of VAT, owing to the lack of specific rules in the applicable tax legislation regarding the criteria and methods of apportionment which would enable that taxable person to determine the share of that input VAT which must be regarded as being connected to his economic and non-economic activities, respectively.[76]

As a result, this ruling of the CJEU had important implications for case I FSK 119/17. The SAC had to review the ruling of the VAC, in which it relied on the resolution of seven judges of 2011, which later, in 2019, proved to contain an interpretation of VAT regulations which was incompatible with EU law (as interpreted by the CJEU). The SAC in case I FSK

73 Resolution of seven judges of the SAC of 24 October 2011, case I FPS 9/10.

74 It was amended later by the Polish legislature, but the problem existed for years 2013–2015.

75 Order of the VAC in Wrocław of 10 June 2017, case I SA/Wr 123/17.

76 Case C-566/17, *Związek Gmin Zagłębia Miedziowego*, EU:C:2019:390; for discussion, see further: Ch. Sterzinger, Steuerpflichtiger, der sowohl wirtschaftliche als auch nichtwirtschaftliche Tätigkeiten ausübt – Gegenstände und Dienstleistungen, die sowohl für Zwecke der Erzielung von mehrwertsteuerpflichtigen als auch von nicht der Mehwertsteuerpflichtigen als auch von nicht der Mehrwertsteuer unterliegenden Umsätzen erworben wurden, *Umsatzsteuer-Rundschau*, 2019, pp. 424–432; F. Huschens, Gemischte – wirtschaftliche und nicht wirtschaftliche hoheitliche – Tätigkeiten, *EU-Umsatz-Steuerberater*, 2019, pp. 45–47.

119/17, properly decided that, prior to 1 January 2006, Polish regulations (lacking the criteria and methods of apportionment) could not be the legal basis for the deduction, in full, of the input value-added tax. This modification of interpretation, however, according to the SAC, could not be sufficient legal basis for an obligation of taxable payers to corrections of the tax due, as it would be contrary to constitutional principles of rule of law and legality. Such limitation of the effectiveness of EU law, as decided by the SAC in this judgment, as a consequence of limitation of temporal effects of the CJEU judgment, has been justifiably criticised in Polish literature.[77]

Finally, the SAC assumes that there is no need to initiate the procedure contained in Article 269 of the Law on proceedings before administrative courts when the issue, relating to the interpretation of EU law, has already been resolved by the CJEU. The SAC consistently accepts that it is pointless to refrain from referring a legal issue to the enlarged SAC panel for hearing, due to the primacy and seriousness of the interpretation of the EU provisions (applicable in the case concerned) covered by a respective judgment of the CJ, in addition to the principle of the effectiveness of EU law, in addition to the economics of administrative court proceedings. That is the case where the legal issue relevant to the dispute has been resolved by the CJEU.[78]

Another interesting example of the non-application of a procedural provision is a situation in which the SAC requires the disregarding of the application of the provision limiting the jurisdiction of administrative courts. As was indicated in the introduction, 'administrative courts shall exercise review of the activity of public administration and employ means specified in statute' (Article 3 § 1 of Law of proceedings before administrative courts). The Law of proceedings before administrative courts also defines the decisions of public administration subject to judicial review. At the same time, the Law indicates the cases, in which the jurisdiction of administrative courts is excluded. The SAC, in recent case-law, has already refused to apply the provision of the Law of proceedings before administrative courts, under which the jurisdiction of administrative courts had been limited to considering the decisions of administrative authorities, where it was necessary to ensure the effectiveness of EU law. Pursuant to Article 58 (1) of the Law on proceedings before administrative courts, 'The court shall dismiss an action: (1) where the case does not come within the jurisdiction of an administrative court'.

77 M. Maliński, Glosa do wyroku Naczelnego Sądu Administracyjnego z dnia 2 lipca 2019 r. (sygn. akt I FSK 119/17) [Commentary on the Judgment of the Supreme Administrative Court of 2 June 2019, Case I FSK 119/17], *Zeszyty Naukowe Sądownictwa Administracyjnego*, 2020, no. 6, pp. 187–196.

78 Judgments of the SAC: of 29 May 2013, case I FSK 147/13; of 18 September 2020, case I FSK 234/18; of 28 August 2020, case I FSK 1921/15; of 26 June 2020, case I FSK 1623/17; of 28 February 2020, case I FSK 1391/17; of 28 February 2020, case I FSK 982/16.

In the dispute between an individual and the consul of the Republic of Poland, concerning the refusal to issue a Schengen visa on the basis of Article 32 (1) of Regulation 810/2009, the VAC refused to accept the complaint for consideration, applying the provision of the Law on proceedings before administrative courts, according to which the jurisdiction of administrative courts had been excluded in this respect (Article 5 (4) the Law on proceedings before administrative courts). The SAC, when considering the appeal against the VAC ruling, doubted whether the exclusion with respect to earlier discussion of the possibility of lodging an appeal against the consul's decision was compatible with EU law.[79] As a result of referring, by the SAC, a question for a preliminary ruling,[80] the Court of Justice held that:

> Article 32(3) of Regulation (EC) No 810/2009 of the European Parliament and of the Council of 13 July 2009 establishing a Community Code on Visas, as amended by Regulation (EU) No 610/2013 of the European Parliament and of the Council of 26 June 2013, read in the light of Article 47 of the Charter of Fundamental Rights of the European Union, must be interpreted as meaning that it requires Member States to provide for an appeal procedure against decisions refusing visas, the procedural rules for which are a matter for the legal order of each Member State in accordance with the principles of equivalence and effectiveness. Those proceedings must, at a certain stage of the proceedings, guarantee a judicial appeal.[81]

The SAC, when deciding the case, found that, due to the inconsistency of Article 5 (4) of the Law on proceedings before administrative courts with Article 32 (3) of the Code on Visas read in conjunction with Article 47 first paragraph the EU Charter of Fundamental Rights, the application of the aforementioned Polish provision should be refused. Consequently, it held that 'there were no grounds for dismissing an action brought for the reason

79 According to Article 32(3) of the Regulation 'Applicants who have been refused a visa shall have the right to appeal. Appeals shall be introduced against the Member State that has taken the final decision on the application for an extension and in accordance with the national law of that Member State. Member States shall provide applicants with information regarding the procedure to be followed in case of review, as specified in Annex VI'.

80 Order of the SAC of 28 June 2016, case II OSK 1346/16.

81 Case C-403/16, *El Hassani*, EU:C:2017:960; for discussion, see further: D. Simon, Indépendance des juges, *Europe* 2018 Avril no. 4 pp. 11–12; L. Coutron, Cour de justice, 13 décembre 2017, El Hassani, aff. C-403/16, ECLI:EU:C:2017:960, Jurisprudence de la CJUE 2017, *Bruylant, Bruxelles. Décisions et commentaires*, 2018, pp. 226–237; J.-Y. Carlier, L. Leboeuf, Droit européen des migrations, *Journal de droit européen*, 2019, no. 3, pp. 114–130; R. Puchta, Warunki dopuszczalności powołania się na ochronę wynikającą z art. 47 KPP [Conditions of Applicability of the Guarantees Resulting from Article 47 of the Charter of Fundamental Rights of the European Union (Remarks Concerning ECJ Judgment of 13 December 2017, El Hassani], *Państwo i Prawo*, 2019, no. 4, pp. 35–52.

indicated by the Court of the First Instance on the grounds of the order under appeal'.[82]

In addition, a similar position was taken by the SAC in the case in which the VAC found inadmissible, in the first instance, an appeal against the refusal to issue a visa for the purpose of exercising an entry within the meaning of Directive 2016/801 on the conditions of entry and residence of third-country nationals for the purposes of research, studies and training.[83]

Taking into account a directly effective provision of EU law in the application of substantive law

A directly effective provision of TFEU as a source of rights for individuals

The first legal problem, after the accession of Poland to the European Union, that was resolved in administrative courts and the case-law of the Court of Justice, was the issue of discriminatory taxation of second-hand vehicles imported from other Member States compared to the second-hand cars purchased in Poland.[84] In answer to the question referred for a preliminary ruling by the VAC,[85] the Court of Justice held, in the *Brzeziński* judgment, that: 'The first paragraph of Article 90 EC [art. 110 TFEU] is to be interpreted as meaning that it precludes an excise duty, in so far as the amount of the duty imposed on second-hand vehicles over two years old acquired in a Member State other than that which introduced such a duty exceeds the residual amount of the same duty incorporated into the market value of similar vehicles which had been previously registered in the Member State which introduced that duty',[86] leaving to the national court to determine whether national legislation produces such an effect. The VAC held in the judgment that,

> in order for the burden of both categories of second-hand vehicles (over two years old) to be the same in Polish legislation, the amount of excise duty imposed on second-hand vehicles originating in another Member State may not exceed the amount of residual excise duty included in the

82 Order of the SAC of 19 February 2018, case II OSK 1346/16.

83 Preliminary reference of the SAC: order of 4 November 2019, case II OSK 2470/19; case C-949/19, *M.A.*, EU:C:2021:186; final decision of the SAC of 13 April 2021, case II OSK 2470/19.

84 On the facts of the case and the EU law element in that case, cf. Chapter 3.

85 Order of the VAC in Warsaw of 22 May 2005, case III SA/Wa 679/05.

86 Case C-313/05, *Brzeziński*, EU:C:2007:33, see also commentaries: E. Bernard, Droit d'accises sur les véhicules d'importation en Pologne, *Europe* 2007 Mars Comm. no. 85 pp. 13–14; B. Makowicz, Polnische 'Akzise' auf eingeführte Gebrauchtfahrzeuge, *Zeitschrift für Zölle und Verbrauchsteuern*, 2007, pp. 129–131; K. Lasiński-Sulecki, Sprzeczność polskich przepisów dotyczących opodatkowania używanych samochodów osobowych z europejskim prawem wspólnotowym [Incompatibility with the Community Law of Polish Regulation on Taxation of Second-Hand Cars], *Przegląd Podatkowy*, 2007, no. 4, pp. 41–43; A. Rigaux, Taxe d'effet équivalent, *Europe* 2017 Décembre no. 12, pp. 23–24.

> market value of a similar second-hand car, which has already been registered in Poland. . . . Excise duty, which differentiates the method of calculating the taxable amount of the second-hand vehicles in such a way, that it does not take into account the actual depreciation of imported cars, while this element is taken into account for domestic cars, infringes the principle of discrimination.[87]

The consequence of the VAC judgment was the need to reconsider the case by a tax authority and to determine the difference in taxation in such a way as to avoid a greater burden on a vehicle imported from other Member States. Whilst the VAC pointed out that the development of the detailed rules for any possible refund of overpaid excise duty falls within the competence of administrative authorities, which should take into account the principles of interpretation of EU law, due to the fact that, this part of excise duty will be refunded, which exceeds the excise duty contained in the value of a similar vehicle previously registered in Poland.[88] However, ultimately, the problem of the amount of refund of the overpaid tax was solved by a special law, which specified how to calculate the difference between the tax paid and the tax due.[89]

The subject matter of the case-law of administrative courts was also the question as to whether it was admissible, in the light of EU law, for the purposes of the annual settlement of the personal income tax, to exclude the possibility of a) reducing the taxable amount by the amount of the social security contributions paid in another State and b) reducing the tax due by the amount of the health insurance contributions paid in another State.

Namely, just after the accession of Poland to the EU, the applicable provision of the Personal Income Tax Law allowed for the deduction from the tax due, the health insurance contributions paid 'under the Polish Law of 27 August 2004 on Health Care Services financed from public funds' (that is to reduce the tax by those amounts), which consequently, due to the applicability of that Law in the territory of the Republic of Poland only, led to the exclusion of the deductibility of contributions paid under legislation of another State (where they have been collected). In practice, this led to taxable persons being prevented from deducting contributions paid in other Member States. As a result of the question referred by the VAC in Wrocław for the preliminary ruling,[90] the Court of Justice in the *Rüffler* judgment held

> that Article 18(1) EC precludes legislation of a Member State which makes the granting of a right to a reduction of income tax by the amount of health insurance contributions paid conditional on payment of those contributions in that Member State on the basis of national law

87 Judgment of the VAC in Warsaw of 6 March 2007, III SA/Wa 254/07.
88 Ibidem.
89 The Law of 9 August 2008, *Dz. U.* [Journal of Laws] 2008, 118, 745.
90 Order of the VAC in Wrocław of 3 October 2007, case I SA/Wr 971/07.

> and results in the refusal to grant such a tax advantage where the contributions liable to be deducted from the amount of income tax due in that Member State have been paid under the compulsory health insurance scheme of another Member State.[91]

In the judgment issued with the due account of the ruling of the CJ, the VAC found that the effect of the interpretation adopted by the CJ was

> to modify a rule of tax law resulting only from the provisions of domestic tax law by taking into account the inadmissibility, established by the Community court, of the restriction on the application of the deduction of the health insurance contribution resulting from the wording of the national provision. That modification consists in removing from that rule of law, those elements thereof, which introduce the limitation to the deduction contested by the taxable person. Under the circumstances of the operation of those provisions of tax law, such an interpretation procedure leads to granting to the taxable person of the personal income tax – who exercises the free movement in Poland (the country of taxation, residence) – the possibility of deducting the health insurance contribution paid in the Federal Republic of Germany from the tax (provided that it has not been deducted from the income of the source country), under the same conditions as the persons paying health contributions directly to the Polish health insurance scheme. The deduction thus structured – according to the panel ruling in the case – provided a full guarantee for implementing freedom of movement of persons within the European Union.[92]

In other words, as a result of the taking into account the directly effective provision of Article 18 (1) TFEU (in relation to the freedom of movement and residence guaranteed under Article 21 (1) TFEU), the basis for the ruling in this case was reconstructed in such a way as to enable the EU citizens, who have exercised their freedom of movement, to include, in their annual tax return, additionally the contributions paid in other Member State.

At the same time, doubts were raised as to the compatibility, with EU law, of a provision of the Personal Income Tax Law, which allowed for the deduction from the taxable amount, the amounts of social security contributions 'laid down in the Law of 13 October 1998 on the social security system'. Therefore, as in the case of tax deductions of contributions paid for health insurance, in this case, due to the applicability of this Law in the territory of

91 Case C-544/07, *Rüffler*, EU:C:2009:258, for commentaries, see further A.-L. Mosbrucker, F. Kauff-Gazin, Fiscalité directe, *Europe* 2009 Juin Comm. no. 214 pp. 9–11; P. Kubicki, Einkommensteuer ermäßigbar durch Abzug der in anderem Mitgliedstaat gezahlten Krankenversicherungsbeiträge, *Europäische Zeitschrift für Wirtschaftsrecht*, 2009, pp. 543–545.

92 Judgment of the VAC in Wrocław of 25 August 2009, case I SA/Wr 946/09.

the Republic of Poland only, it led to the exclusion of the deductibility of contributions paid in accordance with the legislation of another State (where they had been collected). In practice, that led to the prevention of the taxpayers being able to deduct contributions paid in other Member States. As a result of the preliminary questions of the VAC in Poznań,[93] the Court of Justice in the *Filipiak* judgment held that:

> Articles 43 EC and 49 EC preclude national legislation under which the possibility for a resident taxpayer to obtain, first, a deduction from the basis of assessment in the amount of social security contributions paid in the tax year and, second, a reduction of the income tax which he is liable to pay by the amount of health insurance contributions paid in that period, exists solely when those contributions are paid in the Member State of taxation, while such advantages are refused in the case where those contributions are paid in another Member State, even though those contributions were not deducted in that other Member State.[94]

The VAC, in its judgment, taking into account the CJ ruling, held that, the principle of primacy of EU law 'requires a national court to apply Community law and to disapply national provisions incompatible with it'. As a result of the taking into account, as the basis for the ruling, the directly effective provisions of the TFEU (establishing the freedom of establishment, now Article 49 TFEU, and the freedom to provide services, now Article 56 TFEU), the administrative court enabled the inclusion, in an annual tax return, submitted in the territory of the Republic of Poland, the health insurance contributions paid in other Member States. The VAC, when annulling an administrative decision, refusing the possibility to deduct, pointed out that

> the tax authority, when reconsidering the case, will be obliged to take into account the views expressed by the Court in the present judgment and take into account the possibility for the taxpayer to reduce the taxable amount and tax also by social and health insurance contributions paid in the territory of H.[95]

Although the *Brzeziński*, *Rüffler*, and *Filipiak* judgments were not groundbreaking for the development of EU law, they were important from the perspective of the judiciary practice of Polish administrative courts. It is also worth appreciating the fact that the incompatibility of national provisions and, thus, the incompatibility of administrative decisions in specific and individual cases had already been noticed by voivodeship administrative courts, which

93 Order of the VAC in Poznań of 30 May 2008, case I SA/Po 1756/07.

94 Case C-314/08, *Filipiak*, EU:C:2009:719, for commentaries, see further K. Tetlak, *Highlights & Insights on European Taxation*, 2010, no. 2, pp. 65–66.

95 Judgment of the VAC in Poznań of 14 January 2010, case I SA/Po 1006/09.

did not hesitate to refer the preliminary questions to the Court of Justice. Thus, they ensured the effectiveness of the EU law and the protection of the rights, which the individuals derive from EU law even before the conformity of national legislation with EU law was provided.[96]

It is also worth pointing out that the *Filipiak* judgment was an important element of the debate in Poland on the primacy of EU law due to the circumstance that the provisions of the Personal Income Tax Law concerned were declared by the Constitutional Tribunal unconstitutional, but, at the same time, their binding force was maintained until 20 November 2008 (to enable the legislature to amend those provisions in a way that would be compatible with the Constitution).[97] For this reason, the VAC, examining the case of Mr. Filipiak made, in the main proceedings, a reference to the CJ asking whether it was bound by the deferral of the loss of the binding force of the disputed provisions of the Law, as ruled by the Constitutional Tribunal.[98] The Court of Justice held in this regard that:

> Pursuant to the principle of the primacy of Community law, a conflict between a provision of national law and a directly applicable provision of the Treaty is to be resolved by a national court applying Community law, if necessary by refusing to apply the conflicting national provision, and not by a declaration that the national provision is invalid, the powers of authorities, courts and tribunals in that regard being a matter to be determined by each Member State.

and that

> the primacy of Community law obliges the national court to apply Community law and to refuse to apply conflicting provisions of national law, irrespective of the judgment of the national constitutional

96 The Amendment to the Personal Income Tax Law in this respect entered into force on 1 December 2008.

97 Judgment of the Constitutional Tribunal of 7 November 2007, case K 18/16.

98 Some commentators in Poland opined that the second question was a consequence of the wrong interpretation of the Polish Constitution by the referring VAC. It was underlined that even if the Constitutional Tribunal deferred the loss of the binding force of a national provision, the national constitution does not require the national court *to apply it*. Thus, for some commentators it was obvious that VAC is obligated to disapply such a national provision, and that the second question of VAC was not necessary at all; see: P. Bogdanowicz, M. Wiącek, Zasada pierwszeństwa prawa wspólnotowego a kompetencje Trybunału Konstytucyjnego (uwagi na tle postanowienia WSA w Poznaniu z dnia 30 maja 2008 r., sygn. akt I SA/Po 1756/07) [The principle of primacy of Community law and the competence of the Constitutional Tribunal (remarks on case I SA/Po 1756/07], *Zeszyty Naukowe Sądownictwa Administracyjnego*, 2009, no. 3, pp. 55–74; P. Mikłaszewicz, glosa do wyroku WSA w Poznaniu z 14.01.2010 (I SA/Po 1006/09) [Commentary on the Judgment of the VAC in Poznań of 14 January 2010, I SA/Po 1006/09], *Europejski Przegląd Sądowy*, 2011, no. 10, pp. 41–46.

> court which has deferred the date on which those provisions, held to be unconstitutional, are to lose their binding force.[99]

Consequently, the deferral of the loss of the binding force of provisions of the Law declared unconstitutional cannot, according to the administrative courts, be an obstacle to the taking into account the infringement of EU law.[100]

In addition, the freedom of establishment and freedom to provide services were taken into account by the administrative courts in subsequent disputes of taxable persons with the administrative authorities. The problem of deduction also arose in the context of the possibility of exercising the exemption in the personal income tax on revenue obtained from the sale of immovable property, provided that this revenue was reinvested in the purchase of property exclusively in the territory of the Republic of Poland. The VAC held that the pleas in law alleging the infringement of provisions of Article 18, Article 39, and Article 43 TEC (Article 21, Article 45 and Article 49 TFEU respectively) should be upheld and that the Applicant was entitled to an exemption in the flat-rate, personal income tax on revenue derived from the sale of an immovable property in a situation when the expenditure for the purchase of property had been incurred and the property was located in the territory of another Member State of the European Union. The individual interpretation was revoked.[101] The SAC hearing the cassation against that judgment added that,

> in order to avoid a situation, in which the rules of national law lead, in essence, to a restriction on those freedoms, such provisions should be interpreted, both by the courts of a Member State, as well as by administrative authorities, in the manner, which guarantees the primacy of application of Community provisions, thus, in a way that excludes the discrimination of a taxable person depending on, whether the property

99 Case C-314/08, *Filipiak*, EU:C:2009:719, para. 82 and sentence.

100 Judgment of the VAC in Poznań of 14 January 2010, case I SA/Po 1006/09 (*Filipiak*); I SA/Po 371/10; on this dual path and interaction between the request for preliminary ruling and request to the Constitutional Tribunal in particular, see A. Kustra, Odroczenie przez TK utraty mocy obowiązującej przepisu niezgodnego z prawem UE. Glosa do wyroku TS z 19 November 2009 r. w sprawie C-314/08 Filipiak [The Deferral of the Loss of the Binding Force of the Provision Contrary to EU Law. Commentary on the Judgment of the Court of Justice of 19 November 2009 in C-314/08 Filipiak], *Europejski Przegląd Sądowy*, 2012, no. 6, pp. 34–40; P. Wróbel, Dialog of administrative courts with the Court of Justice of the European Union, *Zeszyty Naukowe Sądownictwa Administracyjnego*, 2021, no. 1–2, pp. 175–195, at. 188; as well the judgment of the VAC in Gliwice of 10 January 2012, case I SA/Gl 446/11; similarly judgments of the VAC in Poznań: of 23 June 2010, case I SA/Po 362/10; of 23 June 2010, case I SA/Po 363/10; of 8 July 2010, case I SA/Po 370/10; of 8 July 2010, case I SA/Po 371/10.

101 Judgment of the VAC in Warsaw of 6 May 2010, case III SA/Wa 2286/09.

> purchased is located in the territory of the Republic of Poland, or in another Member State.[102]

Therefore, in practice, the basis for the ruling again was construed on the basis of a national provision with a modification taking into account the prohibition of introducing unjustified restrictions on the freedoms of the internal market.

For example, based on established case-law of the CJEU (and therefore, without reference for a preliminary ruling), the SAC took the view that

> the circumstance of liquidation of a foreign permanent establishment of a Polish company, resulting in inability to settle the loss in the tax system of another EU Member State, requires to adopt (under the freedom of establishment), that under the Corporate Income Tax Law the company is entitled to settle, in the Polish tax system, the loss generated by the permanent establishment operating in another Member State and impossible to be settled in that State.[103]

Directly applicable provisions of Regulations, as the source of rights and obligations

Administrative courts apply, as the basis for the ruling, also the provisions of Regulations. An example is the judgment in which the SAC settled a dispute between a farmer and an agency paying out direct payments *Agencja Restrukturyzacji i Modernizacji Rolnictwa* (Agency for Reconstructing and Modernisation of Agriculture), relating to the refusal of payments as the result of the failure to meet the conditions laid down in Polish legislation. Both the VAC and the SAC, in the course of the instance review, found that a directly applicable provision of the Regulation (Article 130 (3) of Regulation No. 73/2009 applicable then), should be the basis for the dispute resolution, disregarding the additional conditions laid down in Polish legislation. The SAC found that the farmer had met the conditions provided for in Article 130 (3) of Regulation No. 73/2009, which could be directly applicable in the case.[104]

In other cases, administrative courts also heard disputes relating to the conditions which a veterinarian must meet in order to be appointed to the position of a district veterinarian (a function within the public administration). The essence of the dispute, in those cases, amounted to two issues: 1) whether the provisions of the EU Regulation could be directly applicable in such cases and 2) whether national law provisions introducing additional

102 Judgment of the SAC of 14 March 2012, case II FSK 1603/10.

103 Judgments of the SAC: of 28 November 2011, case II FSK 929/11; of 4 April 2012, case II FSK 1819/10; of 12 April 2013, case II FSK 1593/11; of 15 October 2014, case II FSK 2401/12 and recently of 16 May 2017, case II FSK 1003/15.

104 Judgment of the SAC of 8 April 2016, case II GSK 2429/14.

criteria (restrictions) on the appointment of a person to perform veterinary activities comply with the rules of EU law. In one of the judgments, the SAC found that Regulation No. 854/2004 was directly applicable under Article 91 (3) of the Constitution of the Republic of Poland, and there were no normative grounds for relativising the possibility of such an application in the area of national law. The conflict of rules, referred to in Article 91 (3) of the Constitution of the Republic of Poland, means that it is not possible to apply both competing legal regulations at the same time and this, in turn, leads to the conclusion that, for the application of the constitutional conflict-of-laws rule, it is necessary to compare the content elements of the conflicting legal rules applicable in the case. Consequently, the SAC ruled that a veterinarian who is not an inspection employee may be designated to carry out the activities laid down in national law, pursuant to the provisions of points 1–5 of chapter IV, [Division] A, Section III of Annex 1 read in conjunction with Article 5 of Regulation No. 854/2004. In relation to the content of Article 288 TFEU and the constitutional order of the system of sources of generally applicable law, it was on the basis of those criteria that it was needed to establish the applicant's preparation for discharging the duties of an official veterinarian, since the rules of Regulation No. 854/2004 are, in this respect, clear, precise, and fully governing the issue of professional qualifications of the official veterinarian.[105]

The provisions of the Regulations are directly applicable also in those cases where administrative courts review the decisions of public administration authorities regarding the compliance of the products with the requirements resulting from legislation. For example, in one of the SAC judgments, the question at issue in the case was whether it was possible to challenge the order of the District Veterinarian on the provisional securing of goods in the refrigeration chamber owned by the applicant Company, or whether that order could be challenged only in the appeal against the final decision in the case. The SAC had based its decision on the provisions of Regulation No. 882/2004, on official controls performed to ensure the verification of compliance with feed and food law, animal health and animal welfare rules, applicable in that case,[106] and found that, since the administrative authority had applied towards the entity under control, the measure provided for in Article 54 (2) of Regulation (EC) No. 882/2004, consequently, the provision of Article 54 (3) of the aforementioned Regulation had to be applicable. The circumstance that the authority applying the measure under Article 54 (2) (h) of Regulation (EC) No. 882/2004 gave to the ruling the form of an order of a provisional security nature, at the same time, did not amount to the exclusion of right of

105 Judgment of the SAC of 12 October 2016, case II OSK 3262/14.

106 Regulation (EC) No 882/2004 of the European Parliament and of the Council of 29 April 2004 on official controls performed to ensure the verification of compliance with feed and food law, animal health, and animal welfare rules, OJ L 165, 30.4.2004, p. 1 (no longer in force).

the controlled entity to challenge it, in accordance with Article 54 (3) of the aforementioned Regulation.[107]

A directly effective provision of a Directive as a basis for the right to be protected by court

There are numerous examples of cases in which administrative courts, in situations where the incompatibility of national law with EU law is found, derive the right of an individual from the directly effective provision of a Directive, relying, first of all, on the judgment of the CJ in case *Becker*[108] are provided by case-law in tax matters. It should be emphasised that disputes resolved by administrative courts always relate to the relationship between an individual and a State or a State and an individual. If in a dispute with an administration authority, an individual relies on a provision of EU law in order to challenge a provision of national law, there are no doubts in the case-law of administrative courts as to the applicability of a directly effective provision of EU law (the rules resulting from case-law of the CJEU limiting the direct effect of Directives in relations between individuals are not applicable).

The first example is the group of rulings in which the administrative courts examined the issue of the incompatibility of the, then applicable, provisions of the VAT Law in terms of determining the catalogue of services for which the place of supply is considered to be the place of establishment (the then Article 9 (3) (e) of the VI Directive). The dispute concerned the issue as to whether national provisions had transposed correctly the catalogue of those services into Polish law, since it did not take into account IT services. The VAC recognised that, at the time of hearing the case, the aforementioned provision had not been properly implemented in Polish law, an incomplete catalogue of such services in national law, and consequently, in order to ensure the compatibility of the ruling with EU law, found that 'in the circumstances of the present case, the conditions for the direct application of the provision of Article 9 (2) (e) of the VI Council Directive have been met', since 'the rule covered by that provision is unconditional and precise, and the margin of discretion relates only to the means of its implementation'. Consequently, according to the VAC, the company was entitled to directly rely on the provision of Article 9 (2) (e) of the VI Council Directive, which consequently meant that the service provided by the company should be taxed only in the country of residence of that service recipient (customer), which was other than Poland.[109]

In another case, the VAC first had found the incompatibility of the provision of the implementing regulation to VAT Law with Article 27 (1) of the

107 Judgment of the SAC of 18 January 2017, case II OSK 1027/15.

108 Case 8/81, *Becker*, EU:C:1982:7.

109 Judgment of the VAC in Warsaw of 9 February 2006, case III SA/Wa 3203/05, accepted by the SAC in judgment of 8 May 2007, case I FSK 829/06.

Council Directive 92/83/EEC (according to which Member States exempt the products covered by it from the harmonised excise duty under the conditions to be laid down by them in order to guarantee the correct and fair application of such exemptions and to prevent any possible evasion, circumvention of infringement of those provisions, when they are used in the manufacture of vinegar bearing a tariff code CN 2209), since Polish legislation exempted the product at issue only in the case of acquiring in the domestic trade, excluding the intra-Community acquisition. Subsequently, it held that in 'the absence of relevant national provisions, taxpayers may . . . rely on, before courts, the directly applicable rule of Article 27 (1) of the Council Directive 92/83/EEC of 19 October 1992', which in this case meant the possibility of exercising the exemption (which had not been provided for at that time in Polish legislation).[110]

Administrative courts have also accepted that direct effect is produced by Article 5 (3), the second indent of Directive 69/355/EC, which, according to the courts, required, in calculating the amount of capital duty (i.e., the tax on civil law transactions) chargeable on an increase in a company's capital arising from the conversion into shares, following the Republic of Poland's accession to the European Union, of loans taken up by that company prior to that accession, account be taken of the previous taxation of those loans.[111] Consequently, the basis for the case resolution, resulting in allowing the earlier taxation of loans to be taken into account, was the directly effective provision of the Directive.[112]

The Polish administrative courts found directly effective Article 33 (6) of the Council Directive 2008/118/EC of 16 December 2008 concerning the general arrangements for excise duty and repealing Directive 92/12/EEC[113] in the disputes of taxable persons with administration authorities, in the context of national provisions making the refund of excise duty subject to meeting additional conditions not provided for in that Directive. The voivodeship administrative courts took the view that a national provision limited the group of persons entitled to the reimbursement of tax duty in relation to the rules included in Article 33 (1) and 6 of Directive 2008/118. In view of the fact that a national provision was incompatible with the provisions of the Directive, the VAC decided that those provisions could be a source of rights for taxable persons (whereas, in order for a provision of the Directive to be the

110 Judgment of the VAC of 18 October 2006, case I SA/Bd 492/06, accepted by the SAC in judgment of 12 August 2008, case I FSK 952/07.

111 Case C-441/08, *Elektrownia Pątnów II*, EU:C:2009:698; for discussion, see further: A.-L. Mosbrucker, Application dans le temps de la directive sur les droits d'apports, *Europe* 2010 Janvier Comm., no. 39, p. 34; K. Tetlak, *Highlights & Insights on European Taxation*, 2010, no. 2, pp. 114–116.

112 Judgment of the VAC of 7 April 2010, case III SA/Po 123/10.

113 OJ L 9, 14.1.2009, pp. 12–30.

source of a right, it must be precise and unconditional).[114] The VAC found that, 'since the right to a refund of an excise duty in the factual situation, which arose in that case, could not be derived from national law, it should be derived directly from the provisions of the Directive'.[115] The position of the VAC was confirmed in the judgment of the SAC[116] and is widely accepted in case-law of administrative courts.[117]

Personal scope of the application of the principles of primacy and direct effect

As in the context of an interpretation of national law in conformity with EU law, the administrative courts have consistently emphasised that administrative authorities, in addition to courts, are obliged to respect the principle of primacy of EU law over national law and to refuse to apply national law incompatible with Community law.[118]

Taking into account the context in which administrative courts review the activities of the administrative authorities, the obligations of those authorities have been defined separately in the context of issuing the binding tax interpretations and, thus, administrative proceedings, in which a tax authority does not issue an individual administrative decision (does not establish the situation of a given entity in a binding way). Additionally, the administrative courts consistently rule that when issuing the tax interpretations, the administrative authorities are obliged to respect the principle of primacy of EU law.

As the SAC explained, when an EU Directive relates to tax issues (e.g., Directive 2006/112), its provisions are 'tax law provisions' in the meaning of the Polish Tax Ordinance Law (the Law specifying the procedures related to the collection of taxes by administration), and in the absence of their

114 The VAC referred the order of CJEU in case C-275/14, *Jednostka Innowacyjno-Wdrożeniowa*, EU:C:2015:75, para. 33; although that judgment has been issued in the form of an order, due to the *act éclairé*, for administrative courts is one of the most frequently referred sources confirming direct effectiveness of the directives' provisions.

115 Judgment of the VAC in Gdańsk of 24 January 2017, case I SA/Gd 1233/16; in the same vein many others judgments, in particular: of the VAC in Gorzów Wielkopolski of 6 November 2019, case I SA/Go 624/19; of the VAC in Gdańsk of 24 January 2018, case I SA/Gd 1619/17; of the VAC in Poznań of 9 December 2015, cases: III SA/Po 124/15 and III SA/Po 65/15.

116 Judgment of the SAC of 24 January 2020, case I GSK 525/17.

117 Judgments of the SAC: of 23 February 2017, cases: I GSK 1281/15, I GSK 1288/15, I GSK 1837/15; of 27 February 2017, cases: I GSK 1879/15, I GSK 1967/15, I GSK 2260/15 and I GSK 2029/15; of 22 September 2017, case I GSK 1348/15; of 16 February 2018, case I GSK 127/16.

118 For example, judgments: of the VAC in Warsaw of 4 November 2009, case III SA/Wa 832/09; of the VAC in Gliwice of 20 September 2011, case I SA/Gl 549/11; of the SAC: a large group of judgments of 3 April 2007 in cases: I FSK 523/06; I FSK 462/06; I FSK 518/06; I FSK 519/06; I FSK 522/06; I FSK 175/06; I FSK 520/06; I FSK 521/06; of 29 September 2011, II FSK 601/10; of 14 October 2014, case II GSK 1426/13.

implementation or the defectiveness thereof, 'constitute a legal basis on which individuals may rely, however, in the scope of only those provisions of Directives, which are sufficiently clear and unconditional, and thus, formulated in such a way, as to allow their direct application'. In addition, as the SAC specified, if the EU Directive falls within the aforementioned term of 'tax law provisions', the administrative authorities are obliged to take into account its provisions in resolving the respective cases of individuals. This obligation is addressed, in particular, to the Minister competent for public finances, who upon the written request of the party concerned, is obliged to issue, in an individual case, a written interpretation of the provisions of [the applicable] Directive and the implementation thereof into the national legislation on tax on goods and services.[119]

Determination of the direct effect of the EU legislation

In the case-law of the administrative courts, the direct effect of the TFEU provisions, in particular, those from which the freedoms of the internal market are derived, is beyond doubt. For this reason, administrative courts ignore completely the issue as to whether an applicable provision of the Treaty is directly effective and have no difficulty in deriving the rights of taxable persons from the freedom of movement and residence (Article 21 (1) read in conjunction with Article 18 TFEU),[120] the freedom of establishment (Article 49 TFEU), the freedom to provide services (Article 56 TFEU),[121] and the free movement of goods, especially the prohibition of discriminatory taxation (Article 110 TFEU).[122] In addition, the administrative courts have no difficulty in accepting the direct applicability of Regulations provisions.[123]

On the other hand, in relation to the direct effect of the provisions of a Directive, administrative courts refer rather when there has already been the case-law of the CJEU confirming the direct effect of a given provision. In few cases is the direct effect of a Directive provision taken into account when reconstructing the legal basis for rulings and is determined by the

119 Judgments of the SAC: of 11 March 2006, case I FSK 61/09; of 20 December 2018, case II FSK 3523/16.

120 Judgment of the VAC in Wrocław of 25 August 2009, case I SA/Wr 946/09, after the judgment of the CJEU in case C-544/07, *Rüffler*, EU:C:2009:258.

121 Judgment of the VAC in Poznań of 14 January 2010, case I SA/Po 1006/09, after the judgment of the CJEU in case C-314/08, *Filipiak*, EU:C:2009:719; judgments of the SAC: of 28 November 2011, case II FSK 929/11; of 14 March 2012, case I FSK 519/06; of 4 April 2012, case II FSK 1819/10; of 12 April 2013, case II FSK 1593/11; of 15 October 2014, case II FSK 2401/12 and of 16 May 2017, case II FSK 1003/15.

122 Judgment of the VAC in Warsaw of 6 March 2007, case III Sa/Wa 254/07, after the judgment of the CJEU in case C-313/05, *Brzeziński*, EU:C:2007:33.

123 Already mentioned earlier, judgments of the SAC: of 8 April 2016, case II GSK 2429/14; of 18 January 2017, case II OSK 1027/15.

court itself. For example, in the dispute relating to the possibility of exempting from VAT all educational services, regardless of their purpose and nature, the SAC found that Article 132 (1) (i) of Directive 2006/112/EC (*ex* Article 13 part A (1) (i) of VI Directive) was directly effective. In view of finding the incompatibility of a national provision with the aforementioned provision of the Directive, the SAC recalled that a clear, precise, unconditional provision of a Directive could be directly effective, and subsequently found that the provision of the Directive referred to by the applicant met those conditions.[124] Therefore, in this case, the refusal to apply a provision of national law (which had defined too broadly the scope of the VAT exemption) was to be accompanied by the application of the directly effective provision of the Directive, which had defined that scope of the exemption concerned more narrowly.

Administrative courts also refer preliminary questions in order to determine the direct effect of the provisions of Directives. For example, as a result of the preliminary references of the SAC[125] the Court of Justice held that:

> taxable person may, however, rely on the incompatibility of that exemption with point (i) of Article 132(1) of Directive 2006/112 so that that exemption is not applied to it where, even taking account of the discretion granted to Member States, that taxable person could not objectively be regarded as an organization having objects similar to those of an educational body governed by public law, within the meaning of that provision, which is to be determined by the national court. In the latter case, the educational services supplied by that taxable person will be subject to value added tax and that person could then benefit from the right to deduct input value added tax.[126]

Also upon request of the adjudicating panel of the SAC,[127] the Court of Justice ruled on the direct effect of the second subparagraph of Article 2 (3) of Directive 2003/96, finding that 'an individual may rely on it against the competent national authority in the dispute before national courts in order to exclude the application of a national rule which is incompatible with that provision'.[128]

124 Judgment of the SAC of 9 July 2009, case I FSK 1244/08.
125 Order of the SAC of 27 April 2012, case I FSK 54/12.
126 Case C-319/12, *MDDP*, EU:C:2013:778; for discussion, see further: D. Dominik-Ogińska, MDDP. VAT Exemption Educational Services Provided by Private Entities, *Highlights & Insights on European Taxation*, 2014, no. 2, pp. 47–48; A.-L. Mosbrucker, TVA et prestations éducatives, *Europe* 2014 Janvier Com. no. 1, pp. 39–40; D. Ravella, Prestations de services éducatifs rendues par des organismes privés à but lucratif: conditions d'exonération et droit à déduction de la TVA, *Revue Lamy droit des affaires*, 2014, no. 91, pp. 57–58.
127 Order of the SAC of 12 September 2013, case I FSK 454/13.
128 Case C-275/14, *Jednostka Innowacyjno-Wdrożeniowa*, EU:C:2015:75.

It is worth noting that in both the judgments referred to, the Court of Justice emphasised, for the purposes of tax matters and the application of the VAT Directive in the national legal order, a direct link between the effectiveness of a provision of the Directive and the refusal to apply the provision. In the *MDDP* judgment, the Court of Justice stated that:

> according to settled case-law, wherever the provisions of a directive appear, so far as their subject-matter is concerned, to be unconditional and sufficiently precise, they may, in the absence of implementing measures adopted within the prescribed period, be relied on against any national provision which is incompatible with the VAT Directive or in so far as they define rights which individuals are able to assert against the State.[129]

Additionally, in the order *Jednostka Innowacyjno-Wdrożeniowa*, the CJ explained that

> in all cases where the provisions of a Directive, [in terms of its wording], are unconditional and sufficiently precise, may be relied on by individuals before national courts against the State, where the State has failed to implement a directive in domestic law by the end of the period prescribed or where it has failed to implement the directive correctly.[130]

However, it should be stipulated that the administrative courts hardly ever make the refusal to apply a national provision conditional upon that, whether a provision of a Directive, which is the standard for review, is directly effective. On the contrary, most often the refusal to apply occurs after determining that a national provision is simply incompatible with the provision of the Directive.

Determination of incompatibility of a national law provision with the EU law provision

In the case-law of administrative courts, it is accepted without reservations that the principle of primacy has an unlimited scope, since it extends to all rules of Union law in both primary and secondary law, and to all rules of national law.[131] Administrative courts find that Polish law is incompatible with EU law after establishing an EU normative standard on the basis of case-law of the Court of Justice of the European Union. For this purpose, they reconstruct

129 Case C-319/12, *MDDP*, EU:C:2013:778, para. 47.

130 Case C-275/14, *Jednostka Innowacyjno-Wdrożeniowa*, EU:C:2015:75, para. 33.

131 See a large group of judgments of the SAC of 3 April 2007 in cases: I FSK 523/06; I FSK 462/06; I FSK 518/06; I FSK 519/06; I FSK 522/06; I FSK 175/06; I FSK 520/06; I FSK 521/06.

that standard on the basis of established case-law or make references for a preliminary ruling (and as it has been indicated before, they remain active in that regard).

In addition to the cases discussed before, that is, *Sosnowska,*[132] *Oasis East,*[133] *TNT WorldWide,*[134] and *Pieńkowski,*[135] administrative courts made references for a preliminary ruling in the area of telecommunication law,[136] VAT regulating provisions[137] and excise duty,[138] rules relating to indirect taxes on raising the capital,[139] and internal market freedoms (in addition to the judgments referred to previously) on the basis of the free movement of capital[140] and the free movement of goods.[141]

When determining the conflict between a national provision with an EU provision, administrative courts also use the standards established by the Court of Justice in cases upon action, that is, under the procedure of Article 258 TFEU. For example, in order to establish for the purposes of applying excise duty on electricity the moment at which that tax is due, the standard set out in the judgment of the Court of Justice in the case C-475/07,[142] was applied from which it appeared that the provisions of Polish law did not conform with Article 21 (5) of Directive 2003/96/EC.[143]

132 Preliminary reference: see order of the VAC in Wrocław of 22 December 2006, case I SA/Wr 1238/06, case C-25/07, *Sosnowska*, EU:C:2008:395.
133 Preliminary reference: see order of the SAC of 6 August 2009, case I FSK 990/09; case C-395/09, *Oasis East*, EU:C:2010:570.
134 Preliminary reference: see order of the SAC of 4 January 2012, case I FSK 484/11, case C-169/12, *TNT WorldWide,* EU:C:2013:314.
135 Preliminary reference: see order of the SAC of 27 January 2016, case I FSK 1398/14.
136 Preliminary reference: see order of the SAC of 17 September 2008, case C-522/08, *Telekomunikacja Polska,* EU:C:2010:135.
137 See for example: order of the SAC of 14 July 2009, case I FSK 748/08, case C-438/09, *Dankowski*, EU:C:2010:818; order of the SAC of 6 March 2014, case I FSK 516/13, case C-277/14, *Stehcemp*, EU:C:2015:719; order of the SAC of 23 February 2016, case I FSK 1573/14, case C-308/16, *Kozuba*, EU:C:2017:869; order of the VAC in Wrocław, case I SA/Wr 123/17, case C-566/17, *Związek Gmin Zagłębia Miedziowego,* EU:C:2019:390; order of the VAC in Wrocław of 25 April 2018, case I SA/Wr 257/18, case C-491/18, *Mennica Wrocławska*, EU:C:2018:1042.
138 Order of the VAC in Szczecin of 29 May 2014, case I Sa/Sz 1536/13, case C-313/14, *ASPROD,* EU:C:2014:2426.
139 Order of the VAC in Gliwice of 15 March 2010, I SA/Gl 731/09, case C-212/10, *Logstor,* EU:C:2011:404.
140 Order of the VAC in Bydgoszcz of 28 March 2012, case I SA/Bd 1035/11, case C-190/12, *Emerging Markets,* EU:C:2014:249.
141 Order of the VAC in Warsaw of 18 April 2018, case VI SA/Wa 2256/17, case C-387/18, *Delfarma*, EU:C:2019:556.
142 Case C-475/07, *Commission v. Poland,* EU:C:2009:86.
143 Judgment of the VAC in Gliwice of 9 July 2008, case III SA/Gl 116/08, confirmed by judgment of the SAC of 18 May 2010, case I GSK 885/09.

Administrative courts also relied on the judgment in case C-639/11,[144] in which the Court of Justice found that:

> by making registration in its territory of passenger vehicles having their steering equipment on the right-hand side, whether they are new or previously registered in other Member States, dependent on the repositioning of the steering wheel to the left-hand side, the Republic of Poland has failed to fulfil its obligations under Article 2a of Council Directive 70/311/EEC of 8 June 1970 on the approximation of the laws of the Member States relating to the steering equipment for motor vehicles and their trailers, Article 4(3) of Directive 2007/46/EC of the European Parliament and of the Council of 5 September 2007 establishing a framework for the approval of motor vehicles and their trailers, and of systems, components and separate technical units intended for such vehicles (Framework Directive), and under Article 34 TFEU.

That standard was helpful when resolving the dispute as to whether a diagnostician, carrying out technical tests of a vehicle (conditioning the admission of the vehicle in question to traffic operation), could be punished with the withdrawal of the right to perform technical tests of vehicles due to the fact that he had confirmed compliance with the requirements set out in Polish legislation by the vehicle having its steering wheel located on the right side (in Poland cars generally have them on the left side). The SAC, taking into account the incompatibility of provisions laying down the requirements for the admission of vehicles into service with EU law (confirmed in the judgment C-639/11), held that the ruling of the Court of Justice modified the concept of a vehicle that could be registered in Poland and that this fact also affected the assessment of the technical (periodic) inspection carried out by the applicant in cassation and, consequently, the assessment of the authorities' decision to withdraw the diagnostician's authorisation to perform technical examination of the diagnostician. It ordered an administration authority to reconsider the case.[145]

Yet, in another case, the basis for the establishing of, by the SAC, the incompatibility of Polish law with EU law, was the judgment in case *Commission v. Poland*,[146] thus delivered in the direct action pursuant to Article 258 TFEU. The proceedings before the CJEU were initiated by the Commission in the context of Polish legislation, according to which roads in the country were divided into categories and the use of vehicles with different authorised single driving weights was allowed in each category of roads. This was to be confirmed by special driving permits. Without entering into details

144 Case C-639/11, *Commission v. Poland*, EU:C:2014:173.
145 Judgment of the SAC of 14 October 2014, case II GSK 1426/13.
146 Case C-127/17, *Commission v. Poland*, EU:C:2019:236.

(available in the ruling of the CJEU), it suffices to say that, according to the Commission, national rules were not compatible with EU law. This statement was confirmed by the CJEU which ruled that Poland,

> by imposing on transport undertakings a requirement to be in possession of special permits in order to be able to circulate on certain public roads, the Republic of Poland has failed to fulfil its obligations under the combined provisions of Articles 3 and 7 of Council Directive 96/53/EC of 25 July 1996 laying down for certain road vehicles circulating within the Community the maximum authorised dimensions in national and international traffic and the maximum authorised weights in international traffic, as amended by Directive (EU) 2015/719 of the European Parliament and of the Council of 29 April 2015, read in conjunction with points 3.1 and 3.4 of Annex I to Directive 96/53.

In one of the individual cases, the administrative courts were asked to verify the legality of an administrative decision imposing a fine for driving a vehicle without a permit, which was required by Polish rules. Whereas in the first instance, the VAC decided that such an administrative decision valid was (conformed to law), the SAC, under the instance review, decided to take the CJEU ruling in case C-127/17 into account. When explaining its position, the SAC referred to the wording of Article 260 (1) TFEU[147] and, in this context, also to the established case-law of the CJEU according to which national authorities are prohibited to apply a national rule recognised as incompatible with the Treaty and are under obligation to take all appropriate measures to enable Community law to be fully applied.[148] The SAC further explained that this obligation of compliance with the CJEU's ruling is binding for administrative courts and that it requires the SAC to take it into account in the procedure controlling the ruling of the voivodeship administrative court (of first instance). In addition, the SAC declared itself bound by the obligation to respect EU principles of primacy and effective judicial protection. According to the SAC, it was clear from the judgment in case C-127/17 that Polish regulation was not compatible with EU law. As a consequence, Polish rules could not be a legal basis for imposing a fine on a transport enterprise for driving a vehicle without a required permit. The SAC thus decided on discontinuation of administrative proceedings and set the VAC ruling aside.[149]

147 If the Court of Justice of the European Union finds that a Member State has failed to fulfil an obligation under the Treaties, the State shall be required to take the necessary measures to comply with the judgment of the Court.

148 Case 48/71, *Commission v. Italy*, EU:C:1972:65, para. 7; case 103/88 *Costanzo*, EU:C:1989:256, para. 33; case C-101/91, *Commission v. Italy*, EU:C:1993:16, para. 24.

149 Judgment of the SAC of 12 June 2019, case II GSK 5001/16; on the same day still without reference to Article 260 TFEU, see judgment of the SAC of 12 June 2019, case II GSK

What is more, administrative courts refer to the standards resulting from the judgments of the Court of Justice in cases upon action other than against Poland. For example, in order to determine the incompatibility of the provision of the Personal Income Tax Act with the principle of non-discrimination on the grounds of citizenship, free movement of people and freedom of establishment, an administrative court made a reference to the judgment of the Court of Justice C-345/05.[150] On the basis of the standard for review established in that way, the administrative court found incompatible with EU law (the principle of non-discrimination, free movement of workers and freedom of establishment) the provision of the Polish Personal Income Tax Law, which prevented a taxable person from exercising the exemption from taxation of revenue from the sale of the residential premises, partly spent on financing the purchase of a new property outside the territory of the Republic of Poland, and in the territory of the EU Member States.[151]

The results of application of the principles of direct effect and primacy

Results from the perspective of administrative courts

From the perspective of administrative courts, the principles of primacy and direct effect have an impact on the application of the procedural provisions, which are inherently intended to ensure the uniformity of case-law. Due to the fact that those issues have been discussed in detail earlier (see Section 'Non-application of a national provision of procedural law'), at this point, it is only worth mentioning that, in order to ensure the full effectiveness of EU law and, in particular, by taking into account, in domestic case-law, the rulings of the Court of Justice of the European Union, national courts sometimes disregard the SAC rulings issued in the enlarged panels, in particular those provisions, which generally require the voivodeship administrative courts to respect the rulings issued by the SAC, or the regular compositions of the SAC.

Results from the perspective of individuals

The application of the principle of primacy and direct effect in the case-law of administrative courts leads primarily to an improvement in the situation of private entities, in particular, taxable persons in relations with State authorities.

Firstly, the application of those principles may have an impact on determining the **absence of liability**. For example, in the context of tax obligation,

412/17; followed by another 171 rulings of the SAC with reference to this CJEU's ruling, see the most recently judgment of the SAC of 17 May 2022, case II GSK 1900/18.

150 Case C-345/05, *Commission v. Portugal*, EU:C:2006:685.

151 Judgment of the VAC of 4 November 2009, case III SA/Wa 832/09; confirmed by the SAC in judgment of 31 May 2011, case II FSK 141/10.

administrative courts relying on the directly effective Article 9 (2) (e) of the VI VAT Directive (77/388), acknowledged that IT services should be taxed only in the State of establishment of the service recipient [customer]. Therefore, in the context of cases under consideration, those services were taxable in another EU Member State, and not in Poland.[152]

At this juncture, it is worth referring to the group of cases, resulting in establishing the absence of administrative liability in general. In a whole series of cases, administrative courts reviewed the legality of administrative decisions concerning a breach of traffic provisions; it was about driving on the roads with vehicles not meeting the requirements laid down in Polish law. The SAC, in its case-law, assumed that, in order to assess the compliance of inspected vehicles with legislation, administrative authorities should have taken into account not only the provisions of Polish law but also EU law. Since in the course of the judicial review it turned out that a national provision determining the authorised axle load in the VII category cars, providing for 8 tonnes was incompatible with Article 3 and Article 7 of Directive of the Council 96/53/EC, where that load had been provided for as 11.5 tonnes. Thus, according to the SAC, it could not be considered lawful to impose an administrative penalty on driving on roads with a vehicle whose load exceeded 8 tonnes but did not exceed 11.5 tonnes. The SAC, relying on the the judgment of the CJEU in case C-127/17, concluded that there were no grounds for establishing, in national law, so determined an authorised load of a single driving axle of a vehicle as a condition for circulating on Polish national roads.[153] Consequently, administrative courts, on the one hand, refused to apply a national provision setting the maximum load in this category of vehicles contrary to the Directive, and at the same time, applied a standard more favourable to the applicants under the provisions of Directive 96/53/EC, which consequently led also to the exemption from administrative liability (recognising the decisions imposing sanctions to be unlawful) in those cases, where it had been determined by administration authorities exclusively on the basis of national law, incompatible with EU law.[154]

Secondly, the application of the aforementioned principles of EU law may have an impact on determining **the moment when the tax liability arises**. Recognising the *TNT WorldWide* judgment, national courts refused to apply the provision of the Value Added Tax Law, which, for the transport and shipping services, determined the time of the arising tax liability, contrary to Directive 2006/112/EC. As a result of disregarding the provision of the Law [statute] incompatible with EU law, a general rule applicable to all services,

152 Judgment of the VAC of 9 February 2006, case III SA/Wa 3203/05, accepted by the SAC in judgment of 8 May 2007, case I FSK 829/06.

153 Judgment of the SAC of 13 February 2020, case II GSK 3028/17.

154 Judgment of the SAC of 12 June 2019, case II GSK 5001/16; on the same day still without reference to Article 260 TFEU see judgment of SAC of 12 June 2019, case II GSK 412/17; followed by another 171 rulings of the SAC with reference to this CJEU's ruling, see the most recently judgment of the SAC of 17 May 2022, case II GSK 1900/18.

namely, recognising that the tax liability arises at the time of issuing an invoice, was applicable to deciding those cases.[155]

Thirdly, the application of the principle of primacy and direct effect may also lead to **granting/determining/maintaining the right to deduct or reduce tax.** Numerous examples in this regard are also provided by the case-law of administrative courts, taking into account the directly effective provisions of TFEU. In the case-law of administrative courts presented earlier (see Section 'A directly effective provision of TFEU as a source of rights for individuals') of the study, the application of the directly effective provisions of the TFEU led to conferring on taxable persons the rights they had been deprived of under national tax law. The judgments of administrative courts led to the abolition of discriminatory taxation of the second-hand vehicles imported into the territory of the Republic of Poland from other Member States,[156] to enabling personal income taxpayers to include in their annual tax returns health insurance contributions paid in other Member States[157] and social security contributions paid in other Member States,[158] to allowing the taxable persons to exempt from the personal income tax, the revenue obtained from sale of immoveable property, also when the income from this sale has been reinvested in the purchase of a property in other EU Member States (and not only in Poland).[159]

In another line of cases, with due account of the judgment *Oasis East*, as a result of the refusal to apply the provision of the VAT Law, limiting the possibility of deductions form VAT, administrative courts applied instead, another provision of national law, which made it possible, in accordance with EU law, to deduct, from VAT, the expenses incurred by a taxable person.[160] Whereas, as a result of adopting by an administrative court the direct effect of Article 5 (3) of Directive 69/355/EC, the company in the dispute with administrative authorities was granted the right to take into account, for the purposes of the capital duty (in Poland – the tax on civil law transactions) the loans which had been taken by this company before.[161]

In the case-law following the judgment C-335/19 *E.*, the administrative courts disapply the conditions of the reduction of the taxable amount, which stem from national provisions contrary to Article 90 (1) of Directive 2006/112. As a result of the application of the directly effective article of this

155 Judgment of the SAC of 20 November 2013, case I FSK 1749/13.

156 Resulting from case C-313/05, *Brzeziński*, EU:C:2007:33, judgment of the VAC in Warsaw of 6 March 2007, case III SA/Wa 254/07.

157 Resulting from case C-544/07, *Rüffler*, EU:C:2009:258, judgment of the VAC in Wrocław of 25 August 2009, case I SA/Wr 946/09.

158 Resulting from case C-314/08, *Filipiak*, EU:C:2009, EU:C:2009:719, judgment of the VAC in Poznań of 14 January 2010, case I SA/Po 1006/09.

159 Judgment of the VAC in Warsaw of 6 May 2010, case III SA/Wa 2286/09, confirmed in judgment of the SAC of 14 March 2012, case II FSK 1603/10.

160 Judgment of the SAC of 16 March 2011, case I FSK 1588/10.

161 Judgment of the VAC in Poznań of 7 April 2010, case III SA/Po 123/10.

directive and primacy of EU law, the taxpayer had a chance before tax administration authority to obtain reduction, pursuant to EU law.[162]

Fourthly, EU law may affect the **choice of an appropriate tax rate**. As a result of the CJ ruling in the judgment *Pieńkowski*, the SAC found that, in their analysis of the issue as to whether the taxable person was entitled to benefit from the preferential 0% VAT rate, the administrative authority could not deprive of such a right on the sole ground that the conditions for the taxable person to achieve a turnover of over PLN 400 thousand for the previous tax year or to conclude an agreement with an authorised entity have not been met. Since such an additional condition has been found incompatible with Directive 2006/112/EC, it should be disregarded in the basis for the ruling and the right to benefit from the preferential VAT rate should be granted (provided that other conditions compatible with EU are met).[163] On the other hand, the ruling of the CJ in *Polska Jednostka Wdrożeniowa* case made it necessary to disregard, in the disputes with the authorities, the provision of the Law [statute] under which one of the types of fuel additives was to be taxed at the highest possible tax rate. Consequently, in the basis for the ruling, another national provision should be taken into account according to which the appropriate rate for fuel to which an additive has been added should be applied to that additive. That resulted in the application of the lower tax rate and, therefore, an advantage to a taxable person.

Finally, taking into account EU law by administrative courts may lead to the **modification of the conditions specifying the procedure for payment or tax refund**. In cases decided taking into account the *Sosnowska* judgment, the refusal to apply a provision of national law [statute], under which an administrative authority had 180 days to reimburse the excess tax, where one category of taxable persons was concerned (those who had just started their operation), led to the need to apply (under national law) a general, 60-day time limit for the refund of excess tax applicable in relations with all taxable persons (and therefore, a solution more favourable for a taxable person).[164] Whereas, in terms of the excise duty taking into account directly effective Article 33 (6) of Directive 2008/118/EC, administrative courts held that, in view of the incompatibility of the Polish provision with EU law, the provision of the Directive was the basis for demanding a refund of excise duty.[165]

162 Judgment of the SAC of 17 June 2021, case I FSK 2261/15.

163 Judgment of the SAC of 10 May 2018, case I FSK 1398/18; also many other judgments in the same vein, for example, judgment of the SAC of 10 May 2018, case I FSK 1602/14.

164 Judgment of the VAC in Wrocław of 29 September 2008, case I SA/Wr 1238/06; accepted widely also in other cases, for example, judgment of the VAC in Opole of 13 July 2009, case I SA/Op 92/09, judgment of the SAC of 14 October 2010, case I FSK 1741/09 (until the provisions were modified).

165 Judgments of the SAC: of 23 February 2017, cases: I GSK 1281/15, I GSK 1288/15, I GSK 1837/15; of 27 February 2017, cases: I GSK 1879/15, I GSK 1967/15, I GSK 2260/15 and I GSK 2029/15; of 22 September 2017, case I GSK 1348/15; of 16 February 2018, case I GSK 127/16.

In the recent case-law of administrative courts, in particular of the SAC, of particular importance is the right to a fair trial provided for by Article 19 (1) TEU and Article 47 of the Charter of Fundamental Rights. On the one hand, in specific cases, the SAC derives the need to guarantee the right to a trial, which may require the need to disregard the application of the provision of the Law on proceedings before administrative courts and direct applicability of Article 47 CFR.[166]

Conclusions

Even in the early case-law of the SAC, including an EU element, it was emphasised that

> in the event of incompatibility between a rule of national law and a rule of Community law, a court of a Member State should issue a judgment on the basis of the rule of Community law and refuse to apply a national law rule. In that case, incompatibility of the rule is understood as a condition under which it is not possible to fulfil, at the same time, the rules belonging to both legal systems in question, having at least partially, a common scope of application.[167]

Thereafter, the administrative courts have consistently adopted that, in the event of a conflict between EU and national rules which cannot be remedied by the interpretation of national law in conformity with EU law, in accordance with the principles of primacy (supremacy) and direct effect of EU law, a national court is obliged to refuse to apply a provision of national law which is contrary to EU law more favourable to an individual.[168] It is also worth emphasising that, for Polish courts, a standard that is important in the context of the principle of primacy is also the judgment of the CJ in the *Filipiak*[169] case. In reference to that ruling, the courts generally accept that the principle of primacy of Union law obliges a national court to apply that law and to derogate from the application of provisions of national law conflicting with it, irrespective of the

166 Resulting from case C-403/16, *El-Hassani*, EU:C:2017:960; for discussion, see further J.-Y. Lebeuf, Droit européen des migrations, *Journal de droit européen*, 2018, pp. 95–110; R. Puchta, Radosław: Warunki dopuszczalności powołania się na ochronę wynikającą z art. 47 KPP [Conditions of Applicability of the Guarantees Resulting from Article 47 of the Charter of Fundamental Rights of the European Union (Remarks Concerning ECJ Judgment of 13 December 2017, El Hassani], *Państwo i Prawo*, 2019, no. 4, pp. 35–52; this was accepted in order of the SAC of 19 February 2018, case II OSK 1346/16; resulting from case C-949/19, *M.A.*, EU:C:2021:186, order of SAC of 13 April 2021, case II OSK 2470/19.

167 See a large group of judgments of the SAC of 3 April 2007 in cases: I FSK 523/06; I FSK 462/06; I FSK 518/06; I FSK 519/06; I FSK 522/06; I FSK 175/06; I FSK 520/06; I FSK 521/06.

168 For example, judgment of the SAC of 16 March 2011, case I FSK 1588/10.

169 Case C-314/08, *Filipiak*, EU:C:2009:719.

judgment of the national constitutional court, which defers losing the binding force of those provisions, which have been held unconstitutional. They also accept that the examination of the compatibility of national law with EU law is based on the dispersed review standard, where it is for each court, ruling on an individual case, to consider the conflict between the rules of national law with Community law.[170] The case-law has also emphasised that administrative courts are obliged to review the activities of public administration in a way that makes it possible to eliminate decisions that are incompatible with EU law. It is for this reason that the national court, which is responsible, within its competences, for the application of EU law legislation, is obliged to ensure the full effectiveness of those rules, without applying conflicting provisions of national law.[171]

The administrative courts have accepted, in line with the position of the CJEU, that the function of both principles is to ensure the effectiveness of EU law in a situation, where it is not possible through the interpretation in conformity with EU law.[172] This function is performed in administrative courts in various ways, which (similarly as in the chapter on case-law of the Supreme Court) can be grouped into cases that use both principles in a way consisting of:

- the omission of a provision of substantive law;
- the omission of a provision of procedural law;
- taking into account a provision of EU law in the process of applying national substantive law.

The case-law, referred to in this chapter, reflects a considerable judicial practice of administrative courts in all three aspects.

Literature

Bartosiewicz A., Wyrok Trybunału Sprawiedliwości, C-335/19, E. Sp. z o.o. Sp. k. przeciwko Ministrowi Finansów, a ograniczenie w czasie możliwości skorzystania z ulgi na złe długi [Case C-335/19 E. Sp. z o.o. Sp. k. przeciwko Ministrowi Finansów and Restricting the Time Limit to Benefit from the Exemption on 'Bad Doubts'], *Przegląd Podatkowy*, 2020, no. 12, pp. 24–28.

Bernard E., *Droit d'accises sur les véhicules d'importation en Pologne*, Europe 2007 Mars Comm, no. 85, pp. 13–14.

Bogdanowicz P., Wiącek M., Zasada pierwszeństwa prawa wspólnotowego a kompetencje Trybunału Konstytucyjnego (uwagi na tle postanowienia WSA w Poznaniu z dnia 30 maja 2008 r., sygn. akt I SA/Po 1756/07) [The Principle of Primacy of Community Law and the Competence of the Constitutional Tribunal (Remarks on

170 For example, judgment of the SAC of 15 February 2010, case I OSK 672/09; the *Filipiak* judgment appears in 462 cases, including 152 cases of SAC.

171 Judgment of the SAC of 12 March 2020, case II GSK 3028/17.

172 For example, judgments of the SAC: of 14 January 2010, case II FSK 2018/09; of 16 March 2011, case I FSK 1588/10; of 20 November 2013, case I FSK 1749/13.

Case I SA/Po 1756/07)], *Zeszyty Naukowe Sądownictwa Administracyjnego*, 2009, no. 3, pp. 55–74.

Carlier J.-Y., Leboeuf L., Droit européen des migrations, *Journal de droit européen*, 2019, no. 3, pp. 114–130.

Coutron L., *Cour de justice, 13 décembre 2017, El Hassani, aff. C-403/16, ECLI:EU:C:2017:960, Jurisprudence de la CJUE 2017*, Bruylant, Bruxelles. Décisions et commentaires, 2018, pp. 226–237.

Dąbrowska P., *Skutki orzeczenia wstępnego Europejskiego Trybunału Sprawiedliwości* [Effects of the Preliminary Ruling of the European Court of Justice], Dom Wydawniczy ABC, 2006.

Dauter B., Komentarz do Art. 183 [Commentary to Article 183], in B. Dauter, A. Kabat, M. Niezgódka-Medek (eds.), *Prawo o postępowaniu przed sądami administracyjnymi. Komentarz* [The Law on Proceedings before Administrative Courts], Wolters Kluwer, 2020, p. 663.

Dauter B., Komentarz do Art. 190 [Commentary to Article 190], in B. Dauter, A. Kabat, M. Niezgódka-Medek (eds.), *Prawo o postępowaniu przed sądami administracyjnymi. Komentarz* [The Law on Proceedings before Administrative Courts. Commentary], Wolters Kluwer, 2020, p. 709.

Dominik D., Commentary to the Judgment of the CJEU in Case C-395/09, Oasis East sp. z o.o., EU:C:2010:570, *Highlights & Insights on European Taxation*, 2010, no. 8, pp. 73–74.

Dominik D., Commentary to the Judgment of the CJEU in Case C-395/09, Oasis East sp. z o.o., EU:C:2010:570, *Highlights & Insights on European Taxation*, 2011, no. 1, pp. 62–63.

Dominik-Ogińska D., Commentary to the judgment of the CJEU in Case C-169/12, TNT Worldwide, EU:C:2013:314], *Highlights & Insights on European Taxation*, 2013, no. 8, pp. 86–87.

Dominik-Ogińska D., MDDP. VAT Exemption Educational Services Provided by Private Entities, *Highlights & Insights on European Taxation*, 2014, n° 2, pp. 47–48.

Heinrichshofen S., Verzögerte Auszahlung von Vorsteuern bei Unternehmensgründungen, *EU-Umsatz-Steuerberater*, 2008, pp. 53–54.

Huschens F., Anmeldung von Vorsteuerüberhängen – Erstattungsfristen und Forderungen nach Sicherheitsleistungen, *EU-Umsatz-Steuerberater*, 2008, p. 25.

Huschens F., Gemischte – wirtschaftliche und nicht wirtschaftliche hoheitliche – Tätigkeiten, *EU-Umsatz-Steuerberater*, 2019, pp. 45–47.

Kabat A., Komentarz do Art. 269 [Commentary on Article 269], in B. Dauter, A. Kabat, M. Niezgódka-Medek (eds.), *Prawo o postępowaniu przed sądami administracyjnymi. Komentarz* [The Law on Proceedings before Administrative Courts. Commentary], LEX, 2019.

Kamiński M., Konstruowanie wzorca legalności decyzji administracyjnej na podstawie prawa UE przez polskie sądy administracyjne, cz. I [Reconstructing by Polish Administrative Courts of the Standard of Legality for Administrative Decision Pursuant to EU Law, Part I], *Europejski Przegląd Sądowy*, 2011, no. 4, pp. 22–27.

Kamiński M., Konstruowanie wzorca legalności decyzji administracyjnej na podstawie prawa UE przez polskie sądy administracyjne, cz. II [Reconstructing by Polish Administrative Courts of the Standard of Legality for Administrative Decision Pursuant to EU Law, Part II], *Europejski Przegląd Sądowy*, 2011, no. 5, pp. 22–27.

Kmieciak Z., Wykonanie przez Naczelny Sąd Administracyjny w ramach kontroli instancyjnej wyroku Trybunału Sprawiedliwości – Glosa do wyroku Naczelnego Sądu Administracyjnego z dnia 12 czerwca 2019 r., II GSK 5001/16 [Implementation of the Judgment of the CJEU by the Supreme Administrative Court in the Second Instance Proceedings (Control of the Ruling of the Court of First Instance) – Commentary to the Judgment of the SAC of 12 June 2019, II GSK 5001/16], *Orzecznictwo Sądów Polskich*, 2020, no. 3, pp. 144–150.

Kubicki P., Einkommensteuer ermäßigbar durch Abzug der in anderem Mitgliedstaat gezahlten Krankenversicherungsbeiträge, *Europäische Zeitschrift für Wirtschaftsrecht*, 2009, pp. 543–545.

Kustra A., Odroczenie przez TK utraty mocy obowiązującej przepisu niezgodnego z prawem UE. Glosa do wyroku TS z 19.11.2009 r. w sprawie C-314/08 Filipiak [The Deferral of the Loss of the Binding Force of the Provision Contrary to EU Law. Commentary on the Judgment of the Court of Justice of 19 November 2009 in C-314/08 Filipiak], *Europejski Przegląd Sądowy*, 2012, no. 6, pp. 34–40.

Lasiński-Sulecki K., Sprzeczność polskich przepisów dotyczących opodatkowania używanych samochodów osobowych z europejskim prawem wspólnotowym [Incompatibility with the Community Law of Polish Regulation on Taxation of Second-Hand Cars], *Przegląd Podatkowy*, 2007, 4, pp. 41–43.

Lebeuf J.-Y., Droit européen des migrations, *Journal de droit européen*, 2018, pp. 95–110.

Makowicz B., Polnische 'Akzise' auf eingeführte Gebrauchtfahrzeuge, *Zeitschrift für Zölle und Verbrauchsteuern*, 2007, pp. 129–131.

Maliński M., Glosa do wyroku Naczelnego Sądu Administracyjnego z dnia 2 lipca 2019 r. (sygn. akt I FSK 119/17) [Commentary on the Judgment of the Supreme Administrative Court of 2 June 2019, Case I FSK 119/17], *Zeszyty Naukowe Sądownictwa Administracyjnego*, 2020, no. 6, pp. 187–196.

Mikłaszewicz P., Glosa do wyroku WSA w Poznaniu z 14.01.2010 (I SA/Po 1006/09) [Commentary on the Judgment of the VAC in Poznań of 14 January 2010, I SA/Po 1006/09], *Europejski Przegląd Sądowy*, 2011, no. 10, pp. 41–46.

Militz M., Wyrok w sprawie TNT Express Worldwide – analiza skutków wyroku 'na dziś' i 'na przyszłość' [Case TNT Express Worldwide – Analysis of the Implications 'for Today' and 'for Tomorrow'], *Przegląd Podatkowy*, 2013, no. 8, pp. 12–18.

Mosbrucker A.-L., Application dans le temps de la directive sur les droits d'apports, *Europe,* 2010 Janvier Comm. no. 39, p. 39.

Mosbrucker A.-L., Kauff-Gazin F., Fiscalité directe, *Europe,* 2009 Juin Comm. no. 214, pp. 9–11.

Mosbrucker A.-L., Taxe sur la valeur ajoutée, *Europe,* 2010 Novembre Comm. no. 11, pp. 32–33.

Mosbrucker A.-L., TVA et prestations éducatives, *Europe,* 2014 Janvier Comm. no. 1, pp. 39–40.

Nieskens H., Ausfuhrlieferung von Gegenständen im persönlichen Reisegepäck, *Umsatz-Steuerberater*, 2018, no. 2, pp. 41–42.

Puchta R., Warunki dopuszczalności powołania się na ochronę wynikającą z art. 47 KPP [Conditions of Applicability of the Guarantees Resulting from Article 47 of the Charter of Fundamental Rights of the European Union (Remarks Concerning ECJ Judgment of 13 December 2017, El Hassani)], *Państwo i Prawo*, 2019, no. 4, pp. 35–52.

Ravella D., Prestations de services éducatifs rendues par des organismes privés à but lucratif: conditions d'exonération et droit à déduction de la TVA, *Revue Lamy droit des affaires*, 2014, no. 91, pp. 57–58.

Rigaux A., Taxe d'effet équivalent, *Europe*, 2017 Décembre no. 12, pp. 23–24.

Simon D., Indépendance des juges, *Europe*, 2018 Avril no. 4, pp. 11–12.

Simon D., Remboursement des excédents de TVA et lutte contre la fraude, *Europe*, 2008 Octobre Comm. no. 337, pp. 36–37.

Sterzinger Ch., Steuerpflichtiger, der sowohl wirtschaftliche als auch nichtwirtschaftliche Tätigkeiten ausübt Gegenstände und Dienstleistungen, die sowohl für Zwecke der Erzielung von mehrwertsteuerpflichtigen als auch von nicht der Mehwertsteuerpflichtigen als auch von nicht der Mehrwertsteuer unterliegenden Umsätzen erworben wurden, *Umsatzsteuer-Rundschau*, 2019, pp. 424–432.

Tetlak K., Commentary on Case C-314/08, Filipiak, EU:C:2009:719, *Highlights & Insights on European Taxation*, 2010, no. 2, pp. 65–66.

Tetlak K., Commentary on Case Elektrownia Pątnów II, C-441/08, EU:C:2009:698, *Highlights & Insights on European Taxation*, 2010, no. 2, pp. 114–116.

Wróbel P., Dialog of Administrative Courts with the Court of Justice of the European Union, *Zeszyty Naukowe Sądownictwa Administracyjnego*, 2021, no. 1–2, pp. 175–195.

10 The principles of primacy and direct effect of EU law in the case-law of the Constitutional Tribunal

Monika Domańska

Introduction

The principles of direct effect and the primacy of EU law are paramount for the EU legal order. Constitutional plurality, however, implies the existence of converging but distinct legal orders with competing claims of authority.[1] The main question is how domestic legal systems enable the influence of EU law on national law and to what extent they accept limitations of power that follow from sources other than the domestic ones, thereby breaking the 'chain of authority' in all-encompassing legal ordering.[2]

In the case-law of the Constitutional Tribunal, there are not many examples of references to the principle of direct effect and the principle of primacy of EU law as legal instruments which serve to ensure the effectiveness of EU law in the domestic legal order. When looking for reasons for the position of the CT discussed earlier, two circumstances should be taken into account. Firstly, the case-law of the CT explains how to remove hierarchical conflicts in the process of constitutionality review (carried out by the CT) and how to ensure that the norms of national law and EU law are compatible. Secondly, the principle of primacy of EU law and the principle of direct effect, as functionally related principles, are perceived by the CT as an instrument of the judicial application of the law, serving to issue individual decisions in a given case. In turn, the judicial application of law (including EU law) lies outside the sphere of competence of the CT.

1 N. Walker, The Idea of Constitutional Pluralism, *Modern Law Review*, 2002, 65, p. 320; D. Halberstam, Constitutional Heterarchy: The Centrality of Conflict in the European Union and the United States, in: J.L. Dunoff, J. Trachtman (eds.), *Ruling the World? Constitutionalism, International Law, and Global Governance*, Cambridge University Press, 2009, p. 326; M. Poiares Maduro, Courts and Pluralism: Essays on a Theory of Judicial Adjudication in the Context of Legal and Constitutional Pluralism, in: J.L. Dunoff, J. Trachtman (eds.), *Ruling the World? Constitutionalism, International Law, and Global Governance*, Cambridge University Press, 2009, p. 356.

2 N. Walker, Constitutionalism and Pluralism in Global Context, in: M. Avbelj, J. Komárek (eds.), *Constitutional Pluralism in the European Union and Beyond*, Hart Publishing, 2012, p. 17.

DOI: 10.4324/9781003376019-13

Nevertheless, the principles on which the EU legal order is based, including the primacy of EU law and the principle of direct effect, already in the pre-accession period influenced the development of many assumptions and examples concerning the coexistence of national and EU law within the structure of the legal system binding in Poland. These experiences have remained relevant in the subsequent case-law of the CT. They have significantly altered the interpretation of the applicable concepts and principles relevant to the functioning of the state, including the application of sources of law by national courts and the scope of the constitutional review procedure by the CT. In the context given earlier, that is, in the context of the hierarchical relationship between legal orders, the Constitutional Tribunal most often analyses the principle of the primacy of EU law.

Highlighting the point discussed earlier is essential for the analysis to be carried out. Firstly, this problem affects the layout of the considerations presented, which deviates from that which is characteristic of courts applying the law. Secondly, a particular discrepancy can be observed in the case-law of the CT on this issue, resulting from a change in the opinion of the CT as to the possibility (competences) of making an assessment and establishing its specific results as to whether the legislative bodies of the European Union, whilst issuing legal acts, acting within the framework of delegated competences (in the opinion of the CT, exceeding such framework results in legal acts issued outside such competences not being covered by the principle of primacy of the EU law).[3] The CT signalled a cautious attitude towards the primacy of EU law but, at the same time, supported the EU integration process as such.[4]

It is worth noting that both, at the very beginning and in the most recent judgments, the justification for this expressed position of the CT was the principle of preserving sovereignty in the process of European integration and the requirement to preserve Poland's constitutional identity. However, what has fundamentally changed is the direction of the findings of the CT as to the definitional scope of these concepts and thus to the possibility of *ultra vires* review of acts of EU bodies and institutions.

3 See judgments of the CT in cases K/18 and P 7/20.

4 N. Walker, Constitutionalism and Pluralism in Global Context, in: M. Avbelj, J. Komárek (eds.), *Constitutional Pluralism in the European Union and Beyond*, Hart Publishing, 2012, p. 17; M. Claes, Negotiating Constitutional Identity or Whose Identity Is It Anyway?, in: M. Claes et al. (eds.), *Constitutional Conversations in Europe*, Intersentia, 2012, p. 210; K. Kowalik-Bańczyk, Sending Smoke Signals to Luxembourg – The Polish Constitutional Tribunal in Dialogue with the ECJ, in: M. Claes et al. (eds.), *Constitutional Conversations in Europe*, Intersentia, 2012, p. 267. It should be also pointed out that in Poland, the constituent understood very well that, considering the far-reaching consequences, the decision to join the EU should be made by a qualified majority so as to give it more political legitimacy, see M. Wyrzykowski, EU Accession in Light of Evolving Constitutionalism in Poland, in: G.A. Bermann, K. Pistor (eds.), *Law and Governance in an Enlarged European Union*, Hart Publishing, 2004, pp. 441–442.

Legal bases for the reception of the principles of primacy and direct effect into the national legal order – the perspective of the scope of competence of the Constitutional Tribunal

At the time when Poland was still a country associated with the European Communities, the relationship between the Polish Constitution and EU law (including the scope of possible collisions between the two legal orders and the methods of resolving them) was the subject of analyses of the Polish, legal doctrine. There have been some opinions that the EU law takes precedence over the Constitution of the Republic of Poland,[5] in addition to that of the Constitution and the EU law have an equal position in the hierarchy of sources of law,[6] and that the Constitution of the Republic of Poland occupies a higher place in such a hierarchy.[7] After Poland acceded to EU structures, this issue still raised many doubts.

From the point of view of the discussed issue, the starting point, for any considerations carried out in this respect, is to determine the place of the Constitution and international and supranational law in the constitutional system of sources of law. The Polish Constitution is a normative act that contains general and abstract norms. In accordance with Article 8 para. 1 of the Constitution, it is the supreme law of the Republic of Poland, and its provisions shall apply directly unless it provides otherwise (Article 8 para. 2). This provision expresses the principle of supremacy of the Constitution and its direct application.

In principle, it should be noted that the national legislator is also bound by international law. This obligation results from Article 9 of the Constitution, according to which the Republic of Poland shall observe international law

5 For example, J. Barcz, Konstytucyjnoprawne problemy stosowania prawa Unii Europejskiej w Polsce w świetle dotychczasowych doświadczeń państw członkowskich [Constitutional and legal problems of the application of European Union law in Poland in the light of the experience of Member States], in: M. Kruk (ed.), *Prawo międzynarodowe i wspólnotowe w wewnętrznym porządku prawnym* [International law and community law in the internal legal order], Wydawnictwo Sejmowe, 1997, pp. 217–218; P. Błachut, P. Mikuli, Uwagi o stosowaniu ustaw przez sądy w przypadku ich kolizji z prawem wspólnotowym [International law and community law in the internal legal order], in: M. Kruk, J. Wawrzyniak (eds.), *Polska w Unii Europejskiej* [Poland in teh European Union], Zakamycze, 2005, pp. 273–274.

6 A. Wyrozumska, Ratyfikacja traktatu akcesyjnego w drodze referendum [Ratification of the Accession Treaty by referendum], in: J. Barcz (ed.), *Czy zmieniać konstytucję? Ustrojowo-konstytucyjne aspekty przystąpienia Polski do Unii Europejskiej* [Should the constitution be changed? System and constitutional aspects of Poland's accession to European Union], Instytut Spraw Publicznych, 2002, pp. 91–93.

7 L. Garlicki, Kilka uwag o konstytucyjnych aspektach Polski przystąpienia do Unii Europejskiej [A few remarks on the constitutional aspects of Poland's accession to the European Union], in *Konstytucja. Wybory. Parlament. Studia ofiarowane Zdzisławowi Jaroszowi* [Constitution. Elections. Parliament. Studies dedicated to Zdzisław Jarosz], Liber, 2000, pp. 63–65 and pp. 68; K. Kubuj, Konstytucyjne podstawy uczestnictwa państwa w integracji europejskiej na tle porównawczym [Constitutional basis for State participation in European integration on a comparative basis], in: M. Kruk (ed.), *Konstytucja RP z 1997 r. na tle zasad współczesnego państwa prawnego. Zagadnienia wybrane* [The Constitution of the Republic of Poland of 1997 on the background of principles of the modern rule of law. Selected issues], Wyższa Szkoła Handlu i Prawa im. R. Łazarskiego w Warszawie, 2006, pp. 91–91.

binding upon it. In principle, there can be no doubt as to the precedence over laws of such international agreements whose ratification is subject to prior consent expressed by law, as expressly stated in Article 91 para. 2 of the Constitution. Moreover, the law established by an international organisation also takes precedence over laws since, in accordance with Article 91 para. 3 of the Constitution of the Republic of Poland, if it results from an agreement ratified by the Republic of Poland constituting an international organisation, the law established by it is applied directly, taking precedence in the event of a conflict with laws. For obvious reasons, the Constitution of the Republic of Poland does not expressly speak about EU law. Nevertheless, it is the content of Article 91 para. 3 of the Constitution that should be directly referred to with regard to the relationship arising from the relational application of the Constitution and secondary EU law.[8]

As a result of the accession of Poland to the EU, all national courts have started to play a 'dual' role. They have become both organs of the state, called upon to perform the tasks set out in the Constitution and EU bodies, which should ensure compliance with EU law within the framework of their competencies. Judicial application of the law, including the application of the principles of primacy and direct effect of EU law as mechanisms of effective protection of rights stemming from EU law, as has been emphasised many

8 It is underlined in doctrine

> Considering the interaction between international and national law, in legal commentary the prevailing view is that the monist system is predominant in Poland (incorporation doctrine). This statement is based on art. 9(1) of the Constitution. The jurisprudence of the national courts is not entirely clear on this matter, and there have been rulings based on a dualist approach (transformation doctrine).

S. Biernat, M. Kawczyńska, The Role of the Polish Constitution (Pre-2016): Development of a Liberal Democracy in the European and International Context, in: A. Albi, S. Bardutzky (eds.), *National Constitutions in European and Global Governance: Democracy, Rights, the Rule of Law*, Springer Open, 2019, p. 784. As for literature see respectively: S. Biernat, M. Niedźwiedź, Znaczenie prawa międzynarodowego i unijnego dla prawa administracyjnego i administracji publicznej w świetle Konstytucji RP [The Role of International Law and the EU for Administrative Law and Public Administration in the Light of the Constitution of the Republic of Poland], in: R. Hauser, A. Wróbel, Z. Niewiadomski (eds.), *System Prawa Administracyjnego* [The System of Administrative Law], Vol. 2. C.H. Beck, Warszawa, 2012, p. 121; A. Wyrozumska, Zapewnianie skuteczności prawu międzynarodowemu w prawie krajowym w projekcie konstytucji RP [Ensuring the Effectiveness of International Law in National Law Under the Draft Polish Constitution], *Państwo i Prawo*, 1996, no. 11, p. 24; R. Szafarz, Skuteczność norm prawa międzynarodowego w prawie wewnętrznym w świetle nowej Konstytucji [The Effectiveness of Norms of International Law in the Light of the New Constitution], *Państwo i Prawo*, 1998, no. 1, p. 3; A. Wasilkowski, Transformacja czy inkorporacja? [Transformation or Incorporation?], *Państwo i Prawo*, 1998, no. 4, p. 86; and A. Wyrozumska, *Umowy międzynarodowe. Teoria i praktyka* [International Agreements, Theory and Practice], Wydawnictwo Prawo i Praktyka Gospodarcza, 2006, pp. 592–599; A. Wyrozumska, Prawo międzynarodowe oraz prawo Unii Europejskiej a konstytucyjny system źródeł prawa [International Law, European Union Law and the Constitutional System of Sources of Law], in: K. Wójtowicz (ed.), *Otwarcie Konstytucji RP na prawo międzynarodowe i procesy integracyjne* [The Openness of the Polish Constitution to the International Law and Integration Processes], Wydawnictwo Sejmowe, 2006, pp. 45–50.

times, remains beyond the competence of the CT. Thus, the position of the CT, from which it assesses the effectiveness of the principle of primacy and the direct effect of EU law, depends on the scope of its competence and occurs when removing hierarchical contradictions from the legal system. Both the scope of normative acts, subject to review and the adopted review norms, are essential here. It should be noted that the CT notes many debatable issues concerning the relationship between Polish law and EU law in the context of the principle of primacy of the latter over the entire national legal order. These doubts continue to arise from the wording of the provisions of the Constitution of the Republic of Poland in force, from which it is possible to interpret both the basis for the primacy of the EU primary law and secondary law, in the case of a collision with laws and sub-legislative acts (Article 91 paras. 2 and 3 of the Constitution), in addition to the unquestionable principle of the supremacy of the Constitution in the system of sources of law binding in Poland (Article 8 para. 1 of the Constitution). In this respect, it should be emphasised that the CT takes the standpoint of the supremacy of the Constitution over EU law. In this regard, Poland joined several other countries which have challenged the unconditional dominance of EU law.[9]

The CT most frequently expresses its opinions when assessing the mutual relations between Union law and the Constitution. First of all, it is necessary to point to the judgment of the CT on *the Treaty of Accession* (K 18/04);[10] the judgment on *the Treaty of Lisbon* (K 32/09),[11] or the judgment in case SK 45/09,[12] in which the CT used a special mandate to protect the integrity of the national constitution and offered resistance to the unconditional primacy of EU law.

The analysis of the newest jurisprudence of the CT reveals that the principle of primacy of EU law appears when it comes to assessing the impact of the application of this principle by national courts. It means that the CT is analysing the way of judicial application of this principle (by national courts) but hidden behind the context of the consequences of the collision of norms assessed by the CT. This position was most clearly expressed in the most recent decisions of the Constitutional Tribunal, that is, in the judgment in case P 7/20[13] and in case K 3/21.[14] It should be emphasised in this place of this analysis that

9 Similarly for Germany, Denmark, France, Hungary, and Italy. See A. Albi, Supremacy of EC Law in the Member States, *European Constitutional Law Review*, 2007, no. 3, pp. 25–67; M. Claes, *The National Courts' Mandate in the European Constitution*, Hart Publishing, 2006; F.C. Mayer, Multilevel Constitutional Jurisdiction, in: A. von Bogdandy, J. Bast (eds.), *Principles of European Constitutional Law*, 2nd ed., Hart Publishing, 2009.

10 Judgment of the CT of 11 May 2005, case K 18/04.

11 Judgment of the CT of 24 November 2010, case K 32/09.

12 Judgment of the CT of 16 November 2011, case K 45/09.

13 Judgment of the CT of 14 July 2021, case P 7/20. See also the analysis see the chapter: The effect of consistent interpretation of national law in the case-law of the Constitutional Tribunal in this volume.

14 Judgment of the CT of 7 October 2021, case K 3/21. See also the analysis see the chapter: The effect of consistent interpretation of national law in the case-law of the Constitutional Tribunal in this volume.

these rulings confront the current position of the CT with the jurisprudence of the CT before 2016. Due to the lack of competence of the Constitutional Tribunal to activate mechanisms characteristic for judicial application of the law, the CT stood in position that national courts are to decide on questions relating to the application or interpretation of EU law, and they must comply with the requirements of the institutional guarantees set out in the principle of effective judicial protection. The position was reflected, for example, in the order P 16/17,[15] in which the CT stated that

> Poland has been a member of the European Union since 1 May 2004, which implies the necessity for its organs to also take into account the provisions of European law (the so-called primary law, treaties and other interstate agreements and the so-called derivative law, provisions of direct and indirect effect, enacted by entities authorised to do so) when resolving specific factual situations.[16]

In the judgment P 37/05,[17] the CT emphasised that

> the fundamental problem in the case in question lies in the sphere of application and not in the sphere of validity of the law. Judges in the process of applying the law are unconditionally subject to the Constitution and laws. Related to this principle, the conflict-of-laws rule is expressed in Article 91 para. 2, which imposes an obligation to refuse to apply the law in the event of a conflict with an international agreement ratified by law. The principle of primacy also applies to Community law (Article 91 para. 3 of the Constitution).

Constitutional courts, including the CT of Poland, are in doctrine identified as 'the key sites' of 'high-profile constitutional clashes over the implications of Europe's supranational arrangements'.[18] The CT cannot, by definition, take a more activist approach within legitimation strategy, and it is embedded in the constitutional system and, as a rule, it takes a position in line with the strategy derived from the constitutional system as a whole. Nevertheless, the CT explains

15 Judgment of the CT of 17 July 2019, case P 16/17.

16 But in case K 33/03 the CT explained the way EU directives effects in national legal order by stressing that:

> the present case cannot be viewed in isolation from the European Union rules on biofuels in the broad sense. Directive 2003/30/EC of 8 May 2003 on the promotion of the use of biofuels or other renewable fuels for transport is of primary importance here. It should be recalled that European directives do not have a direct binding effect (unlike regulations) and are only binding as to their objectives, not the means of achieving them.

17 Judgment of the CT of 19 December 2006, case P 37/05.

18 N. Walker, Constitutionalism and Pluralism in Global Context, in: M. Avbelj, J. Komárek (eds.), *Constitutional Pluralism in the European Union and Beyond*, Hart Publishing, 2012, p. 21.

the mandate of ordinary courts explicitly acknowledging that the court, if there is no doubt as to the content of the Community law rule, should refuse to apply the conflicting statutory provision and apply the Community law rule directly, or, if it is not possible to apply the Community law rule directly, seek to interpret national law in accordance with Community law.[19] Where doubts arise as to the interpretation of Community law, the national court should refer the matter to the CJEU for a preliminary ruling. The Tribunal points out that the national court does not then decide to set aside the rule of national law but

> refuses to apply it in so far as it is obliged to give precedence to the rule of Community law. The act in question is not null and void and is binding and applicable to an extent not covered by the Community legislation in question or its temporal scope.

Such a division of competencies between the CT and national courts within the scope of interpretation and application of the EU provisions should be considered as established and unquestionable in the case-law of the CT, although some rulings of the CT issued after 2016 do not confirm this statement.

The principle of primacy of EU law and the principle of supremacy of the Constitution in the case-law of the Constitutional Tribunal

The Constitutional Tribunal does not recognise the possibility of questioning the validity of a constitutional norm by the mere fact of enacting and binding an EU regulation that cannot be reconciled with the constitutional norm. In the opinion of the CT, a change/adjustment of the constitutional norm to the EU law norm is possible, whereas it is impossible to recognise the inconsistency of the constitutional norm with the EU law, which would necessitate the elimination of that norm from the Constitution and perhaps, under certain assumptions, the application of a provision of the Union law in its place. It follows, from the statements of the CT, that the principle of supremacy of the Constitution in the Polish legal system (Article 8 of the Constitution) is one of the most important guarantees of state sovereignty. In the opinion of the Constitutional Tribunal, this principle is also not restricted when Poland joins the structures of international organisations. According to this principle, all legal acts must comply with the Constitution, including the normative acts of international law and EU law.[20] This applies both to acts of law-making and of the application of the law. The conformity order also covers actual actions by public authorities taken on the basis and within the limits of the law. With regard to the law-making authorities, the principle of supremacy of the Constitution formulates the prohibition of enacting legal norms inconsistent with the Constitution.

19 Case P 37/05.

20 The CT has a special mandate to protect the Constitution, and it is inclined to be more critical to the primacy of EC law doctrine.

Due to the existence and interaction of the national and EU legal systems as two autonomous legal orders, the Constitutional Tribunal is aware of their collisions. It recognises that it is for the individual authorities, within their respective spheres of competence, to take such measures as will eliminate these conflicts while respecting the principles governing the application of such rules. First of all, the CT mentions an interpretation of national law that is friendly to EU law (K 18/04 *The Treaty of Accession*).

The procedure established by the line of case-law of the Constitutional Tribunal (cases K 18/04, K 32/09, SK 45/09) in the event of a conflict between the norms of the Constitution and provisions of EU law establishes clear boundaries, which it deems impassable, that is, it is forbidden to recognise the supremacy of the EU law over the constitutional norm; it is forbidden to replace the constitutional norm with an EU law norm; it is forbidden to limit the scope of the constitutional norm to the area not covered by the regulation of EU law.

The impact of the European integration process on the sphere of state sovereignty constitutes a form of restriction on the exercise of the sovereignty of Member States, as stated by the CT in its judgment, case K 32/09. The previous discussion, however, does not collide with the applicable constitutional norms, that is,

> by virtue of the primacy of legal force resulting from Article 8 par. 1 of the Constitution, the Constitution enjoys in the territory of the Republic of Poland the primacy of validity and application. . . . The transfer of competencies may not violate the provisions of the Constitution, including the principle of the supremacy of the Constitution in the system of sources of law. . . . In the opinion of the Constitutional Tribunal, 'the Constitution remains – by virtue of its special power – the 'supreme law of the Republic of Poland' in relation to all international agreements binding the Republic of Poland. This also applies to ratified international agreements on the transfer of competence in certain matters'.

The position of the CT, that the adopted hierarchy of sources of law has a guarantee function and constitutes an element of national identity and state sovereignty, is well established.[21] The performance of the CT as an agent engaging in a cooperative relationship, assessing European primacy claims against constitutional core values, constitutional identity, has to be seen from a wider perspective. The CT in Poland but also in Germany[22] and several other courts (in Denmark, France, Hungary, Italy) have compelled the EU to intensify the protection of fundamental rights at the EU level and to accommodate national

21 K. Kowalik-Bańczyk, Sending Smoke Signals to Luxembourg – The Polish Constitutional Tribunal in Dialogue with the ECJ, in: M. Claes et al. (eds.), *Constitutional Conversations in Europe*, Intersentia, 2012, p. 268.

22 See *Solange I* [1974] 37 BverfGE 271; *Solange II* [1986] 73 BverfGE 378.

identity narratives in its own legal system.[23] On the basis of Article 4 (2) TEU, the CJEU has the mandate to deviate from the uniform application of EU law, taking into account the claim of a Member State that its national identity is at stake.[24]

The fundamental rights enshrined in the provisions of the Constitution are also protected by the Constitution and, despite the fact that the Constitution sets the minimum scope of protection, it is, hierarchically, the most important act of national law, whose guarantees cannot be breached by EU law. The previous considerations were clearly illustrated in judgment case P 1/05[25] led to the amendment of Article 55 of the Constitution. The Constitution was amended by introducing a new provision regulating the fundamental basis for the application of the European Arrest Warrant in the Polish legal order. In this way, the compatibility of national and EU regulations was 'secured'. The change to the Constitution, brought by the previous judgment of the Constitutional Tribunal, is the only such change that has been made as a result of taking into account the content and objective of the norm (act) of EU law. This is an effective and, at the same time, a compromise between the inclusion of EU law within the cognition of the Constitutional Tribunal and the need to preserve the supremacy of the Constitution in the system of domestic sources of law. On the one hand, the Constitution upheld its supremacy in the hierarchy of domestic norms, and, on the other hand, the possibility of ensuring the effectiveness of specific EU solutions, in the event of a collision with other regulations of national law, was opened.

At this point, it is worth noting the judgment of the CT in case SK 45/09,[26] in which the Tribunal ruled on the compliance of the EU regulation[27] with the Constitution. A Union regulation, which is an act of Union law binding in its entirety and directly applicable in all Member States, has been recognised by the CT as a legal act pursuant to Article 91 para. 3 of the Constitution takes precedence in the event of a conflict with laws. However, the CT pointed out that the Polish Constitution retains primacy and precedence over all legal acts binding in the Polish constitutional order, including EU law. In view of the previous discussion, it is permissible to examine the constitutionality of the provisions of Union regulations, as the former is the highest law in the national hierarchy of sources of law. In the analysed judgment, the CT also presented its standpoint in the case of the consequences of a possible ascertain-

23 M. Claes, Negotiating Constitutional Identity or Whose Identity Is It Anyway?, in: M. Claes et al. (eds.), *Constitutional Conversations in Europe*, Intersentia, 2012, p. 207.

24 P. Popelier, Europe Clauses' and Constitutional Strategies in the Face of Multi-level Governance, *Maastricht Journal of European and Comparative Law*, 2014, 21, no. 2, p. 12.

25 For more details, see the Section 'The effect of consistent interpretation of national law in the case-law of the Constitutional Tribunal' in this volume.

26 Judgment of the CT of 16 November 2011, case K 45/09.

27 Specifically, Articles 36, 40, and 41 and Article 42 of Council Regulation (EC) No 44/2001 of 22 December 2000 on jurisdiction and the recognition and enforcement of judgments in civil and commercial matters (OJ L 12, 16.1.2001, pp. 1–23) with Article 8, Article 32, Article 45, Article 78, and Article 176 of the Constitution of the Republic of Poland.

ment of a breach of the norms contained in the part of the Constitution regulating the scope of guarantees of individual freedoms and rights. The Tribunal held that the effect of such a collision could not be the loss of validity of the unconstitutional norms but

> the deprivation of derived EU law acts of applicability by Polish authorities and of legal effects in Poland. The effect of the judgment of the CT would therefore be to suspend the application on the territory of the Republic of Poland of the norms of EU law which are inconsistent with the Constitution.

The Tribunal pointed out, however, that 'a declaration of incompatibility of EU law with the Constitution should be of an *ultima ratio* nature and should only occur when all other means of resolving a conflict with the norms of the EU legal order have failed'. The statement of the CT also included a fragment about maintaining the hitherto position concerning the expected possibilities of actions to be taken by the Polish legislator in the event of inconsistency between the Constitution and the EU law (as in the judgment case K 18/04 or P 1/05), emphasising, at the same time, that the decision to withdraw Poland from the EU should be reserved for exceptional cases of the most severe and irremediable conflict between the foundations of the constitutional order of the Republic of Poland and the EU law.

The adoption of the Lisbon Treaty did not change the principle of the supremacy of the Polish Constitution over EU law. From the point of view of the current Constitution of the Republic of Poland, this act is an international agreement, referred to in the Constitution, which has been ratified with the consent expressed by law or referendum. In the decision K 32/09,[28] characterised by long digressions on the concept of sovereignty and by a sort of comparison with the doctrines of the other constitutional courts, it admitted the possibility of carrying out the *ultra vires* control over the EU acts, sending an indirect message to the CJEU in order to preserve the untouchable core of its own Constitution.[29]

In the recent case-law of the Constitutional Tribunal, it is emphasised[30] that, as a result of the negotiations on the Treaty of Lisbon, it was not decided (despite such proposals) to include in the principle of loyal cooperation *expressis verbis* the principle of primacy of EU law over national law (including the Constitution) in those areas where competences were transferred from the Member States to the EU. This argument is made in order to highlight the differences which characterise the application of the rules of EU law and, against this background, the implementation of CJEU decisions – in terms of delegated powers

28 Judgment of the CT of 24 November 2010, case K 32/09.

29 As pointed out in G. Martinico, O. Pollicino, *The Interaction between Europe's Legal Systems. Judicial Dialogue and the Creation of Supranational Laws*, Edward Elgar, 2012, p. 107.

30 Judgment of the CT of 14 July 2021, case P 7/20.

and retained powers (with particular reference to those which cover the organisation of justice in the broad sense).

In the context discussed earlier, it is worth noting that the CT, in its current composition (i.e., after 2016), clearly favours such an interpretation of the principle of loyalty that it considers it to be one of the foundations of EU law, subject to constant interpretation by the CJEU, which is characterised by a clear evolution towards the priority of the application of EU law even over the constitutions of the Member States. The CT emphasises (P 7/20) that, in this area, in characteristic judgments, the CJEU has held that the courts of the Member States must refrain from applying national law where this is necessary in order to give direct effect to an EU law, *van Gend en Loos* C-26/62; *Costa v. Enel*, C-6/64; *Simmenthal* C-106/77; *Factortame* C-21/89. Due to the fact that these judgments concerning direct effect and primacy of application of the EU law by national authorities only in the area of the common market (i.e., customs duties, taxes, administrative charges), that is, competences whose delegation is not in doubt as they were at the basis of creation of the European Economic Community, the Constitutional Tribunal did not find that these judgments violate the limits of the principle of loyalty established in Article 4 (3) TEU together with Article 19 TEU.[31] Quite differently, however, the CT has already assessed the judgment of the CJEU in joint cases C-585/18, *A.K.*,[32] where the CJEU referred to the principle of direct effect and the primacy of EU law to judgments concerning the independence of courts and judges as well as the organisation of the judiciary in Poland. Equally critical, the CT[33] assessed the statement of the CJEU in the judgment in the joined cases ref: C-83/19, C-127/19, C-291/19, C-355/19, and C-397/19,[34] in which it was held that the principle of primacy could not be precluded by internal rules on the delimitation of jurisdiction, including those of a constitutional nature. The CJEU held that, in accordance with the principle of the primacy of EU law, the fact that a Member State refers to provisions of national law, even of constitutional rank, cannot affect the unity and effectiveness of EU law.

The position of the present composition of the Constitutional Tribunal concerning the relation of the principle of the primacy of EU law to constitutional norms, which is presented in the latest jurisprudence, is largely based on the interpretation of the 'national identity' clause introduced by the Treaty of

31 Judgment of the CT of 14 July 2021, case P 7/20.

32 Joined cases C-585/18, C -624/18 and C-625/18, EU:C:2019:982.

33 Judgment of the CT of 14 July 2021, case P 7/20.

34 Joined cases C-83/19, C-127/19, C-291/19, C-355/19 and C-397/19, *'Forumul Judecătorilor din România' and othersv. Inspecția Judiciară and others*, EU:C:2021:393. H. Dumbrava, The Rule of Law and the EU's Response Mechanisms in Case of Violation: a Romanian Case Study: C-83/19, *ERA-Forum: scripta iuris europaei*, 2021, pp. 437–452.

Lisbon in Article 4 sec. 2 TEU.[35] The reference to 'national identity' opens the way to questioning the absolute character of the principle of primacy of EU law in the relational model of coexistence between EU law and constitutional national law. Within the constitutional boundaries of the functioning of the constitutional court, in certain circumstances, this clause may be interpreted as allowing this court to define the area of constitutional boundaries for the principle of primacy of EU law.[36]

Conflict between the foundations of the constitutional order and EU law in the case-law of the Constitutional Tribunal after 2016

One of the most important, current problems, related to the functioning of Poland in the EU, is the issue of the split in the jurisprudence of the Constitutional Tribunal concerning the resolution of conflicts between the provisions of the Polish Constitution and the primacy of EU law. In the light of the previous analyses, it would seem that the solutions and findings developed by the Constitutional Tribunal over the years substantially eliminate doubts concerning the resolution of such conflicts. However, the reform of the organisation of the judiciary in Poland, which has also encompassed the Constitutional Tribunal, has resulted in a different line of interpretation being adopted in the jurisdiction of the Constitutional Tribunal for many notions that have an impact on the assessment of the maintenance of the supremacy of the Constitution in the system of sources of law and that affect the exercise of constitutionality review of legal acts by the Constitutional Tribunal (e.g., such notions as constitutional identity, democratic state of law, sovereignty). Moreover, the Constitutional Tribunal acknowledged its jurisdiction to review the acts of EU bodies and institutions, undertaking *ultra vires* review as to whether the CJEU, in ruling on interim measures,[37] did not go beyond the norms lying within the scope of competences conferred on the EU by the Republic of Poland (Article 4 (1) TEU), whether it did not violate the Polish constitutional identity (Article 4 (2) TEU), whether it took into account the essential functions of the state (Article 4 (2), second sentence, TEU), and whether it did not go beyond the limits of the principles of subsidiarity and proportionality (Article 5 (1) TEU).

35 L. Besselink, National and Constitutional identity before and after Lisbon, *Utrecht Law Journal*, 2010, 6, no. 3, pp. 36–49; A. Bogdandy, S. Schell, Overcoming Absolute Primacy, Overcoming Absolute Primacy: Respect for National Identity Under the Lisbon Treaty, *CML Review*, 2011, pp. 1417–1454; A.S. Arnaiz, C.A. Llivina (eds.), *National Constitutional Identity and European Integration*, Cambridge-Antwerp-Portland, 2013.

36 See A. Sołtys, Cechy i charakter prawa unijnego oraz problem jego konstytucjonalizacji [Features and nature of EU law and the problem of its constitutionalization], in: S. Biernat (ed.), *Podstawy i źródła prawa Unii Europejskiej. System Prawa Unii Europejskiej* [Fundamentals and sources of European Union Law. System of EU Law], C.H. Beck, 2020, pp. 231–232.

37 Order of the CJEU of 8 April 2020, case C-791/19 R, EU:C:2020:277.

A change in the position of the CT on the effectiveness of the instrument of a question for a preliminary ruling expected by the EU order, in addition to the application of the principle of primacy of EU law in the circumstances of an irremediable conflict between the foundations of the constitutional order and EU law was initiated by the judgment issued in case P 7/20.[38] The position expressed in this judgment is equally a questioning of the hitherto existing and applied division of competencies between the Constitutional Tribunal and the CJEU in the context of a binding interpretation of the law, as well as the first explicit ruling on the incompatibility of EU primary law with the provisions of the Constitution. In this case, the Disciplinary Chamber of the Supreme Court submitted a legal question to the Constitutional Tribunal in which it alleged that the second sentence of Article 4 (1) TEU, in conjunction with Article 279 TFEU, as unconstitutional to the extent that these provisions result in 'the obligation of an EU Member State to implement provisional measures relating to the form and functioning of the constitutional organs of its judicial power'. This question was formulated as a reaction to the judgment of the CJEU of 19 November 2019, in the joined cases C-585/18, C-624/18, and C-625/18,[39] which considered the question of the independence of the National Council of the Judiciary and the Disciplinary Chamber of the Supreme Court.[40]

The Constitutional Tribunal judgment (14 July 2021, P 7/20) clearly indicates that the ruling was aimed at excluding, from the application of the principle of primacy of EU law, the effects of the CJEU ruling (considered to be issued *ultra vires*) on the imposition of interim measures in response to the introduction into the Polish legal system of provisions concerning the organisation of the Supreme Court in the framework of the ongoing judicial reform. The Constitutional Tribunal made it clear that

> the interim measures imposed on Poland on 8 April 2020, contrary to the first sentence of Article 4(2) TEU, encroach in a clear and significant manner on constitutional regulation, thereby infringing the Polish constitutional identity, of which the Polish administration of justice is an inherent part. No authority may exempt Polish citizens, particularly Polish judges, from the obligation to apply the Polish Constitution.

In the justification of the judgment in question, the CJEU clearly emphasised that 'the principle of supremacy (supreme legal force) of the Constitution clashes with the principle of primacy of application of Community law

38 Judgment of the CT of 14 July 2021.
39 Joint cases C-585/18, C-624/18, C-625/18, A.K. and others, EU:C:2019:982.
40 More on the ruling in question in the part of the study devoted to the pro-EU interpretation of domestic law in the case-law of the Constitutional Tribunal.

stemming from the case-law acquis of the CJEU'. In the situation of a contradiction between a Community law norm and a constitutional norm, the Constitutional Tribunal firmly takes the position of the validity of the principle of supremacy of the Constitution in the meaning given by Article 8 para. 1 of the Constitution.

When conducting the *ultra vires* review of the norms established by order of the CJEU 8 April 2020, the Constitutional Tribunal stressed that such *ultra vires* review, which is by its very nature exceptional, is exercised with restraint and by means of a sympathetic interpretation, and EU acts, including judgments of the CJEU, may be considered to have been issued *ultra vires* when the infringements are clear and substantial, as well as when they flagrantly violate the principles of proportionality and subsidiarity. In the opinion of the Constitutional Tribunal, the finding of such a circumstance leads to the conclusion that acts issued *ultra vires* do not enjoy the privilege of their direct application on the territory of Poland before the provisions of national laws (Article 91, para. 3 of the Constitution). In the opinion of the Constitutional Tribunal in case P 7/20, direct effect (direct applicability) and primacy are not inherent features of EU law nor the result of an EU *case-law* but are merely the effect of a domestic act of ratification, that is the emanation of the will of the sovereign acting on the basis of a domestic constitution. Hence, it is unacceptable in Poland to apply EU law that exceeds the scope determined by the act of ratification and the Constitution, as determined by the ruling of the Constitutional Tribunal.

Referring to the position discussed earlier, the Constitutional Tribunal emphasised in the conclusions of its justification that this ruling

> cannot be interpreted as a negation of the principle of primacy of EU law or the principle of the direct effect of EU law. On the contrary, both above principles are permanent elements of the Polish legal order. They are contained in Article 91 pars. 1–3 of the Constitution. However, the two principles above must be understood and applied only in conjunction with and within the limits of the principle of delegation of competencies, as they are interdependent. The validity and application of any two of the three fundamental principles (primacy, direct effect and delegation) distort the meaning and purpose of the treaties.

An essential feature of this ruling influencing its assessment is a ruling of scope and application. A 'range decision' is understood to be a decision of the Constitutional Tribunal, whose operative part contains the phrase: 'to the extent that' (or its equivalent). The effect of a restitution scope judgment is not the loss of binding force of the entire provision under review but rather the 'cutting out' from its scope of the fragment it contains, which is deemed to conflict with the Polish Constitution. In turn, an application judgment is a judgment, in the operative part of which the Constitutional Tribunal states the compatibility or non-compliance of the challenged regulation with the

Constitution and decides on the legal consequences of this judgment for legal situations shaped before the date of its pronouncement. The Constitutional Tribunal often formulates guidelines for the legislator and the courts on implementing the judgments of the Constitutional Tribunal in the justifications of its judgments.

It should be emphasised that the recognition by the Constitutional Tribunal of the incompatibility of provisions of primary EU law with the Polish legal order does not entail the repeal of the validity and application of EU provisions in Poland. Nor is the Constitutional Tribunal competent to set aside the application of Article 91 paras. 2 and 3 of the Constitution, which provides for the primacy of the application of Union law. Thus, the judgment of the Constitutional Tribunal in case P 7/20 raises many legal doubts about its effects in the sphere of the case-law of Polish common courts.

The previous verdict of the CT has, however, it may seem, set a particular direction of case-law, within the framework of which the present composition of the Tribunal presents the view on the absolute supreme power of the Constitution on the territory of Poland, including its priority of validity and application also in relation to ratified international agreements, EU treaties and *acquis communautaire* (including the effects of CJEU judgments). This position is reflected in the judgment of the CT issued in case K 3/21.[41] At the time of this analysis, the grounds for the judgment had not yet been prepared and, as a result, it is difficult to comment on the main reasons for the decision, but it suffices to point out that the formula of the scope and interpretative character of the judgment adopted in the judgment results in the CT declaring the application of the reviewed provisions of the TEU in individual cases to be unconstitutional. These cases are, in fact, the circumstances of the application and understanding of EU law, corresponding to specific rulings of the CT issued in Polish cases and defining the norm of adequate legal protection on the basis of Article 19 TEU. In this matter, however, under the provisions regulating the principles of constitutional review exercised by the CT, the Tribunal has no competence to examine the compatibility with the Constitution of individual judicial decisions. This applies to both national judgments and those of the CT. In terms of its core competencies, the case-law of the latter, that is, ensuring respect for the law in the interpretation and application of treaties, has been assessed by the CT as 'a practice of progressive activism'.[42]

The Constitution, as the supreme law and the criterion for verifying the compliance of international (EU) law with Polish law, especially constitutional

41 Judgment of the CT of 7 October 2021, case K 3/21. For the operative part of the judgment in details, see Section 'The cognition of the Constitutional Tribunal to consistent interpretation in the procedure for review of constitutionality of legal norms'.

42 In the context of this analysis, it should be pointed out that the rulings of the CT issued in cases K 3/21 and P 7/20 will be – most probably – confirmed in other proceedings which are pending before the CT, e.g., K 7/18, K 5/21, K 8/21.

law, is not a subject of controversy. The crux of the problem, however, lies in the assessment of the effects of this control. The principle of constitutional supremacy cannot be the basis for violating international (EU) law that is binding on a state and does not release the state from international liability for such violations.

In the case of a constitutional unconformity found by the CT, it should be eliminated by changing the constitutional norm or an international norm (act). The judgments of national, constitutional courts do not discharge the state from its international obligations. These courts also do not have the competence to assess the legality of acts of international bodies with the founding treaties of a given organisation. National judgments or opinions stating 'suspension of the application' of international standards, including EU ones, or their removal from the national system of legal sources as a result of a decision by the politicised CT are manipulative and express acceptance of violations of binding law. The competence to put an end to the application of international norms belongs to state bodies other than the CT.

The CT's recent rulings (P 7/20, K 3/21) are causing a schism in case-law on this matter and are creating conditions of competition between the CT and the CJEU. Within the same (new) line of case-law, the CT seeks to impose an obligation on Polish courts not to recognise CJEU rulings handed down in Polish cases concerning the independence of the courts and the impartiality of judges and to exclude from the principle of primacy and direct applicability CJEU rulings relating to the system and jurisdiction of Polish courts and procedure before Polish courts.

Conclusions

The analysis of the decisions of the Constitutional Tribunal leads to the conclusion that the Constitution occupies the highest place in the hierarchy of sources of law in Poland and that it enjoys priority in terms of validity and application. Additionally, in the conditions of EU membership, the Constitution is the supreme law in Poland (K 18/04, K 32/09, K 45/09, SK 45/09, K 3/21). Thus, on the one hand, it is assumed that the supremacy and primacy of the Constitution concerning all legal acts binding in the Polish legal order may not be questioned (Article 8 para. 1 of the Constitution). On the other hand, it is possible to assume that the principle of primacy implies the obligation of each body applying legal regulations to assess the existence of a collision between the norms of EU and national law. The latter finds direct support in Article 91 para. 3 of the Constitution. The Constitutional Tribunal clarifies that the EU Member States have, side by side, two autonomous legal orders. They interact with each other, which gives rise to many collisions. However, it is the national courts which, in the process of applying the law, have both the right and the obligation to refuse to apply a national rule which conflicts with provisions of EU law and thus satisfy the principle of the primacy of European Union law and its direct effect.

The Constitutional Tribunal has repeatedly stated its competence to examine the compatibility of EU law with the Constitution. This concerned both primary and derived EU law and acts of national law implementing EU law. In this case-law, a characteristic element of the deliberations is the argumentation 'safeguarding' the supremacy of the Constitution and a clear distinction between the role and tasks of the Constitutional Tribunal and the CJEU. If, however, an irremovable contradiction did indeed arise, the Constitutional Tribunal takes the view that a constitutionally empowered Polish authority would have to make a decision: either to amend the Constitution (P 1/05 is an illustration) or to bring about changes in EU law, or to withdraw Poland from the EU.

According to the model of constitutional judiciary, adopted in Poland, the Constitutional Tribunal does not have the competence to examine the compliance with the Constitution of individual judicial decisions (of Polish and supranational courts) in addition to making a final, and binding, interpretation of EU law (which results from the division of competence between the Constitutional Tribunal and the CJEU). However, the Court's recent rulings (P 7/20, K 3/21) are causing a schism in case-law on this matter and are creating conditions of competition between the Constitutional Tribunal and the CJEU. Within the same (new) line of case-law, the Constitutional Tribunal seeks to impose an obligation on Polish courts not to recognise CJEU rulings handed down in Polish cases concerning the independence of the courts and the impartiality of judges and to exclude from the principle of primacy and direct applicability CJEU rulings on interim measures relating to the system and jurisdiction of Polish courts and procedure before Polish courts.

Literature

Albi A., Supremacy of EC Law in the Member States, *European Constitutional Law Review*, 2007, no. 3, pp. 25–67.

Arnaiz A.S., Llivina C.A. (ed.), *National Constitutional Identity and European Integration*, Cambridge-Antwerp-Portland, 2013.

Barcz J., Konstytucyjnoprawne problemy stosowania prawa Unii Europejskiej w Polsce w świetle dotychczasowych doświadczeń państw członkowskich [Constitutional and legal problems of the application of European Union law in Poland in the light of the experience of Member States], in M. Kruk (ed.), *Prawo międzynarodowe i wspólnotowe w wewnętrznym porządku prawnym* [International law and community law in the internal legal order], Wydawnictwo Sejmowe, 1997.

Bartosiewicz A., Wyrok Trybunału Sprawiedliwości, C-335/19, E. Sp. z o.o. Sp. k. przeciwko Ministrowi Finansów, a ograniczenie w czasie możliwości skorzystania z ulgi na złe długi [Judgment of the Court of Justice, C-335/19, E. Sp. z o. o. Sp. k. against the Minister of Finance, and the limitation in time of the possibility of usingbad debt relief], *Przegląd Podatkowy*, 2020, no. 12, pp. 24–28.

Besselink L., National and Constitutional Identity before and after Lisbon, *Utrecht Law Journal*, 2010, no. 6, pp. 36–49.

Biernat S., Kawczyńska M., The Role of the Polish Constitution (Pre-2016): Development of a Liberal Democracy in the European and International Context, in A. Albi, S. Bardutzky (eds.), *National Constitutions in European and Global Governance: Democracy, Rights, the Rule of Law*, Springer Open, 2019, pp. 745–793.

Biernat S., Niedźwiedź M., Znaczenie prawa międzynarodowego i unijnego dla prawa administracyjnego i administracji publicznej w świetle Konstytucji RP [The Role of International Law and the EU for Administrative Law and Public Administration in the Light of the Constitution of the Republic of Poland], in Hauser R., Wróbel A., Niewiadomski Z. (eds.), *System Prawa Administracyjnego* [The System of Administrative Law], vol. 2. C.H. Beck, 2012, pp. 89–125.

Błachut P., Mikuli P., Uwagi o stosowaniu ustaw przez sądy w przypadku ich kolizji z prawem wspólnotowym [Comments on the application of statutes by courts in the event of their conflict with Community law], in M. Kruk, J. Wawrzyniak (eds.), *Polska w Unii Europejskiej* [Poland in the European Union], Zakamycze, 2005, pp. 273–274.

Bogdandy A., Schell S., Overcoming Absolute Primacy, Overcoming Absolute Primacy: Respect for National Identity Under the Lisbon Treaty, *CMLRev.*, 2011, pp. 1417–1454.

Claes M., *The National Courts' Mandate in the European Constitution*, Hart Publishing, 2006.

Claes M., Negotiating Constitutional Identity or Whose Identity Is It Anyway?, in M. Claes et al. (eds.), *Constitutional Conversations in Europe*, Intersentia, 2012, pp. 205–235.

Dumbrava H., The Rule of Law and the EU's Response Mechanisms in Case of Violation: A Romanian Case Study: C-83/19, *ERA-Forum: Scripta Iuris Europaei*, 2021, pp. 437–452.

Garlicki L., Kilka uwag o konstytucyjnych aspektach Polski przystąpienia do Unii Europejskiej [A few remarks on the constitutional aspects of Poland's accession to the European Union], in L. Garlicki (ed.), *Konstytucja. Wybory. Parlament* [Constitution. Elections. Parliament], *Studia ofiarowane Zdzisławowi Jaroszowi*, Liber 2000.

Halberstam D., Constitutional Heterarchy: The Centrality of Conflict in the European Union and the United States, in J.L. Dunoff, J. Trachtman (eds.), *Ruling the World? Constitutionalism, International Law, and Global Governance*, Cambridge University Press, 2009, https://ssrn.com/abstract=1147769.

Kowalik-Bańczyk K., Sending Smoke Signals to Luxembourg – The Polish Constitutional Tribunal in Dialogue with the ECJ, in M. Claes et al. (eds.), *Constitutional Conversations in Europe*, Intersentia, 2012, pp. 267–285.

Martinico G., Pollicino O., *The Interaction between Europe's Legal Systems. Judicial Dialogue and the Creation of Supranational Laws*, Edward Elgar, 2012.

Mayer F.C., Multilevel Constitutional Jurisdiction, in: A. von Bogdandy, J. Bast (eds.), *Principles of European Constitutional Law*, Hart Publishing, 2009, pp. 399–440.

Miąsik D., *Zasady i prawa podstawowe. System Prawa Unii Europejskiej* [Principles and Fundamental Rights. System of EU Law], T. 2, C.H. Beck, 2022, pp. 91–116–157.

Poiares Maduro M., Courts and Pluralism: Essays on a Theory of Judicial Adjudication in the Context of Legal and Constitutional Pluralism, in J.L. Dunoff, J. Trachtman (eds.), *Ruling the World? Constitutionalism, International Law, and Global Governance*, Cambridge University Press, 2009, pp. 356–380.

Sołtys A., Cechy i charakter prawa unijnego oraz problem jego konstytucjonalizacji [Features and nature of EU law and the problem of its constitutionalization], in

S. Biernat (ed.), *Podstawy i źródła prawa Unii Europejskiej. System Prawa Unii Europejskiej* [Fundamentals and sources of European Union Law. System of EU Law], 2020, C.H. Beck pp. 199–287.

Szafarz R., Skuteczność norm prawa międzynarodowego w prawie wewnętrznym w świetle nowej Konstytucji [Effectiveness of international law norms in municipal law under the new Constitution], *Państwo i Prawo*, 1998, no. 1, pp. 3–12.

Walker N., Constitutionalism and Pluralism in Global Context, in M. Avbelj, J. Komárek (eds.), *Constitutional Pluralism in the European Union and Beyond*, Hart Publishing, 2012.

Walker N., The Idea of Constitutional Pluralism, *Modern Law Review*, 2002, 65, no. 3, pp. 317–359.

Wasilkowski A., Transformacja czy inkorporacja? [Transformation or incorporation?], *Państwo i Prawo*, 1998, no. 4, pp. 80–92.

Wyrozumska A., Prawo międzynarodowe oraz prawo Unii Europejskiej a konstytucyjny system źródeł prawa [International Law, European Union Law and the Constitutional System of Sources of Law], in K. Wójtowicz (ed.), *Otwarcie Konstytucji RP na prawo międzynarodowe i procesy integracyjne* [The Openness of the Polish Constitution to the International Law and Integration Processes], Wydawnictwo Sejmowe, 2006.

Wyrozumska A., Ratyfikacja traktatu akcesyjnego w drodze referendum [Ratification of the Accession Treaty by referendum], in J. Barcz (ed.), *Czy zmieniać konstytucję? Ustrojowo-konstytucyjne aspekty przystąpienia Polski do Unii Europejskiej* [Should the constitution be changed? System and constitutional aspects of Poland's accession to European Union], Instytut Spraw Publicznych, 2002.

Wyrozumska A., *Umowy międzynarodowe. Teoria i praktyka* [International Agreements, Theory and Practice], Wydawnictwo Prawo i Praktyka Gospodarcza, 2006.

Wyrozumska A., Zapewnienie skuteczności prawu międzynarodowemu w prawie krajowym w projekcie konstytucji RP [Ensuring the Effectiveness of International Law in National Law Under the Draft Polish Constitution], *Państwo i Prawo*, 1996, no. 11, pp. 17–26.

Wyrzykowski M., EU Accession in Light of Evolving Constitutionalism in Poland, in G.A. Bermann, K. Pistor (eds.), *Law and Governance in an Enlarged European Union*, Hart Publishing, 2004, pp. 437–450.

11 Conclusions

Monika Domańska, Dawid Miąsik, Monika Szwarc

The concept of 'EU case' in the Polish courts

The overview of judgments of the Supreme Court and the administrative courts, including the Supreme Administrative Court on issues relating to the concept of 'EU cases', has evidenced a proper understanding of the spectrum of the various types of proceedings that fall within the scope of EU law and, hence, demand the application of its principles by national courts. However, both the Supreme Court and administrative courts rarely focus their attention on the reasoning for the judgments to which they have applied EU law on explaining the type of the EU element that made a case an EU case. Thus, the terms such as 'the EU case' or 'governed by EU law' or 'scope of application of EU law' are rarely used. The Polish courts of different types of jurisdiction analysed in this monograph have had no difficulty in identifying the EU rules applicable in the cases in question. Therefore, while they generally follow the guidelines resulting from the concept of the EU case, they refer to it only in dubious cases, as demonstrated by II UZ 10/18 or III UZP 3/17 in the case-law of the Supreme Court, by III SA/Wa 679/05, I SA/Wr 971/07, I SA/Gl 446/11, I SA/Bd 1035/11, in the case-law of the voivodeship administrative courts and by II FSK 1308/11, in the case-law of the Supreme Administrative Court.

The basic function of the EU case concept, in the case-law of the Supreme Court and administrative courts, has been the same: to identify EU cases and to provide guidelines to respectively: national courts of lower instances and administrative authorities, on when they should adjudicate as EU courts and have to respect various principles of EU law.

The concept of the EU case also provided the Supreme Court with additional arguments in favour of changing the established case-law in order to assure compatibility between Polish and EU legal standards.[1]

1 The resolution of a panel of seven judges of the SC of 28 September 2016, case III PZP 3/16; judgments of the SC of 14 April 2010, case III SK 1/10; of 21 September 2010, case III SK 8/10; of 7 July 2011, case III SK 52/10.

DOI: 10.4324/9781003376019-14

Some differences may be noted in respect of the types of EU cases. Whilst both the Supreme Court and administrative courts adjudicate most often in proceedings that are governed by EU law in the form of directives, the administrative courts more regularly adjudicate in cases with a cross-border element. The administrative courts, immediately after the accession, began to correctly identify those cases in which the directly effective provisions of the TFEU, guaranteeing the freedoms of the internal market, should be incorporated as the grounds for the ruling. This is particularly evident in the area of non-harmonised taxes. On the contrary, cases that belong to this category before the Supreme Court are not governed by the provisions of the Treaty but by the directly effective regulations applicable to cross-border situations in cases concerning the coordination of social security systems and cooperation in civil matters.

Failure to decode the scope of EU law in cases adjudicated by the Supreme Court and administrative courts has been rare. The clearest examples are delivered by the case-law discussed in III UZP 3/17 (*Pawlak*) in the case-law of the Supreme Court and by I FSK 2008/15 and I FSK 1588/16 in the case-law of the administrative courts. A number of proceedings before the Supreme Court were identified in which the European element was either omitted by the courts of lower instance or ignored by the professional representative filling the appeal for cassation on behalf of the party. The situation, in the context of administrative courts is different. In general, the voivodship administrative courts, at least just after the accession, were provoked by claimants to reflect on EU elements in their adjudication activities. In cases such as *Brzeziński*, *Rüffler*, and *Filipiak,* the pleas grounded in EU law were formulated by the claimants and their legal representatives. It is also a rule that administrative authorities are very reluctant to apply EU law in handled cases, in particular to accept the arguments of the applicant concerning non-conformity of national provision with EU law, not to mention to analyse this issue using their own initiative. Therefore, the European character of such cases is clear from the beginning since provisions of EU law either are invoked in the decision itself or are raised in appeal by the party challenging the decision. Apart from that, parties involved in judicial administrative proceedings are much more often represented by professionals from the beginning of the case. This significantly increases the number of cases where the link with EU law is raised, either by the claiming party itself or by the administrative authority defending its decision. Therefore, in comparison to the practice of the Supreme Court, the issue of *ex officio* application of EU law has not received that much attention in the case-law of the administrative courts concerning the scope of the application of EU law.

A significant number of the cases decided by the Supreme Court, and reported in this monograph, concern the impact of EU substantive law on the national civil procedure. The Supreme Court had to weigh up not only between the principle of effectiveness of EU law and national procedural autonomy (as in the case of *ex officio* application of EU law by that Court itself) but also various issues resulting from the indirect influence of substantive provisions of EU law on the application of Polish civil procedure code (e.g., EU rules on the internal market of postal services versus national rules on delivery of pleadings to the court).

Both administrative courts and the Supreme Court have also identified non-obvious EU cases, when the dispute between the parties itself falls generally outside of the scope of EU law and, as a result, only an incidental issue is governed by EU law. In respect of the Supreme Court, II UK 504/17, serves as a good example (a right to the social security pension fell outside the scope of EU law but the issue of proper representation before lower courts was governed by EU rules on the free movement of legal services).

In the area of 'EU cases' falling into the categories of 'reverse discrimination' and 'a reference to EU law in national legislation', it remains to be seen how the Supreme Court itself and lower courts will try to apply the judgment of the ECJ, C-585/18 *A.K., and others*, in cases that do not strictly fall within the scope of the application of EU law. On the other hand, the Supreme Administrative Court, which is not formally bound by the resolution of the formation of the combined Civil Chamber, Criminal Chamber, and Labour Law and Social Security Chamber of 23 January 2020, BSA I-4110-1/20, has never applied the reasoning adopted in that resolution even before a large number of nominees from the notorious National Council for the Judiciary, in operation since 2018, began serving as administrative judges. Hence, the standard of protection of the right to a fair trial before administrative courts may not fulfil the requirements stemming from Article 47 CFR and Article 6 ECHR.

Since imposing on Poland an obligation to adapt its national law to the standards resulting from the EU (Community) legal order, the CT has also considered the EU (Communities) *acquis* in its case-law. Within that practice, the definition of 'the EU/Community case' has started to be developed in the CT case-law.

The Constitutional Tribunal referred to the content of EU (Community) regulations even before Poland's accession to the EU in order to strengthen the chosen direction for interpretative considerations (K 2/02). On the basis of the analysis of the case-law of the Constitutional Tribunal, one may be tempted to conclude that the CT takes EU law into account both directly and indirectly, thus creating a line of judgments 'in cases with an EU element' and a line of judgments 'in EU cases'.

Due to the special competence of the Constitutional Tribunal, which does not coincide with the competence of common courts or supreme courts in Poland (the Constitutional Tribunal does not apply the law but performs a constitutional review of legal norms), EU cases decided by the Constitutional Tribunal have – already in the documents initiating the proceedings – a clearly marked EU law context, as it is directly connected (has an impact) with the substantive examination of the case. The Constitutional Tribunal does not examine *ex officio* whether EU law is applicable. Within the scope of cases decided by the Constitutional Tribunal, there are no judgments in which the necessity to take EU law into account for the purpose of determining hierarchical compliance of norms was not noticed beforehand by the entities submitting the case for consideration by the Constitutional Tribunal. Thus, as regards the analysis of the issue focusing on the concept of an 'EU case', it may be stated that the CT includes in this category all those cases in which it issues rulings resolving legal issues related to Poland's membership in the European Union and the place of EU law in the Polish legal order (K 41/05; K 18/04, K 32/09). More narrowly, these are cases in which the considerations relating to EU law are closely connected with the subject matter of the review established in the case (P 1/05).

A characteristic feature of the case-law of the CT in the EU cases *sensu largo* is limiting of the deliberations contained on the grounds of the issue currently being decided in a case concerned. It is strictly related to the limits of the constitutional claim.

The principle of consistent interpretation in Polish courts

All the Polish courts under consideration have accepted the principle of consistent interpretation of Polish law with EU law. Whilst the Supreme Court and administrative courts have accepted, and used the obligations resulting from consistent interpretation in such a form and, to the extent as established in the case-law of the Court of Justice of the European Union (CJEU), the Constitutional Tribunal took a different view. Even prior to the accession, the CT opted to favour such an interpretation of the Polish constitution that would be 'friendly' towards EU law. The Constitutional provisions and rules were to be understood, as much as possible, in such a manner as to avoid conflict between the basic law and EU law. The principle of interpreting domestic law in a 'Europe-friendly' manner is clearly phrased in the case-law of the Polish Constitutional Tribunal. The CT has developed a constitutional principle of EU-friendly interpretation of legislation, and it accepts that it can rely on Union law and the judgments handed down by the CJ in interpreting the Polish constitution (K 18/06).

All the courts under consideration have treated, to date (with the exception of the CT in the latest judgments, especially since 2020), that the duty of consistent interpretation of national law is a principle and not an exception. All courts have stressed that national courts must try to align Polish law with EU law by means of interpretation before they seek recourse to the other principles of EU law such as primacy and direct effect. Hence, the latter principles are treated as the principles of EU law of the last resort by means of their application. All courts have assumed that the effectiveness of EU law should be ensured, in the first place, using the interpretation of national law in conformity with EU law and, should it be necessary and possible to choose between various interpretative methods and results, priority should be given to such an interpretation of Polish provisions that will guarantee the useful effect of EU legislation provisions. Only when a conflict between the EU and national legal norms cannot be resolved, by means of consistent interpretation, will a Polish court be obliged to disapply the provision of national law that is contrary to EU law.[2]

The administrative courts, in addition to the Supreme Court, rightly accept that the obligation of consistent interpretation extends to all the provisions of national law and, at the same time, arises in all 'EU cases' on all the issues governed by EU law. Courts from both jurisdictions take account of the case-law of the CJEU, as a source of binding interpretation when reconstructing the European interpretative standard to which interpretation of Polish law should be aligned.[3]

In the case-law of the Constitutional Tribunal, it should be noted that EU law can act as a benchmark for interpretation by the Constitutional Tribunal. In such a case, the CT may establish the contradiction of the object of review with EU law (the consistent interpretation does not remove the contradiction) and then examine the review model (constitutional norm) in such a way as to eliminate the provision that is contrary to EU law from the national legal order. Furthermore, the Constitutional Tribunal may establish that the object of review (a norm of national law simultaneously implementing the objectives of the EU regulation) is consistent with the EU law and then interpret the review model (constitutional norm) in such a way as to maintain the object of review as a norm binding in the national legal order.

In the case-law of the Constitutional Tribunal, such a configuration is also accepted, in which the EU law is the review model and the object of review. In the first case, the EU law norm is the benchmark for reviewing national law. In the second case, EU law is examined for compatibility with the Constitution. In all types of conducted reviews of constitutionality, the Constitutional Tribunal applies methods of interpretation of law recognised in national law, taking into account the content, scope, and limits of the obligation to apply pro-EU interpretation, also specified in the case-law of the CJEU.

Both the Supreme Court and administrative courts make use of consistent interpretation in two types of legal reasoning. The first one encompasses interpretation undertaken with a view to ensuring the respect of the principle of the uniform interpretation and application of EU law. This type of legal interpretation is focused on safeguarding the fact that the terms used in national provisions, adopted to implement EU law, are interpreted in a way that is consistent with the terms applied in a given EU legal act and the interpretation thereof in the case-law of the CJEU. Hence, in the case-law of the Supreme Court, this

2 Judgments of the SAC: of 14 January 2010, case II FSK 2018/09; of 16 March 2011, case I FSK 1588/10.

3 Judgment of the SAC of 2 April 2009, case I FSK 4/08.

type of consistent interpretation was for some time called an 'EU-oriented' interpretation. The other approach to consistent interpretation takes place when it is necessary to resolve a conflict between the provisions of national law and the provisions of EU law. In these situations, the courts explicitly refer directly to the concept of consistent interpretation and the relevant case-law of the CJEU, when they have established incompatibility of Polish law with EU law *ex officio* or must address the claim made by the party. The analyses of case-law lead to the conclusion that the use of consistent interpretation prevails in the first of the situations presented, which well serves the full effectiveness of the provisions of EU law.

Both the administrative courts and the Supreme Court have been eager to use the principle of consistent interpretation in all those cases, when the provisions of Polish implementing EU law reproduced, even partially, the wording of the implemented sources of EU law. Even when certain words used in Polish, legal language had a certain, established meaning, the courts were ready to either depart from the previous interpretation or to interpret a provision containing such words autonomously (and consistently with EU law) strictly for the purposes of a specific legal act. The best example here is provided in the case-law of the Supreme Court using the issue of understanding under the concept of 'damage' (which, under Polish law, had been traditionally limited to various types of loss incurred in the property – material damage) also personal injury in the form of the loss of enjoyment of a holiday.[4]

Courts from both jurisdictions were also less successful in reaching the result required by conforming interpretation when the national implementing act did not introduce autonomous legal definitions of the concepts used in it but referred to legal definitions that had already been specified in other Polish acts whose provisions were not covered by the scope of EU law.[5]

Despite these convergences in approach, a number of differences can be noted. The use of consistent interpretation by the Supreme Court happens more regularly in comparison to administrative courts. This can be explained by the short list of limitations placed upon the principle of consistent interpretation and its application by the ECJ on one hand and the type of proceedings before the Supreme Court: consistent interpretation is often used in proceedings between individuals where, for obvious reasons, principles of direct effect and, hence, primacy, could not be invoked if the contentious issue is governed by EU law, taking the form of a directive. It should also be emphasised again that the principle of consistent interpretation is used by the Supreme Court in vertical and horizontal relations, both to the benefit and detriment of individuals. However, the application of the interpretation, in conformity with EU law, to the detriment of individuals, is rare. It is mostly applied when there is a judgment of the Court of Justice

4 Resolution of the SC of 19 November 2010, case III CZP 79/10.

5 See resolution of the SC of 9 September 2015, case III SZP 2/15.

establishing a certain interpretation of EU law (to the detriment of the individual) given in reply to a preliminary reference from the Supreme Court.[6] In comparison with the case-law of the Supreme Court, the administrative courts do not have to seek various interpretative methods in order to produce a maverick (yet not *contra legem*) interpretation of national law to secure the effectiveness of EU law. Since all the cases adjudicated by them concern disputes between individuals and administrative bodies, the administrative courts may easily resort to principles of primacy and direct effect, should they encounter any difficulties in aligning Polish law with EU law by means of interpretation.

From a practical point of view, an important difference concerns the practical effects of consistent interpretation. Whilst the Supreme Court accepts that the use of consistent interpretation may lead to obligations being imposed on an individual, the SAC seems to, somehow, equate such an outcome as being *contra legem*. The prohibition of imposing an obligation on an individual, by means of consistent interpretation, does not have any grounds in the case-law of the Court of Justice, which has consequently held that consistent interpretation may not lead to the 'effect of determining or aggravating the liability in criminal law of persons who act in contravention of the provisions of that directive'.[7] The consistent interpretation is not excluded in other cases, when it would result in the aggravation of a situation of an individual in a specific proceeding, in particular in imposing an obligation.[8]

Another difference can be noted in the approach to the limits of consistent interpretation. Both the administrative courts and the Supreme Court accept the boundaries resulting from the established case-law of the CJEU, pursuant to which 'the obligation on a national court to refer to the content of a directive when interpreting and applying the relevant rules of domestic law is limited by general principles of law, . . . and that obligation cannot serve as the basis for an interpretation of national law *contra legem*',[9] with specific emphasises given to such general principles of law as the principle of legal certainty and the principle of non-retroactivity.[10] The administrative courts in many rulings held also that 'there is no obligation of interpretation if it was to lead to a denial or rejection of national law, thus, to

6 See in particular cases III SK 28/13 and III UZP 3/17, where the Supreme Court initially (at the point of making the reference) rejected the possibility of aligning national law with EU law through the use of consistent interpretation.

7 Case 80/86, *Kolpinghuis Nijmegen*, EU:C:1987:431.

8 Again for further reading, see A. Sołtys, Obowiązek wykładni prawa krajowego zgodnie z prawem unijnym jako instrument zapewniania efektywności prawa Unii Europejskiej [The Obligation to Interpret National Law in Conformity with EU Law as an Instrument to Ensure Effectiveness of EU Law], Wolters Kluwer Polska, 2015, pp. 387–392.

9 For example, judgments of the SAC of 8 October 2014, case I FSK 1512/13; of 14 May 2015, case I FSK 382/14.

10 For example, judgments of the SAC: of 29 March 2018, case I FSK 1069/15; of 4 April 2015, case I FSK 1872/14; of 2 July 2019, case I FSK 119/17.

interpretation *contra legem*'.[11] Whilst the Supreme Court generally adopted the same approach and remains cautious when the consistent interpretation of Polish law would lead to a *contra legem* textual interpretation of national law, that court seems to be much more eager to adopt even courageous legal interpretation that would serve the effectiveness of EU law. In such cases, the Supreme Court uses two methods in its legal reasoning. In the first one, when selecting national provisions that will form a legal base suitable for consistent interpretation, the Supreme Court would be willing to consider the application of provisions of Polish law that would normally not be applicable in the case.[12] The second one is adopted in cases when the duty of consistent interpretation relates to the provisions of Polish law which are not provisions of substantive law, and hence their extensive or restrictive interpretation (depending on the requirements of EU law) does not change the scope and content of rights and obligations of individuals as determined by Polish law.[13]

The analysis of the judicial practice of Polish courts, in the area of consistent interpretation, revealed that there are still some challenges facing both the Supreme Court and administrative courts in terms of the understanding and application of the '*contra legem*' exception when consistent interpretation is a tool to resolve a conflict between a provision of national law and a provision of EU law. Administrative courts, and even the Supreme Court, still rely mostly on the literal (textual, grammatical) method of the interpretation of Polish provisions, ignoring other methods of interpretation, should the results of this interpretation be clear, even though they lead to the formulation of a legal norm, incompatible with a legal norm derived from EU law. This approach is widely referred to in the context of the *contra legem* limitation of consistent interpretation. Whilst Polish academia has been very critical of this approach and suggested a bolder use of the combined methods of interpretation, advocated by the domestic legal theory[14] and accepted, at least, in some cases by all highest courts, there are not so many judgments in which such an approach was adopted. We believe the III UZP 3/17 is a good example of a judgment delivering a comprehensive set of arguments that should be used by Polish courts to fulfil their duties under the principle of consistent interpretation even in the case that, at a first glance and following textual interpretation, they are not susceptible to such an interpretation.

11 For example, judgments of the SAC: of 8 January 2009, case I FSK 1798/07; of 5 February 2009, case I FSK 1880/07; of 27 May 2009, I FSK 358/08; of 8 May 2009, I FSK 1509/08.

12 See in particular case III SK 28/13.

13 III UZP 3/17.

14 A. Sołtys, *Obowiązek wykładni prawa krajowego zgodnie z prawem unijnym jako instrument zapewniania efektywności prawa Unii Europejskiej* [The Obligation to Interpret National Law in Conformity with EU Law as an Instrument to Ensure Effectiveness of EU Law], Wolters Kluwer Polska, 2015, pp. 544–547.

The obligation of consistent interpretation exercised by the Constitutional Tribunal within the framework of constitutional review is subject to implementation at many levels. Constitutional norms appear as the benchmark for interpretation, benchmark, and object of review. The effectiveness of the duty of consistent interpretation, and thus of ensuring the effectiveness of EU law in the domestic legal order, depends on the correctness of detailed findings by the CT, that is, the scope of application of EU law in the context of the subject matter of the review; the correct EU standard of interpretation (taking into account the position of the CJ); and the application of the rules of interpretation inherent in the duty of consistent interpretation when interpreting in a conforming manner the subject matter of the interpretation and the standard of interpretation. Importantly, these findings are interrelated and conditional as to effectiveness. Each of the review patterns carried out may lead to a change in the interpretation of the reviewed norm and a change in its scope of application.

It should be stressed that the boundaries of the consistent interpretation in an approach which is representative of the judgments of common courts and which is taken from the case-law of the CJ are not an explicit subject of consideration by the CT but are rather conducted on the margins of the reconstruction of the EU benchmark. However, it should be stressed that the limits of consistent interpretation in the case-law of the Constitutional Tribunal are established not only by reference to the linguistic meaning of the constitutional norms being interpreted but also by taking into account the guarantee functions of these regulations. In its judgment in case K 32/09, the CT presented a fundamental position on the question of respecting the limits of the obligation of interpretation in conformity with EU law:

> From the point of view of this principle, in reconstructing the standard (norm) by which constitutionality is assessed, one should make use not only of the text of the Constitution itself but – to the extent that this text refers to terms, concepts and principles known to European law – one should refer to these very meanings. . . . Under no circumstances may an interpretation favourable to European law lead to 'results which are contrary to the clear wording of the constitutional norms and impossible to reconcile with the minimum guarantee functions performed by the Constitution'.

A significant change in the direction of the CT case-law with regard to the maintenance of constitutional dialogue, and thus the division of competencies between the CT and the CJ, as well as with regard to the effectiveness expected by the EU order, of the instrument of consistent interpretation, binding interpretation of provisions of EU law – including the effectiveness of the instrument of the preliminary ruling – but also other means of protection of rights stemming from the EU order, was very clearly visible when the Constitutional Tribunal examined case no. P 7/20. This new direction is increasingly evident and goes far beyond an isolated departure from established case-law. This judgment and subsequent judgments (K 3/21) provide a basis for the assumption that the current composition of the Constitutional Tribunal considers that it has sufficient competence to review the constitutionality of any 'normative act', that is, one that expresses a general and abstract manner of proceeding, regardless of the form and entity that issued it (the question at issue in the case was the scope compatibility with the Constitution of a rule ordering the Republic of Poland to enforce interim measures ordered by the CJEU concerning the system of courts, their jurisdiction and the procedure before the courts). In this way, the Constitutional Tribunal reviewed the general and abstract norms derived from the second sentence of Article 4 (3) TEU in conjunction with Article 279 TFEU with the provisions of the Constitution constituting, in this case, the norm of review for EU provisions.

It should be assumed beyond any doubt that it is this new direction of the CT's judicial activity that will constitute in the nearest future the greatest challenge for Poland as a Member State of the EU in terms of fulfilling the obligation to ensure axiological consistency of the national and EU legal system and respecting the limits of competences of relevant national and EU institutions, and in particular of the CT and the CJ.

The principles of primacy and direct effect in Polish courts

The review of the case-law of the Supreme Court and administrative courts highlighted the importance of the consistent interpretation of national law as the main tool of securing the effectiveness of EU law. With the exception of cases governed by directly effective provisions of the founding treaties or regulations, the use of the principles of direct effect and primacy has always been preceded by an attempt to interpret national provisions that should form the legal basis of the judicial decision in conformity with EU law.[15] Hence, the limited number of cases of the Supreme Court in which both principles under consideration have been applied. The larger number of such cases in the case-law of the administrative courts can be explained by a far larger number of cases with the same legal issues concerning the decisions of tax or customs authorities (e.g., taxes imposed on imported cars) based on the provisions of Polish law that were found to be incompatible with EU law either by the courts alone or with guidance from the CJEU in preliminary rulings resulting from preliminary references originating from Polish courts. Only in the event of a conflict between EU and national rules, which cannot be remedied by the interpretation of national law in conformity with EU law, is a national court obliged to refuse to apply a provision of national law that is contrary to EU law more favourable to an individual.[16]

15 See in particular case III PK 53/19.

16 For example, judgments of the SAC of 16 March 2011, I FSK 1588/10; of 14 January 2010, case II FSK 2018/09; of 16 March 2011, I FSK 1588/10; judgments of SC case I UK 182/07; III PK 53/19.

Both the Supreme Court and the administrative courts have, so far, accepted the principles of primacy and direct effect as they had been formulated by the CJEU. Although, they have also rooted this acceptance in the Polish Constitution. This acceptance has not only been expressed in their judgments presented in this monograph but also in some preliminary references, which considered various practical aspects of the principle of primacy and its operation. For example, in the reference for a preliminary ruling in *Filipiak*,[17] administrative courts accepted that the principle of primacy of Union law obliges a national court to disapply the provisions of national law conflicting with it, irrespective of the judgment of the national constitutional court which deferred the loss of the binding force by those provisions. On the other hand, in C-585/18 *A.K. and others*, the Supreme Court expected the CJEU to confirm that EU law requires the Supreme Court to examine the compatibility of the way in which the Disciplinary Chamber of the Supreme Court was constructed and staffed with the requirements stemming from Article 47 CFR and Article 19 TEU, and empowers that court to disapply provisions of national law granting the competence to hear a particular case to the Disciplinary Chamber.

The Polish courts under consideration have accepted, for a very long time, that the effectiveness of EU law demands an *ex officio* examination of the compatibility of national law with EU law by each court and even administrative authority, ruling on an individual case.[18] In executing the assessment required by the principle of primacy, the courts under consideration mostly base their reasoning on the previous case-law of the CJEU. Only a few preliminary references, which resulted in the obligation to use the principle of primacy, have been made.

The courts have also respected the link between the principle of primacy and the principle of direct effect and have refused to apply Polish provisions only if they were contrary to a provision of EU law capable of producing a direct effect. The direct effect of the provisions of EU law has been determined by the Polish courts mostly on the basis of the *acte éclairé* doctrine.[19]

The Polish courts under consideration in this monograph have secured the effectiveness of EU law by recourse to the principle of primacy in various ways. Depending on the legal situation, a national court adjudicates the case (or incidental issues falling within the scope of EU law) either on the basis of other provisions of national law (compatible with EU law) or on the basis of directly effective provisions of EU law or on the legal basis formed from provisions of both EU and national law. In order to construct the legal base for the judicial decision that would produce a legal norm compatible with EU law, Polish

17 Case C-314/08, *Filipiak*, EU:C:2009:719.

18 For example, judgments of the SAC of 15 February 2010, case I OSK 672/09; judgment of the SAC of 12 March 2020, case II GSK 3028/17.

19 See, for example, case III PK 53/19.

courts have been forced to: 1) disapply provision of substantive law (mostly), 2) disapply provision of procedural law, and 3) add to the legal base of their judicial decision a directly effective provision of EU law and apply it with other national provisions that are compatible with EU law.

In the practice of the Supreme Court, the exclusionary effect of the principle of primacy has been the most important.

The substitution effect in the form of replacing a national provision, incompatible with a provision of EU law, seems to be rarely used with the best examples provided by III PO 7/18, III PO 8/18, and III PO 9/18 discussed previously.

In the case-law of the Constitutional Tribunal, one does not find many examples of references to the principles of direct effect and the principle of primacy of EU law, which confirms the thesis that removing collisions between the Constitution of the Republic of Poland and EU law and ensuring compatibility of legal norms should consist, in the first place, of applying the obligation of consistent interpretation. In turn, the invoked principles expressing the EU mechanism defining the judicial rule of refusal to apply a provision of national law contrary to EU law and direct application of EU law are not frequent subjects of consideration by the Constitutional Tribunal. This is primarily because the principle of primacy of EU law and the principle of direct effect – as functionally related principles – are perceived by the CT as an instrument of judicial application of the law. However, the principles on which the EU legal order is based, including the primacy of EU law and direct effect, have changed the interpretation of the applicable concepts and principles relevant to the functioning of the state, including the application of sources of law by national constitutional authorities. Against this background, many problems have emerged concerning the relationship between Polish law and EU law in the context of the principle of the latter's primacy over the entire national legal order. In the context discussed earlier, that is, in the context of the hierarchical relationship between legal orders, the Constitutional Tribunal analyses the principle of the primacy of EU law.

The Constitutional Tribunal does not recognise the possibility of questioning the validity of a constitutional norm by the mere fact of introducing into the law system an EU regulation which is contrary to it. The procedure established by the line of case-law of the Constitutional Tribunal (cases no. K 18/04, K 32/09, SK 45/09) in the event of a conflict between the norms of the Constitution and provisions of EU law establishes clear boundaries, which it deems impassable, that is, it is forbidden to recognise the superiority of the EU law over the constitutional norm; it is forbidden to replace the constitutional norm with an EU law norm; it is forbidden to limit the scope of the constitutional norm to the area not covered by the regulation of EU law.

The position of the Constitutional Tribunal that the adopted hierarchy of sources of law has a guarantee function and constitutes an element of national identity and state sovereignty is well established. Moreover, the fundamental rights enshrined in the provisions of the Constitution are also protected by the Constitution. Furthermore, even though the Constitution sets the minimum scope of protection, it is hierarchically the most critical act of national law, whose guarantees cannot be breached by EU law. The considerations discussed earlier were clearly illustrated in judgment case no. P 1/05 which led to the amendment of Article 55 of the Constitution (EAW).

The change to the Constitution brought about by the aforementioned judgment of the Constitutional Tribunal is the only such change that has been made as a result of taking into account the content and objective of the norm (act) of EU law. This is an effective and, at the same time, compromise solution between the inclusion of EU law within the cognition of the Constitutional Tribunal and the need to preserve the supremacy of the Constitution in the system of domestic sources of law. In this context, it should be stated that the abolition of the principle of supremacy of the Constitution of the Republic of Poland and the introduction of the absolute precedence of EU law over all Polish law (its inclusion with the Constitution) may be recognised only after a possible amendment of the Constitution, through the explicit adoption of a provision providing for the primacy of EU law, taking into account its specific hierarchy of sources of law.

One of the most important current problems related to Poland's functioning in the EU is the issue of the split in the already mentioned case-law of the Constitutional Tribunal concerning the resolution of conflicts between the provisions of the Polish Constitution and primacy of EU law. A change in the position of the CT on the application of the principle of primacy of EU law in the circumstances of an irremediable conflict between the foundations of the constitutional order and EU law was initiated by the judgment issued in case no. P 7/20. This is the first clear ruling on the incompatibility of EU primary law with the provisions of the Constitution. However, the verdict given earlier of the CT has already been set out – as can be seen from subsequent decisions, for example, case no. K 3/21 – a particular direction of case-law, within the framework of which the present composition of the Tribunal presents the view on the unquestionable supreme validity of the Constitution on the territory of Poland in the conditions of a conflict of norms. The CT noted that 'the principle of the primacy of the Constitution clashes with the principle of the primacy of the application of Community law resulting from the case-law of the CJ'.

An analysis of the judgments of the Constitutional Tribunal concerning the principle of primacy of EU law and direct effect leads to the conclusion that the most recent judgments of the Constitutional Tribunal, that is, P 7/20 and K 3/21, cause a split in case-law and lead to the positioning of the Constitutional Tribunal and the CJ as competing bodies in terms of their jurisdiction. It is undoubtedly the effect of these rulings, which seek to impose an obligation on Polish courts not to disregard CJ rulings made in certain 'Polish cases', by excluding them from the principle of priority and direct applicability, that will be the greatest challenge to the domestic judiciary in the nearest future.

It should be noted that challenges to both principles under consideration result from the activity of both the National Council for the Judiciary and the President who pack Polish courts with nominees susceptible to fail the test established in C-585/18 *A.K. and others* and from the politically motivated interpretation of the Polish Constitution that has been adopted by the Constitutional Court since 2018. This interpretation has a direct impact on the scope of application of the principle of primacy as the CT has developed a habit of declaring, as unconstitutional, any obligation or right stemming from EU law that is considered to be hostile by the ruling coalition.

Index

www.ingramcontent.com/pod-product-compliance
Lightning Source LLC
LaVergne TN
LVHW021119300926
849160LV00010B/787
9781032452241